Comprehensive Curriculum for Gifted Learners

Joyce VanTassel-Baska
The College of William and Mary

John Feldhusen
Purdue University

Ken Seeley
The Clayton Foundation

Grayson Wheatley
Purdue University

Linda Silverman
Gifted Child Development Center

William Foster
Rutgers State University

Allyn and Bacon, Inc.

Boston London Sydney Toronto

We wish to thank Linda Avery, Dr. James Hersberger, Nancy Mincemoyer, Dr. Paul Plowman, and Dr. Harry Passow for helpful critiques and editing suggestions on parts of the manuscript.

We also wish to thank Janice Lackey and MaryLou Mattes for faithfully typing and proofreading drafts of individual papers.

And last, we wish to thank our families who have tolerated our group habits of long meetings over several weekends to bring this project to closure.

The Keystone Consortium

Library of Congress Cataloging-in-Publication Data

Comprehensive curriculum for gifted learners / Joyce VanTassel-Baska . . . [et al.].
    p.   cm.
Includes bibliographies and index.
ISBN 0-205-11259-5
    1. Gifted children–Education–United States–Curricula.
2. Curriculum planning–United States. I. VanTassel-Baska, Joyce.
LC3993.9.C66 1988
371.95′3–dc19   87-27082
                                                            CIP

Page 23: Extract of poem from "The Hollow Men" in *Collected Poems 1909–1962* by T. S. Eliot, copyright 1936 by Harcourt Brace Jovanovich, Inc.; copyright © 1963, 1964 by T. S. Eliot. Reprinted by permission of the publisher.
Page 77: Extract of poem reprinted by AMS Press, Inc., New York.
Pages 190–191: Material from G. W. Ford and L. Pugno, *The Structure of Knowledge and the Curriculum*, 1964.

Printed in the United States of America
10 9 8 7 6 5 4   92 91 90 89

Contents ━━━━━━━━━

Preface _____

This book on curriculum for gifted learners has been designed to give practitioners in gifted education an overall grasp of the theoretical bases and practical applications for curriculum work with the gifted. At the same time, it seeks to provide specific procedures to follow and concepts to consider in creating curriculum experiences for these learners. The authors have attempted to be practical yet avoid a "cookbook" rendering of a complex set of issues. A guide to the organization of the material and to the thinking of the authors regarding some of the issues may serve as an appropriate way to begin the book.

The opening chapters of this book outline the process of curriculum making—those procedures necessary for practitioners to undertake in developing a total curriculum for the gifted. From an understanding of this process, the reader can form an impression of the issues, concepts, and processes involved in curriculum development before examining curriculum from a specialized point of view in a given area of inquiry. Chapters on theory, research, and practice, the curriculum development, and the design process comprise the first three chapters of the book. The next two chapters provide an intensive view of both the macro approach to developing curriculum through scope and sequence and the micro approach to developing curriculum through units. These five chapters, taken together, provide the framework for all of the chapters that follow in that they lay out the blueprint and specifications for any area of the curriculum to be considered.

The next four chapters address the core curriculum areas treated in all schools as their general education. These chapters on the verbal arts, social science, science, and mathematics attempt to delineate important considerations in planning, developing, and implementing curriculum for the gifted in these areas. Each chapter has been conceptualized (1) to address broad goals of a gifted program in that content domain K–12, (2) to present the current state of the art regarding curriculum for gifted learners in that content area, (3) to provide specific examples of exemplary curricula in those fields at various levels, (4) to offer guidelines for implementing the curriculum, and (5) to recommend resources that should prove useful to readers in acquiring relevant curriculum materials. These content chapters also attempt to establish the relationship of the three curriculum models introduced in Chapter 1 to each area. The reader can then readily translate ideas on content acceleration, process skill enrichment, and interdisciplinary themes to curriculum.

Section Three focuses on important curriculum areas frequently not found in programs for the gifted but that are important fundamental areas of exploration for them. These areas include humanities, the arts, affective curriculum, leadership, and thinking skills. Chapters 6 through 9 show the reader various approaches to incorporating and integrating these important topics within a program of study for gifted learners. These areas of the curriculum can be seen as distinctive domains of study in themselves and also as significant threads within

**FIGURE 1 Sample Content and Process Overlaps in Key Areas of the
                  Curriculum**

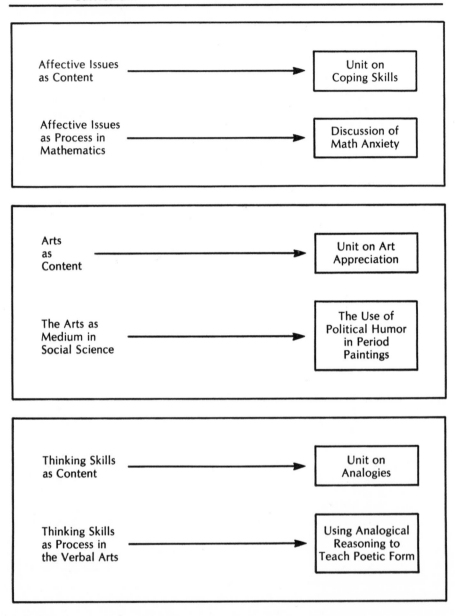

more traditional content; thus they can be viewed as both content and the means by which content is communicated. Figure 1 presents this dual purpose.

The next three chapters focus on the important relationships of curriculum to classroom and school district implementation. These relationships include classroom instructional strategies, computer technology, and instructional leadership in the context of school programs for the gifted. The importance of these support structures to the framework of curriculum for the gifted cannot be underestimated, for they represent the major pathways to curriculum delivery.

The final chapter of the book presents a synthesis of total curriculum experiences for gifted learners. It focuses on a set of guiding principles behind the planning and development of specialized curriculum for this population.

Introduction _____

How do we help a gifted student to excel? The answer to this question is a complicated one. We believe that what happens to a child in school has a significant effect on the process.

The quality and character of a school's curriculum is a vital ingredient to the eventual realization of a child's capacity. Two key propositions underlie the curriculum ideas we are about to share. First, *gifted and talented students, like all students, have the right to a continuity of educational experience that meets their present and future academic needs.* Second, *when an organized, thoughtful curriculum plan is in place and when that curriculum is supported by an articulate, informed educational leadership, the probability of capturing the interest and energy of our ablest young thinkers is markedly enhanced.*

The provision of curriculum and instruction for gifted learners occurs by planned intent rather than by serendipity. We want these students to excel, to enhance their capabilities in relation to the demands of the academic experience. Such is the responsible course for professional educators.

These propositions are stated with a clear understanding that a vital aspect to the successful accomplishment of these ends relate directly to the quality of the ongoing exchange between the learner and teacher. We know that good things can happen for our ablest learners if they have good teachers at critical stages of development. Certainly, an organized educational curriculum is another key ingredient in this complex blending of circumstance so central to the transformation of a gifted learner's initial capacity for intellectual activity into a mature competence for academic and professional accomplishment.

Beliefs and Assumptions

The authors feel strongly about certain issues regarding appropriate curriculum for the gifted and use these beliefs as strong underpinnings to the book. The basic premises on which this book was created are:

1. All learners should be provided curriculum opportunities that allow them to attain optimum levels of learning.

2. Gifted learners have different learning needs compared with typical learners. Therefore, curriculum must be adapted or designed to accommodate these needs.

3. The needs of gifted learners cut across cognitive, affective, social, and aesthetic areas of the curriculum experience.

4. Gifted learners are best served by a confluent approach that allows for accelerated and advanced learning, and enriched and extended experiences.

5. Curriculum experiences for gifted learners need to be carefully planned, written down, and implemented in order to maximize their potential effect.
6. Curriculum development for gifted learners is an ongoing process that uses evaluation as a central tool for future planning and revision of curriculum documents.

This book does not treat the traditional "curriculum models for the gifted," such as Bloom's Taxonomy, Guilford's Structure of the Intellect, the Williams Model, or Renzulli's Enrichment Triad, as fundamental models for conceptualizing curriculum. Since the authors' view of these models departs somewhat from the conventional view in the field of gifted education, it seems useful to state and clarify it here. We believe these models help practitioners to organize curriculum experiences at various levels, but they do not help them to decide on appropriate content for gifted learners. Several individual chapters reference these models, and they are used by the authors as teaching or instructional tools rather than as curriculum models per se.

The authors acknowledge that there are at least three different curricula operative in schools: the "intended" curriculum that is written down, the "delivered" curriculum that is implemented, and the "received" curriculum that is evaluated at least partially through student performance. In order to ensure a reasonable relationship among these perceptual differences, ongoing monitoring and evaluation of both learner outcomes and curriculum content and process must occur. Although this issue is treated procedurally in Chapters 2 and 3, it needs to be considered here as a major premise of the book. Figure 2 presents the dynamic and multiple shifts that any written curriculum makes once it is enabled through the process of instruction to enter the arena of learning.

Furthermore, the authors of this book view curriculum as a set of planned experiences for a targeted population, rather than as an evolving process in the

FIGURE 2 The Operationalizing of Curriculum

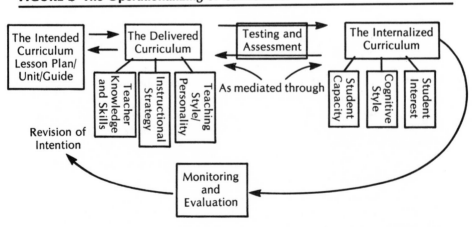

context of the classroom. Whereas we value and hold in place the dual perspective of static curriculum and dynamic instruction, we have chosen to filter this "simultaneity" model through the various lenses that shape curricular experiences in schools, with the predominant focus being at the level of overall curriculum planning and organization. Although classroom activities are highlighted throughout the topical chapters, the intent has been to focus on appropriate learning goals and objectives within key areas of learning.

The Integrated View

An important perspective for developing appropriate curriculum for the gifted learner in a comprehensive manner is to see it as an integrated set of experiences. The authors have chosen to present this perspective through the metaphor of a house. Figures 3A, 3B, 3C, and 3D illustrate this framework. The house of comprehensive curriculum for the gifted has four sides that are each characterized by fundamental realms or doors of learning: cognitive, affective, social, and aesthetic.* Each door has a curriculum that unlocks a given realm of learning and allows access to more specific domains of study.

On each side of the house are windows that look in on rooms of individual study. The roof of the house is characterized as development and design, those organizational elements of curriculum work that both help define and protect the structure. The foundation of the curriculum house is knowledge, which is the basis for all sides of learning. The support structures of the curriculum house are threefold: instructional strategies, computer technology, and instructional leadership. These structures serve as props to keep the total structure grounded in the operational day-to-day functions of schools. On the cognitive side, the humanities are viewed as the connective tissue among the knowledge domains, representing the major contributions of each knowledge area. Thus they serve as the hallways between rooms and the corridor that connects all rooms. The verbal arts, science, the social sciences, and mathematics are the rooms of study unlocked through a thinking skills curriculum. On the affective side of learning, the key to unlocking these rooms is an affective curriculum. Access to the rooms of self-concept, social skills, motivation, sensitivity, and purpose in life is then acquired. Turning to the social learning side, the turnkey is a leadership curriculum that unlocks the spaces of group dynamics, styles, traits, moral development, and ethical decision making. Our final side of learning is aesthetic learning, accessed primarily through the expressive arts of music, graphic arts, drama, and dance, but with an interconnecting corridor to the fine arts areas.

Although all sides of the house are equally important in addressing the needs of gifted learners, this book focuses more strongly on the cognitive, which represents the front side of most school curricula at the present time. In furnishing and decorating a house, one usually starts with the essential rooms so that daily functions can be performed easily. Thus we have chosen to focus on the

---

* Psychomotor learning with its domains of study are not treated formally within this book, although it is recognized by the authors as an important realm of learning.

FIGURE 3A The House of Curriculum: Cognitive View for the Gifted

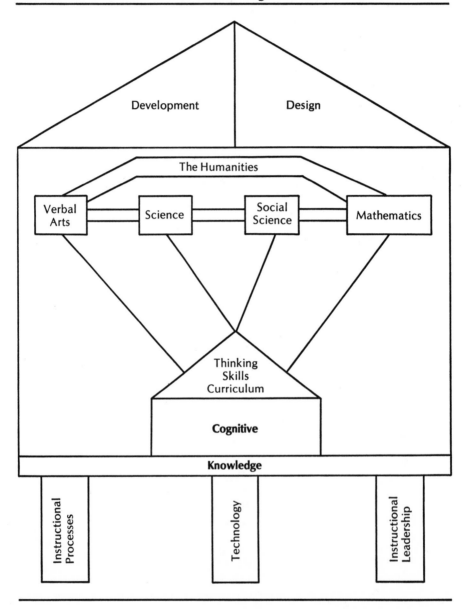

domains of study viewed by schools as essential curriculum so that the majority of time gifted learners spend in school is not dysfunctional.

This house of curriculum reveals other relationships of importance. As one moves inside the house from any entrance point, it becomes clear that a perceptual shift has occurred. Now the sides of the house lose their meaning as one

FIGURE 3B The House of Curriculum: Affective View for the Gifted

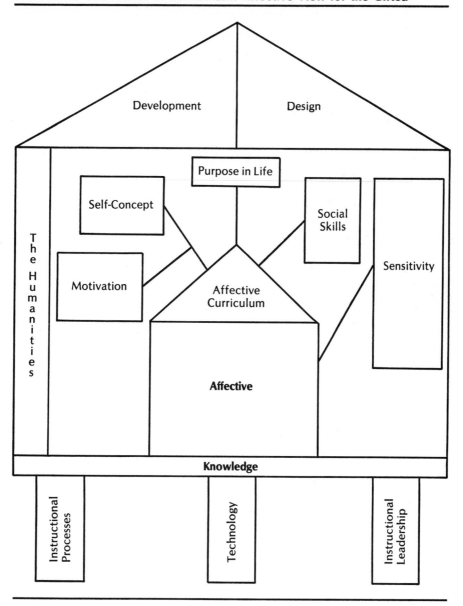

begins to explore the floor plan, room by room. Connections can be made across realms of learning as desired or needed, for each room has four walls that now can represent the four sides of learning, using a single domain of study as a focal point. Thus mathematics curriculum can be viewed as an aesthetic, social, and affective experience as well as a cognitive one, and ethical decision making can

FIGURE 3C The House of Curriculum: Social View for the Gifted

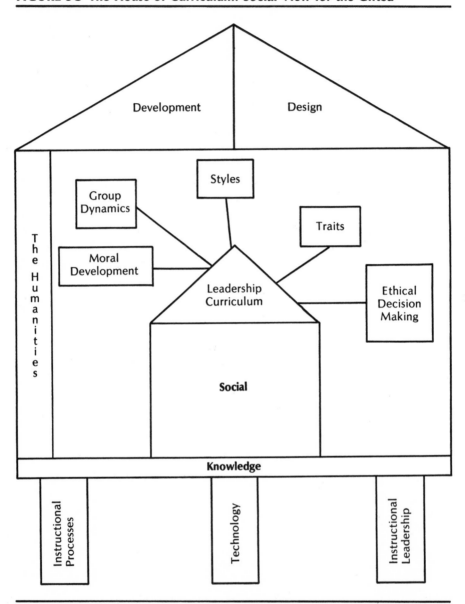

be treated in the cognitive realm of the social studies as well as a separate area of social learning. As the occupant of the house of curriculum, we hold four keys that serve to provide access to particular sets of rooms, yet they are intrinsically valuable as well. Thinking skills curriculum can be seen as a strand running through each traditional domain of study, and as a distinctive piece of curricu-

FIGURE 3D The House of Curriculum: Aesthetic View for the Gifted

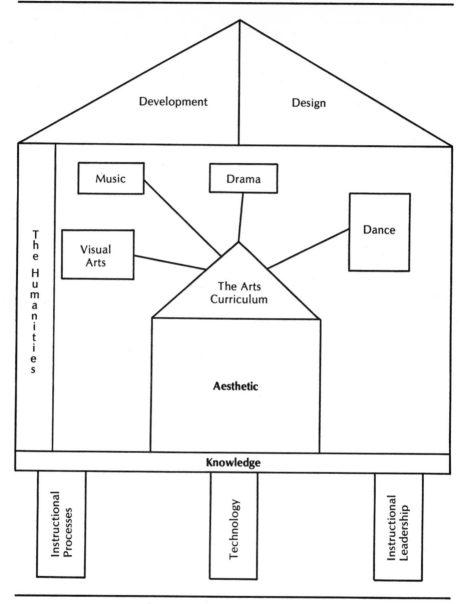

lum in its own right. Leadership curriculum for the gifted can be woven through other curriculum areas or represent a singular focus in the curriculum. So too is the case with affective curriculum and the arts.

This metaphor of a house represents the superstructure of an ideal curriculum for gifted learners that can be adapted to meet their needs at all stages of development. It also accounts for the multifaceted and adaptable aspects of any curriculum area and its shared interdependence with other areas. Furthermore, it envisions a comprehensive approach to curriculum making and doing in several realms. In practical terms, this perspective implies that schools are addressing the broad needs of gifted students in cognitive, affective, social, and aesthetic realms through a program of study that includes all domains of study from kindergarten through grade twelve. The authors strongly believe that this vision of curriculum must become a shared vision so that comprehensive curriculum becomes the norm in programs for the gifted and not the exception, as it currently is. We invite you to explore the house of comprehensive curriculum as it unfolds.

Joyce VanTassel-Baska

1 Curriculum for the Gifted: Theory, Research, and Practice

Joyce VanTassel-Baska

In human affairs the logical future, determined by past and present conditions, is less important than the willed future, which is largely brought about by deliberate choices.

—René Dubos

Over twenty years ago, national reports ushered in a new era for educational and curricular change, predominantly in science and mathematics. Today, educators again are faced with a barrage of reports that describe deficiencies in the current instruction in mathematics and science and in other content disciplines as well. *A Nation at Risk* (National Commission on Excellence in Education, 1983) reports on the abysmal failure of public education in exposing students to full secondary programs in science and mathematics. The Carnegie Report (1986) further documents the need for more advanced course taking in these subjects by larger numbers of the secondary school population. The College Board's *Project Equality* (1983) outlines maximum competency skills in academic areas that require mastery in today's technologically advanced world. The most stringent recommendations on curriculum are reported by the National Science Commission (1983), which prescribes four full years of science and mathematics for the majority of students in our schools.

Implementing such recommendations would require a massive change in course-taking patterns. A recent study completed for the California State Department of Education (Harnischfeger and Wiley, 1983) found that only 5 percent of California's secondary school graduates and only 2.2 percent of those in Illinois would meet the standards for course taking set forth in the National Science Commission Report, even excluding the recommendation on computer coursework.

Some of the preeminent educational thinkers in the United States today have published treatises on the nature of ideal schooling. Adler's *Paedaeia Proposal* (1984) advocates a basic liberal arts education for all, with a focus on traditional content and the objectives of knowledge acquisition, thinking skill development, and aesthetic appreciation. From an administrative perspective, Goodlad's *A Place Called School* (1983) explores fundamental deficiencies in how schools are organized to carry out instructional tasks. The instructional focus of Bloom's (1980) work on mastery learning provides a model for the systematic and progressive development of skills in various domains of knowledge.

Based on the proliferation of reports on problems and remedies, it is clear that American education is experiencing significant pressure for reform and curricular change. In particular, there is renewed interest in focusing efforts on the academically talented, where educational success can increase performance benefits to the institutions that serve these students well. The visibility provided to the achievements of the gifted can also enhance the educational enterprise for those who are less able.

Although many local programming efforts have not been responsive to the perceived needs of a modern technological society, programming for the gifted and talented can provide a starting point to upgrade these efforts, particularly in areas that national reports have cited as most deficient: mathematics, science, technology, and foreign language. The practical application of theoretical ideas about curriculum for the gifted must be sensitive to the current organizational structure of the schools, the present K–12 curriculum needs, and the recommendations for change being advocated by these major studies. By responding to this challenge in the education of the gifted, local school districts can begin to address issues of excellence that can have qualitative and quantitative impact.

The Forces That Drive Curriculum

We have just emerged from a "dry spell" in curriculum work in this country. Very few large-scale curriculum projects have been undertaken or funded since the splurge of the National Science Foundation in the 1960s. However, curriculum development is now in the forefront of educational reform. Leading the way is the Amoco Foundation's $50 million grant to the University of Chicago to change the shape of American mathematics education at the elementary and secondary levels over a five-year period. A new round of NSF funding also promises innovative science and math curriculum, with a heavy focus on technological application.

What has caused this resurgence of interest in curriculum? One of the social forces at work is our concern as a nation for meeting future workforce needs. Wirsup (1986) reported on the dismal status of America's students in math and science when compared to their Russian, Japanese, and West German counterparts. Numerous reports over the last few years continue to document similar deficiencies in performance. At the national level there has been a pronounced shift in focus from issues like discipline and community involvement to hard questions about the content and sequence of curriculum. The egalitarian philosophy that dominated the last twenty years of educational policy altered curriculum standards, reduced requirements, and created an elective system that spawned low test scores and gaps in traditional knowledge, and contributed to widespread illiteracy. A concomitant focus on the education of the handicapped has sparked an examination of our educational priorities. The billions of dollars allocated to tailoring educational programs to the special needs of handicapped children as a result of the passage of PL 94–142 have raised our consciousness about schooling in general, as well as education for our most gifted and talented.

All of these educational forces have coalesced to create a climate for curriculum reform.

Juxtaposed with these forces in our educational system is new research that affects the progress of curriculum change. New data about how and when children learn are available to shape the curriculum process. Studies on information processing, cognitive mapping, individual differences, and cognitive styles have contributed to understanding how children learn and how curriculum should be altered. The infusion of critical thinking and problem solving as major areas to be included in the curriculum for all students is indicative of this impact.

Curriculum is also being affected by larger social and political contexts. Computer technology has found its way into the curriculum as a "basic" subject rather than as a peripheral. Global interdependence has become a major organizing theme of special programs in all content areas, not just social studies. On the other side of the ledger, moral majority advocates have brought about the dissolution of values education, and other educational foci that encourage free and open inquiry by students.

Goodlad (1979) posits that curriculum decision making is done at two levels, each in isolation from the other. School boards effect curriculum policy and teachers implement classroom curriculum. Little curriculum leadership is provided at a middle level by building principals or central office staff. Consequently, curriculum implementation as a standardized process does not occur in most public school settings. Even skeptical parents are not likely to challenge teachers in an area heavily loaded with issues of expertise and academic freedom.

But curriculum is still mostly driven by the inertia of the status quo, a system of skill-based areas of inquiry that proceed on a continuum from first grade to twelfth grade, frequently with little examination of the "why" of a curriculum offering at a particular point in the sequence. For example, algebra was not in the school curriculum sixty years ago, and now the debate rages as to its appropriateness at the ninth-grade level where it was initiated and has tended to stay. Reading continues to follow a similar illogical path of development based on a curriculum model that ignores individual readiness issues.

Since curriculum is at a point of potential change, it behooves educators of the gifted to take a strong role in defining what it should be for the most able, the process by which it is formulated, and the diversity of products or outcomes to be anticipated. It is through appropriate curriculum design and delivery for the top 5 percent of the population that the whole of curriculum can be upgraded and enhanced. Curricular work for the gifted can spearhead higher standards and more rigorous methodologies in addressing the needs of the rest of the student body.

A CURRICULUM PHILOSOPHY FOR THE GIFTED

It is important for school district personnel to consider what philosophy guides their thinking regarding appropriate curriculum for the gifted. Since most gifted programs are not comprehensive at this evolutionary stage of development, educators should be cognizant of what theory drives the nature of their curricular offerings to gifted learners. Eisner and Vallance (1974) present five conceptions of curriculum that have shaped the thinking of educators in this century. The roots of each of these conceptions can also be found in extant curriculum for the gifted, and represent strong philosophical orientations for what our view of curriculum for the gifted might be. A sixth orientation related to career preparation is also considered here.

1. Curriculum as the development of cognitive process. This orientation in the education of the gifted has focused on process skill development and has led to the adoption of curriculum materials organized around higher level thinking skills. Having its roots in faculty psychology, it has fostered a content-independent model of curriculum that uses cognitive skills as the centerpiece of all learning activities. Implicit in this view is the assumption that learning cognitive skills will translate across, apply to, and enhance any field of inquiry a student may encounter. Many pull-out programs for the gifted, which reflect this orientation, have emphasized critical thinking, creative thinking, and problem solving as the substance of their curriculum, treating these process skills as content dimensions in their own right.

2. Curriculum as technology. This approach to curriculum also is process-oriented, but focuses on the organization of curriculum into student inputs and output. This view of curriculum relies heavily on stated behavioral or performance objectives with measurable outcomes that can be tested in order to determine educational progress or achievement. Much of the curriculum work done for the Title IV-C gifted projects utilized this orientation to a great extent. Small-scale curriculum unit projects also tend to favor it as a way to organize the written work of curriculum making in a formal manner.

3. Curriculum as personal relevance. This orientation promotes a child-centered model that requires curriculum experiences to be tailored to individual student needs at particular points in time. The interest of students in specific areas guides the curriculum. The goal of such curriculum is to be personally engaging and to offer consummatory experiences that will provide growth at each student's level of understanding. The curriculum models in gifted education employed by Renzulli (1977) and Feldhusen and Kolloff (1978) both favor this orientation. Gifted students become responsible for their own curriculum through contracts with a facilitator who assesses interest, ability, and maturity factors. Independent investigations are shaped by this information, and the interaction of student and facilitator form the central core of curriculum experiences.

4. Curriculum as social reconstruction. This view of curriculum holds that the purpose of educational institutions is that of agents for social change and that the content of curriculum should be viewed within the larger social and cultural realm. Topics to be studied are chosen to promote community action programs needed in a student's immediate environment and to promote individual and collective social responsibility. Engaging students in social actions such as drafting a piece of legislation, taking a poll of neighborhood opinions regarding nuclear energy, or organizing a school anti-pollution campaign typify the curricular experience as part of social reform. Work in the education of the gifted that best exemplifies this orientation is the curriculum for global futures and the theme of global interdependence developed at the Center for Global Futures in Muncie, Indiana. Whole school districts also have organized curriculum this way to serve the high-school gifted student, such as Glenbrook Academy in Northbrook, Illinois, and Morgan Park High School in Chicago.

5. *Curriculum as academic rationalism.* This curriculum orientation has its roots in the western tradition of rational humanism. Specifically, it adheres to an ideal of education as a way of providing students with an understanding of great ideas and an ability to analyze and synthesize past achievements. It further espouses a belief in the structure of knowledge as embodied in the organization of academic and artistic fields of inquiry, and seeks to instruct students within those content disciplines. Most of the "durable" curriculum that is regularly used in gifted programs flows from this general orientation. The special National Science Foundation curriculum projects in mathematics, science, English, and social studies (MACOS) that were developed in the 1960s were all rooted in this orientation. Programs like Junior Great Books and Philosophy for Children also adhere to this view.

6. *Curriculum as a precursor to career/professional life.* This view of curriculum has its roots in both the professional school and vocational school models that have influenced curriculum offerings over the last twenty years. A strong focus on the practical and the utilitarian has been a preoccupation at secondary and postsecondary levels. In the field of the gifted, this orientation may best be seen through the career education models (see Hoyt and Hebeler, 1974) that have appeared to help students view curriculum as a preparation for their future. The work experience programs for the gifted, loosely termed *mentorships* and *internships,* also have a utilitarian "real-world" focus. In these programs, students relate to the practicing professional in his or her domain and come to understand and appreciate their own potential as future practitioners of a particular craft.

Although educators are free to choose among these curricular philosophies, the most effective comprehensive programs incorporate several if not all of them. Whereas the academic rationalist's view most closely accommodates the current curricular organization of schools, and has guided most long-term curriculum efforts, it should not be considered in isolation of other perspectives.

It may be useful, however, to develop a philosophy of curriculum for the gifted to ensure its incorporation into school district policy and practice. The following statements represent a sample philosophy regarding curriculum for the gifted that captures the spirit of many of the competing orientations previously described.

1: SAMPLE GENERAL CURRICULUM PHILOSOPHY FOR THE GIFTED

There are over two million school-age children in the United States, who, because of their outstanding ability, are called *gifted and talented.* They come from all kinds of cultural and socioeconomic backgrounds. Once stereotyped as physically weak and mentally unbalanced, gifted and talented children are now generally viewed as healthy and well-adjusted. However, they differ in many ways from children with average abilities.

Education for the gifted and talented requires an understanding that their differences are both real and legitimate. Curricula are planned for them, not on the basis of content that suits the majority of pupils, but on the basis of their advanced accomplishments and interest, which require different content and different opportunities. Like all other students, their educational experiences must be appropriate for *them*.

An adequate curriculum must be diverse, advanced, and complex enough to reflect the abilities of the gifted and talented. The content of such a curriculum should provide interest and challenge, not opportunities to mark time and do "good" work. The hallmark of education for the gifted and talented is careful planning of individual opportunities for advanced learning that are suitable to exceptional minds and talents. Such education enhances development; it does not restrict or postpone it. It accommodates the school to the students, rather than the reverse. In short, it recognizes the child's right to learn and advance his or her unique potential for self-actualization as well as society's need for outstanding contributions.

2: SAMPLE LOCAL SCHOOL DISTRICT CURRICULUM PHILOSOPHY FOR THE GIFTED

Our curriculum philosophy for the gifted and talented recognizes, first of all, the importance of quality curriculum for all students at all stages of development. Second, it recognizes that differences exist among individual learners at given stages of development that can best be addressed through differentiated curriculum experiences. Third, our philosophy acknowledges that the gifted are only one population for which such developmental differences in cognition might be addressed in curriculum areas. Moreover, we advocate differentiated curriculum for gifted learners in those areas where the diagnostic tools available to us can discern significant differences from the typical learner at a given stage of development.

For intellectually gifted learners, the resultant curriculum modifications needed would be comprehensive and affect all curriculum areas in the school program. For students talented in only one or two areas, modifications would be limited to those areas. Our curriculum for gifted learners would ensure a balanced focus on opportunities for accelerated and enriched experiences within traditional areas of learning, opportunities for learning the skills underlying the thinking process, opportunities for experiences that promote an understanding of the world's people and their relationship to each other, opportunities for exploring personal futures, and opportunities for the independent quest of knowledge in areas of interest to the student.

We believe that gifted students have a right to educational experiences that address their needs. In providing for those needs, we address the whole child with a total curriculum that integrates realms of learning within and across planned experiences, that provides for a progressive development of knowledge and skills, and that enhances an appreciation of humanity.

Conceptualizing an appropriate curriculum for the gifted involves exploring some key questions about the curriculum framework. The following four questions are critical in considering curriculum issues for the gifted.

WHAT SHOULD BE THE NATURE OF EXPERIENCES PROVIDED TO GIFTED LEARNERS?

Although the field of gifted education is not prolific with intervention studies, the body of literature on acceleration (see Daurio, 1979) places it in the category of an appropriate experience for some gifted learners. Generally, there is consensus in the literature that students operating two standard deviations above the norm on an appropriate measure can profit from accelerative experiences. Much descriptive literature has been written about enrichment experiences that speak of broadening a student's view of the world of knowledge (Gallagher, 1985; Kaplan, 1979; Renzulli, 1977; Feldhusen and Kolloff, 1978). Counseling has also been mentioned as important to the emotional and social growth of the gifted learner as well as an important underpinning to any devised academic program (Gowan, Demos, and Khatena, 1965; Colangelo and Zaffran, 1979; Piechowski, 1984). Although acceleration, enrichment, and counseling represent the major interventions used with the gifted over the last eighty years, it remains to be determined which are most effective under what circumstances with which gifted learners. Shouldn't the nature of appropriate experiences reflect the purpose for which special programs are developed for this population; namely, to nurture high potential students so they can become creative, productive adults and future leaders in society? Given this as a purpose, what clustering of experiences over time is most apt to produce the desired result?

WHO SHOULD PROVIDE SERVICE TO GIFTED LEARNERS?

Much of the research on eminent adults tends to suggest that important individuals, not schools or teachers per se, have had a profound effect on intellectual and artistic attainments. Usually such individuals were part of the family unit—a mentor, a tutor, or a special teacher. Bloom (1985) notes that schools served only as gatekeepers regarding the talent development process for individuals in his study. The effectiveness of the talent search model over time (Benbow and Stanley, 1983) suggests that a collaborative effort between higher education institutions and elementary/secondary schools can benefit many highly gifted learners. Such data raise issues about the generalizability of these findings to other groups of gifted learners. Can less gifted students profit as much from such intervention techniques? Can less gifted students benefit from access to college work? These data also challenge the role of the local school in talent development, and even more, the role of the typical classroom teacher. Are special qualities necessary to work with gifted learners, even given an effective training program? Should the focus be on training teachers or on training potentially effective individuals? What kind of training emphasis might be most appropriate—in-depth work in a specialty area such as science, the development of effective instructional procedures and strategies, or understanding the nature and needs of the target population? What criteria might be used to determine the appropriateness of individuals and/or institutions in working with the gifted?

WHAT CONSTITUTES A HIGH-QUALITY EDUCATIONAL PROGRAM FOR GIFTED LEARNERS?

Since quality education is a concern for all students in our schools, what standards of excellence can be employed that would ensure that the most able have the opportunity to be the most productive? There is a need to focus on some key issues in deciding what constitutes educational quality for this population. The most obvious is the quality of the facilitator (teacher, mentor, etc.) working with such students. How can one balance the need for high-level competence with the need for personal qualities that provides a context for role modeling, and where can such individuals most likely be found? Quality programs are also visible by their curriculum, the degree to which it responds to the needs of the learner, that it is dynamic, that it is sufficiently advanced and challenging, and that it is well-planned and organized with attention to scope and sequence. And finally, quality programs can be discerned through their regard for efficiency and effectiveness—that student growth gains are measured, and that levels of proficiency are well-defined within a time frame that is sufficient for student progress. The challenging issue is how to develop and implement such programs in a context that provides the comprehensive range of services needed on an articulated basis over time. What cooperative models might be developed among institutions to effect such program development? Or can individual schools reorganize and reallocate resources to provide it? Is there consensus around what markers constitute an appropriate program for differing populations of gifted learners?

HOW CAN "QUALITY" PROGRAMS BE EVALUATED?

The dearth of literature on the effects of program intervention (Weiss and Gallagher, 1982) may be as indicative of ineffectual means to measure program treatment as it is of low-quality programs. What evaluation approaches are most appropriate to use in the context of special gifted programs? Can evaluation data be effectively used to engender greater support for special programs? Of the evaluation models used in extant intervention studies (i.e., quasi-experimental, comparison, goal-based, product review, attitudinal), which appears most promising for future work?

Research on Curriculum for the Gifted

Research into appropriate curriculum for the gifted child is rather meager. Until the Sputnik era of the late 1950s, which resulted in programs that addressed specific content areas, few ideas about differentiated curriculum for the gifted were systematically studied. Even though special classes had been in operation since 1919 in selected locations such as New York and Cleveland, the actual differences in instructional strategies, content, or materials were not examined. Grouping based on intelligence and achievement was the predominant strategy employed, although individual grade acceleration was practiced to some extent, and curriculum outlines and sometimes units were prepared for use with the identified gifted students (Hollingworth, 1926; Hall, 1956).

Over the last twenty years, however, educators in the field of the gifted have formulated some general principles about appropriate curriculum for the gifted children. Ward (1961) developed a theory of differential education for the gifted that established specific principles about appropriate curriculum. Meeker (1969) used the Guilford Structure of Intellect (SOI) to arrive at student profiles that highlighted areas of strength and weakness so that curriculum planners could build a gifted program to improve weak areas. Curriculum workbooks were structured to address this need in the areas of memory, cognition, convergent thinking, divergent thinking, and evaluation. Renzulli (1977) focused on a model that moved the gifted child from enrichment exposure activities through training in thinking and research skills into a project-oriented program that dwelt on real problems to be solved. Gallagher (1985) stressed content modification in the core subject areas of language arts, social studies, mathematics, and science. Stanley, Keating, and Fox (1974) concentrated on a content acceleration approach to differentiate programs for the gifted. Recent writings, including Feldhusen and Kolloff (1978), Kaplan (1979), and Maker (1982), have stressed a confluent approach to differentiation of curriculum for the gifted that includes both acceleration and enrichment strategies. Passow et al. (1982) formulated several cardinal curriculum principles that reflect content, process, product, behavioral, and evaluative considerations.

For the most part, research on curriculum for the gifted has been minimal and what has been undertaken has failed to demonstrate convincing effectiveness with gifted children in comparison to other groups (Gallagher, 1985). Part of the reason is that most of the research has tended to be descriptive in nature, documenting what occurred in classrooms rather than attempting to assess the match between learner needs and curriculum intervention (Kaplan, 1979). Exceptions to that have focused almost exclusively on proficiency gains within a content dimension (Keating, 1976; Benbow and Stanley, 1983). And, ironically, much of the curriculum developed in the late 1950s and early 1960s (e.g., BSCS biology, IPS science, MACOS, Project Physics) that could have been effective with gifted learners was used with *all* students, whereupon it failed. Thus excellent curriculum materials disappeared from use in public schools because they were not successful with all students.

Title IV-C programs constituted another source for curriculum developed specifically for gifted learners and field-tested for its effectiveness in a controlled setting. However, loss of funding and lack of widespread dissemination caused much of this work to become fugitive literature and almost unattainable for replication efforts.

The work of curriculum laboratories like CEMREL in St. Louis and CIRCE at the University of Illinois has resulted in excellent curricula for the gifted; however, adoption of these curricula frequently requires a more controlled environment to demonstrate success than is typical in most public school settings. Thus widespread adoption appears to be unfeasible to many practitioners.

Practical Curriculum Models for the Gifted

Although research on curriculum for the gifted provides a paucity of evidence regarding effectiveness, three relatively distinct curriculum models have proven successful with gifted populations at various stages of development and in various domain-specific areas. They are: (1) the content mastery model, (2) the process/product research model, and (3) the epistemological concept model.

THE CONTENT MODEL

The content model emphasizes the importance of learning skills and concepts within a predetermined domain of inquiry. Gifted students are encouraged to move as rapidly as possible through the content area; thus content acceleration dominates the application of this model in practice. When a diagnostic-prescriptive instructional approach (D→P) is utilized, students are first pretested and then given appropriate mateirals to master the subject area segments prescribed.

The D→P instructional approach has proved effective in controlled settings, but has not been widely practiced in regular classrooms for the gifted. Several reasons appear to account for this. Like any individualized model, it requires a highly competent classroom manager to implement it. When used appropriately, each student may be working on a different problem, chapter, or book at the same time. Regardless of the rhetoric surrounding individualization, very little is actively practiced in basic curriculum areas. A second reason is that most pull-out gifted programs do not focus on core content areas and therefore negate the possible employment of the model. Third, the approach has not been particularly valued by many educators of the gifted because of its insistence on utilizing the same curriculum and merely altering the rate. The lecture-discussion approach to the content model is more widely practiced at the secondary level, but its effectiveness is highly dependent on teachers being well-versed in the structure as well as in the content of their discipline. Too frequently the content model disintegrates into learning the exact same skills and concepts as all learners are expected to do in the school context, only tediously doing more exercises and drills in a shorter period of time.

In the D→P approach, teachers and teaching assistants act as facilitators of instruction rather than as didactic lecturers; although many content-based programs for the gifted place a strong emphasis on lecture and discussion. The curriculum is organized by the intellectual content of the discipline and is highly sequential and cumulative in nature, making a proficiency-based model for measuring achievement very feasible.

The D→P approach to the content model has been utilized effectively by talent search programs across the country, particularly in mathematics (Keating, 1976; Benbow and Stanley, 1983). VanTassel-Baska (1982) has shown the effectiveness of the model in teaching Latin, and foreign language teachers have used the model for years to ensure English syntactic mastery in their students. Clearly, it represents the most individualized instructional approach to basic curriculum for the gifted, and it embodies a continuous progress philosophy that schools readily understand.

The more typical approach to content-based instruction, however, is one that presets an early mastery level for students, frequently requiring more advanced skills and concepts to be mastered one year earlier than normal. The content model uses existing school curriculum and textbooks, so it is not costly to implement. Although it responds to the rate needs of groups of students, allowing the able to advance a little more quickly through the traditional curriculum, it may still leave the highly gifted unchallenged.

In fairness to the content-based model, teachers who use it successfully have made important alterations in the organization of the subject matter being taught. For example, in the fast-paced Latin program, the concepts that are spread out incrementally over the first three chapters of the book are synthesized into a matrix study sheet, presenting students with all five Latin cases, three genders, and two numbers in their various combinations all at once. Homework is assigned only from the third unit, where all the interactions of gender, number, and case may be practiced. Thus thirty hours of instructional time may be reduced to four or five at the most, and gifted students can master the important concepts governing Latin syntax in an economical fashion.

What appears as a simple process of moving more quickly through the same basic material becomes more sophisticated in actual practice. The effective teacher reorganizes the content area under study according to higher level skills and concepts. The focus of student prescriptive work is in larger increments that carry with them a holistic picture of the topic under study.

The content mastery model for curriculum and instruction also has the capacity to cover the regular skill-based curriculum in reading and mathematics in approximately one-third the time currently expended. This condensation process occurs as a result of two curriculum modifications. Students move through skill areas at a rate commensurate with their capacity. By testing for proficiency and assigning work based on documented increased levels of development, and by reorganizing basic skill areas into higher level skill clusters, mastery learning time is conserved, and more efficient and challenging learning experiences are promoted.

The first approach might be accomplished through the following modifications:

Reading Curriculum Topic: Word Attack Skills

Typical Learner Sequence:	Recognizing and sounding out consonants →	Recognizing and sounding out → vowels	Phonemes, prefixes, and suffixes
Gifted Learner Sequence:	Pretest on reading →	Analysis of skill gaps inhibiting reading →	Prescription of work on phonemes, prefixes, and suffixes

The second approach would be accomplished through this additional modification, again in the reading curriculum:

Typical Learner Sequence:	Topic:	Work Attack Skills
	Subtopics:	Recognizing and sounding out consonants; recognizing and sounding out vowels, phonemes, and prefixes and suffixes.
Gifted Learner Sequence:	Topic:	Reading Comprehension (whole words)
	Subtopics:	Word attack skills
		Prefixes and suffixes
		Root words

Through these two modifications, gifted students can master the typical skill-based curriculum in less time and at an appropriate level of complexity and

challenge. For much of the elementary reading, mathematics, and language curriculum, this approach is both feasible and efficacious for gifted learners.

THE PROCESS/PRODUCT MODEL

The process/product model places heavy emphasis on learning investigatory
skills, both scientific and social, that allow students to develop a high-quality
product. It is a highly collaborative model that involves teacher-practitioner-
student as an interactive team in exploring specific topics. Consultation and
independent work dominate the instructional pattern, culminating in student
understanding of the scientific process as it is reflected in selective exploration
of key topics.

Reported in the literature under the rubric of the enrichment triad and the
Purdue model (Renzulli, 1977; Feldhusen and Kolloff, 1978), this approach to
curriculum for the gifted is also successful. At the secondary level, special science programs for the gifted have used the model (VanTassel-Baska and Kulieke, 1987), and institutions like Walnut Hills High School in Cincinnati, Bronx
High School of Science in New York, and the North Carolina School of Math and
Science have practiced the model as a part of their high-powered science programs for years.

The model engages the student in problem finding and problem solving and
puts the student in contact with adult practitioners. In the field of science, for
example, scientists from Argonne National Laboratory work with academically
talented junior-high students during the summer to help them develop research
proposals for project work during the following academic year. Students are
actively involved in generating a research topic, conducting a literature search,
selecting an experimental design, and describing their plan of work in a proposal. The proposal is then critiqued not only by the instructor but also the
scientist. In this way, then, students focus on process skill development in scientific inquiry and strive to develop a high-quality product. Figure 1.1 delineates
the three stages of the inquiry process used in the Northwestern-Argonne program.

The process/product model for gifted curriculum differs from the content-
based model in that content is incidental. Student interest is the mainspring for
what "content" will be studied. The nature of the evaluation effort is product-
based rather than proficiency-oriented, and the focus is on studying selected
topics in-depth rather than moving through a given domain of inquiry in a fast-
paced manner.

Although the model has worked well in pull-out programs for the gifted and
as a part of a total science program at the secondary level, it does present organizational problems for many schools. Critics contend that the single focus of this
model creates confusion around the curricular scope and sequence of learning at
any given level of instruction. Furthermore, the model at the elementary level
tends to devalue core content elements in the traditional curriculum, and to
overvalue independent learning strategies at that stage of development.

Nevertheless, it is the curriculum and instructional model most closely al-
lied with the recommendations of national teacher groups in both science and
mathematics who tend to favor a student-directed, hands-on, inquiry-based pro-

FIGURE 1.1 Three Stages of the Inquiry Process

Pre-Inquiry (Level 1 Skills)

___ 1. The student acquired scientific knowledge relevant to the questions being asked.

___ 2. The student drew relationships among things he or she observed.

Methods of Inquiry (Level 2 Skills)

___ 1. The student plans to use the techniques of identifying objects and object properties.

___ 2. The student plans to use the technique of making controlled observations.

___ 3. The student plans to examine changes in various physical systems.

___ 4. The student plans to order a series of observations.

___ 5. The student plans to classify various physical and biological systems by coding and tabulating data.

___ 6. The student plans to use the techniques of ordering, counting, adding, multiplying, dividing, finding averages, and using decimals.

___ 7. The student plans to demonstrate the rules of measurement as applicable to specific physical and biological systems (i.e., length, area, volume, weight, temperature, force, or speed).

___ 8. The student plans to conduct an experiment by identifying and controlling variables.

___ 9. The student has created operational definitions for the variables under study.

___ 10. The student stated a testable research hypothesis.

___ 11. The student plans to manipulate some type of materials.

___ 12. The student followed the specified proposal format.

Interpretive Inquiry Skills (Level 3 Skills)

___ 1. The student transformed the observed results into graphs, tables, diagrams, and reports.

___ 2. The student drew relationships among things he or she observed.

___ 3. The student generalized from his or her observations.

___ 4. The student interpreted tabular and graphical data.

___ 5. The student used the skills of interpolation and extrapolation to make predictions based on his or her data.

___ 6. The student made inferences based on his or her data.

___ 7. The student related data to statements of hypotheses.

___ 8. The student related previous work to his or her own.

___ 9. The student used the specified project format.

___ 10. The student developed some limitations of his or her study.

Source: Center for Talent Development, Northwestern University.

cess of problem solving, where students are engaged in the act of constructing knowledge for themselves.

THE EPISTEMOLOGICAL MODEL

The epistemological concept model focuses on talented students' understanding and appreciating systems of knowledge rather than the individual elements of those systems. It reflects a concern for exposing students to key ideas, themes, and principles within and across domains of knowledge so that schemata are internalized, synthesized, and amplified by future examples. The role of the teacher in this model is as questioner, raising interpretive issues for discussion and debate. Students focus their energies on reading, reflecting, and writing. Aesthetic appreciation of powerful ideas in various representational forms is viewed as an important outcome of this model.

This model is very effective with gifted learners for several reasons. First, the intellectually gifted child has unusually keen powers to see and understand interrelationships. The whole structure of conceptual curriculum is based on constantly interrelating form and content. Conceptual curriculum is an enrichment tool in the highest sense, for it provides the gifted with an intellectual framework not available in studying only one content area, but exposes them to many ideas not covered in traditional curricula. Furthermore, it provides a basis for students' understanding the creative as well as the intellectual process through critically analyzing creative products and being actively engaged in the creative process itself. It also provides a context for integrating cognitive and affective objectives into the curriculum. A discussion of ideas evokes feelings; a response to the arts involves aesthetic appreciation; and the study of literary archetypes creates a structure for self-identity.

Many writers in the field of gifted education have lauded the epistemological approach to curriculum (Ward, 1961; Hayes-Jacob, 1981; Maker, 1982; Tannenbaum, 1983). Some extant curriculum has been organized around the model at both elementary and secondary levels. The College Board Advanced Placement Program relies heavily on this curriculum approach in its history (both American and European) and literature and composition programs. The Junior Great Books program, Philosophy for Children, and Man: A Course of Study (MACOS) are elementary programs using the approach. Each of these programs stresses the use of Socratic questions to stimulate an intellectual discussion among students on an issue or theme. Creating analogies across a field of inquiry is encouraged, and interdisciplinary thinking is highly valued. Recent curriculum development efforts for the gifted have also attempted to utilize the epistemological framework (VanTassel-Baska and Feldhusen, 1981; Gallagher et al., 1984), and larger curriculum projects in the past, such as CEMREL's mathematics program at the secondary level and the Unified Mathematics program at the middle school level, have utilized a holistic approach to the organization of content.

Secondary humanities programs have often been the reservoir for the use of this model with talented learners. One approach to framing discussions within the humanities is to structure questions about a work of art (whether it be music, painting, or literature) that asks students to examine an "art" object from a variety of perspectives. For example, the following questions might be posed about this poem:

A brilliant star

    f
   a
    l
    l
     s

from the darkened sky.

1. What is it? (What's the subject matter?)
2. What is it made of? (What is its form?)
3. What ideas does it convey? (What does it mean?)
4. What is its context? (How would you categorize it historically?)
5. How do you relate to it? (What is its personal value?)
6. How good is it? (What is your evaluation of its artistic merit?)

Through these several lenses, then, gifted learners can explore the humanities as a collection of creative products assembled by individuals over the centuries, and reflect on their relationship to each other in specific dimensions. Appreciation for the arts can be strengthened through "seeing" the products from various points of view.

Although the concept-based model of curriculum offers the advantages of a unified view of a field of inquiry often undertaken by scholars in individual disciplines, it requires well-trained teachers to implement it effectively. Teachers need to possess in-depth knowledge about a field of inquiry, have the capacity to make appropriate connections to other disciplines, and be able to maintain a consistent vision around the exploration of concepts.

Unfortunately, schools have never really known how to treat such curriculum organizationally. At the secondary level, should students receive an English credit or a social studies credit for a humanities course? Should humanities be offered only at senior level as an elective or earlier as a mandatory course? The very strength of this curriculum and instructional model as an integrating force frequently collapses in the organizational decision making over "where it fits." As with the other two models discussed, developing a scope and sequence within the epistemological orientation is also necessary to allow for appropriate student exposure and progressive development in the realm of ideas.

The concept-based model for curriculum and instruction differs considerably from the nature of the previous two models. See Figure 1.2.

The concept-based model is organized by ideas and themes, not subject matter or process skills. It is highly interactive in its instructional context, which contrasts with the more independent modes of instruction used in the other two models. Concern for the nature and structure of knowledge it-

FIGURE 1.2 Contrasting Curriculum/Instructional Models for the Gifted

A. (Content)	B. (Process/Product)	C. (Concept)
Fast-paced	In-depth on selected topics	Epistemological
Proficiency-based	Product-based	Aesthetics-based
D → P approach	Resource-oriented	Discussion approach
Organized by intellectual content	Organized around scientific process	Organized by themes and ideas
Teacher as facilitator	Collaborative model	Socratic method

self is a major underlying tenet. The evaluation of students engaged in this model typically requires evidence of high-level aesthetic perceptions and insight rather than content proficiency or a culminating product of high quality.

The explication of these three models is useful in understanding how the confluent approaches to curriculum that are currently advocated might be implemented in the context of school-based programs. Clearly, it is not advantageous to select one model over another when planning appropriate curriculum over a span of years, for each approach responds to different characteristics and needs of gifted learners. Acceleration and in-depth as well as broad-based enrichment opportunities are all valuable for the gifted.

Effective curriculum and instruction for the gifted has reached a stage of evolution where existing theoretical and research-based models need to be systematically translated into practice at the local level. Competition among these models has dissipated the effect of building a strong differentiated program for the gifted that addresses all of their intellectual needs within the core curriculum as well as at all levels outside it. The synthesis of the content, process/product, and concept models provides a clear direction for meaningful curriculum work. See Figure 1.3.

FIGURE 1.3 School-based Curriculum Model Linkages on an Academic Year Cycle

Modification of Core Curriculum	Extended Core Curriculum	Curriculum Integration
D → P	Process/Product	Epistemological
Content Approach	Research Approach	Concept Approach
A	B	C
Allows for speeded, compressed, economized version of regular curriculum	Allows for development of generic problem-finding/ problem-solving skills in selected curriculum contexts	Allows for idea discussion/ generation within and across disciplines

Time distribution in one academic year: ⅓

Conclusion

Curriculum development for the gifted begins with a clear understanding of theoretical and research bases from which current practice derives its substance. It is important to understand the forces that contribute to the growth or demise of a particular curriculum trend and to be able to consider curriculum for the gifted in the larger context of curriculum for all students.

The field of gifted and talented education currently espouses two viewpoints regarding curriculum. One view places value in capturing curriculum on paper with appropriately delineated objectives, activities, and evaluation procedures; planning a child's curriculum in advance of the school year; and teaching toward predetermined program goals and objectives. The second view places value in developing curriculum based on the perceived and stated interests of the child; planning situational contexts that contribute to student choice in objectives and activities for the school year; and teaching toward the emergent needs of the child in the context of the classroom.

Although each view has been incorporated into functional programs for the gifted, each carries with it a different perception of the role of curriculum in the overall education of the child. This book places credence in planned and well-described written learning experiences for the gifted, yet it does not seek to devalue the role of the learner or the teacher as each may uniquely interpret and activate those activities through the instructional process. The view of curriculum presented here is a synthesis of seemingly opposing views, an integration of perspectives that will best benefit schools and the gifted students they serve.

It is now time to take a broader and more circumspect look at what makes a curriculum effective for gifted learners. We must examine the relationship between what the curriculum currently provides and what the specific needs of the gifted population are, and to develop new curriculum documents where discrepancies exist. We must examine the relationship of curriculum to instructional strategies to see that it is implemented effectively in classroom settings. We must attend to issues of standards for curriculum for the gifted and the means by which those standards can be met and documented. We need to be clear about what should be included in a curriculum for the gifted and why it is appropriate. Thus topics like the new technology, process skills, product development, and counseling need careful consideration. We also need to be cognizant of our overall curriculum design and to give attention to areas such as scope and sequence and monitoring and evaluation. And last, we should carefully consider the type of leadership necessary to undertake major curricular work. Clearly, the task of curriculum development is complex and arduous, but it is the most important area of work that remains to be done in the field of gifted education.

References

A Nation Prepared: Teachers for the 21st Century (1986). Carnegie Forum on Education and the Economy. New York: Carnegie Corporation.

Academic Preparation for College (1983). Project Equality, The College Board, New York.

Adler, M. (1984). *The Paedaeia Proposal*. New York: MacMillan.

Benbow, C., and Stanley, J. (1983). *Academic Precocity*. Baltimore, Md.: Johns Hopkins University Press.

Bloom, B. (1980). *All Our Children Learning*. New York: McGraw-Hill.

Bloom, B. (1985). *Developing Talent in Young People*. New York: Ballantine.

Colangelo, W., and Zaffran, R. (1979). *New Voices in Counseling the Gifted*. Dubuque, Iowa: Kendall-Hunt.

Daurio, S. (1979). "Educational Enrichment versus Acceleration: A Review of the Literature." In W. C. George, S. Cohn, and J. Stanley (Eds.), *Educating the Gifted: Acceleration and Enrichment*. Baltimore, Md.: Johns Hopkins University Press, pp. 13–63.

Educating Americans for the 21st Century: A Report to the American People and the National Science Board (1983). The National Science Board Commission on Precollege Education in Mathematics, Science, and Technology.

Eisner, E. W., and Vallance, E. (Eds.). (1974). *Conflicting Conceptions of Curriculum*. Berkeley, Calif.: McCutchen.

Feldhusen, J., and Kolloff, M. (1978). "A Three Stage Model for Gifted Education." *G/C/T 1*: 53–58.

Gallagher, J. (1985). *Teaching the Gifted Child*. (3rd ed.). Boston: Allyn and Bacon.

Gallagher, J., et al. (1984). *Leadership Unit*. New York: Trillium Press.

Goodlad, J. I. (1979). *Curriculum Inquiry: The Study of Curriculum Practice*. New York: McGraw-Hill.

Goodlad, J. I. (1983). *A Place Called School*. New York: McGraw-Hill.

Gowan, J., Demos, J., and Khatena, J. (1965). *The Guidance of Exceptional Children*. New York: David McKay.

Hall, T. (1956). *Gifted Children: The Cleveland Story*. Cleveland: World Publishing.

Harnischfeger, A., and Wiley, D. (1983). *Time and Learning in California Schools: Student Achievement in California Schools*. 1982–83 Annual Report, California Assessment Program. Sacramento: California State Department of Education.

Hayes-Jacob, H. (1981). "A Model for Curriculum and Instruction: Discipline Fields, Interdisciplinary, and Cognitive Process." Unpublished doctoral dissertation, Columbia University.

Hollingworth, L. (1926). *Gifted Children*. New York: World Book.

Hoyt, K., and Hebeler, J. (1974). *Career Education for Gifted and Talented Students*. Salt Lake City, Utah: Olympus.

Kaplan, S. (1979). "Language Arts and Social Studies Curriculum in the Elementary School." In H. Passow (Ed.), *NSSE Yearbook, The Gifted and the Talented*. Chicago: University of Chicago Press.

Keating, D. (1976). *Intellectual Talent*. Baltimore, Md.: Johns Hopkins University Press.

Maker, C. J. (1982). *Curriculum Development for the Gifted*. Rockville, Md.: Aspen.

Meeker, M. (1969). *The Structure of Intellect: Its Interpretations and Uses.* Columbus, Ohio: Charles E. Merrill.

National Commission on Excellence in Education (1983). *A Nation at Risk.* Washington, D.C.: U.S. Department of Education.

Passow, H., et al. (1982). *Differentiated Curricula for the Gifted/Talented.* Committee Report to the National/State Leadership Training Institute on the Gifted and Talented. Ventura County, Calif.: Office of the Superintendent of Schools.

Piechowski, M. (1984). "Two Developmental Concepts: Multilevelness and Developmental Potential." *Counseling and Values 18:* 86–93.

Renzulli, J. (1977). *The Enrichment Triad.* Wethersfield, Conn.: Creative Learning Press.

Stanley, J., Keating, D., and Fox, L. (1974). *Mathematical Talent.* Baltimore, Md.: Johns Hopkins University Press.

Tannenbaum, A. (1983). *Gifted Children.* New York: MacMillan.

VanTassel-Baska, J. (1982). "Results of a Latin-based Experimental Study of the Verbally Precocious." *Roeper Review 4*(4) (April–May): 35–37.

VanTassel-Baska, J., and Feldhusen, J. (Eds.). (1981). *Concept Curriculum for the Gifted.* Matteson, Ill.: Matteson School District #162.

VanTassel-Baska, J., and Kulieke, M. (1987). "The Role of Community in Developing Scientific Talent." *Gifted Child Quarterly 31*(3), 111–115.

Ward, V. (1961). *Educating the Gifted: An Axiomatic Approach.* Columbus, Ohio: Charles Merrill.

Weiss, P., and Gallagher, J. (1982). *Program Effectiveness, Education of Gifted and Talented Students: A Review.* Chapel Hill: University of North Carolina.

Wirsup, I. (1986). "The Current Crises in Mathematics and Science Education: A Climate for Change." In VanTassel-Baska (Ed.), *Proceedings from the 9th Annual Research Symposium.* Evanston, Ill.: Phi Delta Kappa.

Section One

The Process of Curriculum Making ─────────

2 Curriculum Planning and Development ━━━━━

Joyce VanTassel-Baska

Between the idea
And the reality . . .
Falls the shadow.

—T. S. Eliot

The process of curriculum planning and development is complex, dynamic, and generative in nature, and our approach to the task should reflect that reality. A stage theory approach will guide the reader in examining the nature of the processes involved in the overall curriculum development scheme. Figure 2.1 details the overall process of school district curriculum planning and development for the gifted. A brief description of each stage follows as a preview to extended commentary.

Each local school district should individually address curriculum development for gifted learners. A sound approach to begin a curriculum development plan should address the following areas:

Stage I Planning	At this stage, the program coordinator for the gifted and a local committee should examine the basic issues and key questions regarding curriculum for the gifted. A general focus and direction should be delineated, a statement of curriculum philosophy developed, and general goals and objectives conceptualized.
Stage II Needs Assessment	This assessment should indicate areas of need in regard to curricular development within the district. Questions such as "At what levels does appropriate curriculum for the gifted exist?" and "Where are the gaps?" are ways of beginning to focus on priority areas of need.
Stage III Curriculum Development Teams and Scope of Work	Based on the district curriculum needs assessment data, it is important to develop a work plan that sets parameters around the tasks to be undertaken. If an appropriate mathematics curriculum needs to be de-

FIGURE 2.1 Curriculum Development Model

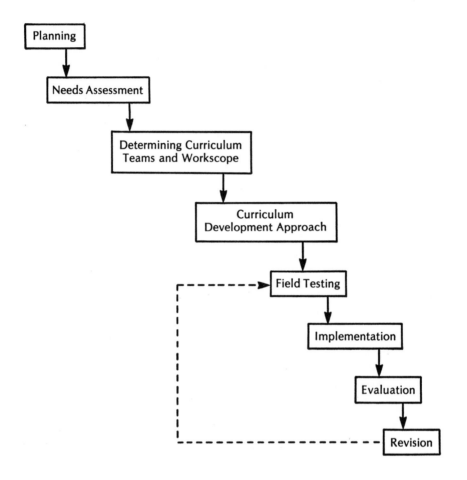

veloped, focusing on primary level first may be most efficacious, followed by intermediate level, and so on, since the task of developing curriculum is time-consuming and somewhat costly to the district. The district also needs to decide who will be responsible for working on curriculum development for the gifted. A model approach would be to (1) select a district team comprised of a primary, intermediate, middle school, and high-school teacher and a principal; (2) work with a content specialist who can provide expertise in the areas of the curriculum being developed; and (3) assign the writing tasks to one person with some written contributions from others on the team and agreement about the outline.

Stage IV **Curriculum Develop-** **ment: Adoption,** **Modification, and** **Development**	Basically, districts have three general approaches to use in developing curriculum for gifted learners. They can: (1) adopt already existing curriculum for gifted learners available from other school districts, state departments, and commercial sources; (2) modify and revise the existing curriculum to make it more appropriate; or (3) develop new curriculum units to supplement the current curriculum. More than one approach should be utilized and may be advantageous for school districts that are just beginning their work in curriculum development for the gifted.
Stage V **Field Testing**	A new curriculum developed for gifted learners should be field tested for a specified period of time in the gifted program. An assessment of its effectiveness should then be made so that the curriculum development team can make appropriate modification and revisions.
Stage VI **Implementation of** **New Curriculum**	The task of implementing a new curriculum needs to be perceived as gradual, with well-defined time specifications for each phase of the process. Consideration must be given to preparing the teaching staff for working with the curriculum, seeing that appropriate materials are available, and developing a plan for monitoring progress.
Stage VII **Evaluation**	Evaluating a new curriculum is an important task but one that frequently is overlooked in the curriculum development process. Program problems are frequently related to an unchallenging, superficial, or insufficient curriculum for gifted learners. Thus developing a curriculum evaluation design is crucial to the success of any new curriculum venture.

General Assumptions Regarding Curriculum Development

It is useful to begin by discussing the underlying assumptions behind a school district's need to plan and develop a curriculum for gifted learners.

Assumption #1: *The regular school district curriculum, as it is currently conceptualized, written down, and operationalized, is inappropriate for talented learners.*

We recognize that the needs of gifted learners are atypical in respect to several core areas: rate (Keating, 1976), capacity for in-depth learning (Renzulli,

1977), capacity to manipulate conceptual schemata (Sternberg, 1985), and need for diversity and challenge in learning experiences (Passow et al., 1982). This recognition leads us to realize that most school curricula are organized around the needs of typical learners, where the spiral effect of incremental learning modules, coupled with heavy doses of reinforcement around a given skill or concept, constitutes the pattern for basic text materials and classroom instruction. Thus one of the first issues to be addressed in assessing the curriculum for the gifted is how to modify or adapt the general curriculum within core areas to respond better to the atypical needs of the gifted. Clearly, accelerative, enriched, and conceptual reorganization must occur if the core curriculum is to be meaningful for the gifted during their K–12 experience. Let us take an example of such modification at the secondary level in the area of Latin.

Typical Learner:	Focus on learning vocabulary and syntax through mythologically and historically based translations and exercises (in grade 9)	Course organized by textbook unit approach, using incremental skill development techniques *Unit I*—Nominative case Feminine nouns and singularity *Unit II*—Genitive case and Dative case Masculine nouns and plurality *Unit III*—Accusative and Ablative cases Neuter nouns, etc.
Gifted Learner: Patterns in Latin	*Accelerative* Focus on learning in Grade 7 Latin as a language that represents Western cultural traditions	*Enriched* *Conceptual*— Course organized by syntactic ideas and key cultural systems *Units of Study*— Gender, Number, and Case; The Function of Nouns in Latin; Man as Myth Maker; Explanations of the Universe

Assumption #2: *General school curriculum needs to be modified for the gifted by deletion as well as by addition.*

Our traditional approach to modifying curriculum for the gifted has been either to speed it up or to add to it. Neither modification in isolation responds to learner needs, only to administrative efficiency. The fundamental problem lies in a lack of attention to reviewing the appropriateness of all aspects of the curriculum. An example from elementary mathematics may be useful to make this point. Most math texts organize fractions as a unit separate from decimals and percents rather than seeing these manipulations as different ways of expressing relationships and inequalities. For gifted learners, deleting unnecessary practice with only one type of problem and adding the concept of ratio and proportion in an applied problem-solving mode is a critical modification. Thus approaches to curriculum development cannot ignore the proper adaptations needed to make the core curriculum, in whatever setting it may be delivered, more appropriate for gifted learners.

Assumption #3: *Curriculum development for the gifted has to be viewed as a long-term process that involves adaptation of the current curriculum, infusion of appropriate extant curricula for the gifted, and the development of a new curriculum.*

Most curriculum work that has been done for the gifted has taken an isolationist perspective. It was conceptualized and written with the idea that it was to be "the curriculum for the gifted." Consequently, committees of writers struggled with key models and concepts as they strove to create a "new" curriculum—one that was appropriate only for the gifted in some special setting. What that approach fosters, however, is a fragmentation of curriculum experiences for the gifted. Frequently such curriculum is organized on a faulty understanding of the models and concepts it purports to convey. Some of the best curricula that exist for the gifted were not written with their special needs in mind. The major curriculum projects of the 1960s in science, mathematics, English, and social studies have proven very successful with gifted populations even though they were not so intended. The Junior Great Books program and Philosophy for Children, both widely used curricula in gifted programs, were not developed expressly for the gifted. Yet use of such tested curriculum material can save districts the time and expense of trying to reinvent what would clearly be an inferior wheel. More effort needs to be expended in bridging the district core curriculum to appropriate adaptations of it for gifted learners. To conceptualize curriculum development as a short-term activity is to misunderstand the nature and scope of the process that needs to be undertaken.

Assumption #4: *Curriculum for the gifted needs to be written down and communicated appropriately within a school district.*

A curriculum only has a recognizable shape or form when it is written. What goes on in a classroom between teacher and learner is instructional process, not curriculum. What curriculum provides is a sense of purpose and direction in areas of educational value that both teacher and student explore. A curriculum for the gifted should provide educational personnel and the community with an understanding of what areas of investigation are valuable, how students will meet their learning objectives, and by what means they will be evaluated. A curriculum for the gifted places emphasis on purpose, means, and end somewhat equally and in a manner that the lay public can understand. The obligation to communicate what is distinct about a program for the gifted is paramount and the strength of that distinction lies in effective curriculum planning.

Stage I: Planning

Local district program planners need to be sensitive to several major issues in examining the area of planning curriculum for gifted learners. Clearly, curriculum philosophy is important as it was discussed in Chapter 1. But other issues also affect the planning effort. One issue is the very *definition* being used for curriculum. For purposes of this book, curriculum is defined as a set of organized experiences appropriate for gifted learners that are written down and adopted for use in a school district. In this sense, then, curriculum represents a formal codifying of the goals, objectives, and activities of a gifted program.

A second issue of concern is with the appropriateness of a district's *basic curriculum* for the gifted. At the point that curriculum development work is undertaken, it is wise to examine the current curriculum and make appropriate modifications in the core content areas before developing a new curriculum.

A third issue focuses on the selection of *appropriate goals* to address in developing a curriculum for gifted learners. Objectives need to flow from the overall goals of the program. Model goals for gifted learners might be:

GIFTED PROGRAM GOALS

1. To provide for the mastery of the basic skills of reading and mathematics at a pace and depth appropriate to the capacities of able learners. Students will participate in a diagnostic-prescriptive model of reading and mathematics instruction that would allow for individual rates of mastery, regardless of age or grade.

2. To promote critical thinking and reasoning abilities. Students will be instructed in the areas of inference, deductive and inductive reasoning, analogies, and evaluation of arguments. These reasoning tools will be applied to all areas of the curriculum.

3. To provide an environment that encourages divergent thinking. Students will be encouraged in the development of originality, fluency, flexibility, and elaboration in their thought processes.

4. To foster inquiry and challenging attitudes towards learning. Students will be able to develop a commitment to learning as a lifelong process and to learn education, civic, social, and personal responsibilities.

5. To develop high-level oral and written skills. Students will become confident in expressing ideas through class discussions, panel discussions, debates,

and oral reports; students will learn expository and creative writing skills and technical report writing.

6. To develop research skills and methods. Students will be able to understand the scientific method and its application to all areas of inquiry.

7. To develop an understanding for systems of knowledge, themes, issues, and problems that frame the external world. Students will be able to interrelate ideas within and across domains of study.

8. To develop self-understanding. Students will be able to understand their strengths and weaknesses in various contexts.

9. To facilitate opportunities for learning that are external to the school but provide an important match to the needs of learners. Students will be able to gain access to educational advantages provided by resources outside the environment of the school.

10. To enhance opportunities for future planning and development. Students will be able to develop goals and apply structure to the tasks of life planning for the future.

Such goals then need to be translated into measurable objectives that become the focus of the curriculum delivery system. Specific objectives may be formulated for both teachers and learners since behavioral change is required for both in order to address stated goals.

A fourth issue of planning is that of *articulation*. Gifted students need to be exposed to increasingly complex and difficult material as they progress through school. Attention to the progressive development of skills and concepts is an essential component of curriculum development for this population. Articulation of skills and concepts in core curriculum areas is but part of the task; skills such as critical thinking, creative thinking, problem solving, and research all need to be structured hierarchically so that higher level skills are taught through a developmental system. Product requirements also need to be articulated across content and grade level dimensions.

Tyler (1949) posits four fundamental questions that have particular relevance for educators of the gifted:

1. *What educational purposes should the school seek to attain?* This question is central to the development of curriculum for the gifted. The selection of educational objectives establishes initially the degree of differentiation the curriculum is apt to have. The following list of questions must be answered by curriculum developers regarding appropriate objectives for gifted learners:

a. Do the educational objectives help gifted learners develop proficiency at a sufficient level of difficulty?

b. Do the objectives help gifted learners become creatively productive?

c. Do the objectives help gifted learners become self-actualized human beings?

d. Do the objectives contribute to the gifted student taking responsibility for his or her own learning?

e. Do the objectives allow the gifted learner to develop advanced skills, concepts, and knowledge about a field of inquiry?

f. Do the objectives focus on economically organized systems of learning within content dimensions?

g. Do the objectives allow for cross-discipline comparisons?

Embedded in these questions are the major principles of differentiation of curriculum for the gifted: pacing, economy, self-directed learning, diversity, and challenge.

2. *How can learning experiences be selected that are likely to be useful in attaining these objectives?* Whereas the first question reflects on the scope of any given curriculum, this second basic question poses the problem of planning specific experiences for learning within a given curriculum area. Learning experiences can promote or inhibit retention, interest, satisfaction, and internalization of a given problem. In the education of the gifted, inquiry-based lessons, group problem-solving settings, independent investigations, and group discussion all characterize instructional techniques that contribute to good learning experiences. In the curriculum development process, those that most effectively move students toward prescribed educational objectives are selected and organized.

3. *How can learning experiences be organized for effective instruction?* The sequencing and continuity of learning experiences for the gifted is a major issue in examining overall curricular experiences. The program model chosen to deliver curriculum and instruction is critical. Pull-out models, unless they replace or introduce key areas of learning, lessen the concentrated amount of instructional time in such a way that the impact of given learning experiences is diminished. By the same token, daily contact in a given curriculum area may be equally inefficient for some learning areas. Nevertheless, curriculum planners need the flexibility of time to develop effective instructional models for the gifted learner. Criteria for effective organization must take into account vertical reiteration, progressive development of skills and concepts, and horizontal relationships of ideas and theories. Phenix (1964) argues that content selection and organization should adhere to these principles:

a. Drawn from the fields of disciplined inquiry

b. Chosen for representativeness of a given field

c. Exemplified methods of inquiry in a given field

d. Aroused the imagination

4. *How can the effectiveness of learning experiences be evaluated?* This fourth question raises the issue of evaluating curriculum in some systematic way. At the present time, gifted education has not set about evaluating learning gains in an effective manner, let alone the experiences and processes by which those gains may have been reached. Nonetheless, the development of methodologies and instruments to assess the effectiveness of curriculum with gifted learners is integral to the task of responsible curriculum development. Criteria for initial consideration may include the following areas:

a. Appropriateness for level of ability and age range

b. Rich and complete treatment of topic

c. Allowance of diversity in learning through the use of multiple sources and the presentation of varying perspectives

d. Enhancement of opportunity for small-group discussions

e. Enhancement of opportunity for independent investigations

f. Increase in interest and motivation for the topic under study

Whereas a curriculum for the gifted relies heavily on general curriculum theory to define itself, it is helpful to codify those aspects of curriculum work that are critical in the development of curriculum materials for the gifted. These principles are derived from a review of general curriculum standards but are also relevant to the gifted population. Curriculum for the gifted should be:

1. Guided by a philosophy of curriculum that states general purposes
2. Tailored to the needs of talented learners
3. Rooted within and across domains of knowledge
4. Balanced between skill development and concept development
5. Articulated across a span of years
6. Monitored for effectiveness with a selected group of learners

These six principles are important to consider at the planning stage since the administrative support must be available to ensure that these processes can be implemented at subsequent stages in the curriculum development model.

Stage II: Needs Assessment

One of the most crucial and practical aspects of the curriculum development process is a thorough needs assessment. This author has proposed the use of a needs assessment model that linked student needs to program components, and linked developmental concerns to the nature and extent of staff development that was necessary for an effective program operation (VanTassel-Baska, 1979). Other perspectives on needs assessment more precisely focus on decision making in the area of curriculum.

PERSPECTIVES ON NEEDS ASSESSMENT

Both state and national needs assessments have been conducted in the field of gifted education in recent years. These surveys have highlighted areas that practitioners have identified as requiring more attention in the future. It is interesting to note that half of them directly bear on aspects of curriculum development.

1. Need for more special programs (Gallagher et al., 1982)
2. Need for comprehensive programs that are articulated across grade levels (Illinois Office of Education, 1978; Richardson Study, 1985)

3. Need for in-service training for teachers (Gallagher et al., 1982)

4. Need for increased financial support bases (Gallagher et al., 1982; Illinois Office of Education, 1978)

5. Need for curriculum development (Gallagher et al., 1982; Richardson Study, 1985)

6. Need for valid instructional materials (Gallagher et al., 1982)

7. Need for more research (Gallagher et al., 1982)

8. Need for demonstration programs (Gallagher, 1982; Richardson Study, 1985)

9. Need for consistency in identification procedures and standards (Gallagher et al., 1982; Richert, 1982)

10. Need for consistency in program delivery based on student needs rather than district resources (Illinois Office of Education, 1978)

11. Need for consistent and selective criteria for choosing teachers of the gifted (Seeley, 1985)

12. Need for philosophical and psychological support from professional colleagues (administrators and teachers) (Gallagher et al., 1982; Richardson Study, 1985)

However, needs assessment must also occur at the local level in order to determine what currently exists in the curriculum for gifted students and what needs to exist. This task can be accomplished through asking students, parents, administrators, teachers, and others to comment formally on this aspect of the district's educational plan. Once it has been ascertained that a percentage of the district's gifted population is not receiving appropriate curriculum or that existing curriculum is not adequate to the needs, the mechanism is in place to begin formal curriculum work.

How can a needs assessment be done? What are its most important components? It is useful to start with a list of questions that can be answered by a good needs assessment.

1. Based on the characteristics of gifted children in this district, what are the educational needs for which we are responsible?

2. What are the gaps in our current program that must be addressed in order to provide appropriate intervention for gifted students?

3. What kinds of technical assistance do we need in order to proceed with the curriculum development task?

DETERMINATION OF STUDENT NEEDS

In order to plan effective special programs for gifted students, school districts must understand the special needs of the population involved. Gifted and talented students need:

1. Activities that enabled them to operate cognitively and affectively at complex levels of thought and feeling.

2. Opportunities for divergent production.

3. Challenging group and individual work which demonstrates process/product outcomes.

4. Discussions among intellectual peers.

5. A variety of experiences that promote understanding of human value systems.

6. The opportunity to see interrelationships in all bodies of knowledge.

7. Special courses in their area of strength and interest which accelerate the pace and depth of the content.

8. Greater exposure to new areas of learning within and outside the school structure.

9. Opportunities to apply their abilities to real problems in the world of production.

10. To be taught the skills of critical thinking, creative thinking, research, problem-solving, coping with exceptionality, decision-making and leadership (VanTassel-Baska, 1979).

This needs list can be used by districts in three major ways to document their student needs:

1. Districts can rank order this list of needs according to the percent of students demonstrating each of them, and according to the degree of each need (mild, moderate, severe) as ascertained by professional staff.

2. Districts can use the list as a student survey in current gifted programs to ascertain which needs gifted students feel are being met and which ones are not.

3. Districts can survey parents regarding their perceptions of the extent to which their children's needs were or are being met.

Figure 2.2 contains a form that can be used by school districts for any of the stated purposes to ascertain a current picture of curriculum needs of their gifted students.

Needs assessment, then, has two important components: the identification of all needs and the prioritization of areas of need with which to start. A needs assessment tells you what is considered most important by various constituency groups most affected by special programs. If time, resources, and other constraints do not preclude it, proceeding to address these highest areas of identified needs should be viewed by program coordinators as very appropriate. The process by which the needs assessment data are obtained can also build support for and involvement in the overall curriculum development effort.

In addition to viewing curriculum needs from a student perspective, it may be helpful to gain a larger picture of district needs in curriculum for the gifted by assessing what is and has been done in the name of "curriculum for the gifted." How good is the current curriculum? Is there already written curriculum for gifted students at some levels? Questions such as these may be important to answer also as part of the needs assessment process. The form in Figure 2.3 may assist in capturing an understanding of current and future curriculum needs in the district. It may also help determine priorities for targeting resources for curriculum development work.

A third way of viewing the issue of curricular needs assessment has to do with the nature of curricular documents that will be needed as the gifted pro-

FIGURE 2.2 Needs of Gifted Students

Please rate the following according to the extent they are incorporated into our current program for gifted learners.

	To a great extent				Not at all	
	5	4	3	2	1	
1. Basic cognitive skills:						Cannot judge
a. Critical thinking	5	4	3	2	1	0
b. Creative thinking	5	4	3	2	1	0
c. Problem solving	5	4	3	2	1	0
d. Research	5	4	3	2	1	0
e. Decision making	5	4	3	2	1	0
2. Basic affective skills:						
a. Tolerance of self and others	5	4	3	2	1	0
b. Constructive use of humor	5	4	3	2	1	0
c. Coping with being different	5	4	3	2	1	0
d. Discriminating between the real and the ideal	5	4	3	2	1	0
e. Using their high-level sensitivity	5	4	3	2	1	0
3. To be challenged by mastery level work in areas of strength and interest	5	4	3	2	1	0
4. To be challenged by exposure to new areas	5	4	3	2	1	0
5. To be challenged by the opportunity to see interrelationships	5	4	3	2	1	0
6. To be challenged by experiences that promote understanding human value systems	5	4	3	2	1	0
7. To be challenged through discussions with intellectual peers	5	4	3	2	1	0
8. To be challenged by activities at complex levels of thought	5	4	3	2	1	0
9. To be challenged through opportunities for divergent production	5	4	3	2	1	0
10. To be challenged by the opportunity for real-world problem solving	5	4	3	2	1	0

gram evolves. One way to think about document needs is to conceptualize all of the relevant school groups who have a role to play in the curriculum development process, and then decide what written documents would best facilitate their role in curriculum. Figure 2.4 presents an example of what a typical school district might need, based on the various educational groups involved.

In summary, a needs assessment strategy must recognize (1) generic needs of the field of gifted education, (2) specific curriculum needs of gifted students, (3) discrepancies between what existing curriculum for the gifted currently provides and what it should provide, and (4) specific curriculum documents needed to codify and guide curriculum efforts. All of these elements are useful in ascertaining what appropriate curriculum for the gifted might be. As practitioners, we

FIGURE 2.3 Curriculum Needs Assessment

1. Describe the current operating gifted programs in the district at each level:

   K–3   *4–6*   *7–8*   *9–12*

2. Do you have a differentiated curriculum for the gifted at each level?
   ____Yes ____No Comment:

3. If yes, has gifted curriculum been evaluated for its effectiveness with gifted students?
   ____Yes ____No Comment:

4. Have gifted students assessed their curriculum?
   ____Yes ____No Comment:

5. Have teachers assessed the current curriculum for the gifted?
   ____Yes ____No Comment:

6. What are the perceived gaps in the current curriculum in general?

   K–3   *4–6*   *7–8*   *9–12*

7. What are the gaps for gifted students?

   K–3   *4–6*   *7–8*   *9–12*

8. Areas of need for curriculum development:

   K–3   *4–6*   *7–8*   *9–12*

---

need to clarify better what we do with gifted learners and why we do it, and to develop a meaningful curriculum based on sound efforts of assessment.

Stage III: Determining Curriculum Development Teams and Scope of Work

As one examines the possibility of developing meaningful curriculum for the gifted, it becomes apparent that if the curriculum is content-based or interdisci-

FIGURE 2.4 Curriculum Needs Based on Relevant Groups

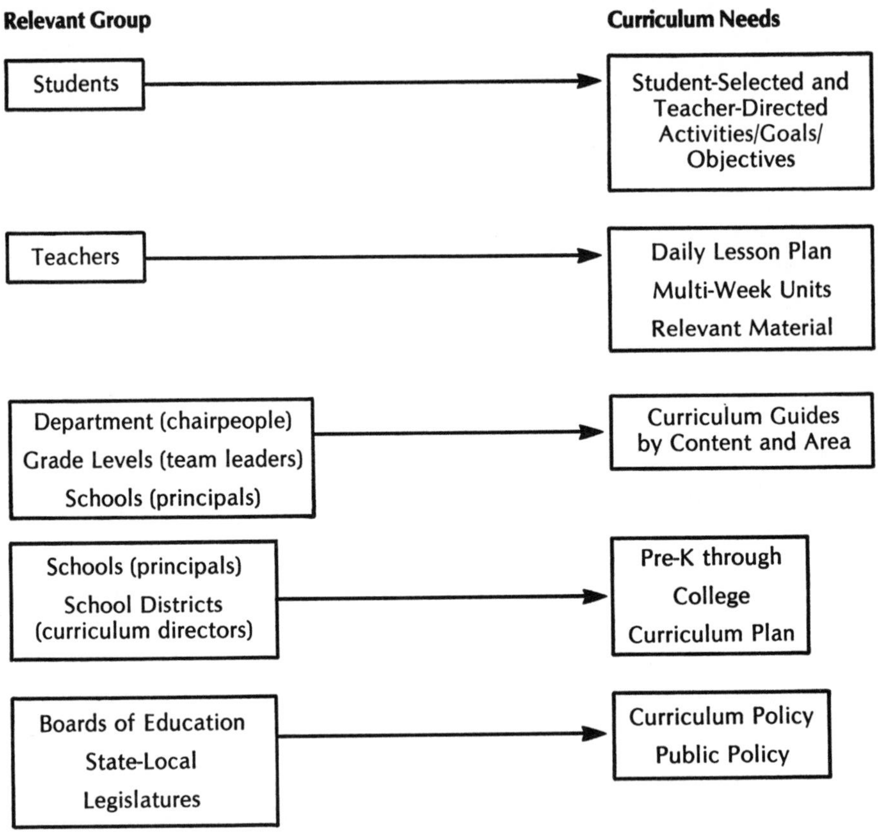

Relevant Group   **Curriculum Needs**

| Students | → | Student-Selected and Teacher-Directed Activities/Goals/Objectives |

| Teachers | → | Daily Lesson Plan / Multi-Week Units / Relevant Material |

| Department (chairpeople) / Grade Levels (team leaders) / Schools (principals) | → | Curriculum Guides by Content and Area |

| Schools (principals) / School Districts (curriculum directors) | → | Pre-K through College Curriculum Plan |

| Boards of Education / State-Local / Legislatures | → | Curriculum Policy / Public Policy |

plinary in nature, curriculum developers must be well-acquainted with the content areas to be examined and have the ability to construct an organizational schema that focuses on the most important skills, concepts, and "cutting edge" ideas in that field.

An individual teacher may or may not have these insights. Consequently, it is useful to develop a team approach to curriculum development that utilizes teachers in deciding the direction of curriculum work. Such a team approach to curriculum making allows the strength of each individual member to show. Good teachers know intuitively what is workable for the gifted in the classroom and can translate ideas at an appropriate level for gifted learners. Content experts, who may be university professors or practicing professionals, know their particular field of inquiry and are engaged in active research within it; thus they can supply key ideas and concepts that can provide the curricular structure. Figure 2.5 shows the relationship of teachers and scholars in this type of curriculum effort.

FIGURE 2.5 Content Expert Model for Curriculum Development

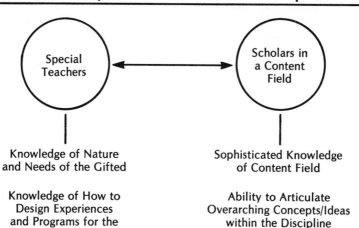

Another model to consider for curriculum team work is one that utilizes the key ideas of scholars but does not involve them integrally in the curriculum development process. Shane (1981) shared the work of scholar teams and their views on important content curriculum for the year 2000 in the key areas of the natural sciences, life sciences, chemistry, geology, and the social sciences.

School districts might solicit outside experts in various fields to provide key ideas and concepts in a given field of inquiry. Then within the school district, curriculum teams can shape those ideas to an advanced curriculum for the gifted. The outside expert might critique the work of the teams regarding the way the ideas were translated in respect to consistency and appropriateness.

A third approach is the more typical consultant model where the curriculum team is led by an educator within the school district, and outside consultants participate at particular stages of the process. This model may be preferable if the focus of the curriculum work is on planning rather than writing, and the mode of teamwork is discussion and deliberation.

Whichever model is preferred within a given school district, it is important to involve individuals with expertise outside the domain of a given district. There are several good reasons for this:

1. The consultant/scholar/expert can provide an objective assessment of any curriculum issue or problem; frequently school political issues tend to dominate curriculum deliberations.

2. He or she has an in-depth knowledge of the key area being considered. For example, in considering an appropriate sequence of mathematics courses for gifted students at the secondary level, a consultant in mathematics can share major approaches to organizing such courses, where exemplary programs based on those approaches may be operating, and

the advantages and disadvantages of any given sequence from the viewpoint of higher education.

3. He or she can facilitate the discussion of a key topic. Curriculum teams need to read about the issues they are addressing and to discuss them in depth. Curriculum generalists in schools may have limited backgrounds in many specific areas of the curriculum and find it difficult to lead team deliberations in those areas of the process.

ORGANIZING STRUCTURES FOR CURRICULUM WORK

The make-up of district curriculum teams should be determined by the scope of the curriculum effort. If the task is to be a comprehensive one, for example restructuring a K–12 curriculum for the gifted, then there will be a need for multiple teams that are guided by a central steering committee. See Figure 2.6.

A clear distinction also needs to be drawn between data-gathering tasks, planning, and writing tasks when considering the composition of committees. Curriculum writers and data gatherers should be a subset of the committee, or, if warranted, a separate task force that works with the committee.

The number of people on a curriculum development committee is a crucial variable. This author can remember being the head of a curriculum council of over 100 people in a local school district. Clearly, curriculum issues were not handled by group discussion or even by ultimate consensus. Ideal sizes for curriculum planning committees range from six to twelve people, depending on the size of the district and the scope of the effort. A data-gathering and writing task force may be best conducted by one to four individuals.

Representation on the committee, of course, is another critical variable. The individual in a school district who is responsible for curriculum leadership for the gifted program should chair the committee, be able to communicate the work of the committee with clarity, and be able to move the agenda along a predetermined schedule to ensure that the committee work will be implemented. Involv-

FIGURE 2.6 District Curriculum Steering Committee

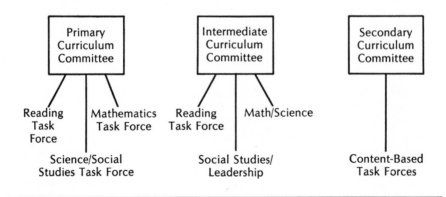

ing building-level administrators in the committee work is vital. One principal can represent his or her counterparts on such curriculum committees. Teacher involvement is also critical but should be reserved for teachers who have knowledge and experience in working with gifted learners in a variety of classroom settings.

Representation by content disciplines rather than grade level only may be an important consideration for teacher selection since the education of the gifted as it is translated through school curriculum needs to be at an advanced level and have a clear emphasis on maximum rather than minimum competency issues. Selecting primary teachers based on their understanding of reading or mathematics rather than their teaching style is preferable. There are two reasons why curriculum work for the gifted should always be conducted across grade levels rather than only at one level. One is that gifted students' capabilities obscure the boundaries of typical grade level designations so that primary program planning is more efficacious than kindergarten planning. A second reason is that the task of developing scope and sequence in the curriculum is simplified by structuring committees in this fashion. This procedure thereby reduces the potential number of assessment points for smoothing out the curriculum to three occurrences—after third grade, after sixth grade, and after eighth grade.

SCOPE OF WORK

It is important to consider several factors when deciding on the parameters of the curriculum development effort: time, resource allocation, and readiness for change.

TIME

The process model presented in this chapter for school district curriculum development is a generative one that builds toward continued improvement and refinement. Yet the reality of schools dictates that priorities change, study committees dissolve, and the world of education goes on. The curriculum leader must determine a realistic time schedule that can be balanced against the current need for curriculum work so that major writing, revisions, and recommendations can take place while the support mechanisms are in place in the district. It is important, however, to stress that curriculum development in any form will take a minimum of three years' commitment on the part of the district and key personnel working on committees. A more realistic time frame for considering comprehensive curriculum development for the gifted would be five years.

RESOURCE ALLOCATION

A second concern in determining the scope of work is the issue of resource allocation. What human and material resources are available to carry out curriculum development tasks over a three-year period? Has the district allocated the necessary budget to provide staff development seminars and consultant time at the planning, writing/adapting, and implementation stages of the project? Does the budget allow for released time for teachers to attend meetings or provide extra stipends for additional work time? Is there a product development allocation so that curriculum guides can be easily disseminated once they are developed? All of these questions are critical to the work scope since constraints around resources can adversely affect the overall process.

READINESS FOR CHANGE

Decisions about the scope of work should also consider in what areas of the curriculum there is a readiness for change on the part of staff. Sometimes at the secondary level, for example, a given department expresses real interest and enthusiasm for "tinkering" with the curriculum, whereas other departments show no such interest. If choices can be made, it may be wiser to capitalize on such organized enthusiasm rather than to effect widespread involvement in curriculum work at a particular time. No instructional leader can expect a staff to be thrilled with the idea of curriculum change. Thus smaller, well-targeted efforts that prove successful may be superior to a comprehensive effort that is blocked because a staff was not ready to be involved.

With these issues in mind, a school district may wish to go through a checklist to determine the scope of work and to set priorities within it (see Figure 2.7).

Stage IV: The Curriculum Development Approach: Data-Gathering, Adapting, and/or Writing

School district practitioners should look askance at any suggestion that appropriate curriculum for the gifted must be developed completely from scratch. Too much time, energy, and resources have already been used by school districts on an individual basis to create their own unique curriculum for the gifted or to allow individual teachers freedom to "do their own thing" with the gifted curriculum. That is not to say that some units may not need to be developed as the process goes on, but creating new units is clearly not a first step.

DATA GATHERING

Gathering extant curriculum that may be appropriate for gifted learners, even though it is not marketed by publishing companies as materials for the gifted, is the first step. Procedurally, this involves the following:

1. Contact appropriate commercial publishers regarding texts in areas under study. Obtain materials they feel are appropriate for "high-ability learners." Review and critique.

2. Contact curriculum libraries on university campuses to compile a list of their materials that are geared to gifted learners. Some of these materials may not be found through any other services and therefore constitute "fugitive" literature.

FIGURE 2.7 Checklist of Priorities for Curriculum Work

	Yes	No
1. Is there a grade-level cluster (i.e., primary, intermediate, etc.) in greater need of curriculum for gifted than others? Name it_____.	—	—
2. Is there a content area in greater need of curriculum adaptation for the gifted learners than others? Name it_____.	—	—
3. Is there a curriculum area not currently offered to the gifted that the needs assessment data point to as important for inclusion? Name it_____.	—	—
4. Is there a current curriculum for the gifted that needs revision? Name it _____.	—	—
5. Is there a need for a process/product orientation (Model B) to the curriculum for the gifted?	—	—
6. Is there a need for an epistemological orientation (Model C) to the curriculum for the gifted?	—	—
7. Is there an area of the general curriculum being studied that could provide resources to the curriculum development task for the gifted? Name it_____.	—	—
8. Is there access now to consultants/scholars in a particular field of inquiry that could aid in the curriculum development task?	—	—
9. Is there a department or small cadre of people in the district who are most ready to move on curriculum change? Name them_____.	—	—
10. Do the gifted coordinators/teachers of the gifted have clear preferences for areas to focus on in the curriculum? Name them_____.	—	—

Based on the number and nature of positive responses to these questions, list the top three priority areas for curriculum work in the district:

(1)_____   (2)_____   (3)_____

3. Contact state consultants for the gifted who should be able to provide lists of curriculum developed in their state for the gifted through Title IV-C projects or state and local efforts.
4. Procure sample materials developed for gifted learners from companies specializing in curriculum for this population. Trillium Press is one example (see Appendix B for others).

5. Review curriculum guides from such prepackaged programs as Junior Great Books; Philosophy for Children; Man: A Course of Study; College Board's Advanced Placement Program.
6. Contact at least five established gifted programs across the country and gather ideas on effective curricula.
7. Establish a set of criteria for judging curriculum materials. (The list of principles for gifted curriculum at the end of this chapter might be adapted for this purpose.)
8. Determine what may be usable from all of these sources for your program and the degree to which it may need to be adapted or supplemented.

ADAPTATION OF EXISTING CURRICULUM

Another task that a curriculum development team must consider is modifying the core curriculum to make it more appropriate for gifted learners. After completing the data-gathering process, it will become clear that most published curricula designed solely for gifted learners are not sufficient in breadth or depth to carry a program for a school year. There is no way to avoid the difficult task of reorganizing and restructuring the school's basic curriculum in order to make it more appropriate for able learners. The following model suggests a procedural way to accomplish this task:

CONTENT MODIFICATION MODEL FOR GIFTED LEARNERS

Step 1 Examine general curriculum guide for required knowledge and skills in given content areas, at various stages of development.
Step 2 Compress scope and sequence of skill mastery by 30 to 50 percent through reorganization according to higher level skills.
Step 3 Develop additional knowledge and skill areas appropriate for the gifted at various levels.
Step 4 Integrate process skill development and independent work for the gifted into each level.
Step 5 Identify key issues, problems, and themes that might be worked with at various levels.
Step 6 Add needed curriculum materials or develop through a unit approach.

This content modification approach is particularly useful as an alternative to total curriculum change for several reasons. (1) The content modification approach starts with the state-of-the-art district curriculum; it is familiar, accepted, and usually board-approved, and, in that sense, vested with curriculum policy implications. District curriculum guides are an important point of departure for developing gifted curriculum from both a political and a logical perspective. (2) Content modification allows the curriculum developer to challenge all underlying assumptions currently operating in the school district regarding a segment of curriculum. This challenging of assumptions and restructuring to accommodate specific learner needs is a key exercise in the overall process. (3) This approach keeps the curriculum focus on the content dimensions by which schools are organized and with which staff are somewhat comfortable, yet moves beyond basal text materials and forces schools to alter curriculum scope and sequence in the face of individual learner needs. No special jargon is necessary to talk about the curriculum for the gifted learner. We are all talking about the same curriculum areas: reading, mathematics, foreign language, social studies, science, language arts/English, and so on. (4) The content modification approach allows us to infuse the teaching of such process skills as critical thinking, creative thinking, and research into individual fields of inquiry rather than teach them in isolation. In this way, these skills can adapt to the idiosyncratic nature of individual disciplines rather than be viewed as applicable in all respects to every discipline. Problem solving in mathematics, for example, is quite different from problem solving in political science. The scientific method may not be applicable to the teaching of the American Revolution but it has great significance for the teaching of science content. (5) This approach allows for project development that is meaningful in the context of a student's total program, not just an invention pulled out of a laundry list of activity ideas. Thus reading, discussion, and problem solving in a given content area can be merged with the application of high-level process skills and culminate in a high-quality product. (6) Individual units can always be developed or sought out as needed to fill in important gaps in a given knowledge area or its applied fields. Thus in computer science, a unit of study on computer modeling might be developed to give students a sense of the technologically advanced uses for the computer across disciplines.

Through the use of such a content modification model, coupled with appropriate delivery methods, curriculum for gifted learners can maximize its opportunity for being integrated at a policy level in a given school district. Furthermore, appropriate treatment of the students in all of the basic curriculum areas is achieved, thus eliminating fragmentation, gaps, and general lack of curriculum coordination.

CURRICULUM WRITING: UNIT DEVELOPMENT

Because the task of writing curriculum units is in itself a complex one, Chapter 5 of this book is devoted singly to that process. However, the following outline focuses on salient aspects of unit development from a content, process-product, and concept perspective. Decisions regarding the topics of the units to be developed should flow out of the earlier phases of data gathering and adaptation. As school districts begin to consider the infusion of process/product curriculum and concept curriculum, frequently the need for teaching units emerges. As new topics are added to the core content areas, the need for new units may surface as well. Thus careful planning for unit development needs to be undertaken.

SAMPLE OUTLINE FOR CURRICULUM UNITS

FORMAT ELEMENT	QUESTION IT ANSWERS
1. General instructions on the use of the unit (including grade levels, prerequisite skills, type of learner)	Who is the unit for?

2. Unit rationale and goals	What is the purpose of the unit?
3. Unit objectives	What will students learn from the unit?
4. Specific learner activities (including sample questions for discussion, sample exercises, and study sheets)	What will students do?
5. Dominant teaching strategies	How will teachers carry out instruction?
6. Key materials and other resources	What tools will teachers need to implement this unit in the classroom?
7. Appropriate tests and other evaluative tools such as inventories, checklists, etc.	How will teachers assess student learning?
8. Student self-study material	What aspects of this unit can students explore on their own?
9. Student and teacher references	What books, films, etc., increase understanding about this topic?
10. Relationship of the unit to other aspects of the curriculum	How does this unit fit into the larger curriculum schemata?

Stage V: Pilot Testing or Field Testing of the Curriculum

Whether one is adopting a prepackaged curriculum, adapting a currently existing curriculum, or creating new units of instruction, the stage of piloting or field testing is critical. There is often a "leap of faith" that occurs with the development of a curriculum piece. It is assumed that teachers can use it effectively in the dynamic context of the classroom. Frequently the gulf between intended curriculum and delivered curriculum is great. The field-testing stage thus allows individual teachers as well as outside process observers to monitor the use of a new curriculum in a systematic way. Tracking curriculum efficacy at this stage of development also allows the opportunity for important feedback to curriculum writers who may alter and revise learning segments based on teacher or observer responses.

The following form (Figure 2.8) has been found useful in field-testing specific units developed by teachers of the gifted. Typically a meeting should be scheduled to review the field test data and to make recommendations on how best to utilize it for revision purposes.

Stage VI: Curriculum Implementation

Field testing, disseminating, and institutionalizing curriculum within the political context of schools is a major phase in the curriculum process. The problems that change agents (like curriculum developers for the gifted) incur along the road of implementation are myriad. An effective strategy of curriculum change,

FIGURE 2.8 Field-Test Evaluation Form: Criterial Checklist for Curriculum Units for the Gifted

Check one:	Check one:	Code:
K–3 _____	Social Studies _____	Objective(s) _____
4–6 _____	Math _____	Activities _____
7–8 _____	Science _____	
9–12 _____	Lang. Arts _____	
	Other _____	

Please circle the appropriate response for each.

		To a great extent		Not at all		Does not apply
1. The activities were age appropriate for gifted children. Comment _____		5	4 3	2	1	0
2. The activities were appropriate in terms of level of difficulty and/or complexity for gifted children. Comment _____		5	4 3	2	1	0
3. The activities were of interest to students. Comment _____		5	4 3	2	1	0
4. The activities helped accomplish the specific objective(s). Comment _____		5	4 3	2	1	0
5. The activities were differentiated from the regular school program in a specific content area(s). Comment _____		5	4 3	2	1	0
6. The activities were easy to adapt and/or implement. Comment _____		5	4 3	2	1	0
7. The teacher directions were sufficient. Comment _____		5	4 3	2	1	0
8. The background information and materials/references were sufficient. Comment _____		5	4 3	2	1	0
9. The activities were suitable to teaching the topic chosen. Comment _____		5	4 3	2	1	0
10. The activities encouraged creative production in students. Comment _____		5	4 3	2	1	0
11. The evaluation techniques or procedures were appropriate. Comment _____		5	4 3	2	1	0
12. The unit encouraged teachers to develop additional activities. Comment _____		5	4 3	2	1	0
13. The format facilitated understanding of unit purpose and direction. Comment _____		5	4 3	2	1	0

14. The format facilitated recognition of the interrelationship of   5   4   3   2   1   0
    component parts.
    Comment _____

Length of time to complete unit segments: _____

Suggestions for overall unit on change: _____

Other comments: _____

therefore, must proceed on a double agenda, working simultaneously to change ideas about curricula and to change human dynamics. Taba (1962) delineates key issues in the implementation process:

1. Curriculum change requires a systematic sequence of work which deals with all aspects of the curriculum ranging from goals to means.
2. A strategy for curriculum change involves creating conditions for productive work.
3. Effecting curriculum change involves a large amount of training.
4. Change always involves human and emotional factors.
5. Since curriculum development is extremely complex, it requires many kinds of competencies in different combinations at different points of work.
6. Managing curriculum change requires skilled leadership.

Curriculum implementation should be viewed as the most complex stage of curriculum development, for it involves the translation of ideas from written form into classroom action, the transforming of individuals' thoughts and behaviors to new paradigms, and the accomplishment of this evolution in a reasonable period of time.

One of the first issues of curriculum implementation that confronts educational personnel is deciding on the scope of the implementation effort. Successful implementation of curriculum takes a cooperative and total effort by all staff to ensure a smooth and successful transition. Consequently, it may be useful to limit by grade levels, content disciplines, or schools the unit of analysis to be included at the first stage of implementation.

A second issue in curriculum implementation involves a thorough understanding of the change process on the part of the administrator responsible for instituting it. At a very fundamental level, this recognition involves understanding the school climate into which the curriculum innovation will be placed and having a clear idea about how key actors will respond to the demands placed on them in implementing new curriculum.

A third issue revolves around the selection of staff for the first stage of implementation. Even though the total staff may eventually become involved with several aspects of the gifted curriculum, the number of staff involved with implementation should be limited initially. Criteria for considering staff selection should include: willingness and enthusiasm for the new direction, capacity to adapt curriculum appropriately in the classroom, and an interest in training fellow teachers in the use of the new curriculum. It is also important to select schools on the basis of the interest and follow-through involvement that may be anticipated at the principal level.

Staff development work at this stage of the curriculum development process is another issue vital to the success of the effort. Creating a curriculum that sits on shelves or is thrown away is a waste of everyone's resources. Yet frequently there is a void in the process of curriculum development in sensitizing and training personnel to use a new curriculum, laying out expectations regarding its implementation, and disseminating the work of the curriculum teams. These tasks need to be accomplished as part of the implementation stage.

Staff development of new curriculum should occur in segments. Initially, the implementation plan should be presented, followed by the curriculum teams who field tested the materials serving as presenters or discussants regarding its use. The use of outside consultants may be useful if they were involved in the earlier development stages of the project. A two-day period of time should be set aside for this orientation session. Follow-up sessions at three-month intervals should focus on strengths and weaknesses in the curriculum as it is being tried out. Classroom monitoring observations should also be conducted. If possible, teachers implementing the curriculum should be videotaped and those tapes used as a part of the curriculum critique. In this way classroom dynamics become the focus for judging curriculum efficacy.

It is rare that curriculum implementation can occur without some problems. One common problem is the lack of supplementary materials to carry out the implementation tasks at the most effective level. How do we go about accessing appropriate materials at this stage of the curriculum development process? We can maximize the potential for obtaining such materials by taking several steps prior to this stage of the process: establishing lists of types of material needed by teachers and students in the course of using the curriculum, setting criteria for selection of the materials, and budgeting carefully to ensure purchasing power.

Another key issue to consider at the implementation stage is a work plan that charts the progress of this stage of the process. This work plan should chart the implementation schedule according to key turning points in the process, such as when teachers have demonstrated a full understanding of what the purposes are of the new curriculum and the specifics of how to implement it in the context of the classroom. The work plan should also be revised as the process goes along, with notes recorded on problems or issues encountered along the way.

Another important issue to consider at the implementation stage is the monitoring process that needs to occur to ensure that classroom implementation is indeed going on. Are new materials being used? Are teachers applying appropriate strategies in teaching the new curriculum? Do students respond to what is being implemented? All of these questions are important checks on the actual degree of implementation that may be occurring in a given school. It is the responsibility of the administrator of a school and the coordinator of the gifted program to monitor the implementation process according to some predetermined joint agreement.

A final consideration to be made at the implementation stage is to have a process in place that will allow adjustments and adaptations in the curriculum to occur on the spot rather than waiting for the next formal phase of the process. If something is not working, then make the necessary changes and document what

FIGURE 2.9 Central Issues in Curriculum Implementation

1. *Unit of analysis*

    At what grade levels?

    In what content areas?

2. *Understanding change*

    What is the school climate?

    How will individuals respond?

3. *Assessing staff competencies*

    Who are the teachers that are capable of implementation?

    Who are the principals willing to take responsibility?

    Who can do training?

4. *Staff development and innovation*

    What changes are required by staff to implement the program in respect to knowledge, skills, attitudes?

    What type of training will facilitate change?

5. *Selecting supplementary materials*

    What types of materials?

    Criteria for selection?

6. *Sequencing work to maximize success*

    Do teachers understand goals and means equally?

    Is there an implementation schedule?

---

was done. Consequently, fine tuning of the curriculum can occur during implementation rather than being seen as an outcome of evaluation. Figure 2.9 highlights these issues in question form.

Stage VII: Curriculum Evaluation

Since there has been little systematic focus on curriculum work in the field of the education of the gifted, there has been less concern for evaluating the effectiveness of it. Many school districts will choose to assume a defect in their identification protocol rather than examine carefully the nature of the curriculum and its instructional delivery system. Consequently, the quest for the right test goes on and no effort is expended on behalf of a questionable educational treatment. It is as if a doctor constantly questioned his or her diagnosis and test results rather than altering the treatment of a patient who was not responding to one remedy. Such a doctor would not have patients long, yet educators prevail despite neglect of vital educational "treatment."

Evaluating the effectiveness of a curriculum for the gifted is an essential task that should be well-planned and executed. Too frequently, curriculum developers discard what fails without examining the particularities of the situation; likewise, teachers will favor a curriculum unit or segment or a course merely because students like it. The key questions about what makes curriculum effective with a group of atypical learners never get asked.

One excellent way of ascertaining curriculum effectiveness is to pilot test segments of it and then respond to a series of questions like the following:

1. What should be deleted from the unit?
2. What should be added to the unit?
3. What should be changed in the unit?
4. Were the learning experiences appropriately challenging to gifted students?
5. Did gifted students find the unit of high interest?
6. What evidence exists that gifted students gain proficiency at a higher level in a new area?
7. Were the instructional strategies that were employed to teach the unit effective?
8. Were the materials used in teaching the unit appropriate?
9. What are the strengths of the unit?
10. What are weaknesses of the unit?
11. Will the teacher continue to use the unit with gifted students?

The answers to such questions should lead one to revise, modify, or delete the piloted segments from future curriculum.

Another approach to evaluation of curriculum is to establish the content validity of it through experts in the field of inquiry being taught who are also cognizant of the special characteristics and needs of the gifted. Such questions as the following might be posed:

1. Is the knowledge presented in the curriculum materials fundamental to the discipline under study?
2. Are the materials useful and applicable to the educational environments in which gifted students are found?
3. Do the materials provide for progressive skill development?
4. How well do the units articulate to the next level of curriculum?
5. Are the objectives and activities appropriate for academically talented students?
6. Do the materials contain appropriate scope and sequence models for the specified use?
7. Is there internal, logical consistency within and across the units?
8. Are the objectives of the unit clear and attainable for students, given the activities and readings suggested?
9. Are the units appropriately rich in suggested resources, activities, and readings?

Another use of such a list by curriculum developers and teachers is as a set of criteria for deciding what content topics should be stressed, which process skills should be emphasized, and what product outcomes are most suitable.

Still another approach is to set up an evaluation research design that tests the effectiveness of alternate curricula or instructional strategies. In larger school districts the possibility of this approach is feasible and should provide

FIGURE 2.10 Checklist of Curriculum Principles for Use in Developing Gifted/Talented Programs

___ 1. *Continuity* A well-defined set of learning activities that reinforce the specified curriculum objective

___ 2. *Appropriateness for gifted learners* Definition of the curriculum is based on assessment of abilities, interests, needs, and learning styles of gifted learners

___ 3. *Diversity* Provisions for alternative means to attain determined ends within a specified curricular framework

___ 4. *Integration* Integrative use of all abilities that include cognition, emotion, and intuition into the curriculum

___ 5. *Openness* Elimination of preset expectations that limit the learnings within the curricular framework

___ 6. *Independence* Provisions for some type(s) of self-directed learnings

___ 7. *Substantive learning* Inclusion of significant subject matter, skills, products, and awareness that are of consequence or of importance to the learner and the discipline

___ 8. *Complexity* Provision for exposure to systems of knowledge, underlying principles and concepts, and key theories about what students study

___ 9. *Interdisciplinary learning* Provisions for transfer of learning to other domains of knowledge, new situations, etc.

___10. *Decision making* Provisions for student to make some appropriate/relevant decisions regarding what is to be learned and how it can be learned

___11. *Consistent with good teaching/learning methodologies* Inclusion of varied teaching practices that allow for motivation, practice, transfer of training, and feedback

___12. *Creation/recreation* Provisions to apply the creative process to improve, modify, etc., one's creations; to challenge prevailing thought and offer more appropriate solutions

___13. *Interaction with peers and a variety of significant others* Provisions to learn about and meet with individuals who share same and different gifts/talents

___14. *Value system* Inclusion of consistent opportunities to develop and examine personal and societal values and to establish a personal value system

___15. *Communication skills* Development of verbal and nonverbal systems and skills to dialogue, share, and exchange ideas

___16. *Timing* Apportionment of time span for learning activities that is consistent with characteristics of gifted learners for shorter/longer allotments

___17. *Multiple resources* Provision for utilization of a variety of material and human resources in the learning process

___18. *Accelerated/advanced pacing of content* Provision of quickness and aptness of gifted students to master new material

___19. *Economy* Compressed and streamlined organization of teaching material to match learning capacity of gifted students

___20. *Challenge* Provision for a sophisticated level of learning experiences that requires learners to stretch for understanding

helpful information regarding curriculum decision making over time in respect to gifted education.

Figure 2.10 illustrates a set of curriculum principles that may be used to assess the appropriateness of any given set of curriculum experiences for gifted learners. Therefore, the coordinator of gifted programs or the principal may use the checklist to judge the effectiveness of what has been developed.

Conclusion

This chapter has presented a seven-stage model for developing curriculum for gifted learners in a school district setting. Issues and questions have been raised related to each stage of the development process, and useful forms, checklists, and other types of guidelines that may be used by the practitioner have been provided. It is important to note that the curriculum development process has relevance to any area of the curriculum in need of work. In that sense, it is a generic model that can be used by administrators to enhance curriculum renewal efforts in general education as well as in gifted education.

KEY POINTS SUMMARY

- Curriculum development is an ongoing process that involves the several stages of planning, needs assessment, determining the scope of work, adapting or writing curriculum, field testing, implementation, and evaluation.
- Curriculum development efforts require sustained commitment on the part of school personnel and budgetary support for key stages of the process.
- The actual writing of special curriculum for the gifted occurs when available materials are judged insufficient or inappropriate for use.
- The planning phase of the curriculum development process is the most critical one because it sets the focus and direction for the work that will follow, and it codifies the philosophy of the school district regarding appropriate curriculum experiences for gifted learners.
- Adherence to a curriculum development model ensures that a curriculum is dynamic and responsive to the needs of students and sensitive to the realities of the classroom.
- Evaluating curriculum at reasonable time intervals allows the feedback process of revision to be activated, which in turn brings the curriculum back to the stage of rewriting and modification in key design elements.

References

Gallagher, J., Weiss, P., Ogleby, K., and Thomas, T. (1982). *Report on the Education of the Gifted: Survey of Education of Gifted Students*. Chapel Hill:

Frank Porter Graham Child Development Center, University of North Carolina at Chapel Hill.

Illinois Office of Education (1978). *Survey of Provisions for Gifted Children in Illinois.* Springfield, Ill.

Keating, D. (1976). *Intellectual Talent.* Baltimore, Md.: Johns Hopkins University Press.

Passow, H., et al. (1982). *Differentiated Curricula for the Gifted/Talented.* Committee Report to the National/State Leadership Training Institute on the Gifted and Talented. Ventura County, Calif.: Office of the Superintendent of Schools.

Phenix, P. (1964). *Realms of Meaning.* New York: McGraw-Hill Co.

Renzulli, J. (1977). *The Enrichment Triad.* Wethersfield, Conn.: Creative Learning Press.

Richardson Study of Gifted and Talented Education (1985). Fort Worth, Tex.: Richardson Foundation.

Richert, S. (1982). *National Report on Identification,* Assessment and Recommendations for Comprehending Identification of Gifted and Talented Youth. Sewell, N.J.: Educational Improvement Center-South.

Seeley, K. (1985). *Facilitators for Gifted Learners.* In J. Feldhusen (Ed.), *Toward Excellence in Gifted Education.* Denver, Colo.: Love Publishing Co.

Shane, H. (1981). *Content Curriculum for the Future.* Paper developed for College Board, New York.

Sternberg, R. J. (1985). *Beyond I.Q.: A Triarchic Theory of Intelligence.* New York: Cambridge University Press.

Taba, H. (1962). *Curriculum Development, Theory and Practice.* New York: Harcourt, Brace, and World, Inc.

Tyler, R. (1949). *Principles of Curriculum and Instruction.* Chicago: University of Chicago Press.

VanTassel-Baska, J. (1979). "A Needs Assessment Model for Gifted Education." *Journal for the Education of the Gifted,* 2(3), 141–148.

3 Curriculum Design Issues in Developing a Curriculum for the Gifted

Joyce VanTassel-Baska

The proper study of mankind has been said to be man. But . . . in large part the proper study of mankind is the science of design.
—Herbert Simon

The last chapter examined the stages of curriculum development through the perspective of necessary administrative actions to be undertaken in moving the curriculum process along in the context of schools. Another perspective is required to implement curriculum design. To be sure, the design issue is an integral part of the curriculum planning process described in the last chapter as Stage I. Yet it needs to be highlighted separately so that practitioners can understand: (1) the total design process and how the pieces of it interrelate; (2) the application of the confluent approach of content, process/product, and concept models to curriculum making; and (3) the development of a comprehensive curriculum for gifted learners.

A curriculum and instructional design model that is useful for these purposes is based on Kemp's work (1977), which displays the circular nature of the basic design process (see Figure 3.1). Most practitioners will have encountered this type of design model or one similar to it in an introductory course in curriculum and instruction. It frequently serves as the type of model from which teachers learn how to do lesson plans. It also represents the generally understood level of the basic design components that help structure a curriculum for any learner. It is particularly useful in its inclusion of the cell on the nature of the learner's characteristics and needs, which provides the focus for curriculum for the gifted learner. This chapter will discuss each of the design elements in light of key issues of differentiation for the gifted.

Learner Characteristics: A Prelude to Curriculum Dimensions

As we begin this discussion of design issues, it may be helpful to discuss the term *differentiation* as it applies to curriculum for the gifted. The basis for all

**FIGURE 3.1 A Curriculum/Instructional Design Model for Constructing
Curriculum for Gifted Learners**

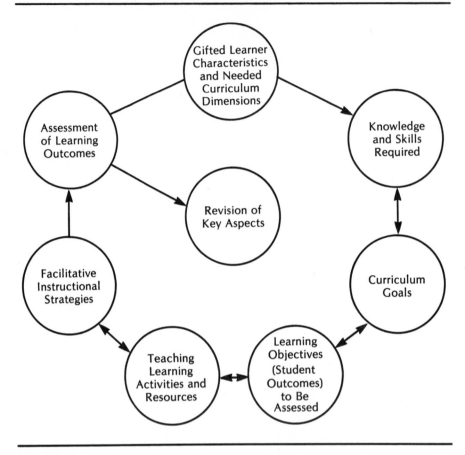

differentiation in the curriculum for these students should emerge from the differences in their characteristics and needs as reflected in formal test data and careful observation of performance behaviors. Fundamentally, the view of differentiation taken in this book is one that emanates from an examination and synthesis of typical characteristics of these learners. Three fundamental differences emerge from the research that distinguish the gifted from more typical learners:

1. The capacity to learn at faster rates (Keating, 1976)
2. The capacity to find, solve, and act on problems more readily (Sternberg, 1985)
3. The capacity to manipulate abstract ideas and make connections (Gallagher, 1985)

Thus a differentiated curriculum should be based on these differences, and simultaneously address all three of them in the learner population if it is to meet their most important albeit diverse needs. The curriculum models presented in Chapter 1 are educational applications of these characteristics in school settings.

Although individual gifted students may vary considerably in their capacities within these three areas, it is the role of the teacher to intensify or slacken the curriculum experience that has been planned in order to accommodate these individual differences. In the diagnostic-prescriptive approach to instruction, for example, there is clearly a methodology to promote an understanding of these differences and to act on them in instructional planning. In problem-solving contexts, the teacher can manipulate the complexity of the problem set and the instructional grouping pattern to accommodate such differences. And in the conceptual realm, the teacher can modify the extent and nature of the concept to be studied and into what areas it will be explored by all gifted students, thus setting the stage for further work on an individual basis. The important issue to be understood here is: *Not all gifted students are alike in respect to their characteristics or needs. So curriculum planning that proceeds from general behaviors of a gifted population needs to be modified appropriately for specific students at each stage of development.* VanTassel-Baska (1981) has used assessment profiles of a gifted population as a basis for a differential approach to the provision of program experiences. The more gifted the learner, the more intensive and extensive should be the experiences, both in respect to contact time and required curriculum resources. The needs of special populations like the disadvantaged, underachievers, and the learning disabled will also affect the nature and extent of the curriculum intervention. Thus individual adaptations need to be considered at this stage of the design process.

Content, Process/Product, and Concept Dimensions

The dimensions within which we design a curriculum for the gifted are based on the characteristics of these learners. In educational practice, they become the basic models discussed in Chapter 1. However, there is a major question to be addressed at this phase of the design process: How does one decide what are the appropriate content topics, process skills/products, and concepts to be studied by gifted learners at any given stage of development? This question needs to be explored according to a set of guided questions for each of the dimensions that practitioners may focus on in their work.

CONTENT

The content dimension determines the particular domain of inquiry to be explored and the aspects of that domain to be addressed. It may delineate the breadth and depth of the curriculum experience. For example, the narrower a content topic, the more likely the student will be able to study it intensively, given a reasonable period of time, as opposed to a broader topic which would require extensive study. Content topics need to be selected according to the following criteria.

1. *Is the content topic important and worthy of the time to be expended on it?* For example, spending six weeks studying designer jeans or the history of teddy bears, two topics actually explored in gifted programs, would be judged less important than topics such as consumer economics or political opportunities in the nineteenth century.

2. *Is the content topic conceptually complex enough to render it meaningful for gifted students?* Gifted students enjoy exploring a topical area, examining it from various perspectives. The topic choice has to be conceptually interesting and complex enough to hold up under intense investigation. Thus the study of magnetism could offer more to the gifted than the study of horseshoes.

3. *Is the content topic relevant to how the world works?* The study of law or a language, it could be argued, is more appropriate for the gifted to study than movie stars of the 1940s since the more general areas of study could provide the gifted with insights into societal systems rather than transitory cultural fads.

4. *Is the content topic likely to be of interest to students?* Although student interest can be gauged formally before curriculum is constructed, it also frequently can be assessed more informally as topics are being considered. What is "likely to be of interest" may be more important than demonstrated interest since interest tends to follow exposure to particular types of experiences. Content topics to be chosen should not deliberately narrow a student's vision of knowledge areas available to be explored.

5. *Is the content topic one that could be taught effectively by the designated instructor?* This constitutes a key question in considering choices of content topics. A teacher must feel comfortable with what is being taught and be well-trained in it. Teachers who do not know a content topic have a great deal of difficulty being creative with that topic. Thus gifted students lose out at the instructional level if the content topic(s) chosen is not well-matched to instructor background. Teachers are unable to answer student questions in any depth or lead them to higher levels of understanding when their own understanding is superficial. Too often students of high ability know more about content areas than their teachers, and are in the awkward position of correcting misinformation the teacher has given the class.

PROCESS SKILLS

Fundamental to our conceptualization of appropriate curriculum for the gifted is the focus on higher level thinking skills that allow such students to learn to think independently of textbooks, materials, and other resources. We also want them to transfer these skills readily from one curriculum area to another and from one dimension (such as academic) to another dimension (such as their personal lives). Thus the curriculum for the gifted needs to be infused and suffused with these lifelong skills. Ideally, those skills that include critical and creative thinking, problem finding and problem solving, and evaluation should be addressed across the K–12 years of schooling. This need, of course, raises the issue of how to organize these skills to ensure maximum internalization and transfer effect. The authors of this book believe strongly that this is more likely to occur if the skills are:

1. Well-defined
2. Consistently addressed over time
3. Taught both within basic content domains as well as intensively as a separate instructional set
4. Organized by scope and sequence from K–12
5. Modeled by the teacher in the classroom
6. Employed as questioning techniques by the teacher

PRODUCT ALTERNATIVES

Both as a tool for evaluation of student synthesis capacities and as a core activity in the curriculum, the selection of projects for students to undertake individually and collectively is important. There is a key set of questions that should be considered when making educational decisions regarding the role of products in a curriculum for the gifted:

1. How and when should independent investigations be undertaken?
2. Should a group of gifted learners create the same type of product under certain circumstances (e.g., an essay written on the same topic)?
3. How should the selection of projects occur? Should teachers generate a list of alternatives for students to choose from or should students work on any project of interest to them?
4. What generative learning processes are important to teach through the product development process?
5. What new knowledge and at what level is it important for students to gain as a result of the work on a given project?
6. How can time allocations both in school and out of school be best utilized for optimal project work?

ISSUES, THEMES, AND CONCEPTS

Central to any vision of comprehensive curriculum for the gifted is the focus on the ideas that have guided the development of civilization as we know it. These large concepts, issues, and themes are those that dominate all areas of knowledge exploration, yet may have specific connotations within a given discipline of thought. So the task of educators of the gifted is to seek out those ideas that can be best utilized with gifted learners at various stages of development both within and across traditional fields of inquiry. There are at least two ways that this might be accomplished:

PROCEDURE A

1. Decide initially on a set of important ideas to explore such as "change," "war," "justice," "honor," "rights," "freedom," and so on.
2. Delineate a content outline that provides the central propositions around those ideas that students should learn.

3. Choose resources and materials that will facilitate the teaching and learning of these propositions.

EXAMPLE: CONCEPT: JUSTICE

CENTRAL PROPOSITIONS:
1. Law is the codified form of justice used by civilized societies.
2. In order for justice to thrive, laws must be interpreted by humans who understand situations and the human condition.
3. One person's justice is another person's punishment.
4. Human behavior has tended to vacillate between practice of the Golden Rule and aggressive territoriality.
5. Justice begins with basic respect for the rights of all persons.

RESOURCES AND MATERIALS:
Film: *Twelve Angry Men*

History of case law

William Golding's *Lord of the Flies*

Harper Lee's *To Kill a Mockingbird*

Visit to local courtroom

Lawyer or judge as a guest speaker

PROCEDURE B

1. Take existing content topics and generate a list of "ideas" found within them.
2. Decide what aspects of the ideas should be explored.
3. Choose supplementary materials to explore the concept more fully.

EXAMPLE: CONTENT TOPIC: GLACIERS
(7TH GRADE SCIENCE TEXTBOOK)

GLACIERS:
1. Move backward or forward over the span of time
2. Leave their imprint on the earth's landscape
3. Form in snow fields above the snow line in mountains and move because of gravity

GENERIC IDEAS TO BE STUDIED FURTHER:
1. Changes in the earth's surface over time
2. How climate affects the environment
3. How the study of natural conditions today can solve mysteries of the past
4. Provide evidence of past Ice Age activity and presage such future activity

TYPES OF MATERIALS:
1. Books on geology, archaeology, ages of man
2. Books on "change" as a concept
3. Films that depict life under different climatic conditions

Both of these procedures are useful in deciding on important concepts to include in a curriculum for the gifted.

It may be helpful to illustrate the transformation of these curriculum dimensions of content, process/product, and concept into a curriculum whole that integrates these four aspects of a differentiated curriculum (see Figure 3.2).

As we examine these curriculum dimensions, we can see the way in which each dimension fits with another to achieve curriculum balance. It is important to note that in this view of the curriculum dimensions, there is equal weighting of each. Big ideas are not valued more than content topics nor are projects a dominating force over the process skills they hope to instill. Rather, there is a comfortable blend of these major components within a curriculum for the gifted.

Knowledge and Skills

How do we go about determining what gifted students should know and be able to do at a given stage of development? We have determined rather imprecisely what typical learners should know at key levels of development. In what skill

FIGURE 3.2 Curriculum Dimensions

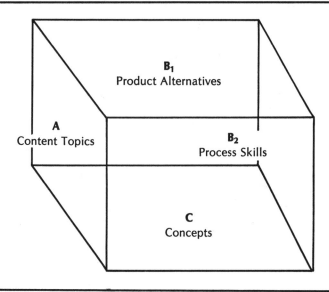

areas should gifted students show proficiency as the result of schooling? At what level of proficiency? These questions are basic to our understanding of how the fundamental process of curriculum design works. In order for teachers to plan classroom experiences effectively, they must have a guide to help them formulate appropriate knowledge areas and skills to be acquired in the context of a gifted program. This means that they must be able to answer the following questions:

1. What are the knowledge and skill requirements for typical learners in my school district at each stage of development?
2. What are the desired knowledge and skill areas for the gifted that are different from these at each stage of development?
3. What is the relationship between the district requirements and the needs of the gifted?

Since what constitutes local school district curriculum can be categorized as knowledge or skills, it may be useful to take an example from a state assessment model to illustrate this issue. By the end of third grade, students in Illinois are expected to possess the following knowledge-skills in the area of mathematical methods:

1. Ability to read, write, and name numbers in several different ways
2. Ability to perform operations with numbers with and without a calculator
3. Application of computational and problem-solving skills to common life situations with or without calculators
4. Measurement in various contexts using appropriate units
5. Estimation of measurements
6. Simple geometric figures and patterns of relationships in two and three dimensions

From the vantage point of gifted learners, these knowledge-skill areas should be addressed at the K–3 level:

1. Counting, calculator, and estimation skills
2. Knowledge of simple probability
3. Knowledge of transformational geometry
4. Basic reasoning and inference skills
5. Knowledge of spatial dimensions
6. Algebraic manipulation skills
7. Basic problem-solving skills
8. Knowledge of modeling techniques

The relationship between the two sets of lists can be described in the following way:

- The state list is more precise, concrete, and specific.
- The state list is simpler for gifted students to master.
- The state list is limited to work in general arithmetic.
- The state list requires less time to master.
- By itself, the state list is inappropriate for gifted learners in mathematics.

Yet, these two sets of required knowledge-skill areas in mathematics at the primary level can be fused to create a powerful knowledge-skill set for the gifted learner:

- Counting, calculation, and estimation skills
- Ability to perform basic computations
- Application of basic problem-solving skills to real life
- Knowledge of simple probability
- Knowledge of transformational geometry: three-dimensional patterns and figures in space
- Basic reasoning and inference skills
- Algebraic manipulation skills
- Knowledge of modeling techniques
- Ability to use the computer as a tool in problem solving

This technique of curriculum alignment is essential to apply as one works out this aspect of the curriculum design so that the regular school curriculum is not abandoned nor viewed as totally inappropriate. Such alignment also forces the practitioner to be very precise about what is needed for each type of learner at a given stage of development, as well as what the curriculum overlaps are for both types of learners (see Figure 3.3).

FIGURE 3.3 Curriculum Alignment Model

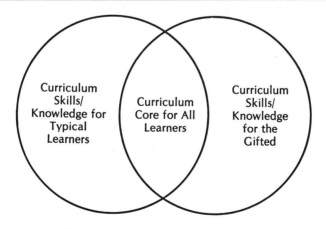

Goals and Objectives: Formulating Student Outcomes

These cells of the curriculum design determine the overall purpose for specific activities undertaken with gifted learners. The objectives also represent an important specification for purposes of evaluation at the student level. They usually answer the question "What do you want gifted students to have gained from their curriculum experiences?" This question needs to be posed against the backdrop of what the regular school curriculum is not providing. As one views this aspect of the design, it is important to keep in mind the cell of learner characteristics and curriculum dimensions so that the formulation of student outcomes is appropriate for gifted learners. It is also useful to understand the shifts in specificity from generating a curriculum goal to a general objective to a behavioral objective that can be measured. The example provided in Figure 3.4

FIGURE 3.4 Goals and Corresponding Objectives

	Examples: Curriculum Goal	Desired Student Outcomes: General Objectives	Behavioral/Objective Translation
Model A	To attain mastery in all areas of learning at a readiness stage of development and at a rate commensurate with capacity	To attain mastery of algebra at a readiness stage of development and at a rate commensurate with capacity	Based on a diagnostic test for placement, gifted students will achieve 90% mastery of algebra topics as assessed by the Cooperative Algebra Test in half the time allotted to average learners
Model B	To develop the higher level thinking skills	To develop high-level inquiry skills (i.e., accurate observation, analysis, and interpretation of data, problem-finding strategies and defining capacities, etc.)	Gifted students will perform at an average of 4.0 on a 5.0 point teacher checklist designed to measure the application of inquiry skills
Model C	To develop the ability to integrate ideas across domains of inquiry	To synthesize ideas about "time" from multiple sources	Gifted students will create a product (i.e., an essay, a slide tape, a musical composition, a painting) that is judged excellent to superior by a panel of "experts"

specifies a goal and corresponding objective for a gifted curriculum for each of the three curriculum and instructional models or dimensions.

The development of goals and objectives appropriate for gifted learners is a critical feature in curriculum design. It is at this stage of the conceptualization process that practitioners are forced to choose what will be emphasized in the curriculum and the reasonable performance level for gifted students in that area. Obviously, goals and objectives need to be generated for all aspects of the program and for all curriculum areas where gifted students will be served. Ideally, gifted students would be served comprehensively across the curriculum, so that goals and objectives would need to be articulated accordingly (see Figure 3.5).

Each of the domains of study in Figure 3.5 is treated extensively in a separate chapter to provide ideas for practitioners in completing this chart. Broad curriculum goals are stated in each chapter, along with sample curriculum that provides illustrative material in respect to student learning objectives.

Activities and Resources

The fourth cell in the curriculum design model focuses on the curriculum experiences that are provided at the classroom level. What activities and materials are selected by the teacher to carry out the stated learning objectives? What criteria might be applied to enhance appropriate choices? A good balance of types of activities should be used with gifted learners: independent, interactive whole group, and interactive small group. Other important criteria for activities and materials include:

1. Activities should be rich and complex enough to serve more than one instructional purpose.
2. Activities should be organized in clusters to build toward the fulfillment of a learning objective.

FIGURE 3.5 CURRICULUM GOALS AND OBJECTIVES BY LEVEL

Domains of Study	K–3	4–6	7–8	9–12
Mathematics				
Social Science				
Verbal Arts				
Science				
Humanities				
The Arts				
Leadership				
Affective				

3. Whole-class activities should be motivational to encourage small group and independent learning.

4. Activities should not be textbook bound.

5. Multiple resources should be available.

6. Print, nonprint, and human resources should be effectively used.

7. Materials resources should be chosen for their congruence with gifted learner objectives.

ANALYSIS OF AN ACTIVITY

For many teachers, the approach to curriculum design that works best is an inductive model where one begins with an activity and builds from it to the more abstract issues of content, process, product, concept, strategy, objective, and purpose. Therefore, the following example has been included to show how this approach can work in thinking through the curriculum design process.

ACTIVITY: THE HOLMES CASE*

Holmes was a seaman on the WILLIAM BROWN, which set sail from Liverpool from Philadelphia in 1841. The ship struck an iceberg some 250 miles from Newfoundland and soon began to sink. Two boats were lowered. The captain, various members of the crew, and a passenger got into one of them and, after six days on the open sea, were picked up and brought to land. The other boat was called the "long-boat"; it was leaky and might easily be swamped. Into it Holmes jumped along with the first mate, seven other seaman, and thirty-two passengers, about twice as many as the boat could hold under the most favorable conditions of wind and weather. Just as the long-boat was about to pull away from the wreck, Holmes, hearing the agonized cries of a mother for her little daughter who had been left behind in the panic, dashed back at the risk of instant death, found the girl and carried her under his arm into the long-boat. The sailors rowed and the passengers bailed, but the over-weighted long-boat, drifting between blocks of floating ice, sank lower and lower as a steady rain fell on the sea. The wind began to freshen, the sea grew heavy, and waves splashed over the bow. Then, after the first mate had twice given the order, Holmes and the rest of the crew began to throw the male passengers overboard. Two married men and a little boy were spared, but the fourteen remaining male passengers were cast over, and two women—devoted sisters of one of the victims—voluntarily leaped to join their brother in his death. The long-boat sailed afloat. The next morning Holmes spied a sail in the distance, exerted himself heroically to attract notice of the passing vessel, and eventually brought about the rescue of everyone left in the boat.

When the survivors arrived in Philadelphia, the mate and most of the seamen, hearing talk of prosecution, disappeared. Holmes was put on trial for manslaughter.

In his charge to the jury as to the law, the judge stated that passengers must be saved in preference to all seamen except those who are indispensable to operating the boat. If no seaman can possibly be dispensed with, then the victims must be chosen from among the passengers by casting lots, provided—as in the case—there is time enough to do so.

---

* This activity is included in the social science chapter as an appropriate activity for gifted learners in grades 4–6. Source of quote is unknown.

Question: If you were to use this case in your teaching of the gifted, what *content topics* might you wish to explore?

Sample response:

- Maritime law (comparable disaster cases)
- Development of law in a society (case law)
- Navy—ships, navigation, historical background
- English society
- Comparative legal systems (moral dilemmas)
- Travel routes (geography, oceanography)
- Law vs. lawless

Question: If you were to use this case in your teaching of the gifted, what *process skills* would you focus on?

Sample response:

- Decision-making skills
- Analysis skills
- Evaluation skills
- Generalization skills

Question: If you were to use this case in your teaching of the gifted, what *issues, themes, or concepts* would you explore?

Sample response:

- Justice (right vs. wrong)
- Spirit of law vs. letter of law
- Comparative perspectives on law
- Conflict and change
- The issues of the individual vs. society
- Value of human life
- Authority
- Moral integrity
- Probability and chance

Question: If you used this activity, what *product alternatives* would you suggest for students?

Sample response:

- Debates
- Mock trials
- Theme papers

- Creative writing pieces (poetry, drama, etc.)
- Reenactment (videotape)
- Role-playing simulation

Question: If you used this activity, what *instructional purposes* would it serve?

Sample response:

- To recognize multiple points of view on a given issue
- To promote the development of decision-making skills
- To establish the relevance of the past to the present and the future
- To explore moral and ethical issues at a personal level
- To demonstrate the relevance of law to the individual
- To gain an understanding of legal procedures
- To promote multiple thinking skills (analysis, synthesis, evaluation)
- To understand the historical context for individual cases

Question: If you were to use this type of activity, what *instructional strategies* would you employ to teach it?

Sample response:

- Inquiry-based discussion
- Speakers/field trips
- Media
- Simulations
- Directed teaching (lecture)
- Small-group problem solving
- Individual/independent learning

At this stage, teachers could generate other activities and resources that would contribute to the curriculum dimensions already conceptualized. Inductively, they have already developed the framework for a unit of study in the social sciences.

Facilitative Instructional Approaches

One can build great curriculum designs and structure meaningful clusters of activities that have relevant content, process, and concept outcomes specified that will still be totally ineffective with gifted learners. Why? Because the piece of the puzzle that is still missing is the instructional glue—the processes and strategies employed by a good teacher to make the curriculum come alive and work in the classroom setting. What are these approaches that work? Research has demonstrated that many strategies are successful with gifted students, so the issue is not *which* strategy but rather "What combination of strategies can be employed?" and "Under what circumstances for maximum effectiveness?" Nevertheless, the following list of instructional processes has been adapted from The Martinson-Weiner Scale of Teacher Behaviors (1974) to provide a universe of successful approaches to facilitating curriculum experiences for gifted learners:

1. Conduct group discussions.
2. Select questions that stimulate higher level thinking.
3. Use varied teaching strategies effectively.
4. Utilize critical thinking skills in appropriate contexts.
5. Encourage independent thinking and open inquiry.
6. Understand and encourage student ideas and student-directed work.
7. Demonstrate understanding of the educational implications of giftedness.
8. Utilize creative thinking techniques.
9. Utilize problem-solving techniques.
10. Synthesize student assessment data and curriculum content effectively.

Assessment: Measuring Student Outcomes

This aspect of the curriculum design wheel is concerned with what happened to the learner as a result of a planned set of curriculum experiences. Did the learner grow in the dimensions anticipated? Did the learner grow to the extent hoped for? Did the learner grow in unanticipated ways? All of these questions are important ones to answer through the assessment process. Equally important from a curriculum perspective, however, are the questions related to curriculum implementation. Was the intended curriculum implemented as it was planned? To what extent were the instructional processes used by the teacher facilitative of student learning?

In the design process, it is anticipated that describing the assessment to be employed will be difficult. And with gifted learners, the task is even more problematic because standardized achievement measures cannot be readily used with that population, and appropriate criterion levels have to be approximated based on good judgment rather than on the typical standard of "nine month's growth in an area based on nine months in school."

Reasonable approaches to assessing the growth of gifted students who have been engaged in a specialized curriculum can be found, however. Kulieke (1986a) has conceptualized a model of alternative evaluation approaches to consider in deciding on student assessment techniques (see Figure 3.6).

Generally, there are some important questions to ask in deciding on an assessment model:

1. *How often should students be assessed?* Clearly, growth in some dimensions takes longer than it does in others. Therefore, timing of the assessment is critical

FIGURE 3.6 A Critique of Evaluation Approaches and Level of Experimental Designs*

	Level 1 "Pre-experimental": One Group Examined at One Point in Time	Level 2 "Time Series": One Group Examined at Two or More Points in Time	Level 3 "Quasiexperimental": Two Nonequivalent Groups Examined at One Point in Time	Level 4 "Quasiexperimental Time Series": Two Nonequivalent Groups Examined at Two Points in Time	Level 5 "Experimental": Two Equivalent Groups Examined at One or More Points in Time
Proficiency Based					
Example: 90% of students have achieved 90% competency on a final test.					
How well can you attribute proficiency to the program?	Poorly	Somewhat poorly	Somewhat poorly	Somewhat well	Well
How well have you assessed program effects?	Poorly	Somewhat poorly	Somewhat poorly	Somewhat well	Well

68

Product Based

Example:
100% of students have completed a final report with a grade of "B" or above.

How well can you attribute the final report to the program?		Well	Well	Well	Well
How well have you assessed program effects?	Somewhat poorly	Somewhat well	Well	Well	

Attitudinal Based

Example:
Students have a greater interest in the subject matter being taught.

How well can you attribute the final report to the program?	Poorly	Somewhat poorly	**Somewhat poorly**	Somewhat well	Well
How well have you assessed program effects?	Poorly	Somewhat poorly	Somewhat poorly	Somewhat well	Well

* From M. Kulieke, *An Evaluation Handbook for Evaluating Gifted Program Impacts* (Evanston, Ill.: Northwestern University, Center for Talent Development, 1986). Reprinted with permission.

to showing learning gains. Some assessment of objectives could occur four times a year; other assessments might occur only once in a three-year period. The nature of the learning task should determine the timing of the assessments. The more complex the task, the longer the period prior to assessment.

2. *On what dimensions of learning should students be assessed?* Many times content-based learning becomes the only dimension to be measured among gifted students. Although it may be easier to show positive change in learning in these areas, it is important to assess what learning is occurring at other levels and in other dimensions.

3. *Who should be involved in the assessment?* The teacher in the classroom is in the best position to handle the details of assessment, but sometimes it is advantageous to use outside experts in a given field. Students should also have input into the assessment process through self-evaluation inventories and some form of "peer review" in certain areas of the curriculum. Whereas the teacher may develop some aspects of student assessment, it is useful to rely on a mix of measures that include standardized tests that may be used pre–post, inventories, and observational checklists that can be utilized by process observers at different points in time, and product assessment.

4. *What are reasonable student growth expectations in a gifted curriculum?* Obviously, this answer depends heavily on the specific objectives of a given program. But it may be useful to delineate a standard for gifted programs compared to regular education programs. For example, consider the following:

IF YOU WOULD EXPECT REGULAR LEARNERS TO ATTAIN:
- Nine months' growth in nine months
- Achieve 3 out of 5 on a product assessment scale
- Produce written essays at an acceptable level
- Demonstrate minimum levels of leadership skills
- Read 5 outside books a year
- Master language usage at a 70 percent level

YOU WOULD EXPECT GIFTED LEARNERS TO ATTAIN:
- Fourteen months' growth in nine months
- Achieve 4 out of 5 on a product assessment scale
- Produce written essays at a superior level
- Demonstrate maximum levels of leadership skills
- Read 10 outside books a year
- Show knowledge of grammar and usage through writing

The issue is to decide on *what is appropriate* based on norms for average learners. Should the gifted be expected to do more, as well as do it better? Or should they be judged according to an entirely different standard—one that gives them credit for being high achievers in a general context, and therefore does not shift its stringency pattern based on the population? For example, the general criterion for passing a course of study is 70 percent correct on a given test measure. Let's say that a special course is available to the gifted in statistics, and the teacher tells the gifted class that the expectation for success will be achieving 70 percent or above on a specially designed test in statistics. Is this an inappropriate evaluation standard for gifted students? In a sense, what we are faced with is a value question. Are there educational experiences, such as learning advanced content, where "passing" would be considered an appropriately high standard for the gifted? Conversely, are some standards too high, such as requiring 95 percent proficiency before moving on to new material? These issues are crucial to discuss in determining criterion levels for success in a gifted curriculum.

GRADING AS A MANIFESTATION OF STUDENT ASSESSMENT

Many teachers of the gifted agonize over the issues of grading gifted students on their work in special programs. In fact, individual assessment is done infrequently in elementary pull-out programs. It is difficult to argue against grading gifted students on their work as well as work habits. Gifted students benefit from clearly knowing their strengths and weaknesses. To deny them this opportunity seems to be a mistake. By the same token, the program administrator needs to know how groups of learners have performed in order to assess the effectiveness of the curriculum plan. Thus grading serves an individual and a systems function in an educational setting.

Should grades be weighted for the gifted? This too is a value question related to the earlier one—should 70 percent be considered an "A"? A clear set of expectations for gifted learners should pervade the curriculum design constructed by practitioners. This set of expectations can then be converted to whatever form of measurement is desired in a given setting. Using the behavioral objectives from earlier in this chapter, Figure 3.7 provides an example for measurement.

In each of these cases, traditional student grading was done that was tied directly to the assessment measures used. Yet different interpretations or values were placed on differing attainment levels for each objective. In algebra, students were encouraged to drop the course if success was not at an 80 percent

FIGURE 3.7 Measurement of Expectations

Behavioral Objective	Assessment Expectations
#1 (related to taking algebra)	To receive an "A" in algebra, gifted students will achieve a 90% score on the Coop Algebra Test by January of the year they take it. To receive a "B," gifted students will achieve an 80% score on the Coop Test by May of the year they take it. Any expectation on the part of the teacher that a gifted student would perform below these levels would lead to another educational placement.
#2 (related to gaining inquiry skills)	The grading range for this aspect of the program is as follows: 4–5 rating = A, 3 rating = B, 2–1 rating = remedial action.
#3 (related to synthesizing ideas in a project)	Excellent/superior ratings = A Good ratings = B Fair ratings = C Poor Ratings = Project or paper to be redone for credit

tested level; in inquiry skills training, a low rating resulted in remedial action in the skill area, and in the conceptual product assessment, a low grade resulted in the student being required to redo the product. Not only is it difficult to identify clear standards for success, it is equally difficult to define and address the problem of failure in gifted classrooms.

A set of guidelines may be helpful at the assessment stage:

1. Recognize the importance of evaluating student performance in gifted programs.
2. Identify acceptable approaches to evaluation based on the curriculum model being used.
3. Set criterion levels for success that consider alternatives to normal distribution scales and yet are sensitive to standards in similar contexts for typical learners.
4. Establish clear standards for performance at the beginning of a curriculum. Be as specific as possible.
5. Use weighted grades or a restricted grading range to provide incentives for gifted learners to elect advanced curriculum at the secondary level.
6. Consider placement out of gifted curriculum experiences on an individual basis rather than based on performance expectation at a given point in time.

MONITORING AS AN ASSESSMENT STRATEGY

It is as important to focus on the degree of appropriate implementation that has occurred with a given curriculum unit or course of study as it is to focus only on the student's learning level. Certainly, there are times that learning is impeded because instructional time has not been adequately used or the emphasis of

FIGURE 3.8 Observation Assessment

Date_____

Time span of observation _____

Name of the teacher _____

Grade level _____

Content area/skill/concept observed _____

What were the students doing? _____

What was the teacher doing? _____

What instructional purpose was being fulfilled? _____

Relationship of observed instruction to written curriculum objectives _____

Other comments: _____

_____

FIGURE 3.9 OBSERVATION FORM FOR USE WITH TEACHERS OF THE GIFTED*

Directions:

Taking into account the content of this class, how proficient do you feel the teacher is at using each of the following teaching strategies? It is recommended that teachers be observed for two 30-minute periods before and after relevant inservice work, using this form as a guide.

	Excellent	Good	Fair	Poor	Very Poor
Conducts Group Discussions					
Teacher withholds own ideas and conclusions.	5	4	3	2	1
Teacher encourages participation of students in discussions.	5	4	3	2	1
Teacher poses interpretive questions for students.	5	4	3	2	1
Selects Questions That Stimulate Higher-Level Thinking					
Students evaluate situations, problems, issues.	5	4	3	2	1
Students ask analytic questions.	5	4	3	2	1
Students generalize from concrete to abstract at advanced levels.	5	4	3	2	1
Uses Varied Teaching Strategies Effectively					
Teacher is sensitive to students' responses.	5	4	3	2	1
Teacher maintains a balance between active and passive activities.	5	4	3	2	1
Teacher deliberately shifts teaching strategies with students.	5	4	3	2	1
Utilizes Critical Thinking Skills in Appropriate Contexts					
Teacher utilizes inductive and deductive reasoning and is able to apply techniques in classroom.	5	4	3	2	1
Teacher encourages student development of inference and evaluation of argument skills.	5	4	3	2	1
Teacher encourages analogical thinking.	5	4	3	2	1

(continued)

FIGURE 3.9 *(continued)*

	Excellent	Good	Fair	Poor	Very Poor
Encourages Independent Thinking and Open Inquiry					
Students compare and contrast different issues, using objective evidence.	5	4	3	2	1
Students engage in lively debate of controversial issues.	5	4	3	2	1
Students and teacher reflect an open/challenging attitude toward knowledge.	5	4	3	2	1
Understands and Encourages Student Ideas and Student-Directed Work					
Teacher encourages students to try new approaches.	5	4	3	2	1
Teacher is tolerant to students' attempts to find solutions to problems.	5	4	3	2	1
Teacher encourages "guesses" by students and facilitates evaluation of guesses by students.	5	4	3	2	1
Teacher helps students to realize that research involves trial and error.	5	4	3	2	1
Demonstrates Understanding of the Educational Implications of Giftedness					
Teacher uses implications of characteristics in the classroom operation, selection of materials, schedules, and questions.	5	4	3	2	1
Teacher uses management procedures that maximize individual differences of students in the learning process.	5	4	3	2	1
Teacher uses advanced organizers for instruction and organizes curriculum around the highest level skill, concept, or idea that a group of gifted learners can master.	5	4	3	2	1

* Adapted from *Martinson-Weiner Rating Scale of Behaviors in Teachers of the Gifted* (Martinson, 1976).

instruction was faulty or the processes of instruction were ineffectual. Gauging the extent of the implementation of a curriculum can best be done by a building principal who, using two different assessment tools, can observe classrooms on a regular schedule. One is a simple chart that records what was observed, its purpose, and the relationship of it to the overall curriculum objectives (see Figure 3.8). The other assessment tool has been adapted by Kulieke (1986b) from the Martinson-Weiner Scale for Rating Teacher Behaviors. It provides a way to monitor the extent to which varied instructional processes are used and how effectively teachers are interacting with gifted learners (see Figure 3.9).

Conclusion

This chapter has explored the key elements of curriculum design, including learner characteristics and curriculum dimensions, goals, objectives, knowledge/skills, activities, and resources; facilitative instructional strategies; and assessment. It has provided approaches to differentiate design cells appropriately for gifted learners. The chapter has also included sample instruments, curriculum, and various models that may aid the practitioner in implementing the curriculum design process.

KEY POINTS SUMMARY

- Curriculum design elements include: learner characteristics and curriculum dimensions, goals, objectives, knowledge, skills, activities, and resources; instructional delivery; and assessment.

- Curriculum design elements that need particular attention in gifted programs are: (1) goals and objectives because they establish the direction for the curriculum emphasis, and (2) assessment because it allows us to ascertain effects of special curriculum intervention.

- Developing a comprehensive curriculum means having an articulated curriculum design in all major domains of study at all stages of the development of the learner.

- The steps in constructing a curriculum can be carried out from the most general level of goals to the most specific level of activities, or it can be constructed in the reverse, from the specific activities to the general goals.

- The integration of the basic curriculum models/dimensions can be achieved at the goal, objective, and activity levels of the curriculum.

- Curriculum alignment at the knowledge and skills level of the curriculum is an important process in integrating the general school curriculum into one appropriate for gifted learners.

- Assessment of student growth and progress in a special curriculum is essential to the individual student and to the program.

- Monitoring the implementation of curriculum and instruction for the gifted is vital to any learning plan.

References

Gallagher, J. J. (1985). *Teaching the Gifted Child.* Boston: Allyn and Bacon.

Keating, D. (1976). *Intellectual Talent.* Baltimore, Md.: Johns Hopkins University Press.

Kemp, J. E. (1977). *Instructional Design.* Belmont, Calif.: Fearson, Pitnam.

Kulieke, M. (1986a). *An Evaluation Handbook for Evaluating Gifted Program Impacts.* Evanston, Ill.: Northwestern University, Center for Talent Development.

Kulieke, M. (1986b). "The Role of Evaluation in Inservice and Staff Development for Educators of the Gifted." *Gifted Child Quarterly, 30,* 3, 140–144.

Martinson, R. (1974). Martinson-Weiner Rating Scale of Behaviors in Teachers of the Gifted in *A Guide Toward Better Teaching for the Gifted.* Ventura, Calif.: Ventura County Superintendent of Schools Office.

Sternberg, R. (1985). *Beyond IQ.* Cambridge: Cambridge University Press.

VanTassel-Baska, J. (1981). *An Administrator's Handbook on Developing Programs for the Gifted and Talented.* Washington, D.C.: National Association of State Boards of Education.

4 Developing Scope and Sequence

Joyce VanTassel-Baska

He builded better than he knew;
The conscious store to beauty grew.

—Ralph Waldo Emerson

Prior chapters have set the stage for both curriculum development and curriculum design work to begin for gifted learners. In this chapter, ideas about organizing the macro picture of curriculum will be shared. What should be the organizational pattern of experiences for gifted learners across the span of years they are in school? How can we concisely describe the nature of these experiences? The answers to these questions are found in the curriculum planning effort of developing scope and sequence.

The organization of a curriculum for gifted learners across the grades is an essential aspect of the work of curriculum development, yet few guidelines exist in the literature surrounding such work. Taba (1962) speaks to the importance of organizing the dimension of learning experiences as well as content topics in delineating a sequence of curriculum for all learners. Smith, Stanley, and Shore (1957) treat the issue as one of essentially grade placement with little attention to ideas about learner needs. Tyler (1949) views scope and sequence as two of the most vital questions one might ask about the curriculum experience: how broadly we define a set of learning experiences and how we order them. Bloom (1958) sees the framing of the curriculum according to key principles and concepts to be an important exercise but is less concerned with the ordering process, believing that the learner reorganizes experiences according to a personal schema. More recent curriculum theorists like Doll, Eisner, and Beauchamp have viewed scope and sequence work as more associated with fundamental issues of substance. Only Maker (1982, 1986) has expressed the importance of considering issues of scope and sequence in a curriculum for gifted learners as integral to the curriculum development process. This chapter addresses important issues and approaches to both thinking about and creating a scope and sequence of learning for gifted students.

Scope usually refers to how expansive a curriculum can be at a given level. Modification needs to occur when curriculum for the gifted is being conceptualized because these students can absorb a larger amount of material and ideas than can typical learners in the same period of time and stage of development. Thus what would constitute scope for average learners for a two-year period in a given content dimension could easily be modified for gifted learners into a one-year continuum. For example:

	7TH GRADE	**8TH GRADE**
Typical learners	Pre-Algebra	Algebra I
Gifted learners	Pre-Algebra	Algebra II
	Algebra I	College Algebra (III)

Sequence generally refers to the order in which content topics, concepts, and skills are placed in the curriculum over a span of years. Implicit in most sequential work in school is the notion of a spiraling curriculum based on reinforcement and concept building from year to year and at subsequent levels.

In practice, however, the notion of sequence often deteriorates into simple repetition of large segments of a curriculum area. This situation creates an acute problem for gifted students who retain information over time, and who do (or have the capability to) master subject matter completely on first exposure. Thus establishing sequential curriculum appropriate for the gifted learner implies attention to:

1. *Limited review of prior material learned.* In most curriculum situations, gifted learners do not need more than two weeks of review at the beginning of a given year. The nature of the review itself is also critical. Key ideas and concepts should be the organizing principle for review work with the gifted, not the small incremental approach so favored by traditional textbooks.

2. *Progressive development in skill acquisition.* Once gifted students have learned the fundamentals in any field of inquiry, it is important that they be allowed to progress at their own rate of mastery rather than be held back by other students or preconceived teacher plans for the rate of "conveying the material." Reading and mathematics curricula are frequently problems in this respect. Students are artificially kept at grade level rather than being allowed to progress more rapidly through the curriculum. There is much higher order skill development work that could be done with these students, but it is rarely attempted. For example, the gifted need work in reading comprehension, analysis and interpretation, inference, and evaluation, all higher order skills that could appropriately be addressed once fundamental reading ability is demonstrated.

3. *Logical ordering of courses based on the underlying organization of the discipline of study.* Part of the difficulty in curricular sequencing occurs because little attention has been paid to the relationship of one year's curriculum to the next, both within and across content dimensions. It is because of this situation that gifted students learn the same facts about English grammar from fourth to twelfth grades. No one in the school takes the responsibility for logical sequencing of curriculum offerings for gifted learners over the span of years these stu-

dents attend school. Schools also are reluctant to go beyond prevailing curriculum norms at any given level. Intelligent sequencing of a program of study for the gifted must involve school staff across levels. Preschool teachers should plan with primary teachers, intermediate with junior high, and high school with universities. Otherwise, these students will continue to be shortchanged.

4. *Concern for progressive development of concepts.* Although the progressive development of skills is important to a curriculum, there also exists as strong a need for appropriately sequenced concepts and ideas. "The change of seasons" is a concept found in much of literature, art, and music. Discussing the concept at a more complex level would require the student to examine the symbolic or metaphoric aspects of "change of seasons," be able to see change in all aspects of nature, and relate to the concept at an intellectual, emotional, and personal level. In this way, then, carefully crafted ideas can be developed at more complex levels of meaning, and continue to challenge the gifted learner.

5. *Increasing complexity in product demands rather than increasing quantity.* Doing a research paper at every grade level may constitute practice in the medium without new challenges. Just as skills and concepts need to be organized progressively, so do special projects and product expectations. Rather than modifying the curriculum for the gifted by *adding* product requirements, closer attention to the nature of the product demand would lead educators to a sequential structuring of product expectations that would require a more complex response on the part of the learner. For example, an assignment to do a written report in seventh grade English on the structural components of a short story might progress to an assignment to do a written critique of a piece of fiction read outside of class in eighth grade.

6. *Flexibility regarding entry and exit points based on age/grade level designations.* A certain blurring of age/grade distinctions must be done if curricula are to be flexible enough to accommodate the diverse learning rates and styles of gifted learners. Preconceived notions about a given body of knowledge being reserved for a certain grade level and inaccessible any sooner is the type of curricular rigidity that impedes and even retards the development of the gifted. Language study is perhaps a good example. The typical age for starting foreign language study in this country is age fourteen, or ninth grade. Gifted students historically could master a foreign language as early as age nine, or fourth grade.

An example of a two-year sequence in Latin typifies many of these issues:

	GRADE 9	**GRADE 10**
Typical sequence	Latin I	Latin II (6-week review)
	Project: Do library research and a report on a famous Roman	Project: Do research and a report on a favorite myth
Gifted sequence	Grade 7, 8, or 9	Grade 8, 9, or 10
	Latin I/II	Latin II/III (2-week review)
	Project: Trace the development of modern romance languages from the classi-	Project: What is language and what causes it to change? Respond to this

cal. What factors led to these changes? Choose a medium to report your findings: research paper, oral presentation, slide/visual display

question by examining the following languages: English, Computer, and Sign

Typically, Latin would be considered a high-school subject where the second year curriculum would begin with a six-week review period of Latin I. Project work would stress library data collecting and the preparation of a written report on a very general topic loosely related to the course of study. For gifted learners, Latin might be studied formally as early as seventh grade (completing two years by eighth grade), or begun at whatever level deemed appropriate. Review work in Latin II could be limited to two weeks and mastery into the next level anticipated in both years. Thus some students might complete three years of Latin in two, due to progressive development in mastering the fundamentals of the content area. Project work would be carried out at a more sophisticated level that requires analytical and evaluative skills. Project demands in eighth grade are more complex but do not necessarily require more time to perform.

Special Issues in Developing Scope and Sequence for the Gifted

There is a set of special issues related to developing a scope and sequence of curriculum for gifted learners that may be useful to discuss. First of all, there is the issue of how to code the curriculum work. The term *coding* used in this context refers to the elements to be included in a written scope and sequence and how they will be organized. This chapter presents varying approaches to that task but a fundamental consideration of curriculum developers must be to make decisions on the most useful approach in their context. Within reason, using the regular curriculum as an indicator or form might be a place to start, but problems abound with being slavish to a given format.

A second more critical issue is the need to start scope and sequence work from a firm grounding in the philosophy, goals, and overall objectives of the gifted program. These general indicators must be stated and be capable of translation during the process of scope and sequence work. It is also necessary to start with a conceptualization of what embodies the core direction and focus of the gifted curriculum within each area of study. Example 4.A at the end of the chapter introduces the key strands to build into a mathematics scope and sequence for gifted learners. It is also linked to an overall philosophy and set of objectives. This level of planning is essential to the ongoing work of scope and sequence development at more discrete levels.

A third issue is related to the level of specificity with which the scope and sequence work is coded. Many general curriculum efforts in this area tend to be extremely precise and prescriptive in what is taught at any given stage of development. Whereas this may be a useful tool for the general classroom where expectations for a preset amount of student learning within a given school year need to be well defined, in working on the same task for gifted learners, greater flexibility and expansiveness is required since expectations are greater. In addition, the chunks of learning that the gifted are capable of handling are much greater than what would be the case for more typical learners; thus the coding of scope and sequence work needs to reflect such a disparity in the level of attainment anticipated.

A fourth issue relates to the infusion of higher level thinking skill development into the curriculum for gifted learners. Virtually all gifted programs have at least one goal that addresses this issue in the curriculum. Yet how to handle the infusion process for scope and sequence purposes needs to be addressed appropriately since process skill development in gifted programs tends to parallel basic skill development in general education programs. Teachers need to know which higher level skills might be taught at what stages of the curriculum. They also need to know how they can be linked together to enhance the capacity of gifted students to utilize them effectively. One way to address this issue is by carefully having all the subskills associated with an area (e.g., critical thinking) and then indicating the grade levels at which such subskills might be taught. Example 4.B at the conclusion of this chapter uses this strategy to present an overview of the teaching of critical thinking in an elementary pullout program. A product like this can be useful to school districts in defining the specific skills they are teaching the gifted learner and at what levels. It can serve as a communication device to regular classroom teachers as well as parents on the overall direction of this aspect of the learning experience.

A final issue to consider in developing scope and sequence for a gifted curriculum is the relative sophistication of the task compared to what is needed in a general curriculum. There are no basal texts for the gifted. Materials do not drive the curriculum experiences. Consequently, there are limited directions to follow in beginning the task. The multiple materials issue is compounded by the multiple objectives within a gifted program that are frequently being worked on simultaneously. Coding in higher level thinking skills and higher level products and key issues, themes, and problems, in addition to capturing the core curriculum within each subject area, is a formidable task. Thus it is important to consider key stages in the process.

KEY STAGES IN THE PROCESS OF DEVELOPING SCOPE AND SEQUENCE

1. Select a small group (two or three) of people to work on scope and sequence issues. These individuals need to be familiar with the regular curriculum and how it is organized across grade levels, understand the salient features of a sound curriculum for gifted learners, and be able to translate skills, concepts, and themes across curriculum areas.

2. Start with establishing a framework for the process to evolve. What are the proficiency requirements of the core curriculum at primary, intermediate, junior high, and high school within each subject matter area? What is the current emphasis of the gifted program at each grade level? What are the guiding goals, objectives, and key content strands to be considered in the curriculum for the gifted? What are the key process, product, and conceptual strands to be nurtured at each level of the curriculum?

3. Pilot test a coding structure that the group can reach consensus on. Use this coding approach to detail scope and sequence for the gifted at one grade level (or across two or three) and across content, process, and product dimensions. Share the product results with various school groups to ascertain its capacity to (a) communicate key features effectively, (b) capture the nature of the curriculum experience sufficiently, and (c) clearly demonstrate the relationship of the curriculum for gifted learners to that provided to more typical learners in the school district.

4. Develop drafts of all curricular areas of the gifted program from kindergarten through grade twelve. Even though the pilot effort was in a narrow band of grade-level designation, work should proceed at the next stage in such a way that the total sweep of the K–12 curriculum is considered. Too frequently school districts run into problems with not extending the scope and sequence effort far enough in both directions in order to continue making appropriate curriculum inferences for the gifted. Attention to prerequisites and postrequisites in planned curriculum experiences is also an important issue at this stage of the process.

5. Test the draft document against the reality of what is currently operative for gifted learners in the school district. Although it is important that the scope and sequence be a planning tool for future efforts and implementation of program pieces, it still must be grounded in what is actually happening to students, particularly at levels where the program has been operative for a while. If there is little resemblance between the document and the curriculum being delivered, then key decisions need to be made regarding where and how revisions in both document and program will occur.

6. Refine the scope and sequence document as new insights emerge about the nature of curriculum experiences for gifted learners in the district. In Chapter 2 of this book, curriculum was presented as constantly evolving and changing in light of classroom instruction and the nature of the learner needs and expectations. Thus scope and sequence must also be viewed as tentative and evolving in nature if it is to represent well a synthesis of the actual and the ideal for gifted learners throughout the span of years they are in school.

7. Continue to monitor the implementation of a planned scope and sequence. There is no substitute for carefully observing the degree of consonance between what a scope and sequence document says is going on and what actually is going on. Little progress can be made toward K–12 articulation without someone assuming this oversight responsibility. Ideally, the gifted coordinator in cooperation with the curriculum director could undertake this effort. Staff development opportunities can best be developed through this stage of the process also as discrepancies in practice are observed.

APPROACHES TO DEVELOPING SCOPE AND SEQUENCE

There are several approaches to scope and sequence that practitioners in gifted programs may wish to consider. Examples of each approach are included at the conclusion of this chapter.

One way to approach scope and sequence work is to limit the grade levels for examination but encompass all core content and process dimensions of the curriculum that are desired. In this approach one would:

1. Begin with the articulation of program goals.

   a. Identify content strands for considerations.

   b. Identify process strands for considerations.

2. Define content topics and student behaviors desired within each content area of the curriculum.

3. Collaborate across grade levels to establish meaningful sequence patterns.

4. Key scope and sequence specifications back to the goal statements to ensure adequate treatment.

This model of scope and sequence work provides a good matrix overview of the curriculum for talented learners. One useful feature is to point out gaps in curriculum materials and the need for curriculum units that have a particular topical focus. Example 4.C at the end of the chapter provides samples of initial curriculum design work for a gifted middle-school program. This work sample was developed by a team of seventh- and eighth-grade teachers from Wilson Middle School, Rockford, Illinois, and illustrates the outlined approach.

The presentation of this curriculum example contains three sections:

1. *Specified program goals provide the superstructure for the content area matrices and the process skill paradigms.* Each aspect of the scope and sequence chart should be able to reflect back to these basic statements.

2. *Content area schemata, organized in matrix form.* Each curriculum matrix reflects global student outcomes intersecting with content topics to be presented. Topics are presented sequentially from left to right with an expectation of increasing levels of difficulty. The Xs reflect the major intersection of content topic and a particular desired student behavior. All content matrices also are keyed to the process skill paradigms that were developed collectively by the team. Organizational approaches varied by content dimensions. Some teams chose to develop a separate matrix at each level (e.g., social studies and science).

3. *Process skill paradigms were developed for the areas of critical thinking, creative problem solving, and research.* All teachers agreed to the definition of these skills, as indicated in the paradigm, and team planning was utilized to promote a common understanding of how each discipline at each level was addressing specific parts of the paradigm. Parameters of project work were delineated on the research paradigm.

A second approach to developing scope and sequence would be to organize the task thematically, according to ideas, and to translate those ideas across grade-level formats. Example 4.D at the end of the chapter, which illustrates the concept of change in *Concept Curriculum for the Gifted*, is indicative of this approach in a K–8 curriculum. Example 4.E, taken from a local school district curriculum effort, presents a K–12 scope and sequence model that has been developed through a thematic approach.

A third approach to scope and sequence development is to define key topics and/or materials that would be appropriate as suggested guidelines for each grade-level cluster. This approach allows flexibility within a range of grades, relative to when something is taught, yet at the same time is suggestive of appropriate levels of difficulty and complexity at these stages of development. Examples 4.F, 4.G, and 4.H are illustrative of this approach in different curriculum areas.

A fourth approach that may be important to consider is based on the Richardson Study Pyramid model cited in Cox, Daniels, and Boston (1986). As this model is applied to curriculum, designating learner experiences according to level of ability and provisional setting as well as grade level represent a more sophisticated multidimensional approach to scope and sequence (see Figure 4.1).

Types of experiences that might describe each aspect of the pyramid comprise Example 4.I at the conclusion of the chapter.

All of these approaches to scope and sequence may be useful for different situations at different stages of the curriculum development process. Often it is useful to key a gifted scope and sequence chart to one for typical learners in a school district to illustrate the nature and extent of differentiation. Other times it may be useful only to reflect a scope and sequence model for the gifted since the linkage to regular curriculum may not exist, as in the case of foreign language at the primary level. A school district needs to decide what approach to scope and sequence is most useful and then proceed to develop it, remembering the impor-

FIGURE 4.1 Pyramid Programming Model

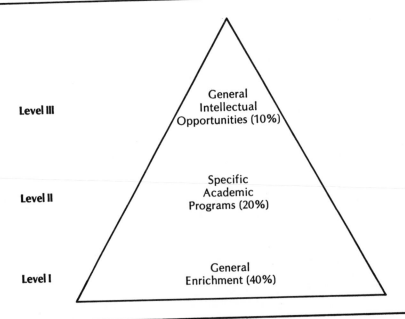

Level III — General Intellectual Opportunities (10%)

Level II — Specific Academic Programs (20%)

Level I — General Enrichment (40%)

tance of working teams that are horizontal as well as vertical in dimension (e.g., teachers working across grade levels but also across content areas to ensure understanding and communication). Under such circumstances, gifted learners become the beneficiaries of well-structured ongoing learning experiences.

Conclusion

This chapter has presented several different ways of thinking about and creating scope and sequence within a curriculum for gifted learners. It has provided samples of school district work in several key areas of content focus but also within process and product dimensions of the curriculum. It has used the latest program research evidence (i.e., the Richardson Study) to create a broader conception of scope and sequence work, moving beyond grade levels and into differentiated levels of experience within a gifted and talented program. In this way, school districts may begin to move toward a broad curriculum planning endeavor that will provide the impetus for systems change on behalf of gifted learners.

The steps in developing a scope and sequence in curriculum can be summarized as follows:

1. Develop overall curriculum goals and objectives.
2. Determine major content, process, and concept strands to be stressed.
3. Examine the school district curriculum guide for scope and sequence in core content areas.
4. Adopt or develop categories of knowledge and skills in the core curriculum learning areas.
5. Decide on an appropriate coding format for reporting.
6. Write a K–12 outline for each relevant strand (i.e., content, process/ product, and concept).
7. Incorporate the outlines into the selected coding format.
8. Cross-reference scope and sequence charts to curriculum goals and objectives.
9. Identify areas within the scope and sequence for curriculum unit development.
10. Reference primary materials to be used for each level and content designation.

Although the order of these steps may vary slightly, they constitute a recommended approach to undertaking scope and sequence efforts in a curriculum for gifted learners.

KEY POINTS SUMMARY

- Developing scope and sequence in curriculum for the gifted provides a way of ensuring vertical and horizontal articulation of learning experiences across the grades.

- Important considerations in building scope and sequence in gifted curriculum are: limited review of learned material, progressive development in skill and knowledge acquisition, attention to the structure of the discipline, and flexibility in age/grade designations.
- Selection of a coding system for scope and sequence work should be based on several criteria, including ease of communication to interested constituencies and consonance in style with the school district's coding for typical learners.
- Curriculum goals and learner objectives should provide the framework for scope and sequence considerations at each relevant grade level.
- Approaching the task of the development of scope and sequence in curriculum for the gifted implies special consideration regarding the need for multiple coding in content, process, product, and thematic dimensions on a K–12 continuum.
- The use of a planning and feedback model is important in implementing the process of scope and sequence development.

References

Bloom, B. (1958). "Ideas, Problems, and Methods of Inquiry." In NSSE *Integration of Educational Experiences.* Chicago: University of Chicago Press.

Cox, J., Daniels, N., and Boston, B. (1986). *Educating Able Learners.* Austin: University of Texas Press.

Maker, J. (1982). *Curriculum Development for the Gifted.* Rockville, Md.: Aspen.

Maker, J. (1986). "Developing Scope and Sequence for the Gifted." *Gifted Child Quarterly,* (4), 151–158.

Smith, B., Stanley, W., and Shore, H. (1957). *Fundamentals of Curriculum Development.* New York: World Book.

Taba, H. (1962). *Curriculum Development.* New York: Harcourt, Brace, & World.

Tyler, R. (1949). *Basic Principles of Curriculum and Instruction.* Chicago: University of Chicago Press.

EXAMPLE 4.A Considerations in Developing a Scope and Sequence of Mathematics Curriculum K–12 ━━━━━━━━━

MY GOAL FOR EDUCATION

I want my students to think with their entire minds, to realize that the compartmentalization of knowledge is done for a pedagogic or systemic classification and that these schemata do not necessarily relate to the knowledge itself. I want my students to be aware of their entire environment, to garner input from all of their senses, and to comprehend the information gathered by the sensory apparatus. I want my students to live full and vital lives.

A PHILOSOPHY FOR MATHEMATICS EDUCATION

I believe mathematics teaching should provide an environment in which students may achieve mathematical knowledge and skills consistent with their capabilities and interests. An acquisition of positive attitudes toward mathematics, the experience of success in learning meaningful mathematics, and the appreciation of the usefulness of mathematics as well as some of its cultural aspects are all part of this philosophy.

In addition to its central role as a major content area, mathematics has another function of high priority: it is a vehicle for the communication of thought. I believe that the study of mathematics can provide conditions of orderly thinking and balance in a student's life.

I believe that the study of mathematics requires consistent effort and self-discipline in order to prepare students for academic success, good citizenship, and occupational and/or professional placement. It is my expectation that success in the discipline of mathematics must encourage students to achieve the best of which they are capable.

I believe in providing a wide variety of mathematical experiences in which students learn to think critically, question perceptively, and evaluate carefully. To acquire these mathematical thought processes, the students should be encouraged to perfect their basic mathematical skills, to gain facility in logical reasoning, and to learn the habit of inquiry.

MY GENERAL OBJECTIVES FOR MATHEMATICS EDUCATION

1. The student should gain knowledge of a body of mathematical facts, concepts, relationships, and recurring patterns.

2. The student should be able to perform basic number operations with reasonable speed and accuracy and to estimate possible outcomes and results.

3. Students should be competent with algorithms, processes, resources, and devices to solve problems efficiently.

4. The student should be able to utilize literal or symbolic expressions for objects, numbers, and ideas when advantageous, and should be able to manipulate them as needed.

5. The student should be able to depict information in sketches, graphs, charts, and tables where appropriate and be able to read information from such presentations.

6. The students should be sufficiently familiar with the role of proof so that they can follow logical arguments and can present and defend ideas themselves.

7. The students should be able to cope with essentially unfamiliar problem situations wherever these situations require the use of mathematical knowledge and techniques known to them.

8. The student should give evidence of a positive attitude toward mathematics by employing it to solve problems.

9. Students should be creative as evidenced by their approach to problems and methods of solution, and by the formulation of new problems for consideration.

10. The student should experience the satisfaction of success after perseverance.

(continued)

THE TOPIC AREA STRANDS

I have arbitrarily divided the body of elementary mathematics into seven topic area strands as listed below. After the listing, each strand will be broken down in greater detail. Here, in no particular order, are my mathematics strands:

1. Counting, Calculation, and Approximation
2. Likelihood and Chance
3. Algebraic Manipulation Techniques
4. Spatial Awareness and Geometric Considerations
5. Logic, Reasoning, and Inferential Systems
6. Algebraic Structures and Analysis
7. Modeling and Problem Solving

Source: David N. Seybold, Chairman, Mathematics Department, South Lyon High School, South Lyon, Michigan. Reprinted with permission.

EXAMPLE 4.B A Scope and Sequence of Critical Thinking Skills for the Gifted, K–8

Objectives	K–2	3–4	5–6	7–8
Critical Thinking				
I. The students will be able to grasp the meaning of a statement.				
The student will be able to point out hidden meanings.	X	X	X	X
The student will be able to determine fact versus opinion.	X	X	X	X
The student will be able to detect inferences in a given sentence.		X	X	X
The student will be able to ask clarifying questions.		X	X	X
The student will be able to apply the meaning to a new set of circumstances.		X	X	X
The student will be able to transfer the meaning of other concepts.		X	X	X
II. The student will be able to judge whether there is ambiguity in a line of reasoning.				
The student will be able to identify vague and/or meaningless words and statements.		X	X	X
The student will be able to identify inconsistent statements.		X	X	X
The student will be able to identify misleading statements.		X	X	X
The student will be able to identify euphemisms.			X	X

Objectives	K–2	3–4	5–6	7–8
The student will be able to recognize that the manner in which words are arranged can lead to misinterpretation.				X
The student will be able to recognize that a word or statement may be interpreted in two or more ways within the same context.				X
III. The student will be able to judge whether certain statements contradict each other.				
The student will be able to analyze the statements on the basis of likenesses and differences.	X	X	X	X
The student will be able to identify meanings which are incompatible in given statements.			X	X
The student will be able to identify implicit as well as explicit deductions.				X
The student will be able to analyze each statement using if . . . then reasoning.			X	X
IV. The student will be able to judge whether a conclusion follows necessarily.				
The student will be able to clearly state the conclusion.		X	X	X
The student will be able to decide if sufficient data is available to warrant a conclusion.			X	X
The student will be able to identify the specific evidence relevant to a particular conclusion.			X	X
The student will be able to recognize if more then one conclusion is valid.			X	X
The student will be able to test validity of a conclusion using the rules of logic.			X	X
The student will be able to identify contradictory data.		X	X	X
The student will be able to decide whether the conclusion may be generalized.			X	X
V. The student will be able to judge whether a statement is specific enough.				
The student will be able to identify the purpose of the statement.		X	X	X
The student will be able to describe the relationship between the purpose of the statement and the degree of detail needed.			X	X
The student will be able to recognize when there is insufficient detail in a given statement.			X	X
The student will be able to state what additional information is needed, if any.			X	X

(continued)

EXAMPLE 4.B (continued)

Objectives	K–2	3–4	5–6	7–8
VI. The student will be able to judge whether a statement is actually the application of a certain principle.				
The student will be able to state a principle.			X	X
The student will be able to relate components of the principle to the statement.				X
The student will be able to recognize any points at which the statement and the principle differ.				X
The student will be able to change the statement to be compatible with the principle.				X
VII. The student will be able to judge whether an observation statement is reliable.				
The student will be able to determine the reliability of the source of the statement.	X	X	X	X
The student will be able to determine if a statement is the result of direct observation.		X	X	X
The student will be able to decide if the statement can be corraborated.			X	X
The student will be able to point out inferences versus facts.		X	X	X
The student will be able to identify bias.		X	X	X
The student will be able to recognize propoganda.		X	X	X
VIII. The student will be able to judge whether an inductive conclusion is warranted.				
The student will be able to understand the process of inductive reasoning.		X	X	X
The student will be able to recognize a simple generalization and decide if it is warranted.		X	X	X
The student will be able to make a generalization from a given set of facts.		X	X	X
The student will be able to relate cause to effect.		X	X	X
The student will be able to decide if enough evidence is presented to establish a hypothesis.			X	X
The student will be able to recognize if a hypothesis can be supported.			X	X
The student will be able to decide if a theory is consistent with known facts and is testable.			X	X
IX. The student will be able to judge whether something is an assumption.				
The student will be able to define assumption as a fact or opinion statement which is taken for granted.			X	X
The student will be able to judge if the assumption is rational.		X	X	X

Objectives	K–2	3–4	5–6	7–8
The student will be able to analyze the reasoning on which the assumption is based.		X	X	X
The student will be able to determine if there is a lack of supporting evidence for a given belief.		X	X	X
X. The student will be able to judge whether a definition is adequate.				
The student will develop and test a definition using the following process:			X	X
Judge if that which is to be defined is placed into a general class.				
Identify that general class.				
Subdivide that general class into successively smaller classes and identify the distinguishing characteristics of each.				
Identify the characteristics which uniquely describe that which is to be defined.				
Compare the two definitions to determine the adequacy of the given definition.				
XI. The student will be able to judge whether a statement made by an alleged authority is credible.				
The student will be able to judge the credentials of the alleged authority, considering the following:			X	X
A good professional reputation and background				
An accepted authority among peers				
The methodology follows accepted means of discovering a procedure in his/her discipline				
The student will be able to judge if the statement contradicts known facts or theories.			X	X

Source: Steve Giannini, Richmond Community Schools, and Jorgena Watson, Nettle Creek School Corporation. Reprinted with permission.

EXAMPLE 4.C A Scope and Sequence of Middle School Curriculum for the Gifted by Goal, Content, Topics, Student Behaviors, and Process Skill Paradigms

GIFTED PROGRAM GOALS (MIDDLE SCHOOL)

1. To provide for the mastery of basic skills while providing for greater depth and breadth of understanding within and across areas of study: Student instruction will differ from the normal course of studies by a pace and level of complexity which are more suited to students of exceptional abilities.
2. To promote critical thinking and reasoning abilities: Students will be in-

(continued)

structed in the areas of inference, deductive and inductive reasoning, analogies, and evaluation of arguments. These reasoning tools will be applied to all
areas of the curriculum.

3. To provide an environment that encourages divergent thinking: Students will
   be encouraged in the development of originality, fluency, flexibility and elaboration in their thought processes.

4. To foster inquiry and challenging attitudes towards learning: Students will be
   able to develop a commitment to learning as a lifelong process and to learn
   their educational, civic, social and personal responsibility.

5. To develop oral and written skills: Students will become confident in expressing ideas through conversations, panel discussions, debates, and oral and
   written reports; students will learn expository, creative writing skills and technical report writing.

6. To develop research skills and methods: Students will be able to understand
   the scientific method and its application to all areas of inquiry.

ENGLISH-LITERATURE, GRADES 7–8

Student Behaviors	Mythology/ Folk tales	Short Story	Biography	Novel	Poetry
Acquiring an understanding of the elements or components of a literary form (i.e., plot, character, theme, setting, sequence)		X		X	
Acquiring an understanding of literary genres and types of literature			X	X	
Developing critical reading skills (analysis and interpretation)		X		X	X
Observing and investigating human motivation	X	X	X	X	X
Developing a sense of identity through reading about character prototypes			X	X	
Developing a literary appreciation of writing styles	X	X	X	X	X

ENGLISH-ORAL COMMUNICATIONS, GRADES 7–8:
CONTENT CATEGORIES

Student Behaviors	Speech	Oral Presentations (individual and panel)	Oral Interpretation	Oral Debate
Developing poise and self-confidence in front of a group	X	X	X	X
Acquiring skills of speech (e.g., voice projection, inflection)	X	X	X	X
Developing critical thinking skills (i.e., inference, deductive reasoning, evaluation of arguments)		X		X
Developing the skills of persuasion and argument				X
Acquiring proficiency in synthesizing thoughts, written ideas, and speech		X	X	X

ENGLISH-WRITING/COMPOSITION, GRADES 7–8:
CONTENT CATEGORIES

Student Behaviors	Paragraph Development	Theme Development	Creative Writing	Technical Report Writing
Understanding the structure of writing (i.e., thesis, supporting evidence, conclusions, transitions)	X	X	X	X
Acquiring the skills of expository writing (e.g., description, narration, persuasion, opinion, thematic organization,	X	X		

(continued)

Student Behaviors	Paragraph Development	Theme Development	Creative Writing	Technical Report Writing
language appropri- ateness)				
Developing the skills of critical review (i.e., proofreading for errors, revising and modifying text)	X	X	X	X
Aquiring the skills of creative writing (i.e., learning to use literary devices, tone, style)	X	X	X	
Acquiring the skills of reporting data accu- rately and com- pletely				X

SOCIAL STUDIES, WORLD CULTURES—GRADE 7

Student Behaviors	Chinese Civilization	Greco/ Roman Civilization	Indian Civilization	Medieval Civilization	Russian Culture
Understanding of cultural patterns and how they develop	X	X			
Acquiring skills in World Geography (i.e., map read- ing, demography)	X		X		X
Relating religious, political, artistic and philosophical aspects of cultures	X	X	X	X	X
Investigating intra and international issues	X	X	X	X	X
Evaluating the con- cept of "progress"	X	X		X	X

SOCIAL STUDIES, THE AMERICAN CULTURE—GRADE 8

Student Behaviors	Pre-Colonial and Colonial/ American Revolution	Industrial Revolution & Expansion	Civil War/ Reconstruction & Recovery	The Depression Era	The "New Deal": The American Dream
Understanding of cause and effect relationships in history	X	X	X	X	X
Understanding of cultural patterns and how they develop	X	X	X	X	X
Investigation of national issues—social, political and cultural			X	X	X
Acquiring the skills of a social scientist				X	X
Developing critical reading skills	X	X	X	X	X

SCIENCE, GRADES 7–12

	7	8	9	10	11	12
Gifted	Advanced Earth Science	Introductory Physical Science (IPS)	BSCS Biology	Chemistry (Chem study)	PSSE Physics (option)	AP Chemistry Anatomy and Physiology
Regular	Earth Science	Life Science (i.e., botany, zoology; human biology)	Introductory Physical Science	Biology	Chemistry	Physics

SCIENCE, GRADE 7: CONTENT AREAS

Student Behaviors	The Nature of Matter (#6, 8, 9)*	Geology (labs)	Meteorology (labs)	Oceanography	Astronomy
Acquiring an understanding of atoms and their relationship to matter	X	X history palentology mineralogy			X

(continued)

Student Behaviors	The Nature of Matter (#6, 8, 9)*	Geology (labs)	Meteorology (labs)	Oceanography	Astronomy
Developing an understanding of the history and development of scientific contributions	X	X	X	X	X
Relating scientific theories to existing scientific evidence	X	X			X
Investigating the role of technology in scientific progress	X	X	X	X	X

* These numbers designate specific chapters to be covered from the 8th grade *IPS* book.

SCIENCE, GRADE 8: INTRODUCTORY PHYSICAL SCIENCE, CONTENT AREAS

Student Behaviors	The Scientific Method (#1, 2, 3)*	Physical Inter-actions (#4, 5)*	The Nature of Energy (#7, 10, 11)*	Physical Science: Applications to Technology (e.g., medicine, engineering, electronics)	The Philosophy of Science: Search for Solutions
Developing re-search skills (see research paradigm for steps)	X	X	X		
Acquiring an understanding of the history and development of scientific contributions	X	X	X	X	X
Investigating tech-nology as it relates to ap-plied fields of study				X	X
Acquiring attitudes and values of a scientist	X	X	X		X
Relating the con-cepts of science to all human inquiry				X	X

* These numbers designate specific chapters to be covered in the *IPS* book.

MATHEMATICS ALGEBRA I—III, GRADES 7–8: CONTENT CATEGORIES

Student Behaviors	Equations and Inequalities	Relations and Functions	Conic Sections and Graphs	Exponents and Logarithms	Sequences, Series and Progressions	Probability, Permutations and Combinations	Applications of Mathematics
Acquiring an understanding of strategies (i.e., look for a pattern, create a model, random search, etc.)	X	X	X	X	X	X	
Developing deductive and inductive reasoning skills (i.e., proofs)		X	X	X			
Developing an understanding of formal logical systems (i.e., syllogisms)	X	X		X	X	X	
Relating mathematical concepts to other fields of inquiry			X	X			X
Developing the skills of research design						X	X

GIFTED PROGRAM RESEARCH PARADIGM: CONTENT DIMENSIONS

Research Skills	English	Social Studies	Science	Mathematics
1. Defining a problem	X	X	X	X
2. Gathering data (library research)	X	X		X
3. Developing a hypothesis			X	X
4. Observing/ experimenting and recording data			X	X
5. Generating conclusions			X	X
Research paper requirements	5-page (grades 7 & 8)	8-page (grade 8 only)	10-page (grade 8 only)	6-page (grade 7 only)

GIFTED PROGRAM CREATIVE THINKING AND CREATIVE PROBLEM-SOLVING PARADIGM

Creative Problem-Solving Skills*	English	Social Studies	Mathematics	Science
Fact-finding (Brainstorming)	X	X	X	X
Problem-finding and defining	X	X		X
Idea-generation and alternative solution-finding	X	X		
Evaluating among solutions	X	X		
Developing a plan of action (acceptance-finding)		X		

* Based on the Parnes and Osborne model.

GIFTED PROGRAM CRITICAL THINKING PARADIGM, GRADES 7–8

Critical Thinking Skills	English	Social Studies	Math	Science
1. Inference	X	X	X	
2. Deductive reasoning	X	X	X	X
3. Inductive reasoning			X	X
4. Analogies	X			
5. Evaluation of arguments	X	X		

Source: Joyce VanTassel-Baska in consultation with middle school staff at Wilson Middle School, Rockford, Illinois.

EXAMPLE 4.D Concept Curriculum for the Gifted

Concept: Change

Content Domain: Social Studies

K–3	4–6	7–8
Key idea: Change can be reflected in the world around us in several areas: 1. Human shelter 2. Clothing 3. Food 4. Leisure 5. Transportation 6. Jobs Key questions: What is change? What causes change? What enhances or impedes change?	Key idea: Change is a product of both time and culture as reflected in the development of great cities. → Key questions: What is a city? What causes a city? What makes a great city?	Key idea: Change can be perceived across cultures and periods of time reflecting mankind's progress. Key → questions: What is a culture? What systems are essential to sustaining a culture? What makes a culture great?

EXAMPLE 4.E Fayette County School Corporation (Connersville, Indiana) Social Studies/Language Arts Content Scope and Sequence for GT Program—Overarching Theme: Humanity Adapts and Develops* ━━━━━━━━

	Level K	Level 1	Level 2
Overarching Concepts	"Understanding Me. A Changing Individual"	"All Kinds of Families"	"From City to Farm"
A Change is continual.	Individuals change.	The family unit changes.	Communities change.
B Communication through language is a necessary element for the functioning of society.	Individuals communicate through language.	Families communicate with their members and society through language.	Communication aids in understanding likes and differences within and among communities.
C Political frameworks are instituted to resolve conflicts and facilitate interaction.	Individuals are expected to follow rules.	Families establish rules.	Communities make and enforce laws.
D Cultures adapt in response to the dynamics of social and physical environment.	Individuals adjust to their surroundings.	Family lifestyles are determined by interaction with the environment.	Communities differ because of their location and their citizenry.
E Economic systems evolve from the management and utilization of scarce resources and the distribution of goods and services.	Individuals learn to use money.	Families use resources to satisfy needs and wants.	Community members depend on each other to provide for their needs and wants through specialization.

Source: Fayette County School Corporation personnel who developed the scope and sequence: Arlene Bliven, Louise Whitaker, Suellen Reed, Alvanell Elkin, Julie Slaubaugh, Sherry Anderson, Susan Shull, Penny Keller, Margie Yeager, Bob Julian, and Karen Armstrong

Level 3	Level 4	Level 5	Level 6
"Tracing Our Community"	"Indiana: Yesterday and Today"	"America, The Melting Pot"	"The Shrinking World"
The local community has changed since its founding.	As the Indiana population grows, economic, political and ekistic structures adapt.	The people immigrating to America contribute to the development of American culture and history.	Interaction of world cultures produces conflict and/or change.
Communication is essential for the development of communities.	As Indiana grew and developed, people devised different methods of communication.	As the U.S. population grew, American literature reflected the impact of cultures and changes in the society.	As world population grew, greater communication among world cultures developed.
City and county governments solve community problems.	The government of Indiana developed social controls with influence from local and national levels.	National government cooperates with state and local administrators to stipulate social controls.	The federal government participates in a system to promote international cooperation.
A community's characteristics are the result of interaction between individuals in a specific environment.	In Indiana, Indian and pioneer cultures adapted in response to interaction between the groups.	American society is a product of the interaction among many cultures.	World cultures are modified by their interactions.
A community determines the use of resources through the market system.	Indiana has developed into an agricultural and industrial state through management and utilization of its resources.	The United States has developed into a leading agricultural and industrial power.	The economic systems rely on the cultural values which determine resources, allocations and output distribution.

(continued)

EXAMPLE 4.E (continued)

	Level 7	Level 8	World History	American History
Overarching Concepts	"World Cultures And Their Interdependence"	"America: The First Century"	"Learning From The Past"	"America: The Plentiful"
A Change is continual.	All societies experience conflict and change.	The development of our heritage is a timeless process in which the past blends into the present and helps shape the future.	World cultures change through the interaction of the values, mores and cultural heritage of many societies.	Out institutions and cultural mores are not static but rather are products of the past, present and future.
B Communication through language is a necessary element for the functioning of society.	Relationships between people require communication.	American heritage and culture is expressed and preserved through written and oral communication.	Language is influenced through contact with and study of other cultures.	Written and oral communication, provides the record of our past and the means to report our present and future.
C Political frameworks are instituted to resolve conflicts and facilitate interaction.	The diverse political systems of the world are the result of the interaction of complex forces.	A democracy depends on participation of a responsible and knowledgeable citizenry.	Formal and informal structures are required to resolve conflicts among countries.	The American political system has evolved as a unique entity.
D Cultures adapt in response to the dynamics of social and physical environment.	Differing environments affect a variety of cultural mores and social institutions.	Our American culture is being determined by the interaction of ethnic background and geographic features.	Through interaction, whether victor or vanquished, civilizations adapt and adopt from others.	
E Economic systems evolve from the management and utilization of scarce resources and the distribution of goods and services.	Developments in one part of the world may influence the economics of other areas of the world.	One of the economic goals of America is economic stability without severe inflation and deflation.	The rise and fall of civilizations rest in part on mismanagement of resources.	The availability of both human and property resources and their use help to explain the development of the American economy.

Sociology	U.S. Government	Economics	Psychology
"Understanding Society"	"U.S. Government: Freedom and Responsibility"	"Buy American?!"	"Psychology At Work"
Relationships among groups are fluid and responsive to past practice, current concerns, and new issues.	Participation by citizens in our political system produces constant changes.	Economic "theories" may be interpreted in different ways according to current trends.	Individuals change as they mature.
Language defines social role and group identification.	Precision and ambiguity of language are elements which determine the effectiveness of language.	Language manipulation is a powerful tool.	Communication plays a role in determining human behavior and attitudes.
Interest groups have played a key role in influencing political decision making.	Our political system enables citizens to control their destinies and preserve their liberties.	Government intervention or lack thereof may alter functions of economic systems.	Resolving conflicts requires the reconciliation of individual differences in attitude, emotions, frustrations and aggression.
Group dynamics affect every phase of our lives and identities.	Our governmental structure has evolved as a result of social dynamics and environment.	Cultural conventions as well as physical environment affect economics.	An individual's perceptions, relationships and behaviors create cultural change.
Households, business, and governments influence economics activities.	Our market system encourages free enterprise which is regulated by the public sector.	Economic growth, that is, a rising standard of living propels use to develop new technologies and resources.	Psychological elements determine economic choices in a market economy.

EXAMPLE 4.F A Topical Approach to Coding Scope and Sequence Work

SEQUENCE OF FOREIGN LANGUAGE OPTIONS FOR THE VERBALLY TALENTED	
K–3	4–6
• Vocabulary work in 3–4 foreign languages • Root words, etymologies • Prefixes, suffixes • Idioms and key phrases	• Formal language study (equivalent of *one* year by end of sixth grade year) • Choice of a classical language—Latin I • Work on vocabulary and syntax • Mythology, history, cultural factors

SEQUENCE OF MATHEMATICS CURRICULUM FOR THE MATHEMATICALLY TALENTED	
K–3	4–6
• Mastery of computational facts and operations • Measurement and estimation • Elementary algebra and geometry • Work with classification, patterns, and probability • Use of calculators for solving problems	• Mastery of fractions, decimals, and percents • Work with metric system • Continue work with algebra and geometry concepts • Basic statistics and probability work • Work with logic and inductive/deductive reasoning • Use of computers for problem-solving

7–8	9–12
• Latin II • Latin III • Analogies • Composition in Latin/English • Roman civilization • Roman/Greek literature	• Latin IV (AP) • 4 years of a second foreign language (modern), culminating in AP

7–8	9–12

• Algebra I
  and
• Algebra II/III
  or
• Unified Math Program/ CEMREL
• Continued work with computers as a problem-solving tool
	• Honors Geometry, Plane and Solid
	• Trigonometry Algebra III Differential Equations
	• Pre-calculus
	• APP Calculus

EXAMPLE 4.G Sequence of Curricular Foci in Verbal Programs

Key Element	K–3	4–6
Literature	-Selected biographies ——————— -*Junior Great Books Series* ————————→ -Oral reading of children's literature -Selected rhymes and poems	-Baskin & Harris *Books for the Gifted Child* -NCTE's *Literature for the Gifted*
Broad-based Reading Skills	-Vocabulary develop-———→ ment -Reading comprehension ——→ -Discussion skills of listening, questioning, ——→ interpreting -Readings in all content areas	-Critical Reading (i.e., inference, evaluation of, arguments) ————→ -Group discussion skills -Readings in all content areas
Composition	-Writing stories (prereading) -Journal writing -Writing to explore new forms	-Writing skills ———— 1) paragraphs 2) themes 3) structure -Journal writing —————
Verbal/Nonverbal Discourse	-Oral reports -Creative dramatics -Role play -Puppet plays	-Panel discussions -Skits ————————→ -Play production
Language	-Vocabulary play -Foreign words and idioms (5 languages) -Sentence patterns	-English grammar & usage -Foreign language offering (4 years) ————

7–8	9–10	11–12
-Interrelated arts -Fry's *Man the Myth-Maker* -*The Perilous Journey* -Selected readings by genre	-AP literature selections ⟶ -Literature club (genre/ ⟶ author approach) -Humanities	-AP literature -World literature (thematic approach)
-Analysis and interpreta- ⟶ tion -Use of symbols and ⟶ analogies (*10 SAT's*) ⟶		
-Expository writing -Critical review and editing	-AP composition -Creative writing	-Technical/research writing
-Debate -Oral interpretation -Speech	-Debate ⟶ -Dramatics ⟶ -Theatrical productions ⟶	
-Linguistics -Etymology	-Semantics -Second foreign language ⟶ (4 years) ⟶	-History and development of language

EXAMPLE 4.H A Scope and Sequence of Topics in Psychosocial Development, Academic Planning, and Career Education for the Gifted Learner, K–12 ━━━━━━━━━━━

K–3	4–6
Strand I • Awareness of famous people and what they do. *Strand II* • Small group work on coping skills and social interaction. *Strand III* • Encouragement in the development of aptitudes at a self-pacing rate. • Avoidance of sex-stereotyping patterns of behavior in play and work.	*Strand I* • Focus on process skill development in the areas of analysis/synthesis/evaluation through examining lives of famous people. *Strand II* • Small group counseling on the skills of group dynamics, leadership, and communication. *Strand III* • Establishment of a mentor program for the most goal-directed students. *Strand IV* • Administration of interest, personality, and ability inventories.

7–8	9–12
Strand I • Establishment of biography clubs that discuss readings.	*Strand II* • Small group counseling on the integration of skills for life-planning.
Strand II • Small group counseling on motivation and task commitment issues.	*Strand III* • Independent study options that provide alternative modalities and content for learning.
Strand III • Encouragement of individual and group projects in a specific field or inquiry. • Continue mentor program and expand.	*Strand IV* • Continued testing and analysis of results.
Strand IV • Individual counseling on results of testing for ability and interest.	*Strand V* • College counseling around choice of institution and course taking.
Strand V • Counseling around high school course options.	*Strand VI* • Course in career area. (Internship for at least one semester.)

EXAMPLE 4.1 Scope and Sequence of Curriculum Experiences by Level of Able Learner ━━━━━━━━━━

PRIMARY (K–3) EXPERIENCES FOR ABLE LEARNERS

LEVEL I
- Attribute blocks and manipulatives
- General problem-solving activities
- Basic research techniques (observing and collecting data, making inferences)
- Creative thinking activities (fluency, flexibility, elaboration, and originality)
- Critical thinking skills (synonyms and antonyms, patterns, sequencing)
- Creative movement activities

LEVEL II

VERBAL	*QUANTITATIVE*
• Junior Great Books or other discussion vehicle using inquiry	• Computer problem solving (LOGO)
• Foreign language exposure activities, from kindergarten on	• Mathematics problem solving
• Focus on vocabulary and reading comprehension skills	• Ungraded math program (diagnostic/prescriptive)
• Writing themes from kindergarten on	• Special mathematics topics (transformational geometry, symbolic logic, etc.)
• Ungraded reading program (diagnostic/prescriptive in nature)	

LEVEL III
- Special class on a selected topic
- Science program (based on original research work)
- Mentorship model (older students work with younger ones)
- Group inquiry on special topics

INTERMEDIATE (4–6) EXPERIENCES FOR ABLE LEARNERS

LEVEL I
- Critical thinking skills (inference, analogy, deductive and inductive, reasoning, evaluation of arguments)
- Creative problem solving (future problem-solving scenarios)
- Special project work on individual topics of choice

LEVEL II

VERBAL
- Philosophy for Children program
- Formal study of a foreign language
- Junior Great Books continued
- Reading comprehension (concepts) and interpretation (inference)
- Writing skills (grammar and usage, formal theme development)

QUANTITATIVE
- Applications of mathematics to technology
- Basic statistics for doing projects
- Ungraded math program continues
- Special math topics (Unified math)
- Transitional mathematics
- Computer problem solving (LOGO)

LEVEL III
- Special topics study
- Science project program with mentor from high school
- Applied intelligence (special class)

JUNIOR HIGH (7–8) EXPERIENCES FOR ABLE LEARNERS

LEVEL I
- Continuation of focus on critical thinking, creative thinking, special project work, and the building of research skills
- Counseling provision that focuses on academic planning and career alternatives

LEVEL II

VERBAL
- Literary discussion group
- Foreign language study (proficiency in one language by eighth grade)
- Verbal reasoning skills
- Writing forms

QUANTITATIVE
- Algebra—I–III
- Mathematical reasoning skills
- Statistics and probability
- Logic
- Computer problem solving (PASCAL)

LEVEL III
- Mentorships (linkage with university personnel)
- Attending high school for special coursework
- Science program expanded to include national laboratory linkage

5 Developing Units of Instruction _____

John Feldhusen

Make no small plans.
—Daniel Burnham

A major aspect of the curriculum development process in the education of gifted learners is the organization of specific units of instruction for use by a teacher with a specified group. The unit is an elaborated element of the broader scope and sequence plan described in the last chapter. The unit is micro, whereas the scope and sequence plan is macro. The unit gives much greater detail about the instructional plan and resource materials.

The unit of instruction is a teaching plan that typically begins with a title that broadly defines a domain of instruction such as "solar energy," "lumbering," "magnetism," "probability," "change in western society," or "beauty as a poetic concept." Early in the planning of a unit, broad goals and specific instructional objectives may be formulated along with a topical or content outline. As a written statement, the unit may also have a narrative exposition that specifies the intended audience (e.g., gifted learners in math at the seventh-grade level), the prospective time frame, suggested teaching methods, and a rationale for how the unit is differentiated to serve the needs and characteristics of the gifted. All of this introductory material sets the stage for the presentation of the unit of instruction.

The unit may be developed for self-instructional use, for implementation in a learning center, for didactic presentation by the teacher, for out-of-school use, as a teaching-learning contract, or as a combination of these approaches with other variants. Regardless of the mode or nature of organization, there are apt to be common ingredients and common adherence to a set of unit development principles. Maker (1986) has presented one such set of principles:

1. It must be flexible, to permit both students and teachers to pursue their individual interests.
2. It should focus on abstract principles and concepts rather than specific facts.
3. It should include process skills such as higher levels of thinking and problem-

solving as a separate scope and sequence that is integrated with the development of content understanding.

4. It should include an emphasis on development of types of sophisticated products integrated with the content and process.

5. It must not restrict the students' opportunities to pursue accelerated content, processes, or products.

6. It must include input from scholars and researchers in academic areas regarding the importance of principles, concepts, skills, and values.

7. It should provide opportunities for exposure to a variety of content areas, skills, values and types of content.

8. It should focus on concepts that are important in several academic areas, with the goal of integrating rather than separating what is learned.

9. It must build upon and extend the regular curriculum for efficiency and articulation in learning, but must not duplicate the regular curriculum.

10. It must include the input of a variety of professionals experienced in curriculum development and those experienced in education of the gifted (p. 152).

We have developed and used the following simplified guidelines for the development of unit planning for the gifted learner.

1. Focus on *major ideas*, issues, themes, problems, concepts, and principles.

2. Emphasize the need for a large knowledge base.

3. When possible, use an *interdisciplinary* approach.

4. Emphasize in-depth *research* and *independent study* with original and high-level products or presentations.

5. Teach *research skills and thinking skills* as metacognitive processes.

6. *Incorporate higher level thinking skills in content study*—in discussions, independent study, research, and writing.

7. *Increase the level, complexity, and pace* of the curriculum to fit the precocity of the students.

8. Teach methods for *independence, self-direction, and self-evaluation* in learning.

The Resource Unit

Example 5.A at the end of the chapter presents one simplified form of an instructional unit for gifted students on "Encounters with the Eminent," which we call a *resource unit*. The compilation of this unit includes all of the resources and information needed, but it does not present any guidelines for teaching the unit. We are simply given an introduction, a statement of the context and how it is differentiated for the gifted, the content or information to be covered; the objectives, discussion topics, and group activities; creative activities for students; the independent studies; mentors; teacher resources; media resources; and the text materials that may be used. This compilation of resources tells the teacher little about the teaching sequence, nor does it discuss methods of instruction except that the lists of objectives, content information, and discussion topics might indeed imply a sequence. Furthermore, in suggesting discussions, creative activities, independent study, field trips, mentors, and speakers, some aspects of teaching methodology are being advocated.

It would be easy to adapt the unit "Encounters with the Eminent" by including still one more organizational topic; namely, a list of materials and resources to be assembled for a learning center. Such a list might be as follows:

1. Pictures of eminent people
2. Sound recordings of their voices
3. Filmstrips on their lives
4. Products that some of them have created
5. Busts and statues of the eminent

The learning center serves several instructional purposes. First, it is an organizer which draws all the resources to one location (usually a table). Second, it is a motivator for gifted students in that the teacher tries to make it stimulating and enticing. Third, it is a technique for making the instruction and its resources readily available for student use. And finally, learning centers, particularly if there are several in a classroom, give gifted students an opportunity to learn how to do independent, small group, and self-directed study.

Content-Oriented Units

Treffinger, Hohn, and Feldhusen (1979) proposed a content-matrix approach to the development of instructional units that has been widely used in the development of units for gifted learners. Their approach begins with the development of a content outline which becomes one of the two dimensions of a matrix. The following example shows such a content outline for a social studies unit on the American colonies:

   I.   Identifying the Colonies
   II.   History, Government, and Politics
   III.   Food, Clothing, and Housing
   IV.   Home Life
   V.   Economics
   VI.   Schools
   VII. Sports, Recreation, and Social Life
  VIII. Religion, Values, and Beliefs
   IX.   Transportation and Communication

Whereas the outline is brief, the elaboration will take place in the later development of objectives and instructional activities for the unit. We call this a *content unit* of instruction because it often focuses on content or discipline-based material.

The second dimension of the content matrix is the type or level of objectives to be written for the unit. Treffinger, Hohn, and Feldhusen recommend a union of the Bloom (1956) *Taxonomy of Educational Objectives, Cognitive Domain* and the creativity concepts of fluency, flexibility, originality, and elaboration. If appropriate, they also advocate using concepts from the *Taxonomy of Educational Objectives, Affective Domain* (Krathwohl, Bloom, and Masia, 1964) and *A Taxonomy of the Psychomotor Domain* (Harrow, 1972). Of course, other dimensions of critical or logical thinking could also be included. Since a majority of instructional units for the gifted are developed for use in academic subjects such as mathematics, science, English, and social studies, the concepts of creativity, cognitive operations, and the Bloom cognitive levels are most often used as organizational guides. The Bloom cognitive levels of application, analysis, synthesis, and evaluation are stressed as most appropriate for teaching the gifted, but a necessary underpinning role of knowledge (content information) and comprehension is recognized as prerequisite and essential learning before gifted students can operate and learn at the higher levels. Figure 5.1 shows a matrix that incorporates the content outline and the dimension for classifying objectives.

FIGURE 5.1 A Matrix of Content by Levels of the Taxonomy

	Knowledge	Comprehension	Creative Thinking	Application	Analysis	Synthesis	Evaluation
I. Identifying the Colonies							
II. History, Government, and Politics							
III. Food, Clothing, and Housing							
IV. Home Life							
V. Economics							
VI. Schools							
VII. Sports, Recreation, and Social Life							
VIII. Religion, Values, and Beliefs							
IX. Transportation and Communication							

The matrix serves as a guide and reminder for the writing of objectives, instructional activities, and evaluation procedures. After several years of experience with groups of teachers developing units of study for gifted learners, we have found that a sound and workable procedure is to have teachers create the matrix framework on large sheets of poster board or newsprint so that there is a large space for each matrix intersect of a level of objectives with a content topic. The matrix then serves as a guide for the writing of objectives in that it graphically shows the union of each topic with each potential level or type of objective that might be written. It is important to note, however, that a teacher who is developing a unit should not feel that there must be objectives at each intersect. Rather, it is the teacher or the development group's task at each intersect to decide which, if any, objectives are needed and, if so, to proceed to write them. We should also note that there may be a need for one or several objectives at an intersect, depending on how complex the topic item is.

Typically a teacher works across the matrix horizontally, staying with a topic and considering all the possible levels of objectives that might be written for that content topic. Many teachers prefer to design the instructional activity and to specify the evaluation procedure as or while they are writing objectives. Whereas it is usually the case that instructional activities must be specified for every objective, evaluation procedures might be specified only periodically, for example, at the end of a content line, as shown in Figure 5.2, where it is called a *checkpoint.*

The design of instructional activities for each objective is facilitated by the immediate presence of the behavioral objective. Mager (1975) urged that the properly stated objective include a transitive verb that specifies the action a student should be able to carry out after learning has occurred and the objective has been achieved. He also suggested that a well-stated objective must specify the conditions under which the student must be able to demonstrate learning and the level or quality of performance expected. Thus a completed objective might be stated as follows:

Able to point out 90 percent of the errors in word usage, spelling, punctuation, or grammar in a specially prepared short essay.

However, many objectives do not lend themselves well to such precision in the specification of the condition of performance or the level of efficiency. For example:

Able to write a short scenario describing health conditions in the future.

This objective could be rewritten to conform to Mager's three criteria as follows:

Able to write, as a homework assignment, a short scenario describing health conditions in the future, with no more than five errors in grammar, usage, punctuation, and spelling.

Many teachers find such elaboration tedious and unnecessary as a guide to teaching.

FIGURE 5.2 Objectives and Activities by Content Topic and Evaluation Checkpoint

	Knowledge Comprehension	Application	Analysis	Synthesis	Evaluation	Creativity
IV. Home Life	Objective: Be able to describe major features of colonial house life. Activity: Read one of the following: Jones: Colonial House Life Arrow: The Colonial Family Hansen: Life in Early America		Objective: Be able to delineate the relationships among colonial children, parents, and other extended family members. Activity: Write a short story depicting colonial family life, and particularly portraying relationships between family members.	Objective: Write a fictional account of a colonial family life. Activity: Write a short story depicting colonial family life, and particularly portraying relationships between family members.	Objective: Compare and evaluate the quality of family life in colonial and western America. Activity: Write an essay comparing the quality of life in colonial and modern America as depicted in your earlier assignment. Checkpoint: Present your short story and essay to several students for critiquing. Revise and critique it yourself. Submit it for teacher evaluation.	Objective: (Already covered in synthesis objective)

The design of the instructional activities for each objective is also facilitated by the teacher-developer's knowledge and flexibility in relation to optional and alternative techniques in teaching, as well as by knowledge of alternative resource materials. Some teachers also choose to offer alternative instructional activities to the student for each objective, thereby accommodating different learning styles and preferences. For example:

Objective

Able to design a survey of energy problems in the community.

Instructional Activities

Design a survey instrument to use in conducting an energy survey and specify the data gathering design.

or

Use an existing energy survey questionnaire, plan a small survey sample, conduct the interviews, analyze results, write a report.

or

Enroll for a mentoring experience in which you work with the staff of a survey research company.

An alternative to writing the objectives, instructional activities, and checkpoints in the boxes on the big newsprint is to use 5 × 8 cards to represent each intersect box, writing the three components on cards. Later, when using the unit with a class, many teachers will also choose to present the unit to students as a card pack, with the intent that students themselves take the pack in hand and do the cards, one at a time, as a method of working through the unit. Alternatively, the student may take one card at a time and use it as a self-instructional guide. The cards and the activities should be coordinated with a learning center or resource file that the student can use to access resources for the learning activities and evaluation procedures.

As an opener for all such teaching units, there should be a statement directed to the student that tells him or her how to use the unit, that stimulates interest, and that gives an organizational statement of how the unit fits into or relates to other learnings and a broader framework. At the close of a unit there should be a similar summary statement regarding what has been learned and its relationship to other learnings.

Some teachers develop units with the intent to share them with other teachers. In such cases there should be an opening statement from the teacher-developer, specifying the targeted grade level of the unit and how the unit is adjusted to the needs of gifted learners. There should also be some guidelines offered on how to teach the unit, how to secure the resources, and how to handle student assessment.

A complete unit following the model presented in *Reach Each You Teach* (Treffinger, Hohn, and Feldhusen, 1979) is presented in Example 5.B. The topic is fairy tales; its target grade levels are grades 2–5. Note that the assessment of student progress or achievement of objectives is called *assessment checkpoint*. Some teachers who used the term *evaluation* in units found that it created confusion with the sixth level of the Bloom Taxonomy, which is also called *evaluation*. Thus we suggest the terms *checkpoint* or *assessment* as alternatives. Treffinger, Hohn, and Feldhusen go on to describe a variety of procedures for evaluating student progress and for keeping records of student progress and achievement.

This author has had extensive experience in helping teachers develop units of the type described here and then later seeing teachers use the units in teaching gifted learners. The settings have included full-time, self-contained classes for the gifted at the elementary level, resource room/pullout programs, regular classrooms with a gifted cluster, and Saturday/Summer extra-school enrichment programs. The units, often combined with learning centers, seem to work well, but an occasional complaint from supervisors is that the unit activities are not high enough in cognitive level nor fast enough in pace to provide the necessary challenge for the gifted. Special efforts are often needed to get teachers to upgrade the level of expectations and the pace at which students should work. Ordinarily, homework should also be expected with these units.

Conceptually Oriented Units

An ideal program for gifted and talented youth involves them in ideational challenges and activity as a vehicle to learn subject matter and as a stimulus for their cognitive development. Wittrock (1974) has described the ideal mode of learning as "generative." He suggests that in generative learning situations the student is interacting cognitively with the subject matter through problem solving, experimentation, and inquiry. Through such interaction the student constructs his or her own knowledge base, which involves much deeper understanding and fluency in using the knowledge. Wheatley (1984) argues that much time is spent in classrooms drilling students on basic skills, teaching rules, and showing students how to use specific algorithms in solving problems. He argues that these basic skills can be taught to gifted students more effectively in the context of exploring concepts, solving problems, discovering new relationships, or conducting an experiment.

Kaplan et al. (1979) presented a set of principles of a differentiated curriculum for gifted learners as follows:

1. Present content that is related to broad-based issues, themes, or problems.
2. Integrate multiple disciplines into the area of study.
3. Present comprehensive, related, and mutually reinforcing experiences within an area of study.
4. Allow for the in-depth learning of a self-selected topic within the area of study.
5. Develop independent or self-directed study skills.
6. Develop productive, complex, abstract, and/or higher level thinking skills.
7. Focus on open-ended tasks.
8. Develop research skills and methods.
9. Integrate basic skills and higher level thinking skills into the curriculum.
10. Encourage the development of products that challenge existing ideas and produce "new" ideas.
11. Encourage the development of products that use new techniques, materials, and forms.
12. Encourage the development of self-understanding, i.e., recognizing and using one's abilities, becoming self-directed, appreciating likenesses and differences between oneself and others.
13. Evaluate student outcomes by using appropriate and specific criteria through self-appraisal, criterion referenced and/or standardized instruments (p. 5).

A number of these principles are relevant guides in designing a conceptually oriented curriculum unit for gifted learners, notably numbers one, six, eight, and nine. That is, such units should focus on broad themes or concepts, involve students in using higher level thinking skills, develop research skills for experimentation and scientific inquiry, and teach basic skills along with higher level thinking activities.

A concept unit, then, begins with the selection of a concept or theme around which the unit will be developed. For the teacher at the elementary or second-ary level, some effort might be exerted to find broad themes or concepts that are particularly relevant or intrinsic to the teacher's discipline or major subject mat-ter area. Thus, a unit on "beauty" may be particularly relevant in language arts, art, or even social studies, whereas a unit on "reasoning" might seem to be particularly relevant for a unit in mathematics or science. However, it should be noted in the list of principles (on preceding page) from Kaplan et al. (1979) that item number two advocates integration of multiple disciplines into the area of study. Thus either of these themes might form the base for an interdisciplinary unit of study for a group of gifted and talented youth. VanTassel-Baska and Feldhusen (1981) developed a set of units for the gifted in grades K–8 on the themes of problem solving, change, reasoning, and signs and symbols. Three of these themes were selected from Adler's (1952) *The Great Ideas: A Syntopicon of Great Books of the Western World.* The *Syntopicon* presents essays on 102 of the great ideas from western world literature. A sample of the concepts is presented in Figure 5.3. These themes present an excellent conceptual framework for developing units of instruction and complete curricula for the gifted.

In his classic work, *Differential Education for the Gifted,* Ward (1961) ar-gued that the curriculum for the gifted should explore the concepts extending over broad expanses of the chief branches of knowledge. He also pointed to the *Syntopicon* as an excellent resource for identifying themes or concepts to be taught. In a highly elaborate set of principles, Ward delineated the nature of a differentiated and appropriate curriculum for the gifted. Such a curriculum, he

FIGURE 5.3 Concepts found in *The Syntopicon*

Aristocracy	Honor	Progress
Astronomy	Immortality	Reasoning
Beauty	Infinity	Religion
Being	Judgment	Revolution
Cause	Justice	Rhetoric
Chance	Knowledge	Science
Change	Labor	Sense
Citizen	Language	Signs and Symbols
Courage	Law	Sin
Custom and Convention	Liberty	Soul
Democracy	Life and Death	Space
Desire	Logic	State
Dialectic	Love	Temperance
Duty	Matter	Theology
Emotion	Metaphysics	Time
Eternity	Mind	Truth
Evolution	Monarchy	Tyranny
Family	Nature	Virtue and Vice
Fate	Necessity and Contingency	Wealth
Form	Oligarchy	Will
Good and Evil	One and Many	Wisdom
Happiness	Pleasure and Pain	World

argued, deals with theory and abstractions and involves gifted learners in the challenges of intellectual activity.

We present in Example 5.C a conceptually oriented unit of instruction for secondary gifted students. The unit focuses on the concept of "inverse" in mathematics. The teachers-developers began by identifying the theme as a part of a larger curricular sequence of experiences in a high-school mathematics class. The teacher proceeded to identify associated subconcepts, ideas, and resources that might become a part of the ideational framework of the unit. That analysis and elaboration took the form of a conceptual network analysis. Out of this analysis, there emerged the more articulate framework for the unit.

In the next stage of developing the concept unit, the teacher-developer gathered resource materials, wrote the objectives for each topic (often using a matrix approach like that described earlier), planned the specific instructional activities and/or alternatives that might be used, and established the assessment or evaluation procedures. In all forms of instructional units for gifted learners, the assessment procedure ought to involve students in learning how to evaluate their own work and experiencing self-assessment prior to teacher evaluation. Gifted learners can develop their own criteria or standards for evaluation of their productions or performances. This can often best be done in small groups. The criteria can then be used by individuals. We have observed a procedure in some gifted classes where children use a checklist of criteria for evaluation of their independent study projects. In other classrooms we have observed groups of children formulating criteria to evaluate student oral presentations. We have also seen gifted classes in which students are doing their own report cards before the teacher does them. In all these situations gifted students are learning to be self-evaluators, free from dependence on teachers and other adults for evaluation of their work.

Steps in Developing a Unit of Instruction

The steps in developing a unit of instruction can be summarized as follows:

1. Selecting content or concepts
2. Developing outline and sequence
3. Gathering ideational resources
4. Developing an overall design
5. Establishing goals
6. Planning and writing objectives
7. Planning and writing activities
8. Specifying evaluation
9. Assembling resources
10. Assembling units

Teachers who are developing units for gifted students may vary the sequence somewhat to suit their own creative styles. For example, some teachers prefer to begin with activities and work backward to objectives and forward to evaluation, but whatever the order, the essential elements of a unit are contained in this model for unit development.

Conclusion

We have described three types of instructional units that can be developed by individual teachers of gifted students or by teams of teachers in a curriculum development project. The procedures set forth in this chapter provide for the development of teaching units, that is, the specific guidelines and materials for classroom interaction with a group of gifted learners. These units can form part of the larger, articulated curriculum plan with grade level, subject matter, scope, and time sequence specifications. Thus the larger plan might specify that the unit on language be used in the fifth-grade gifted resource room in November, to be followed by the solar energy unit in December. Ordinarily, an articulated curriculum plan would cover several years of instruction.

The resource-type unit that was presented first provides a format for organizing all of the components of an instructional unit, but it says little directly about how to teach it. The content-oriented unit, on the other hand, specifies more directly the sequence and procedures or activities for teaching and evaluating achievement of gifted students. The content-oriented unit and the resource unit are both adaptable in respect to focus. However, the concept-oriented unit specifically demands that the substance of the unit be conceptual or thematic in nature while permitting alternative structural approaches.

The unit structures presented in this chapter are a part of the overall curriculum development process presented in Chapter 2, and assist in a small way with the articulation of the entire curriculum.

KEY POINTS SUMMARY

- A unit of instruction is a teaching plan that defines objectives, activities, evaluation procedures, and resources.
- Macro curriculum plans in the form of scope and sequence statements need to be translated into specific teaching units.
- One form of unit is the "resource unit," a compilation and statement of all the information and media resources needed for a unit of instruction.
- Another form of unit is called the "content unit." It provides a more specific sequential teaching plan but focuses mainly on traditional content.
- Conceptually oriented units focus mainly on broad, subsuming concepts. These units are similar to content-oriented units in that they provide a sequential teaching plan.
- Units of instruction are adaptable to all types of programs, levels of instruction, and educational settings.
- Units are particularly effective in learning center environments.

References

Adler, M. J. (1952). *The Great Ideas: A Syntopicon of Great Books of the Western World.* Chicago: Encyclopedia Britannica.

Bloom, B. S. (1956). *Taxonomy of Educational Objectives, Handbook I, Cognitive Domain.* New York: Longman.

Harrow, A. J. (1972). *A Taxonomy of the Psychomotor Domain.* New York: David McKay.

Kaplan, S. N. et al. (1979). *Inservice Training Manual: Activities for Developing Curriculum for the Gifted/Talented.* Los Angeles: National/State Leadership Training Institute on The Gifted and Talented.

Krathwohl, D. R., Bloom, B. S., and Masia, B. B. (1964). *Taxonomy of Educational Objectives, Handbook II, Affective Domain.* New York: David McKay.

Mager, R. F. (1975). *Preparing Instructional Objectives.* Belmont, Calif.: Fearon-Pittman.

Maker, C. J. (1986). "Developing Scope and Sequence in Curriculum." *Gifted Child Quarterly, 30* (4), 151–158.

Treffinger, D. J., Hohn, R. L., and Feldhusen, J. F. (1979). *Reach Each You Teach.* Buffalo, N.Y.: DOK Publishers.

VanTassel-Baska, J., and Feldhusen, J. F. (1981). *Concept Curriculum for the Gifted.* Matteson, Ill.: Matteson School District #162.

Ward, V. S. (1961). *Differential Education for the Gifted.* Columbus, Ohio: Charles E. Merrill.

Wheatley, G. H. (1984). "Instruction for The Gifted: Philosophies and Approaches." In J. F. Feldhusen (Ed.), *Toward Excellence in Gifted Education.* Denver: Love Publishing Co.

Wittrock, M. C. (1974). "Learning as a Generative Process." *Educational Psychologist, 11,* 87–95.

EXAMPLE 5.A Encounters with the Eminent ─────────

A RESOURCE UNIT FOR PRIMARY AND INTERMEDIATE GRADES

DEBBI RUCKMAN
GIFTED EDUCATION RESOURCE INSTITUTE

The primary purpose of this unit, designed for third through sixth graders, is to acquaint gifted students with a series of famous people. Through this study, the students will be able to draw conclusions and parallels which will affect the conduct of their own lives and potential careers. Not only does a gifted child need this insight, he is motivated by it and toward the study of it.

Encounters with the Eminent by its very nature potentially employs a wide variance of content areas through the diverse complex of people who may be studied. In the resource section, major attempts are made to include references about a wide variety of well-known people in many fields, both dreamers and doers, from many differing life-styles and eras, with a great divergence of characteristics. What they all have in common is success: success in career achievements, success in setting goals and attaining them, success in knowing who they are, and success in gaining the confidence needed to excel. Thus, the major theme to impart to the students as they use these persons as role models is SUCCESS.

CONTEXT

Encounters with the Eminent is designed for use with academically talented students in a pullout and/or Saturday setting to typically consist of nine two-hour sessions, with time alloted outside of classroom meetings for investigation and readings. The unit was piloted with a group of third- through fifth-graders. This unit serves as a resource to plan for any type of classroom use, but is particularly suggested for use with the combination of group discussion and activities, learning center (creativity) activities, and independent study.

DIFFERENTIATION

This unit attempts to differentiate curriculum in one or more ways in all areas described by Maker: content, process, product, and environment. Much of the content focuses on different levels of abstractness and complexity than the regular curriculum. A most substantial content modification is in the choice of topic itself: the study of people.

There is opportunity within the unit for many open-ended questions and activities. Students are asked to back up their lines of reasoning with proof. This is a great opportunity for group interaction with peers in the Saturday or resource room setting, and the interdisciplinary nature of the people studied provides great variety in both content and process.

The students will discover how the real problems of real people relate to their own real problems and will be encouraged to evaluate their own products as they use them in some real way with an appropriate audience.

Finally, environmental modifications will depend in part on the setting and the individual teacher leading the unit. The unit is designed to be student-centered with discussions and research taking place in an open and accepting atmosphere.

CONTENT OUTLINE

    I. Characteristics and Achievement
       A. Personal attributes
          1. relationship to personal achievement
          2. relative importance
       B. Intelligence
       C. Creativity characteristics
    II. Interests/Mentors
       A. Favorite books of the eminent
       B. Hobbies of the eminent
       C. Mentors of famous people

   III. Educational Backgrounds
      A. Importance of education
      B. Evaluation of educational needs for professions
   IV. Cultural/Racial and Religious Influences
      A. Cultural/Racial studies
         1. Black
         2. American Indian
         3. Non-American
      B. Religion
   V. Historical Influences
      A. Political implications
      B. Social implications
      C. Wars and their implications
      D. Inventions and their implications
      E. Present and future implications
   VI. Effect of Sex Roles
      A. Past
      B. Present
      C. Future
   VII. Problems Encountered by the Eminent
      A. Troubled homes
      B. Dislike of schools and teachers
      C. Domineering mothers/fathers
      D. Social difficulties/non-acceptance
      E. Handicaps

OBJECTIVES (CONTENT AND PROCESS)

The following list of stated objectives is coded by levels of Bloom's Taxonomy using these abbreviations:

   K = Knowledge
   C = Comprehension
  Ap = Application
  An = Analysis
   S = Synthesis
   E = Evaluation

Following participation in group discussions, group activities, creativity activities, and independent study, the students will be able to:

E   1. Recognize and evaluate the relative importance of personal attributes to achievement.

C   2. Cite examples of famous people who exemplify these personal attributes.

Ap   3. Recognize these attributes in themselves.

An   4. Realize the importance of education in eminent individuals' lives.

E   5. Evaluate educational needs for a given profession.

An   6. Compare and contrast educational backgrounds of famous people with that of their own.

An   7. Analyze the effect political viewpoints and conflicts of an era had on the lives of famous people.

An   8. Recognize how social and moral values are reflected in life histories of famous people.

C   9. Understand how wars have influenced the upbringing of many of the eminent.

An   10. Relate lives of inventors to their inventions.

An   11. Predict how the present and future will become influences on the eminent of tomorrow.

An   12. Perceive how ethnic and religious convictions affect the lives of famous people.

An   13. Assess how male-female roles of past, present, and future relate to the lives of eminent people.

C   14. Recount personal struggles experienced by famous people in home life, school life, and society in general.

E   15. Evaluate the means by which people overcame these problems.

S   16. Develop a plan for overcoming one's own personal hardships.

An   17. Relate reading preferences and hobbies to the achievements of eminent people.

E   18. Evaluate the importance of mentors in the lives of eminent people.

E   19. Determine an appropriate mentor for themselves.

Ap   20. Develop a greater ability to produce ideas fluently, flexibly, originally and elaborately.

S   21. Use the creative problem solving process effectively in the context of solving their own career problems.

An   22. Conduct an independent in-depth study of one or more eminent individuals using a comparison-contrast format.

GROUP ACTIVITIES AND CLASS DISCUSSION TOPICS

1. Using these characteristics—optimism, health, patience, self-confidence, courage, perseverance, willingness to take risks, peer/family support, money, and ability to delay gratification—rank from 1 to 10 in order of importance to a person's success or achievement. Compare your rankings with those of others in the class.

2. List ways to cope with failure.

3. List ways to cope with success.

4. Play "Who's Who in Black History?"—a card matching game.

5. Play the *People Magazine* Trivia Game.

6. Chart the steps you would follow in aiming at a particular famous individual's career.

7. If Thomas Edison would visit Disneyworld, what would he say? Discuss.

8. Describe an experience when you were reluctant to try a new task, sport, or skill. Who encouraged you to do so? How did they do so?

9. Discuss the changing role of women in sports.

10. Play excerpts from Bill Cosby comedy records. Discuss his humor and how it is derived from his life experiences.

11. Rank the following 10 people in relative importance as to their contributions to society: Jesus Christ, Thomas Edison, Ben Franklin, Abraham Lincoln, Christopher Columbus, Albert Einstein, Karl Marx, Sigmund Freud, Mark Twain, and Charles Darwin. Defend your decision.

12. Listen to excerpts from *Cradles of Eminence* by Goertzel and Goertzel. How do the upbringings of famous individuals relate to each other and to you?

13. Discuss: How do today's headlines influence the eminent people of tomorrow?

14. Discuss: What famous women of the past could have used some "women's lib" influence in their lives? How?

15. What famous person of the past would you choose to have as your mentor? What would you have them do? Discuss how your life would be different as a result.

16. Choose a problem encountered in the life of a famous person. In a small group, use the creative problem solving approach to elicit a solution different from the one the person may have actually employed.

17. Brainstorm characteristics other than those named in Activity #1 which are important in achieving success.

18. Brainstorm American Indians, Blacks, or women who would make good mentors.

CREATIVE ACTIVITIES

1. Draw a caricature of a famous person, then do one of yourself. Any similarities?

2. Write a letter of advice to a famous person, counseling him/her on a personal problem.

3. Do a creative talent illustration—what kind of animal, bird, fish, weather, food, plant, flower are you like? Illustrate.

4. Design a birthday card to send to a famous person.

5. Collect quotations of famous Americans and compile a book of them.

6. Make bookmarks or greeting cards for friends using quotations from famous people.

7. Create a recipe of characteristics that make up an eminently successful person.

8. Imagine you are going to interview _____. What would you ask her?

9. Create a trivia game involving a related group of famous people.

10. Design a collection of posters showing people remembered in history in some related way.

11. Complete a time line relating the sequence of events in several famous persons' lives.

12. There is room for one more: Draw your own face between those of Teddy Roosevelt and Abe Lincoln on Mt. Rushmore.

13. Create a legend about yourself. Include what you want to accomplish.

14. Do humorous or serious artistic interpretations of quotations from famous people.

15. Create a work in the style that a famous person you admire uses, either in prose, poetry, song, or the arts.

16. Select a year of the past. Then consider famous persons working during that year (artists, actors, musicians, authors). Design an award given by an actual group of that period. Tell what the award is given for and the criteria by which the persons were judged.

17. A famous person from the past has called and left a message. Who was it for and what was the message?

18. Make a chronological chart of an eminent person's life.

19. Make a time line of world leaders from Queen Victoria to John F. Kennedy. Show the issues involved in their times. Rank the leaders' influence.

20. Write an epitaph for a famous person. Suggestions: Mark Twain, Jesse James, Harry Truman.

INDEPENDENT STUDY

Independent research will be conducted on one or more creative, well-known people using one of the following optional themes.

1. An in-depth study of one famous person, relating that person to yourself in some way.

2. A comparison-contrast study of two or more people of the same era who worked in different fields.

3. A comparison-contrast study of two or more people in the same field of endeavor but who lived in different times.

4. A comparison-contrast study of a female and a male famous in the same field.

5. A comparison-contrast study of three people in the arts who lived in the same era (e.g., Pablo Picasso, Clark Gable, and Louis Armstrong).

6. A comparison-contrast study of two or more people with another well-defined relationship as seen by the student (e.g., father-daughter study of Henry and Jane Fonda).

7. Work through an entire unit from *Creative Encounters with Creative People* by Janice Gudeman. This will include readings, creative encounters, and independent projects.

MENTORS

A mentorship relationship can be developed with people in the community who are successful, eminent people like those studied in the unit. Possible choices could come from the following:

Political—mayor, legislator, judge, attorney

Media—newscastor, sportscastor, actor, comedian

Athletic—player, coach

Arts—musician, painter, sculptor, designer, architect, writer

Military—leader, aviator

Science—researcher, physician, psychologist, professor

TEACHER RESOURCES

Bogojavlensky, A. and Grossman, D. (1977). *The Great Learning Book*. Menlo Park, CA: Addison-Wesley Publishing Company.

DeBono, E. (1976). *The Greatest Thinkers*. New York: G. P. Putnam's Sons.

Feldhusen, J. F. (1984). *The Purdue Creative Thinking Program*. Lafayette, IN: Gifted Education Resource Institute.

Forte, I. and MacKenzie, J. (1976). *Kids' Stuff Social Studies*. Nashville: TN: Incentive Publications, Inc.

Goertzel, V. and Goertzel, M. (1962). *Cradles of Eminence*. Boston: Little, Brown, and Company.

Gudeman, J. (1984). *Creative Encounters with Creative People*. Carthage, IL: Good Apple, Inc.

Holmes, D. and Christie, T. (1978). *Thumbs Up*. Carthage, IL: Good Apple, Inc.

Yapp, M., Killingray, M. and O'Connor, E. (1980). *Greenhaven World History Program: History Makers*. St. Paul, MN: Greenhaven Press, Inc.

MEDIA RESOURCES

The following biographical sketches in filmstrip format can be obtained from the local media center.

George Rogers Clark	Story of Lewis and Clark
Ethan Allen	Story of Abraham Lincoln
Susan B. Anthony	Horace Mann
Johnny Appleseed	Marco Polo
John James Audubon	Story of Father Marquette
Johann Sebastian Bach	James Oglethorpe
Ludwig von Beethoven	William Penn
Daniel Boone	Paul Revere
Story of Admiral Byrd	Captain John Smith
Andrew Carnegie	Robert Louis Stevenson

Buffalo Bill
Columbus
Story of Hernando deSoto
Leif Ericson
Benjamin Franklin
John C. Fremont
Lee and Grant
Nathan Hale
Patrick Henry
John Paul Jones
Francis Scott Key
Dolley Madison

Peter Stuyvesant
Booker T. Washington
Story of George Washington
Roger Williams
Eli Whitney
Joan of Arc
Story of Dr. Lister
Wright Brothers
Sam Houston
Martin Luther King
Ponce de Leon in the New World
Betsy Ross

TEXT MATERIALS

American Heritage (1960). *Men of Science and Invention*. New York: Golden Press.

Asimov, I. (1972). *Asimov's Biographical Encyclopedia of Science and Technology*. Garden City, NY: Doubleday and Company.

Baldwin, G. C. (1973). *Inventors and Inventions of the Ancient World*. New York: Four Winds Press.

Batten, M. (1968). *Discovery by Chance: Science and the Unexpected*. New York: Funk and Wagnalls.

Bell, E. T. (1937). *Men of Mathematics*. New York: Simon and Schuster.

Berger, M. (1968). *Famous Men of Modern Biology*. New York: Crowell.

Block, E. B. (1967). *Famous Detectives*. Garden City, NY: Doubleday and Company.

Bolton, S. (1961). *Famous Men of Science*. New York: Crowell.

Bolton, S. (1962). *Lives of Poor Boys Who Became Famous*. New York: Thomas Y. Crowell and Sons.

Cane, P., and Nisenson (1959). *Giants of Science*. New York: Gosset and Dunlap.

Chandler, M. H. (1964). *Man the Inventor*. Chicago: Rand-McNally.

Chase, A. (1964). *Famous Artists of the Past*. Platt.

Clark, P. (1979). *Famous Names in Science*. Wayland.

Cooper, M. (1965). *The Inventions of Leonardo da Vinci*. New York: Macmillan.

Cottler, J., and Joffe, H. (1969). *Heroes of Civilization*. Boston: Little, Brown, and Co.

Cournos, J., and Norton, S. (1954). *Famous Modern American Novelists*. New York: Dodd, Mead and Co.

Cox, D. W. (1974). *Pioneers of Ecology*. Maplewood, NJ: Hammond.

Eberle, I. (1945). *Famous Inventors for Young People*. New York: Dodd, Mead and Co.

Evans, I. O. (1962). *Inventors of the World*. London: Frederick Warne.

Gies, J., and Gies, F. (1976). *The Ingenious Yankees*. New York: Crowell.

Haber, L. (1970). *Black Pioneers of Science and Invention*. New York: Harcourt, Brace and World.

Hayden, R. C. (1970). *Seven Black American Scientists*. Reading, MA: Addison-Wesley Publishing Co., Inc.

Halacy, D. S. (1967). *They Gave Their Name to Science*. New York: Putnam.

Heath, M. (1956). *Great American Inventors and Scientists.* Menlo Park, CA: Pacific Coast Publishers.

Heyn, E. V. (1976). *Fire of Genius: Inventors of the Past Century.* Garden City, NY: Doubleday and Company.

Hoff, R. and de Terra, H. (1968). *They Explored!* New York: McGraw-Hill Publishing Co.

Hollander, Z. D. (1966). *Great American Athletes of the Twentieth Century.* New York: Random House, Inc.

Hughes, L. (1954). *Famous American Negroes.* New York: Dodd, Mead and Co.

Hughes, L. (1955). *Famous Negro Music Makers.* New York: Dodd, Mead and Co.

Hylander, C. J. (1934). *American Inventors.* New York: Macmillan and Co.

Jacobs, H. D. (1975). *Famous Modern American Women Athletes.* New York: Dodd, Mead and Co.

Johnston, C. H. L. (1909). *Famous Indian Chiefs.* Boston: L. C. Page and Co.

Klein, A. E. (1971). *The Hidden Contributors: Black Scientists and Inventors in America.* Garden City, NY: Doubleday and Co.

Kundsin, R. B. (1974). *Women and Success.* New York: W. Morrow.

Land, B. (1968). *The Telescope Makers: From Galileo to the Space Age.* New York: Crowell, 1968.

Lavine, S. A. (1965). *Famous Merchants.* New York: Dodd, Mead and Co.

Leahy, W. (1975). *Stars of the Olympics.* New York: Hawthorne Books, Inc.

Leipold, L. E. (1971). *Famous American Architects.* Minneapolis, MN: T. S. Denison.

Lovejoy, E. P. (1957). *Women Doctors of the World.* New York: Macmillan and Co.

McKinney, R. J. (1955). *Famous American Painters.* New York: Dodd, Mead and Co.

Marinacci, B. (1961). *Leading Ladies.* New York: Dodd, Mead and Co.

Milne, L. J. (1952). *Famous Naturalists.* New York: Dodd, Mead and Co.

Morrison, E. E. (1966). *Men, Machines and Modern Times.* Cambridge, MA: MIT Press.

Norman, B. (1976). *The Inventing of America.* New York: Taplinger Pub. Co.

Osen, L. M. (1975). *Women in Mathematics.* Cambridge, MA: MIT Press.

Overmyer, G. (1944). *Famous American Composers.* New York: Thomas Y. Crowell Co.

Pickering, J. S. (1968). *Famous Astronomers.* New York: Dodd, Mead and Co.

Ploski, H. A., and Marr, W. (1976). *The Negro Almanac: A Reference Work on the Afro-American.* New York: Bellwether.

Poole, L., and Poole, G. (1960). *Scientists Who Changed the World.* New York: Dodd, Mead and Co.

Poole, L., and Poole, G. (1969). *Men Who Pioneered Inventions.* New York: Dodd, Mead and Co.

Pratt, F. (1955). *All About Famous Inventors and Their Inventions.* New York: Random House.

Rogers, J. A. (1972). *World's Great Men of Color.* New York: Macmillan. Vol. I, Ancients; Vol. II, Modern.

Silverberg, R. (1965). *Scientists and Scoundrels: A Book of Hoaxes.* New York: Crowell.

Stoddard, H. (1970). *Famous American Women.* New York: Crowell.

Truman, M. (1976). *Women of Courage.* New York: W. Morrow and Sons.

Walker, G. (1975). *Women Today: Ten Profiles.* New York: Hawthorn.

Western Electric Co. (undated). *Legacy for All: A Record of Achievements by Black American Scientists.*

Williams, G. (1959). *Virus Hunters.* New York: Knopf.

Wilson, M. A. (1972). *Passion to Know: The World's Scientists.* Garden City, NY: Doubleday and Co.

Yost, E. (1962). *Modern Americans in Science and Technology.* New York: Dodd, Mead and Co.

Yost, E. (1959). *Women of Modern Science.* New York: Dodd, Mead and Co.

EXAMPLE 5.B Fairy Tales ━━━━━━━━━━━━━━━━━━━━━

A CONTENT-ORIENTED UNIT FOR GT STUDENTS IN GRADES 3–4

MARCY CHUDNOV
INDIANAPOLIS, INDIANA

RATIONALE

Fairy Tales are a part of many children's cultural background, and, hopefully most children have read or have had read to them folk and/or fairy tales. This unit teaches not only the components of fairy tales but also compares different versions of fairy tales and illustrates the effect of cultural influences on folk literature. The unit also introduces the concept of stereotypes and encourages the child to transfer knowledge from fairy tales to contemporary life.

DIFFERENTIATION

This unit is differentiated for GT students in several ways. First it assumes that the children will be reading two or three years above their grade level. Second, it engages them in a great deal of higher level thinking activity. Third, it tries to integrate the teaching of basic skills with higher level activity. Fourth, it involves the youngsters in much creative project and production activity. Fifth, the students are expected to engage in self and peer assessment of their work. And sixth, the students are allowed to become self-directing and independent as they go about the activities. At all times the teacher should encourage the children to strive for superior performance and products.

TO THE TEACHER

This unit is intended to be used as one semester's work for middle elementary-high ability students in the reading area. It is assumed that the students will be reading at two or more years above grade level. It is also assumed that the students have a background in folk and fairy tale literature. If you find that some of your students lack a working knowledge of folk and fairy tale literature, it is suggested that you teach to that deficit area before proceeding with the unit.

In order to accomplish the objectives in this unit, many activities have been listed. Hopefully, the children will be able to achieve their objectives using only some of the listed activities. Certainly, the ambitious student is welcome to try all listed activities.

This unit has been designed to proceed from one level of the stated taxonomy to the next in order to encourage higher level thinking processes. Therefore, it is recommended that the teacher use the unit according to this design and not jump from one objective to another. It is also recommended that, if possible, the children view the unit as a gestalt and have the opportunity to learn the system of this particular taxonomy.

TO THE STUDENT

This unit has been designed in hopes that as you progress through its various phases you will increase your knowledge of the origin and purpose of fairy and folk literature and the many elements that combine to make good fairy tale reading.

Many activities are offered to help you understand and master the objectives listed. You are encouraged to be original and creative in your methods of working these activities. Try the unusual! Good luck!

I. Topic: Identification of Fairy Tales—Origin and Purpose

OBJECTIVES AND CORRESPONDING ACTIVITIES

OBJECTIVES

1. Define the term fairy tale.
2. Identify several fairy tales.

1. Knowledge Level

ACTIVITIES

a. Work with some other children in locating some other tales you have not read yet.
b. Read the new fairy tales you have found.

OBJECTIVES

Explain the cultural influences on style of a fairy tale that appears in several versions.

ACTIVITIES

a. Read several different versions of the same fairy story.
b. Listen to the "Cinderella" tape that discusses different versions of this tale.

2. Comprehension Level

c. Share what you have learned about cultural effects on tales with the class.

OBJECTIVES

1. List as many different reasons for the need of fairy tales as possible.
2. List the different attributes of fairy tales.

ACTIVITIES

a. Listen to the teachers lecture on attributes and attribute listing. Take good notes.
b. Brainstorm with small group of classmates and list all the reasons you can think of for writing fairy tales.
c. Divide the list into categories to see if you can compose a new list of attributes common to most fairy tales.

3. Creative Thinking Level

OBJECTIVES

1. Report your findings on the common attributes of fairy tales.

ACTIVITIES

a. Construct a chart listing attributes of fairy tales.
b. Interview other students to find how their lists differ or are similar to yours.

4. Application Level

OBJECTIVES

1. Choose various characters from some of your favorite fairy tales to study in-depth as to character analysis.

ACTIVITIES

1. Role-play these characters and explain their actions to the class.
2. Listen to the teacher-made tape on "Character Analysis" at the learning center.
3. Infer from the list of character attributes the reasons for the actions of the characters you have chosen.
4. Read Chapter 7 in our English book—"Character Analysis."

6. Synthesis Level

ASSESSMENT CHECKPOINT

This topic will be assessed in the following way:

1. *Teacher assessment will be based on:* ability to define a fairy tale, understanding of cultural influences on tales, ability to understand and explain society's need for tales, and ability to list and identify common attributes of fairy tales.

II. Topic: Plot Structure-Theme-Story Line

OBJECTIVES

1. Discover an understanding of plot structure in fairy tales.
2. Read a variety of fairy tales.

ACTIVITIES

a. Take good notes when you listen to the teacher lecture on theme and plot structure.

b. Read: *Blue Beard, Diamonds and Toads,* and *Ricky with a Tuft* for enjoyment.

1. Knowledge Level

c. Discuss with teacher and class: plot development.

d. Match: who, when, and where elements in two or more tales.

e. Match: first, second, and third events in two or more tales.

OBJECTIVES

1. Identify common elements in some fairy tales that you have read for the first time.

ACTIVITIES

a. Make a tape to share your findings.

b. Make a diorama of a tale that you have read.

c. Prepare a radio play of a favorite tale with other students.

2. Comprehension Level

OBJECTIVES

1. Predict many different endings to the "Hansel and Gretel" story.

ACTIVITIES

a. Write or create a chart that allows you to switch elements within this fairy tale.

3. Creative Thinking

b. Create a poster that would tell this story with a different ending.

OBJECTIVES

1. Write a new beginning and ending to a fairy tale.

ACTIVITIES

a. Write a new beginning and ending to the "Hansel and Gretel" story.

b. Experiment with other possibilities in the story line.

c. Record an "up-dated" version of this tale and add it to the learning center.

4. Application Level

OBJECTIVES

1. Compare stories/tales with similar plot structures.

2. Identify themes in several fairy tales that you have read.

ACTIVITIES

a. Write a report in which you compare and contrast stories/tales with different themes.

b. Prepare a commercial that will entice the class to read one tale over another.

5. Analysis Level

OBJECTIVES

1. Relate how the style for a particular fairy tale matches its context.

ACTIVITIES

a. Create your own original dialogue to portray a specific character is a tale. For example: Puss in "Puss in Boots."

b. Infer and demonstrate dialogue to that story that would be relevant to today's contemporary life.

6. Synthesis Level

OBJECTIVES

1. Decide if fairy tales of the past have relevance in our society of today.

ACTIVITIES

a. Participate in a panel discussion that debates the above issue.

7. Evaluation Level

b. Prepare a news item that supports or does not support fairy tales as being relevant to today's contemporary life.

ASSESSMENT CHECKPOINT

This topic will be assessed in the following ways:
1. Class assessment of reports, dialogues, and commercials (a total group score would be used).
2. Self-assessment by students of their own creative efforts in making original tapes, radio plays, posters, and diagrams.
3. Teacher assessment for this topic will be based on: students' understanding of plot structure, knowledge of common elements in fairy tales, and ability to identify themes within tales.

III. Topic: Setting-Locale-Elements

OBJECTIVES

1. Identify elements in story that lead to fantasy.
2. Understand concept of symbolism and how and why it is used.

ACTIVITIES

a. Match similar elements in "The Three Bears" and the "The Three Pigs."

b. Listen to the tape "Rapunzel" at the learning center. This tape will omit certain key elements in the story.

c. Locate and identify the missing elements.

d. Listen and take good notes to the teachers' lecture on symbolism.

e. Work with a small group of classmates and ask each other what symbols are present in "Sleeping Beauty" and "Dick Whittington."

1. & 2.
Knowledge
and Compre-
hension Level

OBJECTIVES

1. Invent your own brand of "fairy tale symbolism."

ACTIVITIES

a. Write a fairy tale of your own using as many different kinds of symbolism as possible.

3. Creative
Thinking

b. Compose a jingle that would go along with your fairy tale.

OBJECTIVES

1. Construct an artistic endeavor that records different types of symbolism.

ACTIVITIES

a. Sketch or paint an illustration depicting the various types of symbolism in "The Emperor's New Clothes."

4. *Application Level*

b. Prepare a diorama that shows the major symbolic event in "Snow White and The Seven Dwarfs."

c. Construct a puzzle that takes one "Down The Symbolic Road."

OBJECTIVES

1. Categorize the many elements you have found in fairy tales.

ACTIVITIES

a. Prepare a graph showing which elements are used more than others.

5. *Analysis Level*

b. Make a chart that separates elements that are used more often from those that are used less often.

OBJECTIVES

1. Combine more of the less-used elements with a few elements that are often used in fairy tales.

ACTIVITIES

a. Create a cartoon depicting the "Jack and The Beanstalk" fairy tale using the above combination.

6. *Synthesis Level*

b. Produce a puppet show for kindergarten students using this new combination of elements.

ASSESSMENT CHECKPOINT

This topic will be assessed in the following ways:

1. Class assessment of graphs, charts, and fairy tales prepared by various students. (using a total group score).

2. Self-assessment by students of their own creative efforts in making original cartoons, puppet shows, and jingles.

3. Teacher assessment for this topic will be based on: understanding of plot structure, knowledge of common elements in fairy tales, and ability to identify themes within tales.

IV. Topic: Characters

OBJECTIVES

1. Observe characters who remain the same in fairy tales and those who show growth and change.

ACTIVITIES

a. Read "Jack and The Beanstalk" to learn how Jack changes as a person.

b. Identify other characters that grow and change in other tales.

c. Listen to the teacher's lecture on character development-take notes.

d. Watch the film "Character Development in Stories."

1. *Knowledge Level*

OBJECTIVES

1. Explain why some changes are necessary in characters.
2. Ask others what their feelings are about various characters they have read about.

ACTIVITIES

a. Read several different fairy tales to see if there are characters in each that show growth and change.

b. Watch the filmstrip on "Characters in Fairy Tales."

c. Ask and observe what other children felt about "the wolf eating grandmother." What did you feel about this? Share your feelings.

2. *Comprehension Level*

OBJECTIVES

1. Develop a storyboard for a roll movie.
2. Dramatize a scene from a story.

ACTIVITIES

a. Illustrate each segment of your storyboard.

b. Share your storyboard with the class.

4. *Application Level*

c. Dramatize the scene from the fairy tale "The Princess and The Pea" when the Princess could not sleep.

OBJECTIVES

1. Compare one character with another as to likenesses and differences.
2. Compare the treatment of animals as characters in fairy tales.

ACTIVITIES

a. Compare and contrast the likenesses and differences between Hansel and Jack.

b. Compare and contrast the initial treatment of Wilbur the Pig to Charlotte the Spider.

5. *Analysis Level*

OBJECTIVES

1. Given different teacher suggested situations, predict how you think a character would act.

ACTIVITIES

a. Estimate how Jack would have acted if he knew there was a mean giant at the top of the stalk *before* he climbed it!

b. Predict what Snow White would have done if she knew:
   1. The old woman was her stepmother
   2. The apple was poisoned

6. *Synthesis Level*

OBJECTIVES

1. Evaluate the possibility/possibilities that would occur if the treatment of animals in fairy tales were exchanged.

ACTIVITIES

a. Decide what would happen in each story if the characterization treatment of animals in "The Three Little Pigs" and "Puss in Boots" were exchanged.

7. *Evaluation Level*

ASSESSMENT CHECKPOINT

This topic will be assessed in the following way:

1. Teacher assessment for this topic will be based on: students ability to discuss character growth and change, likenesses

and differences in characters, and ability to compare and contrast the treatment of and placement of animals as characters in fairy tales.

V. Topic: Events/Time Sequence

OBJECTIVES

1. Observe how the plot develops in several fairy tales that your teacher has read to you.

ACTIVITIES

a. Identify the scenes in sequence in "The Three Little Pigs," "Goldilocks and The Three Bears," and "King Midas."

b. Listen to the tape at the Learning Center that tells the story of Henny Penny out of sequence.

c. Watch the corresponding filmstrip.

1. Knowledge Level

OBJECTIVES

1. Identify the events in some simple fairy tales as to ordinal order.

ACTIVITIES

a. Read several fairy tales that are more complex in nature.

b. Make a chart showing the sequence of events in one tale as compared to another.

2. Comprehension Level

OBJECTIVES

1. Name as many events as possible for a fairy tale.

ACTIVITIES

a. Brainstorm with a small group of children to fulfill the above objective.

b. Decide which events in your list will be good for a fairy tale and which can be deleted.

c. Write your own original tale using events from your brainstorming list—be original in your placement of events into a sequence.

3. Creative Thinking Level

OBJECTIVES

1. Separate the various events in some fairy tales that you have read.
2. Categorize these events.

ACTIVITIES

a. Prepare a graph that classifies the events in fairy tales into distinct categories. Use "Rapunzel," "The Golden Fleece," "The Little Match Girl."
b. Chart your results on a poster board.
c. Report your results to the class.

5. *Analysis Level*

OBJECTIVES

1. Hypothesize what would occur if you could reorder events and time sequence in a given fairy tale.

ACTIVITIES

a. Write a new short version to "The Elves and The Shoemaker" reordering events and time sequence.
b. Superimpose some events from "Goldilocks" to "Henny Penny" and create a new title.

6. *Synthesis Level*

OBJECTIVES

1. Discuss with the class the possibility of reordering events in fairy tales.

ACTIVITIES

a. Have a court trial "Changing Events and Time Sequences in Cinderella" vs. "Not Changing Events and Time Sequences in Cinderella."
b. Conclude whether or not you feel the jury's verdict was right. Write your conclusion as a statement.
c. Write your conclusion as a letter to the judge.

7. *Evaluation Level*

ASSESSMENT CHECKPOINT

This topic will be assessed in the following ways:

1. Teacher assessment for this topic will be based on: Students' ability to discuss and show an understanding of time sequence in tales.
2. Self-assessment by students of their own efforts in writing original tales, making charts and graphs, and writing letters and statements.

VI. Topic: Stereotypes

OBJECTIVES

1. Define the term stereotype.
2. Identify some stereotypes in fairy tales.

ACTIVITIES

1. Listen to the lecture on stereotypes.
2. Discuss with others in a small group about stereotypes in tales.
3. Find some stereotypes in "Cinderella."

1. *Knowledge Level*

OBJECTIVES

1. Match similar stereotypes in several fairy tales.

ACTIVITIES

1. Watch the film on "Fairy Tale Stereotypes."
2. Read some fairy tales that you have not read before and locate stereotypes in them.
3. Watch television during the week and see if you can find similar stereotypes.

2. *Comprehension Level*

OBJECTIVES

1. Manipulate your knowledge of fairy tale stereotypes to people in the news, radio, and television personalities.

ACTIVITIES

1. Write a diary illustrating stereotypes you see each day via the media that compare to those you have met via fairy tales.
2. Illustrate your diary with caricatures of stereotypes.

4. Application Level

OBJECTIVES

1. Imagine what would happen if the Ayatollah was the villain in a fairy tale.

ACTIVITIES

a. Write your own tale combining the characters of "King Midas" with the Ayatollah replacing King Midas.
b. Produce a short play from your original fairy tale.

6. Synthesis Level

OBJECTIVES

1. Evaluate the importance of stereotypes in fairy tales. Are they an ingredient that must be included?

ACTIVITIES

a. Survey the class for their opinion on the question: Are stereotypes an element of fairy tales that must always be written in?
b. Conclude from the results of your survey if stereotypes are really necessary.
c. Make your own value judgment.

7. Evaluation Level

ASSESSMENT CHECKPOINT

This topic will be assessed in the following ways:

1. Self-assessment by students of their own creative efforts in writing tales, diaries, and plays.
2. Teacher assessment for this topic will be based on students' ability to identify and discuss the concept of stereotypes, the ability to transfer tale-type stereotypes to present day stereotypes.

RESOURCE BOOKS FOR THIS UNIT

Baker, A. (1971). *Young Years*. New York: Parents' Magazine Press.
Crosby, N. E., and Martin, E. H. (1981). *Fairy Tales*. Cincinnati, OH: Education for Excellence, 7927 Hickory Hill Lane.

Crosby, N. E., and Martin, E. H. (1982). *Mysteries, Mythology, Fairy Tales, Fables, Legends, the Supernatural.* Buffalo, NY: DOK Publishers.

Crosby, N. E., and Martin, E. H. (1983). *Lucky Legends.* Buffalo, NY: DOK Publishers.

Cushenberry, D. C., and Howell, H. (1974). *Reading and The Gifted Child* Springfield, IL: Charles C. Thomas.

Hoomes, E. W. (1984). *Create-a-Fantasy.* Hawthorne, NJ: Educational Impressions.

Isabelle, J. (1974). *On Children's Literature.* New York: Schoeken Books.

Lipson, G., and Morrison, B. (1977). *Fact, Fantasy and Folklore.* Carthage, IL: Good Apple, Inc.

Polette, N. (1979). *Activities with Folktales and Fairytales.* O'Fallon, MO: Book Lures, Inc. P.O. Box 9450.

Polette, N. (1979). *Approaches to Literature with Gifted Kids.* O'Fallon, MO: Book Lures, Inc. P.O. Box 9450.

Sale, R. (1978). *Fairy Tales and After.* Cambridge, MA: Harvard University Press.

Stewig, J. W., and Sebesta, S. L. (1978). *Using Literature in the Elementary Classroom.* Urbana, IL: National Council of Teachers of English.

EXAMPLE 5.C Mathematical Inverses ━━━━━━━━━━━━━

A CONCEPT UNIT FOR THE MIDDLE SCHOOL

JOHN HYLKEMA
NORTH MONTGOMERY HIGH SCHOOL
CRAWFORDSVILLE, INDIANA

INTRODUCTION

This unit deals with the concept of balance, specifically as it relates to the idea of inverse. The main emphasis is on mathematical inverses. These can be thought of as quantities that cancel one another out, balance, are opposites or reciprocals. There are also inverse operations; these operations neutralize one another and when performed successively return action to the original state. The unit looks at the idea of neutralizing, opposing action as it is manifest in the statistical concept of inversely related variables, the economic concept of revenue neutral budgeting, and the science fiction topic of time and dimension travel. These topics are taken from many different disciplines in order to offer the gifted student the exploration of issues across traditional content boundries indicated by the student's wide interest and need for an holistic outlook at knowledge. Among other possible areas of investigation are the balance formed by opposing political parties, moderation and balance in living our lives, the scales of justice, weight and measurement, and counterbalances used in engineering (e.g., drawbridge).

This unit is differentiated for GT students in that it focuses on conceptual understanding in mathematics, not on mechanical skills. Students are also involved in creative thinking and problem solving as well as project activity. The material should be presented at a high level and fast pace. Finally, it is multi-disciplinary so that GT students can learn the concepts as they relate to several disciplines.

The unit is aimed at GT students with above average ability in mathematics, verbal, and creative skills working at *upper sixth to lower ninth grade levels*. Activities should cover a four to five week period and objectives easily break into instructional units of one to two hours. The activities involve a wide variety of instructional modes including teacher lecture and optional individual or group work to match learner characteristics. Team teaching is a distinct possibility and would involve instructors familiar with math, statistics, economics, and creative arts. Evaluation of some objectives involve student and professional input.

GOALS

This unit deals with the concept of balance. Specifically, GT students will be introduced to the subtopic of inverses and will be able to use them as they relate to mathematics. The student will also examine some analogous ideas from economics and creative arts. GT students will begin to examine the importance of balance in life and philosophy through equal but opposing quantities.

CONTENT OUTLINE

I. Mathematics
   A. Algebra
      1. identities
      2. opposites
      3. reciprocals
      4. operations
      5. solving equations
   B. Geometry
      1. geometric transformations
         a. computer design
   C. Statistics
      1. graphing data
      2. direct variation of variables
      3. inverse variation of variables

II. Economics
   A. Budget Making
      1. revenue neutral

III. Creative Arts
   A. Representations of Abstract Ideas
      1. literature
      2. sculpture, drawing
      3. writing
      4. video, film, television

OBJECTIVE #1

Mathematics: Inverses
(knowledge & comprehension)

Students will be able to state the additive and multiplicative identities, tell how they relate to inverse, state the additive (opposite) or multiplicative (reciprocal) inverse of a number, group the basic operations as inverse pairs.

ACTIVITIES

1. Lecture on identities, inverse quantities, and inverse operations.
2. Divide students into small groups, assign conservative assignment to reinforce lecture topics.

ASSESSMENT CHECKPOINT

1. Have students work in small groups and design a self evaluation procedure for their understanding of the concepts.
2. Quiz over identities, inverse quantities, and inverse operations.
3. Help students who are not satisfied or comfortable with knowledge level.

OBJECTIVE #2

Mathematics: Inverses
(application, analysis, & synthesis)
Students will be able to compare and contrast various experiences to the idea of inverse, and will develop a chess strategy based on that idea.

ACTIVITIES

1. Brainstorm: "What are some things that happen every day that could be explained as inverses?" e.g., The wind blows your hair; you comb it back to original. Your mom cleans your room; you make it comfortable again. You pay for something with a large bill; the cashier counts back change in a particular manner.
2. Discuss, and elaborate on each of the items developed from brainstorming.
3. Teach the rules of chess. Perhaps they could be presented by a knowledgable student. Have students play one another till everyone has the basics.
4. Discuss manifestations of inverses on the chessboard.
5. Assign students to develop a strategy for chess based on "Inverses".
6. Set up a chess tournament in class. Instruct students to attempt to apply and refine their strategy. Highly successful students should teach their strategies to other students.

ASSESSMENT CHECKPOINT

1. Did the student participate in brainstorming and discussions?
2. Student: Was your strategy successful? Were you able to change it to be successful?
3. Encourage self evaluation by each student.

OBJECTIVE #3

Mathematics: Inverses
(knowledge & competition)
Students will be able to use the idea of inverse operation to solve linear equations.

ACTIVITIES

1. Discuss/review the various operations involved in a linear equation and how they are manifested.
2. Brainstorm in small groups ideas for uses of inverses in solving linear equations; examine promising student suggestions, and direct discussion toward preferred method.
3. Assign various equations to be solved by GT students in small groups. Stress that students should be employing the idea of inverses.

ASSESSMENT CHECKPOINT

1. Have students develop one equation each to include on a test over this instructional objective.
2. Have students decide on grading levels after plotting the distribution of test scores.

OBJECTIVE #4

Mathematics (Geometry): Inverses
(application)
Students will be able to perform basic transformations and state the inverse of any given geometric transformation at a 95% success rate.

ACTIVITIES

1. Discovery Lesson: This lesson will lead students through ideas of geometric transformations for a square. Students will be reminded of the topics of identities and inverses and asked for applications of those ideas to transformations.
2. Give students various objects, some two-dimension, others three-dimensional. Have them, individually or in small groups, experiment with transformations of their object looking for identity elements and inverses.
3. Students then will present their findings to the rest of the class and answer and questions that arise.
4. Bring in a computer expert or engineer to discuss geometric transformation in computer graphics and computer aided design.

ASSESSMENT CHECKPOINT

1. The students will be given a teacher prepared test to check on meeting the criterion. Students may elect to use a form of the test that utilizes objects.
2. After taking the test each student is asked to identify his or her weak points and to devise a way of correcting the weaknesses.

OBJECTIVE #5

Mathematics (Statistics): Inverses
(application)
Students will be able to graph data and differentiate between direct and inverse variation of variables.

ACTIVITIES

1. Review/learn basic graphing of data.
2. Collect the following information to be graphed: 1) individual females' height and corresponding years in organized basketball, 2) individual males' height and corresponding years in organized basketball.
3. Collect data from the following "game": Select ten volunteers to shoot paper airplanes at the wastebasket. Begin close, then have volunteers move gradually backward taking ten shots at each distance. Plot percentage made at each distance versus the actual distance.
4. Have students in small groups compare graphs of the data. How are they different? What do they show? How does the concept of inverse apply, if at all, in these instances.
5. Brainstorm for other instances where variables are related inversely.
6. Assign students in small groups to gather and present data relating any two variables as was done in class. They should indicate whether there is inverse or direct variation and how they can tell.

ASSESSMENT CHECKPOINT

1. Do the students correctly graph the information in the assignment? Use small group mutual critiquing.
2. Do students correctly distinguish between inverse variation and direct variation? Use small group mutual critiquing.
3. Have students exchange and critique one another's projects.

OBJECTIVE #6

Economics (Budget Making): Inverses
(evaluation)
Students will be able to give a substantiated opinion concerning revenue neutral budgeting, its viability, applicability, and reliability in various situations.

ACTIVITIES

1. Over a period of 2 or 3 weeks, request that each student bring in articles from newspapers, magazines, and journals that deal with budget making at all levels of government.
2. Assign articles that deal with revenue neutral budgets for student reading. Discuss revenue neutral and other budget making topics.

3. Break students into small groups for the purpose of making budgets. Supply each group with an actual budget that is currently in force. These could be budgets of the school departments, city, township, community organization, or any other group. Ask students to revise the budget for the next fiscal period. To do this, the students will have to investigate the group and its needs. This will be an ideal budget based on the percept that the group will be getting more funds. Next have them develop a second budget based on the idea that no additional funds will be available. Both of these budgets should be sent to the groups involved.

ASSESSMENT CHECKPOINT

1. Was the group's budget well received by the institution involved? Did the institution use any of the ideas suggested? Were the students asked to provide more input into the budget process? Have each group of students, as organized for the activities, critique the budget plans of another group.

2. Close with a critique by the instructor and a discussion of concepts learned from the unit. Each GT student contributes and is evaluated by the teacher.

OBJECTIVE #7

Creative Arts: Inverses
(creativity & comprehension)
Students will be able to creatively interpret the concept of inverse.

ACTIVITIES

1. The students should view any or all of the following:
   STAR TREK—various episodes involving dimension travel
   DR. WHO—episodes dealing with time and dimension travel
   BACK TO THE FUTURE
   TWILIGHT ZONE—the movie and some of the TV episodes

2. Read science fiction involving time and dimension travel

3. Assign the students to write a short story, draw a picture, make a sculpture, or produce a video using the idea of inverse as a starting point.

Note: These activities are aimed at science fiction.
Students that feel more inspired by another area should be encouraged in that direction.

EVALUATION

1. Products are to be judged on the basis of student and teacher generated criteria. Teachers should insist on evidence of creative process, and correct form depending on the medium.

Section Two

Adapting Curriculum in the Traditional Content Areas

6 Verbal Arts for the Gifted ─────────

Joyce VanTassel-Baska

There is no frigate like a book to take us lands away.
Nor any coursers like a page of prancing poetry . . .

—Emily Dickinson

There is little doubt that verbally gifted students have been identified through traditional identification measures. In addition to the heavy verbal emphasis on intelligence tests, lists of characteristics of the gifted population have always included several traits that related to high verbal ability: early reading, large vocabulary, high-level reading comprehension, and verbal interests such as voracious reading on a wide variety of topics (Gold, 1962; Gallagher, 1975; Clarke, 1979). What has not occurred is a systematic study of appropriate curriculum intervention strategies for such students, yet more gifted programs are formulated with a language arts emphasis than any other single area (Illinois Office of Education, 1977). This chapter will delineate some key elements to include in the verbal arts curriculum for the gifted and will cite some exemplary practices for doing so.

Overview of Verbal Program Options for the Gifted

Typical intervention provided for the verbally gifted has been an extension of what is offered to average students in the content area of language arts. Receptive experiences, such as the speaking and listening interactive process, form the core of such programs (Kaplan, 1979). Major differences between regular language arts programs and those for the gifted lie in methodologies and materials, open-ended activities, opportunities for student production, and interrelating several content areas to present relevant experiences. The combination of these four factors represents a holistic view of a language arts curriculum for the verbally gifted.

A program emphasis on the concept of values education for those students gifted in the verbal areas was suggested by Gallagher (1975). He noted the need to develop interpretive and expressive skills through the world of literature, its cultural ramifications, and the value exploration that promotes self-awareness. He argued that verbal ability strengthens student understanding of complex ideas, which is a necessary base for values study and evaluating conflicting ideas.

General support for both formal study of language and classical subjects for the verbally able has been suggested by Ward (1961). The need to have gifted students study language is well expressed by the following general proposition of his differential education of the gifted,

> . . . that the nature of language, its structures and functions, its integral relationship to thought and behavior should be part of the education of the intellectually superior child and youth (Ward, 1961).

A focus on language expression has been advocated through the informal teaching of linguistic elements by Arnold (1962). Some research has been directed toward the need to develop vocabulary in the gifted child as a way of improving overall language facility (Dale and Rozik, 1963), and as a way of enhancing verbal humor and the creative use of language (Pilon, 1975).

Many programs for the verbally gifted focused predominantly on developmental reading and literary discussion of ideas (Drews, 1972). Early programs in New York included biography as a genre for the gifted to direct their reading pursuits, partly out of a bibliotherapy motive (Hollingworth, 1926). California's approach to serving the verbally gifted was traditionally handled through a strong literature program developed throughout the grades (California Department of Education, 1979). Major objectives at each level stressed appreciation, understanding themes, and developing the tools of intellectual inquiry.

Key Components of a Verbal Arts Program for the Gifted

Ideally, several key components should shape a verbal arts program for the gifted. These components or strands might be classified as foreign language, literature, writing and composition, language, and oral discourse. Each will be discussed in the following sections of this chapter.

FOREIGN LANGUAGE

Historically, foreign language programs for the gifted have been viewed as an important part of the overall curriculum for the verbally able. These interventions are now supported by some research findings that suggest the importance of a threshold of mastery in one's own language as a prerequisite to second language learning, but that once the prerequisite is met, the second language is a major enhancement to linguistic competency (Cummins, 1979; Morris, 1971; Bartz, 1977). Foreign language was an integral part of the New York City rapid learner program at the Speyer School in the 1920s. French language and literature were introduced to gifted children, ranging in age from seven to nine years old, and taught to them for a full five years. The rationale for foreign language inclusion in the curriculum was that: (1) early language study would foster future opportunities abroad, (2) early language study would produce early mastery for these students, and (3) early inclusion of foreign language would allow gifted students to take more languages during their school careers (Hollingworth, 1942).

The New York program and a program initiated in 1921 in Cleveland demonstrated great value in the inclusion of foreign language for the gifted child early in the elementary years, although they differed regarding whether it should be viewed as enrichment or as an opportunity for accelerative learning. The Cleveland program tended to blend both approaches in that it accelerated language learning by one year before ninth grade and it provided expanded activities and projects in French from second grade on. The New York classes, on the other hand, focused predominantly on enrichment aspects and did not offer a structured program that moved students ahead in the language. However, Hollingworth noted that the expectation was for students to pursue other foreign languages in high school.

In building a case for teaching Latin to verbally talented students, VanTassel-Baska (1987) has cited valuable intrinsic features of the language itself. Reasons for the choice of Latin as an appropriate foreign language for the gifted are several:

1. Some 60 percent of English words are derived from Latin; thus the study of this language greatly heightens vocabulary power in English.

2. Syntactic understanding is a major goal in learning Latin; it has added value in enhancing linguistic competence in English and in learning other languages.

3. The complexity of the language and its logical consistency make it a challenge to gifted students who enjoy learning new symbol systems, analyzing, and using deductive logic in solving problems.

4. The cultural heritage of the Western world is based on Greco-Roman traditions in art, music, literature, and language. To study Latin is to gain invaluable insight into the Western cultural system.

5. Modern language tends to stress oral/aural skills and language fluency. Latin learning, on the other hand, stresses logical reasoning and analysis through an emphasis on translation and study of form changes at increasing levels of difficulty. In that respect, it represents a verbal analogue to the teaching of mathematics as a cumulatively organized subject area that is amenable to fast-paced instruction. Thus it is an easy subject to modify for precocious students.

6. Unlike most languages, Latin has few irregularities.

Whatever the choice of a second language for the verbally gifted, it is important that they have the opportunity to learn one, and preferably much earlier than the typical school curriculum would allow. The primary grades are a good time to start a modern foreign language. Formal study of Latin or Greek can begin by fourth grade. The goal for these students should be proficiency in *two* foreign languages by high-school graduation. Goals of a foreign language program for the gifted could be:

1. To develop proficiency in reading, speaking, and writing in two languages
2. To learn the culture and traditions that shape language
3. To be challenged by the interrelationships across languages in respect to form and meaning
4. To appreciate and understand language systems

LITERATURE

The literature program for the verbally talented child needs to be very rich from the beginning of the language arts experience in school. Children who are reading by kindergarten need a strong literature program at that stage of their development. The use of a basal reading series typically focuses too much time and attention on mastering the reading process, particularly phonics, rather than on allowing gifted students the opportunity for holistic reading of good literature. One way to combat this problem is to build a strong literature program for the gifted K–12, infusing the best and most challenging selections at each stage of development.

Many good recommendations abound in terms of developing such a program. Baskin and Harris's (1980) *Books for the Gifted Child* offers annotated reading lists chosen deliberately for the intellectually gifted child at the primary and intermediate levels. These authors have developed useful criteria for selecting appropriate literature for the gifted child:

1. The language used in books for the gifted should be rich, varied, precise, complex, and exciting, for language is the instrument for the reception and expression of thought.
2. Books should be chosen with an eye to their open-endedness and their capacity to inspire contemplative behavior, such as through techniques of judging time sequences, shifting narrators, and unusual speech patterns of characters.
3. Books for the gifted should be complex enough to allow interpretative and evaluation behaviors to be elicited from readers.
4. Books for the gifted should help them build problem-solving skills and develop methods of productive thinking.
5. Books should provide characters as role models for emulation.
6. Books should be broad-based in form, from picture books to folktales and myths, to nonfiction, to biography, to poetry, to fiction.

A program like Junior Great Books offers the best of classical and contemporary literature selections for students through junior high school, and the adult Great Books program, coupled with the Advanced Placement Program of College Board in Literature, offer challenging reading bibliographies for gifted students in high school.

The literature program for the gifted should provide more than just reading lists and advanced selections. It should provide the context for discussion among students of key issues, ideas, and themes contained in literature and be a catalyst for student writing, drawing, and performing. It should provide the basis for the critical thinking component of the language arts curriculum, helping students sharpen their analytical, interpretive, and evaluation skills. Thus it may be useful to state some specific goals for a literature program for the gifted, whether it be implemented at the primary, intermediate, or secondary level. Goals of a gifted literature program may include:

1. To expose students to appropriately challenging reading material at their stage of readiness
2. To provide opportunities for small group discussion of literature selections.
3. To develop critical reading behavior in the areas of analysis, interpretation, and evaluation
4. To develop and refine reading comprehension skills

At the elementary level, gifted students can be given carefully selected reading lists for reading at home. Books should be selected with an eye to the criteria listed earlier. In addition, establishing in-class reading clusters is an important tool for discussion. Reading aloud is also a valuable adjunct to such a program. Small group discussions about the following types of questions might be held at the primary level.

1. What happens in your book? Can you number the events? (sequencing events)
2. Who is the most important person in the book? Why? Who is your favorite person in the book? Why? (character development)
3. What new things did you learn from reading this book that you didn't know before? (concept formation)
4. What were your favorite words or sentences in the book? Why? (language awareness)
5. Good books make us feel as well as understand a story. What feelings did you have as you read the book? (identification)
6. How good was this book compared to others you have read? (evaluation) How would you rate it in respect to:
   a. interesting story
   b. characters I liked
   c. good ideas
   d. where it occurred was interesting
   e. new things to think about

Early readers should then be encouraged to read on their own and to think about their book through the way the small group discussions are conducted.

Individualizing a reading program for the gifted in such a way that activities correspond to certain verbal characteristics of students is another way to approach planning a differentiated verbal curriculum. The curriculum activities shown in Figure 6.1 might be appropriate for elementary children who display the set of characteristics listed.

FIGURE 6.1 Applications of Characteristics of the Gifted to Curriculum Interventions

Characteristics of Gifted Learners	Curriculum Implications at the Elementary Level
Reads well and widely	1. Individualize a reading program that diagnoses reading level and prescribes reading material based on that level 2. Form a literary group of similar students for discussion 3. Develop critical reading skills 4. Focus on analysis and interpretation in reading material
Has a large vocabulary	1. Introduce a foreign language 2. Focus on building vocabulary 3. Develop word relationship skills (antonyms, homonyms, etc.)
Has a good memory for things he or she hears or reads	1. Present ideas on a topic to the class 2. Prepare a skit or play for production 3. Build in "trivial pursuit" activities
Is curious and asks probing questions	1. Develop an understanding of the scientific method 2. Focus on observation skills
Is an independent worker and has lots of initiative	1. Focus on independent project work 2. Teach organizational skills and study
Has a long attention span	1. Assign work that is long term 2. Introduce complex topics for reading, discussion, project work
Has complex thoughts and ideas	1. Work on critical thinking skills (i.e., analysis, synthesis, evaluation) 2. Develop writing skills
Is widely informed about many topics	1. Stimulate broad reading patterns 2. Develop special units of study that address current interests

Shows good judgment and logic	1. Organize a field trip for the class 2. Prepare a parent night 3. Teach formal logic
Understands relationships and comprehends meanings	1. Provide multidisciplinary experiences 2. Structure activities that require students to work across fields on special group/individual projects 3. Organize curriculum by issues and examine from different perspectives (i.e., poverty, economic, social, personal, education views)
Produces original or unusual products or ideas	1. Practice skills of fluency, flexibility, elaboration, and originality 2. Work on specific product development

At the secondary level, the pursuit of the stated literature goals may be carried out through close textual analysis of short reading selections. The reading passages that follow are brief but rich in meaning, and the discussion questions lead students to deal with the content in highly complex ways.

1

If we can combine our knowledge of science with the wisdom of wildness, if we can nurture civilization through roots in the primitive, man's potentialities appear to be unbounded. Through his evolving awareness, and his awareness of that awareness, he can merge with the miraculous—to which we can attach what better name than "God?" (Charles Lindbergh)

1. What can you infer are Lindbergh's religious beliefs from this passage?
2. Why should man turn to the primitive?
3. Explicate the last line of the passage.
4. Suppose you were a pilot. Would you rely more on science or instinct to fly a plane?
5. In your opinion, is history important? Why or why not?

2

Man is a blind, witless, low-brow, anthropocentric clod who inflicts lesions upon the earth. (Ian McHarg)

1. What is the meaning of the word *anthropocentric?*
2. What does man do that McHarg does not approve of?
3. Why do you suppose that McHarg feels the way he does about man?
4. In your judgment, has man destroyed nature more than he has honored it?

3

There is little use in devising a system of thought about the nature of the trap if the only thing to do in order to get out of the trap is to know the trap and find the exit. Everything else is utterly useless: Singing hymns about the suffering in the trap . . . or making poems about the freedom outside the trap, dreamed of within the trap . . . The first thing to do is to find the exit out of the trap. The nature of the trap has no interest whatsoever beyond this one crucial point: WHERE IS THE EXIT OUT OF THE TRAP? (Wilhelm Reich)

1. What could the trap be?
2. Why does the nature of the trap have no interest?
3. Suppose you had been told there was no exit. What system of thinking would you employ at this point?
4. Compare the reactions of individuals caught in various kinds of traps:

   a. prisoners of war
   b. welfare mothers
   c. flood victims
   d. a mental patient

By discussing the rich passages provided here, secondary-level gifted students have an opportunity to think about literature at many levels and in diverse ways; to respond at an analytical level, yet to think divergently and evaluatively about what they read.

The two companion units that follow this chapter (Example 6.A) attempt to illustrate how gifted students might handle the concepts of form and function, first in poetry and then in the related art form of photography.

The use of a concept-oriented approach to teaching literature to the gifted is also most appropriate at all grade levels. Figure 6.2 depicts six common themes or ideas found in great literature with some key literary selections that illustrate them. Structuring reading selections around such themes provides gifted students with a breadth of reading experiences not frequently encountered under other approaches, as well as a sense of the unity of key ideas across different works.

WRITING AND COMPOSITION

As with literature programs, writing programs for the gifted must begin as soon as these students enter school. Recent research on emergent literacy (Sulzby, 1985) has stressed the importance of writing as a thinking process that clearly precedes the teaching of formal reading or handwriting in the primary curriculum. This issue is even more critical for gifted students. Although psychomotoric readiness to write may not be in place, young gifted children can clearly begin to conceptualize stories, sequence events, and present their feelings and experience through language. Consequently, an early focus on such writing behavior is important. Techniques for including writing as an activity for young gifted children include the following:

FIGURE 6.2 Literary Themes and Examples for Reading

Literary Themes	Comparative Examples for Student Reading
The role of the supernatural in human destiny (e.g., God, gods, fate, chance)	Greek, Roman, Egyptian, African myths (all levels) Sophocles, Euripedes, Aeschylus, (secondary) Thomas Hardy novels (e.g., *Mayor of Casterbridge*) (secondary)
Natural instinct vs. "civilization" influences	*Lord of the Flies*, William Golding (secondary) *Heart of Darkness*, Joseph Conrad (secondary) *Babbitt*, Sinclair Lewis (secondary) Wordsworth's "The world is too much with us" (secondary)
Self-determination; individual control of destiny	*Bringing the Rain to Kapiti Plain*, Verna Aardema (primary) *The Odyssey*, Homer (middle school) *David Copperfield*, Dickens (middle school) *Sylvester and The Magic Pebble*, William Steig (primary)
Social justice	*To Kill a Mockingbird*, Harper Lee (junior high) *Black Boy*, Richard Wright (junior high) *Diary of Anne Frank*, (junior high) *The Pearl*, John Steinbeck (junior high) *You Be the Judge*, Sidney Carroll (intermediate)
Self-understanding, self-doubt, fears, anxieties	*Time to Get Out of the Bath, Shirley*, John Burningham (primary) *Ordinary Jack*, Helen Cresswell (intermediate) *Smith*, Leon Garfield (intermediate) *Catcher in the Rye*, J. D. Salinger (high school) *A Wrinkle in Time*, (middle school)
Ravages of time; loss of youth; growing old	*King Lear*, Shakespeare *The Picture of Dorian Gray*, Oscar Wilde *Ethan Frome*, Edith Wharton *Miss Rumphius*, Barbara Cooney (primary) *The Yearling*, Majorie Rawlings (intermediate)

1. Have each child compose a story and transcribe it as it is being developed. Read it back for editing changes or additions and elaborations. Share the stories in class.

2. Encourage parents to transcribe stories at home and ask the children to bring the stories to school for sharing.

3. Have students draw a picture to illustrate their story and develop a title for it.

4. Use tape recorders to initially record the story and then transcribe it later.

5. Have students compose a story at the computer or typewriter if they have mastered the device adequately enough.

6. Encourage free story building; provide students with a set of givens (e.g., characters, plot pieces, a setting)

7. Have students respond in writing to a piece of music, a picture, or a poem presented in class.

8. Allow young students the freedom to write without requiring accurate spelling and grammar.

As gifted students begin to handle cursive writing, teachers should encourage them to record their impressions or experiences in a daily journal. In this way, teachers can promote written fluency and handwriting at the same time. Encouraging creative responses to life experiences may also be helpful here. Using poetic form or a brief fable to relate a particular incident may be very stimulating and challenging to gifted students. The following represents a comparative sample of creative journal writing from a first grader in a gifted program. The first sample was taken early in the school year when creative response was first being elicited. The second sample was done in the middle of the school year when the student had moved beyond simple visualization techniques into a more sophisticated approach to explaining natural phenomena through imaginative storytelling.

SAMPLE #1: THE MAGIC CARPET

If I had a magic carpet I could go to the desert. I would go because in the desert there are lots of pyramids.

SAMPLE #2: HOW THE HORSE GOT ITS MANE

Once upon a time horses didn't have tails. All the people thought the horses looked dumb, so the people sewed tails on the horses. But there was this one very dumb horseboy. All the horseboys were supposed to sew the tails on their horses. And when the horseboy was talking to his master, he was not looking where he was sewing. All of a sudden, the master had a smile on his face. The horseboy looked at his horse and he had sewed the tail on the neck. And that's how the horse got their manes.

By the intermediate grades, gifted students need to master the basic skills and techniques of writing, at least as those skills apply to expository writing pieces. Collins (1985) points out that there are six critical strategies that are preconditions to a good writing program. These strategies should be used by teachers in an attempt to acclimate gifted students to the writing process. These six strategies are:

1. Provide opportunities for students to discuss and clarify writing assignments before they begin writing.

2. Provide opportunities for students to get more information about a topic before they begin writing.

3. Provide specific information about the criteria you will use to correct each assignment.

4. Provide opportunities for students to review and revise written work completed earlier in the year.

5. Encourage students to edit each other's papers before they are handed in.

6. Provide opportunities for students to read written work out loud to individuals or to small groups of students.

What are the skills gifted students need to master in a writing program? The most frequently needed skills, even at adult levels, are the following:

1. Pre-writing
2. Paragraph development
3. Theme development
4. Developing introductions and endings
5. Working on supporting details
6. Using figures of speech effectively
7. Editing
8. Revising
9. Rewriting

Donald Hall (Hall and Embler, 1976) remarked in one of his essays that "writing well is the art of clear thinking and honest feeling." For gifted students, learning these techniques is critical for improving their thinking and their self-expression. Perhaps no skill represents a greater deficiency for the gifted than does writing. Colleges have long complained of the lack of skill in this area, even among their best students. Thus a rigorous program of teaching writing skills seems crucial.

One very useful technique to incorporate into a writing program for the gifted is the workshop model for teaching editing, rewriting, and revision, as well as teaching the value of peer critique and the importance of evaluation in the writing process. One structure for the workshop technique follows, based on the Reynolds, Kopelke, and Durden (1984) text:

1. The class reiterates the objectives for a particular assignment.

2. Each student receives a copy of the essay and signs up to discuss a particular objective during the workshop.

3. The author reads the essay to the class and then remains silent until the end of the workshop.

4. Each student praises one aspect of the essay.

5. Each group discusses its designated objectives.

6. The author is given the opportunity to speak a one-sentence defense.

7. The class summarizes the techniques that appear to have worked in the essay.

There are many good texts available that stress language awareness through reading excellent prose selections. With older gifted students, where the goal of the writing program may be to develop a writing style, it may be useful to focus on models of writing to analyze and emulate according to such key issues. Thus reading selections serve several simultaneous purposes:

1. They inform the student directly about an aspect of writing as well as a topic of interest.
2. They focus student attention on a distinctive style.
3. They serve as a model for analysis/emulation.

The following writing sample was obtained from a summer class at North-western University where writing models and a student workshop technique of group discussion and evaluation of individual writing were heavily utilized. The student writer is an anonymous eighth grader.

CAUGHT

Sitting on the floor of a police station eating popcorn and crying once in a while, wasn't what I'd had in mind that frigid and bright blue Saturday morning.

Jason was too calm about being arrested. He just sat, relaxed with his legs spread wide apart. A silver earring pierced his image and his right ear. His head was cocked slightly upward and his mouth frozen tight with a sarcastic grin. I had just wanted to bash his clean head into the wall and break his image, but this was a police station.

The cops also picked up another guy from the El station. This one was from Milwaukee, and I had the experience of sitting next to him in the police car. Everything about him reeked of fermented piss; his clothes, his hair, his breath, and he probably had piss on the brain. The poor foreigner had gone up the wrong set of stairs and jumped the turnstile without realizing it was illegal. Jason and I weren't as creative—we did it on purpose.

I wanted to do it, but Jason didn't, which I thought was strange; he seemed to be so illegal. Jason carried a .38 with cartridges, that he showed me earlier that Saturday. The gun lay in his inside pocket, and with the moves of an expert gunsman, he showed me how to load the thing. Jason carried it for protection, from gangs I guess. He had recently gotten involved with a gang, and I saw the changes, but accepted them.

We went downtown to see a very bad Karate flick, which, ironically, we enjoyed, because we were friends. After the movie, we shot to get the sticky mountains of popcorn, which we loved so much, from a gourmet popcorn shop. It was probably Garrett's, but there's so many, who remembers?

No one was looking, I thought, and I didn't see the sense in paying for the train ride. I grabbed the sides of the turnstile where the prices were lit up and hoisted myself over; Jason followed. I felt like a criminal. I felt like I thought Jason felt. I was smiling, laughing, but Jason shrugged it off. I wanted to knock him off the platform. We were already up there.

The guy was a cop, so we never saw the nice blue suit. He was a plain clothes cop, who used words police officers didn't. "I saw you fucking kids jump that fucking gate." These words didn't freeze me at all, but seemed the proper greeting from a cop. The guy showed us his badge. We played along and looked scared, at least I did. He put the cuffs on and I begged a little, said I wouldn't do it again. Jason said nothing; did he want to get arrested?

The car was parked on the street, with every concerned person looking in. He started the report. I don't know how the watermelon got in my throat, but I was in the car, legs twitching violently, and waiting for the tears. I thought I had wet my pants; the smell shot through my nose and fell limp at the back of my head. It wasn't me. It was the guy from Milwaukee, just shoved in the car.

In between sobs in the cold car, I saw Jason looking out the window, unaffected. At the station his eyes searched towards the ceiling. I followed them to an eye chart on top of the far wall. I began to look at the chart, then at Jason and his coat. A thought kicked me, "would they search us?" The crying stopped, and I ate the popcorn; not tasting one kernel.

They didn't search us, but relief waited. Until my mother cautiously walked in, without an angry stare or disappointed look. Relief was the "Oh Well" smile, which she flashed at me. She simply walked over to the cop, and pointed out her kid. But how could I belong to this woman who forgave so easily?

Jason's parents couldn't be reached, so he left with me and the woman with the "Oh Well" smile. The lady asked a lot of questions, and I thought, "maybe she is my mother." But she didn't wait for the answers, which she seemed to know weren't coming. She couldn't be my mother.

I had cried in the police car and police station, but couldn't in front of this lady. I didn't say a word until Jason got out of the car, and then I spoke to the woman. "I know I'm bad, and it's okay if you don't love me anymore." The words just rolled out with no force or conviction behind them.

The woman's reply is something I don't remember, and I'm not sure that she did reply. I'm sure she sat a bag in my lap and said it had a grapefruit in it. It was yellow, but blushed sweetness. I peeled it methodically in silence, and my head rose to the mirror behind the sun shade. In it I saw the white outlines of dried tears, below my eyes, and the orange of my popcorn-stained lips. I peeled the grapefruit faster now, and ripped through the white skin to pinkness. The taste of popcorn was gone, and the orange lips returned to their original pink hue. Then they smiled, reluctantly, at my mother.

I knew then that Jason didn't have a blushing grapefruit waiting for him at home. It was already too late for him.

This story shows an uncommon sophistication on the part of the young writer in his capacity to capture vivid detail and to let potent imagery tell the story. His choice of words, use of symbols, and direct style all reflect writing ability that has been shaped through internalizing the process of writing.

Another writing model that is important for the gifted to emulate is research writing or technical report writing. Since many of these students will be engaged in conducting research during their school years, it is important that they have the appropriate tools to frame a written research report of their efforts. Thus teaching them the fundamental paradigm for a research paper should be a task of the writing program. The following model has been used effectively for this purpose:

SCIENTIFIC RESEARCH PROPOSAL OUTLINE*

1. *Observation of a Phenomenon*
   Something is noticed and attention is given to the observation.

2. *Problem*
   A problem is defined or a question is asked about the observation. Rather than simply accepting the observation and forgetting it, the questioning mind asks "why"?

3. *Preliminary Information*
   In most types of scientific research, gathering preliminary information involves a literature search through books and journals.

4. *Hypothesis*
   A hypothesis is a possible solution to the problem. It can also be explained as an "educated guess." After reviewing the preliminary information, a hypothesis is formed. The hypothesis must be stated in such a way that is testable. To make a hypothesis statement like, "The flowers are pretty," is not adequate as it does not set up a basis of an experiment since it is not testable.

5. *Experiment/Evidence*
   The sole purpose of the experiment is to test the hypothesis correct or incorrect. An experiment should test only one factor—the fact suggested in the hypothesis while all other factors are kept constant. A controlled experiment involves using two groups of the same kind of item or organism and treating them exactly the same except for the factor being tested. This is the variable. To get the most valid results there needs to be a comparison made to a constant standard. This is the control. Conduct the experiment by comparing a known control to the variable.

6. *Data*
   The results or data are collected from the experiment. Often the data are collected in a numerical form. Numerical data can be recorded in a table and plotted in a graph. Data can also be collected by visual and auditory means. These data may be recorded in the written notes of the researcher.

7. *Discussion*
   The data are analyzed and their meanings are interpreted. Comparisons are often made with the experiments and conclusions of other researchers.

8. *Conclusion/Revisions*
   The conclusion summarizes the results of the experiment. In some cases revisions are necessary to explain the original problem or hypothesis better. Don't be afraid to revise your project.

---

* Modified from A. Devine and J. Staudinger: *Biological Investigations: Laboratory Investigations for Introductory Biology,* 5th ed. (Dubuque, Iowa: Kendall/Hunt, 1979).

Specific goals for a writing program for the gifted then might be:

1. To develop the skills of the writing process, from prewriting through revision
2. To develop an appreciation of style and when to use a particular writing model
3. To develop a set of tools for self-expression and creativity
4. To promote the development of critical and creative thinking skills

ENGLISH LANGUAGE STUDY

A sound verbal arts program for the gifted needs to include a strong language study element that allows students to understand the English language from a variety of perspectives. Appropriate goals for a gifted program in this strand would be:

1. To understand the syntactic structure of English (grammar) and its concomitant uses (usage)
2. To promote vocabulary development
3. To foster an understanding of word relationships (analogies) and origins (etymology)
4. To develop an appreciation for semantics, linguistics, and the history of language

In a language program for the gifted, clearly it is necessary to adopt a diagnostic-prescriptive approach to teaching grammar and usage since these students are capable of mastering the language system much more rapidly than other learners and in a shorter time period than currently is allotted in the regular school curriculum. An overview of the syntactic structure by grade six would allow students time to master the parts within a year. A schemata such as Figure 6.3 might be useful for that purpose.

The teaching of formal grammar is better handled through this matrix approach with gifted learners because:

1. It presents the entire system of English syntax to students holistically so that they can grasp immediately what they are seeking to learn.
2. It saves instructional time by reducing the need for reinforcement and repetition, which is a common approach used by textbooks to ensure mastery.
3. It allows students to focus their attention on what they don't know rather than remediating what they do know.

Another aspect of language study that is critical for the gifted is in the area of vocabulary development. A focus on the study of etymology, word roots, prefixes, and suffixes is an important part of their language learning. Use of vocabulary from foreign languages at the primary level enriches their vocabulary and builds an understanding of cognates in various languages. Learning root words

FIGURE 6.3 A Matrix of Language Syntax

Forms	Function	Selective Combinations in Sentences
nouns	subject predicate nominative direct object indirect object object of preposition appositive	The *girl* went to the *store*. Mary, *the leader,* gave *Larry* her title. The teacher is my *friend*.
verbs principal parts tense, voice, mood	infinitives active passive indicative subjunctive present/past/future present perfect/past perfect/future perfect gerunds	The girl *walked* home. The girl *was walked* home by the boy. etc.
pronouns (he/she/it)	replacement for nouns	*She* left *him* for *it*.
adjectives (comparative)	modifier of nouns	The *pretty* woman disliked the *sad* man.
adverbs (-ly) (comparative forms)	modifier of verbs, adjectives, and adverbs	We scored *poorly* on the test. Sara was *too* small for the task. She moved *very* slowly.
conjunctions	"binders"	We ate *and* slept. She went *but* I stayed.
prepositions	provide indications of place and time	He stood *in* the doorway. We left *at* six o'clock.
Multiple forms (more than one word) phrases, clauses, etc.	modifiers of nouns and verbs	*Being lonely,* she left. He wept *because he knew the truth.*

from Latin through English, for example, can increase English vocabulary twice-fold. The following list has been used in gifted programs:

SAMPLE ENGLISH WORDS	LATIN ROOT	ENGLISH MEANING
REGAL, REGALE, REGALIA	rex, regis	king
TEMPORAL, TEMPORARY	tempus, temporis	time
BELLIGERENT, BELLICOSE	bellum	war
CONVENE, VENTURE	convenio	come together
CAPTIVATE, CAPTURE	captivs	prisoner
TERMINAL, TERMINATE	terminus	end
PERPETUITY, PERPETUAL	perpetua	everlasting
MEDIATOR, MEDIATE	media	middle of
RELIC, RELINQUISH	reliqua	left behind, abandoned
SCRIBE, SCRIBBLE	scribo	write
FORTITUDE	fortis	brave
PAUCITY, PAUPER	paucus	few
PERILOUS, PERIL	periculum	danger
EGOIST, EGO	ego	I
EXEMPLUM	exemplum	model
PETITION, COMPETITION	peto	seek, ask
OMNISCIENT, OMNIPOTENT OMNIBUS	omnis	all
SCIENCE	scio	know
FACILE, FACILITY	facilis	easy
INTERROGATE, INTERROGATORY	inter	between/among
	rogo	ask

Working on analogies can also increase the students' vocabulary as well as deepen their understanding of word and syntax relationships. The examples that follow were taken selectively from the College Board's *10 SAT's*:

yawn: boredom   as   **smile: amusement**
Type of analogy: physical expression to feeling
Strategy: establish precise relationship between a given pair of words

famine: starvation   as   **deluge: flood**
Type of analogy: cause and effect
Strategy: make up a sentence using the given pair of words

pride: lion   as   **pack: wolf**
Type of analogy: group to a member
Strategy: explore multiple meanings and relationships for a given word

By modifying the nature of the language program for gifted learners, educators can focus on their capacity to become linguistically proficient early and to develop a high-powered use of language.

ORAL DISCOURSE

Although it is common to find verbally talented students who have mastered the art of "glibness" without the substance of reflective and profound thinking, it is also common to find the direct teaching of oral discourse in its several forms to be sadly lacking from a verbal arts curriculum for the gifted. Most English classes for the gifted employ individual oral reports and panel presentations, but very few utilize debate, dramatics, and oral interpretation as lively expressive forms in their own right.

These "active" expressive forms are extremely important for verbally talented students as skillful techniques to build higher level thinking capacities and to integrate thought and feeling. Using creative dramatics in the classroom from kindergarten on seems most appropriate for these students. Formal debate can be introduced by fifth or sixth grade, and fullblown "dramatic performances" can be undertaken during the same time.

Focusing on oral communication will widen the scope of understanding the dramatic arts. The visual and auditory channels of communication now come into play in a visible way not found in the other components of an English/verbal arts curriculum, and students can begin to understand in a "hands-on" way the nature of interrelated arts. Therefore, equal time within the curriculum for these types of activities seems justified, rather than treating such areas as only electives within the larger school curriculum.

Interdisciplinary Issues in a Verbal Arts Curriculum

Another important issue in building a verbal arts program for the gifted is to recognize the interrelationship among the key components in the curriculum. The following sample, taken from an Advanced Placement examination in English, points out the degree of interplay among reading literature, composition, and language study. It also represents a good example of a high-level activity for gifted students in respect to analysis, interpretation, and evaluation of an unknown problem. Such activity would be valuable for gifted students throughout the grades 7–12 continuum as an example of advanced content material being incorporated effectively into curriculum at an earlier stage.

Read the following poem carefully. Then write an essay in which you describe how the speaker's attitude toward loss in lines 16–19 is related to her attitude toward loss in lines 1–15. Using specific references to the text, show how verse form and language contribute to the reader's understanding of these attitudes. (Suggested time: 35 minutes)

ONE ART*

The art of losing isn't hard to master;
so many things seem filled with the intent
to be lost that their loss is no disaster.

---

* "One Art" from *The Complete Poems 1927–1979* by Elizabeth Bishop. Copyright © 1976, 1979 by Elizabeth Bishop. Reprinted by permission of Farrar Straus & Giroux, Inc.

Lose something every day. Accept the fluster
of lost door keys, the hour badly spent.
The art of losing isn't hard to master.

Then practice losing farther, losing faster;
places, and names, and where it was you meant
to travel. One of these will bring disaster.

I lost my mother's watch. And look! my last, or
next-to-last, of three loved houses went.
The art of losing isn't hard to master.

I lost two cities, lovely ones. And, vaster,
some realms I owned, two rivers, a continent.
I miss them, but it wasn't a disaster.

—Even losing you (the joking voice, a gesture
I love) I shan't have lied. It's evident
the art of losing's not too hard to master
though it may look like (*Write* it!) disaster.

The activity incorporates a strong emphasis on critical reading behavior, sensitivity to the structure and nuance of language, and using written form to express an evaluative judgment. As a test essay question, it allows teachers to evaluate the extent to which students have developed higher level thinking skills and how well they can operationalize and transfer them to new materials. It could also be used effectively as a discussion or writing activity to help teach these skills.

Another way of treating the interrelationships within the verbal arts is to organize the curriculum according to the concept approach discussed in Chapter 1. In this model, the English program is built around key ideas that are valued in the context of society as well as the disciplines under study. The following outline, taken from a ninth-grade English program for gifted disadvantaged students, is exemplary of this approach.

COMPOSITION AND LITERATURE: CONCEPTS FROM THE (PHOENIX PROJECT) ENGLISH PROGRAM

SEARCH FOR IDENTITY AND PSYCHOLOGICAL SECURITY

This project is concerned with the needs of disadvantaged students with a potential for giftedness but who may be handicapped in skill and self-concept areas. This major theme, man's search for identity and psychological security, directly deals with self-concept. One of the major quests in the humanities, especially in the 20th Century, is this search. This unit will cover a variety of media that deal with self-awareness, i.e., art, poetry, essays, novels, filmstrips, values clarification techniques, and the examination of cultures, races, and lifestyles.

COMMUNICATIONS

Communications is a second important concept, because it is basic and essential to dealing intelligibly with any other subject. Both non-verbal and verbal communication will be explored as well as ambiguities in language.

POWER, AUTHORITY, AND JUSTICE

Having explored his self-concept, the student moves to an exploration of power and authority. These forces often set parameters to his search for identity and fulfillment and are often determinants of his self-concept. The study of the use of power and authority leads into questions of justice and injustice, the ethical perspectives by which we assess the wielding of power and authority. Through literature, they can see microcosmic examples on a personal level of these same polarities.

TOLERANCE

Justice is concerned with actions; tolerance with attitudes. The relationship of the two and of understanding is examined in this unit. Naturally, related topics are bigotry and prejudice, as well as apathy and indifference. Exposure to diverse cultures and religions will also be used as a springboard to understanding this concept.

SURVIVAL

A sharpened awareness of the negative aspects of society leads into questions of chances for, and threats to, survival. Man's essential will to survive and his conquest of almost insurmountable obstacles to survival will be examined in this unit. Ecological problems as well as personal and societal ones are corollary topics in the survival quest.

CHANGE AND THE FUTURE

Where do we go from here? How do we deal with rapid changes and what can we project for the future? The final unit logically looks ahead and attempts to provide tools to help deal with these questions and suggest possible answers.

Issues in Implementing Curriculum for the Gifted in the Verbal Arts

It may be useful to consider the following kinds of issues as one moves toward implementing a gifted curriculum for students in the areas discussed.

1. Using all three curriculum models (A, B, and C) is very important to consider in implementing a verbal arts program. Teaching grammar and usage in English and a foreign language is very well adapted to the Model A approach; teaching writing fits well into a Model B perspective, and the teaching of literature, interrelated arts, and humanities fits a Model C perspective.

2. Grade-level designations should remain flexible in regard to the elements discussed in this chapter. Where possible, programs in the verbal arts should be cross-graded with appropriate testing rather than age determining placement in the curricular structure.

3. Achieving a balance among the verbal arts components is an important issue to consider. Typically, schools handle the problem by focusing differentially at different grade levels. Unfortunately, this approach tends to reduce the effort of

a powerful verbal arts program. Flexible scheduling and varying time allotments for a given set of objectives would be one way of solving that problem. Foreign language learning, for example, could be reduced to two hours per week throughout the year. Teaching grammar could be condensed into one year, and four hours of instructional time in writing twice a week may be preferable. (See the sample schedule.)

Weekly Schedule for English/Language Arts Study K–8

Time Blocks by Hour Per Day	M	T	W	Th	F
1	Literature & Critical Thinking	Writing block (Workshop time)	Literature & Critical Reading	Writing block (Workshop time)	Foreign language learning block
2	Grammar & Usage		Grammar & Usage		

Alternative Weekly Schedule for Including Research Projects

Time Blocks	M	T	W	Th	F
1	Literature & Critical Reading block	Grammar & Usage block	Writing block (Workshop time)	Research Project block	Foreign language learning block
2					

4. Selecting teachers to work in verbal arts programs for the gifted is potentially difficult since one person may not embody all the expertise needed to handle the nature of the programs outlined in this chapter. Using teacher teams and outside resource professionals are two approaches to overcoming that problem. Older gifted students can also work with younger ones as another effective allocation of resources to meet the needs of the gifted.

5. Balancing the type of instructional activities in which gifted students engage is an important consideration. Writing, discussion, student performance, group problem-solving, and reading are activities that need to be included in each week's instructional plan so that no one type of activity dominates the learning process.

6. Use of materials that are wide-ranging is a critical implementation issue. Basal texts and even a single anthology do not offer the rich literary selections needed by the gifted from kindergarten on. Much of the best children's literature is not incorporated into a single source. Thus creating a multiple materials approach is crucial to carrying out the ideas expressed here.

7. Use of discussion-oriented inquiry techniques is a very critical part of a successful verbal arts program for the gifted. The following example of multiple types of questions and inquiry behavior is based on the children's rhyme, "Twinkle, Twinkle, Little Star."

TYPE OF BEHAVIOR	QUESTIONS
cognition	1. What is a star?
evaluation	2. Why do you think the author described it as "like a diamond"?
divergent	3. What if you were a star in the sky. How would you describe what you saw on earth?
evaluation	4. Why do we like to look at stars?
fluency	5. Can you name other things we see in the sky? (Let's make a long list).
analysis	6. How is it that we can see stars?
elaboration	7. How else would you describe stars besides as "diamonds in the sky"?
divergent	8. Pretend you are traveling from star to star. What do you notice that we can't from the earth?
inductive reasoning	9. Stars sometime form patterns called constellations. Here are a few of them. What does each look like? Have you ever seen these patterns? Now you can look for them.
evaluation/analysis	10. What is your favorite pattern of stars? Why?
synthesis	11. Create you own favorite star pattern. Use color, shape, and location to convey your pattern.
flexibility	12. Stars are used in many ways in our world. How many different ways can you name?

8. Good booklists should be available to the gifted at all ages, and teachers should actively encourage students to read particular selections. Examples of books for young gifted children (primary level) that are rich in idea, form, and illustration include:

Barbara Cooney	*Miss Rumphius*
Arnold Lobel	*The Rose in My Garden*
Verna Aardema	*Bringing the Rain to Kapiti Plain* (others by this author are also appropriate)
Eric Carle	*The Very Hungry Caterpillar*
Mercer Mayer	*There's a Nightmare in My Closet*
Margaret Wise	*The Runaway Bunny*
Maurice Sendak	*Where the Wild Things Are*
William Steig	*Sylvester and the Magic Pebble* *Doctor DeSoto*

Esphyr Slobidkina	*Caps for Sale*
Arlene Mosel	*Tiktiki Tembo*
Robert McClosky	*Make Way for Ducklings*
Mitsumasa Anno	*Anno's Journey series*
Ludwig Bemelmans	*Madeleine series*
Jean de Brunhoff	*Babar series*
H. A. Rey	*Curious George series*
Stan and Jan Berenstein	*Berenstein Bears series*
Peggy Parish	*Amelia Bedelia series*
Franklyn Branley	*Flash, Crash, Rumble, and Roll* (other science books also available)

9. Another way of thinking and organizing appropriate verbal arts curriculum is to consider key elements that constitute language arts/English and then decide on particular aspects of these that need emphasis or particular attention because of the needs of gifted students. The following example illustrates this approach in the verbal arts.

KEY ELEMENTS IN A VERBAL ARTS CURRICULUM

1. Literature

    a. Exposure to all genres early

    b. Focus on analysis and interpretation skills

    c. Use of symbols and analogies

    d. Teaching toward critical reading (i.e., inference, evaluation of arguments)

    e. Emphasis on reading comprehension

    f. Learning through group discussion

2. Broad-Based Reading

    a. Biography

    b. Domain-specific reading (i.e., science, mathematics, history)

    c. Reading about great ideas

    d. Emphasis on reading comprehension

    e. Learning through discussion

3. Composition

    a. Free expression of ideas

    b. Writing skills

    c. Expository writing

    d. Creative writing

    e. Technical writing/Research writing

4. Oral Discourse

   a. Speech
   b. Drama
   c. Debate
   d. Oral interpretation

5. Language

   a. Vocabulary development
   b. Linguistic proficiency in English early
   c. *Two* foreign languages
   d. Studies in etymology, linguistics, semantics, etc.

10. As educators are in the process of developing curriculum for the gifted, it is important to attempt to keep a balance between developing objectives that focus on skill building and on idea building. Even in the area of higher order skills, it may be useful to develop higher order ideas to be taught simultaneously. For example, the following passage* could be taught purely as an exercise in the skill of inference. However, the curriculum becomes richer if it also is taught with key ideas in mind.

The most fruitful areas for the growth of the sciences are those neglected areas between the various established fields. Since Leibniz, there has perhaps been no one who had a full command of all the intellectual activity of the day. Increasingly, science has become the task of specialists, in fields which show a tendency to grow progressively narrower. Yet it is the boundary regions of science which offer the richest opportunities to the qualified investigator. At the same time, these regions are most refractory to the accepted techniques of mass attack and the division of labor.

If the difficulty of a physiological problem is mathematical in essence, then physiologists ignorant of mathematics will get precisely as far as one physiologist ignorant of mathematics, and no further. However, if one physiologist who knows no mathematics works together with a mathematician who knows no physiology, the one will be unable to state a problem in terms that the other can manipulate, and the second will be unable to put the answers in any form that the first can understand. A proper explanation of these blank spaces on the map of science can only be made by a team of scientists, each a specialist in one field, but each possessing a thoroughly sound and trained acquaintance with the other fields. In addition, all must be in the habit of working together, of knowing one another's intellectual customs, and of recognizing the significance of a colleague's new suggestion before it has taken on a full formal expression. The mathematician need not have the skill to conduct a physiological experiment but must have the skill to understand one, to criticize one, to suggest one. The physiologist need not be able to prove a certain mathematical theorem, but must be able to describe what is needed to the mathematician.

---

* Reprinted from *Beginning an Advanced Placement Course in European History*, Edition C, 1980, College Entrance Examination Board. Reprinted by permission of the College Entrance Examination Board.

Based on this passage, students might be asked to respond to both types of questions that follow.

SKILL-BASED QUESTIONS

1. What can be inferred from the passage is the reason for the lack of successful exploration in the boundary regions of science?
2. One may interpret the passage as urging what kinds of changes in order for science to advance?
3. Why does the author cite the example of Leibniz?
4. What characteristics should individual members of a research team possess?

CONCEPT-BASED QUESTIONS

1. If you were a scientist, how would you respond to this passage?
2. Do you think great ideas are created in isolation by one individual or by a team of people working together? Can you cite instances of important discoveries that support your point of view?
3. What does the passage imply about:
   a. the nature of knowledge in the world today?
   b. the importance of cooperation and teamwork?
   c. the need to know something about more than one field of inquiry?
4. Why do you think that a technological society like ours today still needs generalists? Do you predict this need will continue or change?

11. The blend of content and process components in a curriculum can only result in creating a more enriched, advanced, and personally relevant type of learning experiences for talented learners. Clearly, our objectives for these students need to reflect strongly the importance of these three dimensions. Figure 6.4 provides an example of such a blend in the literature domain. Figure 6.5 features a discussion outline in drama that fuses content, process/product, and concept considerations within its overall structure.

Conclusion

Verbal arts programs for the gifted should present opportunities for challenging curriculum throughout the K–12 continuum. One way to enhance such possibilities is to redirect and refocus the traditional language arts strands in such a way as to make them more compatible with the characteristics and needs of the gifted learner at the appropriate stage of developmental readiness. Second, it is important to treat the strands of language, literature, writing, and oral discourse as separate domains of study as well as find suitable ways to interrelate them. Even gifted students need to feel they have gained some control over a tool skill such as the writing process or oral communications. The separate and integral study of language and literature again allows a level of competence to precede work in interdisciplinary areas. Third, educators in verbal arts programs for the gifted need to organize subject matter more carefully over the years these students are

FIGURE 6.4 Examples of Objectives Generated by Content, Process, and Concept Perspectives

The identified gifted learner will be able to:

CONTENT OBJECTIVES (MODEL A)

- Recognize various literary devices used by authors to explain mood, style, and purpose
- Identify the mythological allusions found in *The Odyssey*

PROCESS OBJECTIVES (MODEL B)

- Critique selected published works: poems, short stories, cartoons, art forms, and visual media
- Write a research paper that contrasts two authors' styles

CONCEPT OBJECTIVES (MODEL C)

- Develop an understanding of satire through contemporary cartooning of literary works of the past
- Recognize that cultures reflect a unique view of human experience through their literature and art

in school so that needless repetition and redundancy is removed from their curriculum experience. The results of such an effort would be to address the needs of the gifted population directly and in the process to upgrade the entire curriculum for all learners.

KEY POINTS SUMMARY

- The verbal arts need to be examined according to the subject matter strands that constitute them for purposes of curriculum modification for the gifted. These strands are: literature, language (mother tongue and foreign), oral discourse, and writing.
- Content modification according to Model A can best be effected in the teaching of the vocabulary, syntax, and usage principles of a language, whether English or a foreign language.
- Process/product approaches to the curriculum, as exemplified in Model B, are best carried out through the tool skill programs of writing and composition as well as through forms such as debate and dramatics.
- Concept approaches in the verbal arts (Model C) can best be enacted through the literature strand and its opportunities for the treatment of the interrelated art forms of music and art.
- The goal structure for a verbal arts curriculum needs to have content, process/product, and concept focal points so that the derived curriculum

FIGURE 6.5 Drama Discussion Outline

Establishing interrelationships among plays is a helpful tool in teaching and increasing student understanding. For this reason, three plays (*Oedipus Rex, Hamlet, Waiting for Godot*) were chosen for discussion in regard to their common elements.

I. General ideas and/or themes
   A. The element of tragedy
      1. tragic hero (high birth, flaw, downfall)
      2. antihero
      3. theatre of the absurd → no hero, tragic condition
   B. Pride → punishment syndrome (hubris → nemesis)
   C. Man's struggle to overcome fate (the gods)
      1. nobility of man
      2. the folly of man
   D. Moderation (sophrosyne)
      1. balance in the plays
      2. passion vs. reason

II. Characterization
   A. Development
      1. illumination of truth about self and/or situation
      2. immutable condition negates development
   B. Similarities and contrasts among characters
      1. Oedipus/Laius
      2. Hamlet/Laertes/Fortinbras
      3. Pozzo/Lucky

III. Dramatic form
   A. Greek plays (chorus, dramatic irony, staging)
   B. Shakespearean plays (standard five acts, soliloquies, stage techniques)
   C. Theatre of the absurd (idea dominates form as reflected in setting, characters, dialogue, nihilism)

IV. Writing assignment (choose one from the following list)
   A. Analyze a key theme across the three plays
   B. Select a key character and trace his or her development or insight *or* motivational changes throughout the work
   C. Evaluate the effectiveness of the three plays from the perspective of a theater audience.

---

experiences can address differing needs of the gifted simultaneously: the need to move ahead at a rate determined by student capacity, the need to engage in problem-finding and problem-solving learning that leads to product development, and the need to explore ideas, themes, and issues within and across areas of knowledge.

- Providing a greater emphasis on the workshop approach to composition programs for the gifted will surely yield a greater return in terms of frequency of writing and mastery of fundamental writing skills at an earlier stage of development.

- An early emphasis on the experiences of learning a foreign language in the elementary grades and mastering two languages by high-school graduation is an important part of language development.
- Stress on learning vocabulary over spelling and learning writing skills over handwriting are important modifications in a verbal arts curriculum for the gifted.
- Early literature and writing experiences are necessary for the gifted child to thrive in the reading experience. These experiences should be standard in K–3 gifted programs.
- The Advanced Placement Program of College Board in Literature and Composition provides an excellent basis for curriculum work in these areas of gifted students' programs as early as middle school. AP tests in these areas stress analytic and interpretive skills, the ability to generalize and synthesize information, and the capacity to evaluate effectively.

References

Arnold, H. (1962). "Useful Creative Techniques." In S. Parnes and H. Harding (Eds.), *A Sourcebook for Creative Thinking.* New York: Scribner's.

Barbe, W. (1955). "Evaluation of Special Classes for Gifted Children." *Exceptional Children, 22,* 60–62.

Bartz, W. (1977). *The Role of Foreign Languages in Gifted Education.* Indianapolis: Indiana State Department of Public Instruction.

Baskin, B., and Harris, K. (1980). *Books for the Gifted Child.* London: Bowker Publishers.

California Department of Education (1979). *Curriculum Guide for Teaching Gifted Children, Literature in Grades 1–12.* Sacramento: California State Department of Education.

Clarke, B. (1979). *Growing Up Gifted.* Columbus, Ohio: Charles E. Merrill.

Collins, J. (1985). *The Effective Writing Teacher: 18 Strategies.* Andover, Mass.: The Network.

Cummins, J. (1979). "Linguistic Interdependence and the Educational Development of Bilingual Children." *Review of Educational Research, 49*(2), 222–251.

Dale, E., and Rozik, T. (1963). *Bibliography of Vocabulary Studies.* Columbus: Bureau of Educational Research and Service, The Ohio State University.

Drews, E. (1972). *Learning Together.* Englewood Cliffs, N.J.: Prentice-Hall.

Dudley, L., and Feracy, V. (undated). *Humanities.* New York: MacMillan.

Gallagher, J. (1975). *Teaching the Gifted Child,* 2nd ed. Boston: Allyn and Bacon.

Gold, M. (1962). *The Education of the Intellectually Gifted.* Columbus, Ohio: Charles Merrill.

Hall, D., and Embler, D. (1976). *A Writer's Reader.* Boston: Little, Brown.

Hollingworth, L. (1926). *Gifted Children*. New York: World Book.

Hollingworth, L. (1942). *Children above 180 I.Q.* New York: World Book.

Illinois Office of Education. (1977). *A Survey of Provisions in Gifted Education*. Springfield: Illinois Office of Education.

Kaplan, S. (1979). "Language Arts and Social Studies Curriculum in the Elementary School." In H. Passow (Ed.), *NSSE Yearbook, The Gifted and the Talented*. Chicago: University of Chicago Press.

Morris, J. (1971). "Barriers to Successful Reading in Second Language Students at the Secondary Level." In B. Spolsky (Ed.), *The Language Education of Minority Children*. Rowlex: Newbury House.

Pilon, A. (1975). "Come Hither, Come Hither, Come Hither: Words' Worth." *Gifted Child Quarterly, 15*(1), 13–31.

Reynolds, B., Kopelke, K., and Durden, W. (1984). *Writing Instruction for Verbally Talented Youth*. Rockville, Md.: Aspen.

Sulzby, E. (1985). *Emergent Writing and Reading in 5–6 Year Olds: A Longitudinal Study*. Norwood, N.J.: Ablex.

VanTassel-Baska, J. (1982). "An Experimental Study on the Teaching of Latin to the Verbally Precocious." *Roeper Review, 4*(3).

VanTassel-Baska, J. (1987). "The Case for the Teaching of Latin to the Verbally Talented." *Roeper Review, 9*(3), 159–161.

Ward, V. (1961). *Educating the Gifted: An Axiomatic Approach*. Columbus, Ohio: Charles Merrill.

Selected Materials for Use in Verbal Arts Gifted Programs

LITERATURE

LITERATURE: USES OF THE IMAGINATION

Northrop Frye, supervisory editor. Will T. Jewkes, general editor. Harcourt Brace Jovanovich, 1972; 1973. *Primary audience: 7–12.*

Revolutionary in concept and technique, this paperback program for junior and senior high school guides students to discover recurring character, story, and image patterns, or archetypes, in the literature of all cultures and periods. With this approach, literature becomes more meaningful, more accessible as well as easier to teach. Poems, short stories, myths, parables, filmscripts, and songs are presented together with contemporary photographs, painting, posters, and cartoons to show the basic imaginative patterns all people share. For example, the archetype of the martyred hero is illustrated in Benet's "John Brown's Body," the myth of Prometheus, and a eulogy for Malcolm X by Ossie Davis; the rightful kingdom archetype in John F. Kennedy's Inaugural Address, the myths of Perseus, and the song "Aquarius" from *Hair*.

JUNIOR GREAT BOOKS

The Great Books Foundation, 40 East Huron Street, Chicago, Illinois 60611.
Primary audience: elementary gifted students (1–6).

This program provides a structured collection of excellent classical and
modern stories for students to read and discuss in the context of shared
inquiry. Discussion leaders, teachers, or volunteers center discussion on
problems of interpretation in a given selection. Students develop the ability
to think reflectively and independently, to listen to and consider opinions
other than their own. At the same time, they are exposed to excellent literature.

WRITING

The Elements of Style, 3rd ed. W. Strunk, Jr. and E. B. White. New York: Mac-
Millan, 1979.

Rules of usage of English language. Elucidates rules and principles of writing by concentrating on common violations.

The Lively Art of Writing. Lucille Vaughan Payne, In 3 vols.: *Developing Structure, Effective Style, Understanding Forms.* Chicago: Follett, 1982.

Writing through development of mental pictures and distinct verb types,
motion-picture verbs, soundtrack verbs, etc. Encourages students to think
through writing to organize structure.

The Art of Styling Sentences. M. L. Waddell, R. M. Esch, R. R. Walker. Wood-
bury, N.Y.: Barron's Educational Series, 1983.

Examples and diagrams of sentence patterns which form the basics of all
good writing. Chapters and exercises in each chapter.

20 Questions for the Writer: A Rhetoric with Readings, 4th ed. Jacqueline
Berke. New York: Harcourt, Brace, Jovanovich, 1985.

Divides twenty questions into four categories: Imaginative, Informative,
Analytical, Critical. Examples of each type of writing and exercises for same
for students. Seven different ways of defining words and phrases. Appendi-
ces on sentence composition and review of punctuation.

EXAMPLE 6.A Sample Language Arts Teaching Units ━━━━━━

This unit and the one following on photography have been developed to teach the
genre of poetry and its relationship to other artistic forms. It is appropriate for gifted
learners in several respects:

1. It engages students in generative learning immediately by having them "create" poems and photographs.
2. It uses selected poems intensively rather than an anthology extensively.
3. It focuses on higher level thinking tasks about poetry and photography.
4. It uses an interdisciplinary approach.

5. It allows student choice in selecting activities.

6. It encourages original production.

Level: Middle School

Grouping: Special class of gifted/talented learners or cluster grouping

TOPIC: POETRY AS AN ART FORM

Objectives and Corresponding Activities

1. Differentiate the form of poetry from prose.

   a. Share from well-known American poets (Emily Dickinson, Carl Sandburg, Robert Frost, Stephen Spender) several poems with the class by reading them, putting them on an overhead projector, and handing them out.

   b. Discuss differences in form and what helps constitute the form of these specific poems.

2. Interpret several poems appropriately, using analytical and aesthetic approaches.

   a. Through an inquiry approach, discover the meaning of each poem and how form contributes to meaning.

   b. Use a forced relationship approach to demonstrate ways to merge form and meaning.

3. Relate how the form of a poem reflects the meaning of a poem by using your favorite poem as an illustration.

   a. In small groups, have students use the creative problem-solving model to select and analyze a particular poem.

   b. Have students critique "favorite poems" in a group setting, citing form characteristics.

4. Using the poem "Jabberwocky," list examples that demonstrate the relationship of form and meaning.

   a. Have students brainstorm key phrases from the poem.

   b. Discuss the form of the poem.

   c. In small groups, utilize decision-making skills to determine relationship between form and meaning.

5. Utilize one form of poetry discussed and write your own poem.

   a. Review forms of poetry discussed.

   b. Practice writing a poem in class according to a particular form and idea.

   c. Share and critique with the class according to the stated parameters.

6. Set up criteria and judge the student poems in respect to form and meaning.

   a. Brainstorm criteria for judgment of student poems.

  b. Create an evaluation form for each student to fill out.

  c. Conduct poetry readings.

7. Create a poem by writing down an idea (in one line) and passing it on. When it comes back, finish the poem. (To be done in groups of four.)

  a. Group work on creating group poems.

  b. Share group poems and discuss how they differ from individual ones.

  c. Judge which group created the best group poem.

Evaluation Design

This topic will be evaluated through the following approaches:

1. Self-evaluation by students of their creative efforts in poetry and participation in group activities

2. Class evaluation of original poems read (a total group score would be utilized here)

3. Teacher evaluation based on: participation, understanding of poetic form and meaning, and the ability to apply these concepts to poetic reaction

TOPIC: PRINCIPLES OF POETRY

Objectives and Corresponding Activities

1. Identify principles of poetry by specific names: meter, rhyme, form, content, poetic devices.

  a. Read about characteristics of poems in John Ciardi's *How Does a Poem Mean*.

  b. Utilize five sample poems with the class to show how these characteristics are present and operate in the examples.

2. Compare and contrast two poems in respect to these principles.

  a. Read "Ulysses" by Tennyson and "Ozymandias" by Shelley.

  b. Write an essay describing similarities and differences in respect to poetic principles.

3. Read new poems and identify the principles represented.

  a. Read at least two poems by each of the following poets: Lao Tse; Shakespeare, Keats, Dickinson, Frost, Hughes.

  b. In groups, discuss the notion of the principles utilized by each poet and how it determines style.

  c. Present a panel discussion on this topic.

4. Compose a poem utilizing the major principles learned, and in the style of your favorite poet.

a. Through inquiry, arrive at a definition of style and how it manifests itself in poetry.

b. Brainstorm important steps in writing a poem.

c. Create a "best list" of steps in poetry writing.

5. Judge whether the principles are appropriately utilized in each student's poem.

a. Present poems to the class.

b. Have the class guess what author's style is being imitated after each presentation.

c. Discuss the poetic principles that are present.

d. Utilize a discrepancy chart to show what might be missing from the poem that could have been included.

6. Create your own poetic principles and apply them to a poem that you write.

a. Set up a list of steps to be followed in creating a new form of poetry.

b. Read about creativity and the process of creativity.

c. Practice poetry writing.

d. Have a poet in residence share perceptions and insights with the class.

Evaluation Design

This topic will be evaluated through the following multiple approaches:

1. Essays will be evaluated on a scale of 1–5 (with 5 being high) according to the criteria of: applicability of content to the assignment, grammatical form, and fluidity of expression.

2. In-class presentations will be videotaped and critiqued by the class as a follow-up activity.

3. A guest poet will judge original poems.

TOPIC: THE LIVES OF POETS

Objectives and Corresponding Activities

1. Read biographies of two major poets.

a. Brainstorm reasons for life history affecting artistic products.

b. Through inquiry, discover the effects of the culture, the time period and other artists on any particular creation.

c. Choose two poets to study in regard to life and cultural milieu.

2. Explain what each poet's conception of the creative process is.

a. Prepare note cards for an oral presentation on main aspects of biographies.

    b. Prepare oral presentation.

    c. Chart similarities and differences among the poets.

3. Apply conceptions of the creative process to the future.

    a. Do a small-group simulation, pretending students are poets in the year 2500. How would they speak about poetry and the creative process?

    b. Share perceptions of all groups.

4. What do poets see as vital components of their art? Analyze at least two biographies in this respect.

    a. Discuss the personal qualities that make a poet.

    b. Read about Blake and Eliot in this respect.

    c. Write an essay demonstrating your perception of the characters of these two poets. Hypothesize on what contributed to their nature.

5. Pretend you are a famous poet. Create your own epitaph based on how you've lived, what you've done, etc.

    a. Choose one of the poets studied.

    b. Write down important things you know about this poet.

    c. Read excerpts from Edgar Lee Masters' *Spoon River Anthology* for an understanding of poetic epitaphs.

6. Evaluate the lives of poets compared to nonartistic occupations; what differences exist? Chart the differences and indicate *your* values on each dimension.

    a. Develop an interview questionnaire regarding rationale for choice of occupation.

    b. Interview at least two people not in artistic fields.

    c. In small groups, discuss findings and use the creative problem-solving model to develop a chart of major results.

    d. Share group results and discuss.

Evaluation Design

This topic's objectives will be evaluated through the following procedures:

1. Class evaluation of oral reports via a structured instrument devised and field-tested by students themselves.

2. Teacher analysis of group interaction via a Flanders-type analysis on individual students.

3. Teacher-evaluated essay, on a 1–5 scale (5 being high) based on the criteria of: analysis of topic, synthesis of information, and evaluation of contributory factors to character formation of poets.

4. Have the class choose the five best epitaphs and critique them in respect to predetermined criteria.

TOPIC: PHOTOGRAPHY AS AN ART FORM

Objectives and Corresponding Activities

1. Understand the elements of photography.

   a. Examine several photographs in class, taking notes on elements that interest you.
   b. Discuss aspects of interest.
   c. Categorize the areas of interest.
   d. Show a set of slides and have the class pick out the key elements in each photograph.

2. Create a montage from a variety of photographs.

   a. In groups, build a montage around the theme of love.
   b. Use morphological analysis to determine a theme, a mode of treatment and resources to be utilized for individual montages.
   c. Provide an outline of project procedures.

3. Describe photographic materials and techniques.

   a. Introduce the tools of a photographer.
   b. Take the class on a tour of a dark room.
   c. Provide hands-on experience with developing techniques.
   d. Have a photographer discuss the technical aspects of his or her job.

4. Analyze photographs in respect to meaning, method, and use of symbols.

   a. Show slides of photographs and discuss how development techniques contribute to visual meaning.
   b. In small groups, prepare a series of photographs that demonstrate good fusion of aesthetics and technique along with a rationale for each.
   c. Individually, choose a favorite photograph and write an analysis of it, reflecting the issues discussed in class.

5. Judge the relative quality of photographs, given the criteria of technical competence, aesthetic content, use of symbols, clarity of ideas, and composition.

   a. Review and discuss terminology used in evaluation.
   b. In small groups, determine photographic quality in five photographs, using the stated criteria.
   c. Have groups present their decisions to the class.
   d. Debrief through a discussion of group differences in perception of quality.
   e. Assign selected readings from Robert Pirsig's *Zen and the Art of Motorcycle Maintenance* that deal with the issue of "quality."

6. Produce a photographic essay.

    a. Have students shoot a complete roll of 35mm film and develop it.

    b. Prepare a presentation for the class on the best series of pictures taken and what they represent.

    c. Conduct a contest and award 1st, 2nd, and 3rd prizes for the best photographs as judged by a class panel.

Evaluation Design

This topic will be evaluated through a three-tiered approach:

1. Level one evaluation will consist of each student completing a self-evaluation form for each major activity completed.
2. Level two evaluation will consist of teacher evaluations of all written and oral presentations.
3. Level three evaluation will consist of peer ratings on the photographic contest.

TOPIC: PRINCIPLES OF PHOTOGRAPHY

Objectives and Corresponding Activities

1. Discern the principles of photography.

    a. Conduct a class discussion on *aesthetics* in respect to meaning and application; then discuss similarly the term *technique*.

    b. Write an essay describing how the principles of poetry and photography are alike and how they are different.

2. Create a photograph that allows you to analyze all the photographic principles.

    a. Do a group simulation on "If you were photographing a tornado that destroyed a town and claimed 100 lives, how would you organize for maximum effect?"

    b. Each group gives an oral report.

    c. Debrief around similarities and differences in interpretation of the event.

    d. Prepare a checklist of photographic procedures and principles to use in creating a picture.

    e. Submit completed checklist and sample photograph.

4. Select a theme and create a photographic essay around it.

    a. Brainstorm lists of possible subjects for photographic essays.

    b. Select a subject and outline alternative approaches to dealing with it photographically.

    c. Shoot and develop photos.

    d. Synthesize photo material for display.

Evaluation Data

This topic will be evaluated by the following devices:

1. Teacher rating sheet on group participation
2. Teacher rating of written essay on a 1–5 scale (5 being high)
3. Panel of three photographers (one professional and two amateur) to judge photo displays, utilizing a predetermined checklist
4. Peer evaluation of photographs illustrating basic principles

TOPIC: LIVES OF PHOTOGRAPHERS

Objectives and Corresponding Activities

1. Understand the cultural and personal factors influencing the work of Steiglitz, Steichen, and Adams.

   a. Read biographical excerpts on each photographer.
   b. Prepare a group chart of major influences on each photographer.
   c. Share with the class and compare charts.

2. Compare the life and times of Steiglitz, Steichen, and Adams with their photographic style.

   a. Analyze the style of each photographer by listing special techniques or unusual, distinctive approaches to treatment of a subject.
   b. Compile a class list of these techniques.
   c. Write an essay reflecting on the relationship of style to personal and social factors.
   d. Compile and present a portfolio to the class that typifies each photographer's work.
   e. Evaluate the portfolio in respect to: adherence to style and comprehensiveness of the effort.

Evaluation Design

This topic will be evaluated by:

1. Teacher rating of portfolios and essays
2. Peer judgment regarding charts of major influences
3. Checklist of biographic materials read, to be completed by the students

7 Social Studies Curriculum for the Gifted _____

Joyce VanTassel-Baska and John Feldhusen

Like Huck, we observed, we judged, we imitated and evaded as we could the dullness, corruption, and blindness of "civilization."
—Ralph Ellison

The framework for conceptualizing the social sciences is a key issue in making decisions about curriculum focus within this broad field for gifted learners. Scriven's model of the tripod is a useful image for perceiving the major areas of knowledge and how they relate to each other (see Figure 7.1). He states:

> I picture the social sciences as a rectangular surface supported on a tripod. The three legs are the three subjects that have some claim to being foundational social sciences, two of which have acquired a primary place in the curriculum. The three subjects are geography, history, and one that is primarily not in the secondary curriculum but in theoretical discussions of the structure of the social science—psychology.
>
> Now, why are these three primary? This is the reason: geography is the study of the spatial distribution of man and his large-scale effects on the earth. History is the study of his temporal distribution and achievements, and psychology is the study of the internal organization of the human entity.
>
> On these three legs rest the social sciences as they are commonly conceived. But, these legs will not hold together, they could not support anything were it not for the general application of methodology, the laws of logic, and mathematics (in particular, statistics). The methodology is that which enables you to get somewhere from the basic observations; the logic enables you to sustain consistency and examine analytically; the mathematics enables you to squeeze intelligible laws out of the complex data of the social sciences.
>
> On the tripod rests the surface that represents the standard social sciences of the academic curriculum: sociology, government, economics, and anthropology. They depend in varying ways on geography, history, and psychology, and I've tried to represent their varying degrees of dependency by their position.
>
> In the center of all this, at the pivot point of the whole system, is the subject of ethics itself. The reason for this location is a very simple one; this is the point of support for any practical action: action in general rests on this surface and has to be supported by it, if it is to be defensible at all. So behavior, or action, or plans of

FIGURE 7.1 Model for the Social Sciences

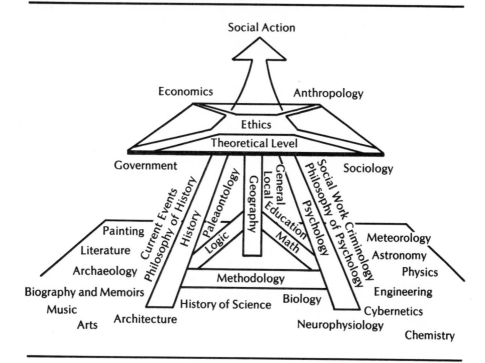

various kinds, since they involve other people (thinking now of behavior in the social area), automatically involves ethics.

Scriven's model raises several issues of importance for decision making regarding curriculum for the gifted learner. The study of any part of the social sciences culminates in a consideration of ethics, which in turn provides the basis for social action. If we find Scriven's model representative, then a natural blend of content and idea can occur in the social science curriculum for the gifted. For all areas of study, ethical behavior becomes an integral part of the learning process. Furthermore, interdisciplinary curriculum efforts within the social sciences are essential to maintaining an appropriate perspective on any one area of study. Economics cannot be studied exclusive of its methodology, its relationship to government and other fields of study, and its impact in the social action arena. Thus curriculum for the gifted learner must provide this mosaic of relationships. The implication of using this model as a guide for curriculum development is that all social science curriculum for the gifted should be treated in an interdisciplinary manner, regardless of the particular area under study.

Yet there abound singular perspectives on what constitutes án appropriate approach to a social science curriculum. These perspectives may be characterized as:

- *The emphasis on history vs. the emphasis on culture.* Those who argue for an historical emphasis in social science curriculum tend to view history as the centerpiece for study, thus inhibiting a broader range of knowledge exploration. Those who favor the cultural approach would relegate history to a less important role and emphasize particular cultures as the basis for study.
- *The emphasis on chronology vs. the emphasis on systems.* The chronologists see history as the unfolding of events in absolute time, whereas those who favor the systems approach prefer viewing past time on the basis of major issues, ideas, or events that emerged out of a larger pattern.
- *The emphasis on content vs. the emphasis on process.* Educators who favor strong content-based instruction in the social sciences view each area as capable of being mastered as a separate entity, whereas educators who favor the process approach believe that the fundamental learning for students from social science curricula is critical inquiry.

Based on the capacities of gifted learners to handle a blend of curriculum approaches, it is reasonable to suggest that distinguishing features of social science curricula for these students be in the scope of exposure to key areas of study, the understanding and concern for developing critical inquiry as the basis for ethical decision making leading to social policy, and the multiple perspectives view within and across each area of study. Key social studies goals for gifted programs might include:

1. To develop critical thought and the spirit of inquiry
2. To understand and accept a world cultures view
3. To appreciate the interrelationship of social science disciplines and institutions
4. To gain knowledge of significant developments in human history and the social systems of which they are a part
5. To develop research skills

Model Curricula in the Social Studies

Barr, Barth, and Shermis (1977) asserted that citizenship education is a major goal of the social studies. Thus, at any grade level the social studies curriculum should focus on issues central to life in the United States and in the world, and should prepare students to think through the major issues and problems facing our society. A knowledge base is implied in these assertions—students should know about the major concepts, principles, themes, problems, and issues that permeate our culture, and they should acquire the skills to analyze, evaluate, and synthesize ideas about them.

Shaver (1984) described the jurisprudential approach to social studies education. In this method and curriculum, students study, analyze, and evaluate major political ethical issues in our society. He argues that the approach is uniquely appropriate for the gifted because of their heightened capacity to read far beyond ordinary textbook content, to deal with moral and ethical issues at a high and abstract level, to use critical thinking skills in analyzing issues, and to verbalize their analyses in interaction with other gifted students. Shaver summarizes the rationale for the jurisprudential approach as follows:

1. Social studies education is basically citizenship education.
2. Citizenship education ought to reflect the nature of the society and of the policy decisions to be made by the society.
3. Our society is pluralistic with a variety of frames of reference, resulting in continous disagreement over the political-ethical issues which are at the heart of policy disputes.
4. Because political-ethical decisions must rest in part at least on one's view of what is morally desirable, values are crucial to their justification.
5. Values are defined differently and, when in conflict, weighted differently by people with different frames of reference.
6. Social studies education should, among other things, help students to analyze public issues in order to make better decisions as citizens; and an appropriate analytic frame must include consideration of values and value conflict, as well as questions of fact and language use.

Shermis and Clinkenbeard (1981) analyzed social studies texts and the study questions included in these texts. They concluded that although there was a shift over the years toward higher level questions, there is still major adherence to questions at the knowledge and comprehension levels. Shermis and Clinkenbeard argue that gifted learners have a special need for high-level thinking experiences, and that social studies teachers must go beyond the standard text questions in designing discussions, case studies, and Socratic dialogues.

Schug (1981) argues that the whole community can be used as a laboratory to develop social studies curricula for the gifted. He suggests that social studies programs for the gifted should begin with a community advisory committee drawn from business, labor, agriculture, the arts, political parties, and so on. The curriculum can be developed around issues and problems in the community. The following are activities for civics, economics, and history courses:

CIVICS

- Visit or participate in meetings of the school board, city council, courts, public hearings, or state legislature.
- Interview public officials such as the mayor, county commissioners, city council members, school board members, or officials in local, state, or federal agencies.
- Invite a member of Congress or the state legislature as a class guest speaker.
- Do volunteer work at local political party headquarters.
- Conduct opinion polls about local public issues or candidates during an election.

- Establish a youth citizenship club whose goal is to encourage studying issues, candidates, and political participation.
- Interview candidates for office about their stands on youth-related issues.

ECONOMICS

- Develop a local consumer price index to measure inflation.
- Interview labor leaders and business people about collective bargaining.
- Produce video tape documentaries about community economic problems.
- Arrange for field trips to a local bank, factory, or human service agency.
- Interview bankers, real estate salespeople, or stock brokers about savings and investment.
- Establish an economic enterprise such as manufacturing and selling products or providing community services.
- Interview student employers about the operations of their business.
- Develop and conduct consumer tests of products purchased at local stores.
- Develop land-use maps to identify the relationship between resources, transportation, and the location of industrial and commercial firms.
- Develop a price comparison survey of products of interest to young people.
- Invite business people in multinational corporations to serve as guest speakers to discuss economic interdependence.

HISTORY

- Arrange field trips to local museums, historical societies, or historical sites.
- Develop oral history collections by doing tape-recorded interviews with senior citizens.
- Do volunteer work at local museums or historical societies.
- Write local histories based on written records, photographs, and interviews with resource people.
- Find and analyze historical artifacts such as weapons, tools, kitchen utensils, arrowheads, toys, clothing, letters, diaries, books, catalogs, or photographs (junk yards, garages, junk shops, and attics are often valuable sources of historical artifacts).
- Arrange a field trip to an old cemetery where students record dates of births and deaths and make inferences about past life spans, epidemics, and health care.
- Video tape interviews with senior citizens talking about life in the past.

Barth and Shermis (1981) presented an extensive curriculum guide to social studies curricula for the gifted and talented. The guide presents material for social studies activities in grades K–12. After each section of activities, there is a section on differentiating to meet the specific needs and characteristics of gifted learners. Here, for example, is the learning objective and activity for an eighth-grade American History course whose overall goal is to "Develop a knowledge base for understanding the ever-changing relationship between human beings and their environment: past, present and future" (p. 40).

Learning Objective: Examine the status of blacks prior to and during the Civil War, and compare and contrast the status and role of blacks prior to, during, and after Reconstruction.

1. Learning activity: *"Jim Crow and You"*
   a. Duration of time: one or two sessions
   b. Materials: selections of Jim Crow laws, a student-made list of daily activities
      Suggested readings:
      The Reign of Jim Crow (AEP)
      Impact of Our Past (McGraw Hill)
      Promise of America (Vol. 2 Scott Foresman)
   c. Description
      1) Ask students to compile a list of activities they might experience during a typical day. (Example: riding a bus to school, buying lunch in the cafeteria).
      2) After reading about Jim Crow laws, ask students to review their list and identify in some way those activities that would have been affected if the same Jim Crow laws applied to them today.
      3) A reaction discussion on the students' feelings about Jim Crow laws could follow.
      4) A coordinated activity could include posters, pictures, written articles, etc., on Jim Crow law and segregation.

Here is a part of their discussion of how to use the activities with the gifted.

How Do These Activities Work with the Gifted?

I Urge You will involve gifted children in some risk-taking and unusual circumstances. While normal children will say "I urge Abraham Lincoln to free the slaves," one can reasonably expect gifted children to urge the appointment of Grant—a general with a superior sense of economic warfare—as General of the Army of the Potomac in 1861. The use of conventional categories in *What's In A Name* is a standard teaching strategy, but one can expect bright children to invent justifications for categories that are likely to go well beyond the conventional response. One can hardly predict what gifted children will do with *Jim Crow and You* which asks for a contemporary application of segregation laws. At the very least, gifted students will go beyond expressing feelings and deal with some of the complex reasons for racism, discrimination, bigotry, etc.; some will want to compare our experience with that of South Africa (p. 45).

Flachner and Hirst (1976) developed curriculum guides for the Astor Program, an early childhood program for the gifted. *200 Years: A Study of Democracy* presents the outline for social studies activities in the program. One of the objectives states, "Children will learn that the United States developed from the combined skills and cultures of people from many levels" (p. 17). The unit begins with Walt Whitman's *I Hear America Singing* and then suggests the following activities:

1. What are some of the vocations and skills the colonists had? From what countries had they come? What work had they done in their former countries?

2. What contributions in skills and work did various ethnic groups make to the growth of America?

For each set of activities, quotations from relevant literature are included, to be used as a basis for discussions and projects with gifted learners. The quotations are from excellent literature, which is much more advanced and complex than generally would be used at the early childhood level. Activities and questions for discussion are at similarly high levels. These guides can be used with young gifted children in various settings, including cluster groups and self-contained programs.

A number of curriculum guides have been developed, and operational program models have been implemented at the Burris Laboratory School at Ball State University, Muncie, Indiana, to serve the special needs of gifted learners. The operational model is generally in the form of a seminar for gifted students characterized by high-level discussions, attention to higher level thinking skills, a focus on issues and problems, much indepth research and project activity, and gifted learners reporting their studies in a variety of creative communication modes. In one of the curriculum guides "A Curricular Approach for Global Futures," Keener (undated) presents the complete curriculum for a futures-oriented course designed especially for gifted learners. The outline for that course follows:

CLASSROOM APPROACHES AND GENERIC GLOBAL
FUTURE CONCEPTS
REFLECTIVE THINKING AND GLOBAL FUTURES
CONCEPTS AS CLASSROOM STRATEGY
GLOBAL FUTURES CONCEPTS AS CONTENT AND
STRUCTURE

Systems

Interdependence

Culture

Lifestyle

Dignity of Man

Change

Populations

Scarcity/Allocation

Energy

Habitat

Institution

Sovereignty

Conflict

Power

Communication

A SAMPLER OF GLOBAL FUTURES ACTIVITIES
INITIATORY/EXPLORATORY ACTIVITIES

Pervasive Global Futures Issues

Generic Global Futures Concepts

Characterizing Global Futures Concepts

What Do Global Futurists Talk About

Projecting My Future

DEVELOPMENTAL/INVESTIGATIVE ACTIVITIES

Individual or Small Group Investigation of an Alternative Global Future

Delineating the Global Futures Investigation

Reporting Research Theses in Global Futures

Individualized Research Theses and Projects/Products

Simplifying a Demographic Abstraction

Nuclear Holocaust Survival Skills

Appropriate Technologies for Developing Economies—Role Playing

Another of the curriculum guides from the Burris-Ball State project, *Environmental Studies from a Global Perspective,* was authored by James E. Adams (undated). The outline of topics for that curriculum follows:

Natural Systems

Emergence of Human Systems

Population and Resources

Issues and Options

About the Future

The California State Department of Education (1977) has published three levels of curriculum guides for educational programs for gifted learners in the social sciences. These guides provide objectives, learning activities, and lists of resources for a curriculum that stresses learning skills, cognitive processes, and affective outcomes in history, political science, economics, anthropology, sociology, psychology, cultural geography, and physical geography. The curricula focus on process within the content topics outlined.

The closest curricular adaptation that has been made of the Scriven conceptual model of the social sciences is the K–12 gifted program used in Chicago Public Schools, Comprehensive Gifted Centers and Magnet High Schools. Because these programs are self-contained, the curriculum can differ substantially from the general curriculum for all students and can be effectively articulated across grade levels. Their social studies curriculum focuses on nine strands: geography, psychology, economics, history, political science, sociology, anthropology, philosophy, and research skills. These strands are targeted for different emphases at various grade levels from kindergarten through grade twelve. The program takes a strong stance on providing students with a sense of the structural nature of the disciplines that make up the social studies, with a focus on the language of the discipline, its theories, and key concepts that define it. At no grade level is only one strand treated; rather, there is a multiple approach used at each. Only at the level of activities would a teacher make adaptations because the student is younger. The course descriptions present an intellectual purpose at each level of the curriculum (see Example 7.A at the conclusion of this chapter).

The Art of Inquiry

In the teaching of the social sciences, perhaps more than any other set of disciplines, the employment of good inquiry techniques is vital since learner outcomes are dependent on developing a critical inquiring mind. Use of a questioning model (see Figure 7.2) may be helpful in preparing social studies discussions. The instructor should be careful to include questions that require several types of thinking processes: memory/cognition, convergent, divergent, and evaluation. Yet, as the example illustrates, the questions are carefully structured to lead from concrete data to abstract speculating, from specific information about one historical event to an understanding of issues that apply to many events. A set of questions may be useful to consider in evaluating individual inquiry-based techniques to question-posing:

1. Do the questions lead to problem formulation?
2. Do they aim toward *student* explication of the problem?
3. Are students called upon to analyze their explanations and to test their hypothesis?
4. Are the questions open-ended?

The following questions have been developed around specific social studies topics to provide teachers of the gifted with a sense of the level, complexity, and nature of appropriate questions for gifted students. Each set of questions* represents a blend of convergent, divergent, and evaluative questions.

AMERICAN STUDIES

1. "The Crusades was the opening chapter in the story of the discovery of America." Explain this statement.
2. If you were a European of the sixteenth or seventeenth-century pe-

---

* These questions are adapted from *A Handbook for the Teaching of Social Studies*, 2nd ed., by The Association of Teachers of Social Studies in the City of New York/United Federation of Teachers. Copyright © 1985 by Allyn and Bacon, Inc. Reprinted with permission.

FIGURE 7.2 Varied Questioning Types and Examples

Question Types	Examples
Memory/Cognition	
These questions are typified by the characteristic of one right answer, are factual in nature, and begin with words like *who/what/when*.	Who directed Civil War activities for the North? What year did the Civil War begin? When did Lee surrender?
Convergent	
These questions are typified by multiple right responses that are analytical in nature, and tend to begin with *why/how*.	Why was the Civil War fought? How did the war begin?
Divergent	
These questions are hypothetical in nature, often creating scenarios or simulations for students to respond to. There are no right answers to this question type, which frequently begin with words like *what if/pretend*.	What if the South had won the war; how would life be different today? Pretend you are a slave during the Civil War. What might you consider in deciding to join the abolitionist movement?
Evaluative	
These questions call for the exercise of student judgment and/or opinion. No right answers are anticipated, and questions begin with words like *in your opinion* or *which is best*.	Which policy is better: • to avoid war at all costs • to fight for principles one believes in In your opinion, is war a part of the human condition?

riod, why would you be willing to leave your home to come to a strange and dangerous New World?

3. The Constitution of the United States has been called "a bundle of compromises." Why?

4. You are a leader of a newly independent nation of Latin America. How would you feel about the issuance of the Monroe Doctrine?

5. An historian stated, "Geography determined which states would secede from the Union." What did he mean?

6. If you lived in the 1850s, would you have considered John Brown a hero or a murderer? Why?

7. Some historians believe that the Civil War could have been avoided; others feel it was irrepressible. With which view do you agree? Why?

8. How may the art and literature of a period of American history give us a picture of life during that period? Give specific examples.

9. You are an urban planner. What problems must you solve to create cities in which people can live good lives?

10. You are a civil rights leader and you are asked, "How has the Civil Rights Movement changed between 1960 and 1980?" How would you answer this question?

11. If you had been alive in 1920, would you have favored or opposed United States entrance into the League of Nations? Why?

12. In 1973, President Nixon declared that the United States had achieved "peace with honor" in Vietnam. What is your view of this statement? Why?

ETHNIC STUDIES

1. The United States presents an example more of a "salad bowl" than of a "melting pot." Do you agree or disagree? why?

2. Why do you think black Americans have adopted more of the white man's customs and culture than the American Indians?

3. How are the problems of Mexican-Americans similar to or different from those of black Americans and Indians?

4. If you were a Japanese person living in California in 1942, how might you have felt if you had been placed in a concentration camp?

GOVERNMENT

1. It has been said that the exposure of the Watergate conspiracy and its results prove that the American constitutional system works. Explain why you agree or disagree with this point of view.

2. If you had lived in the days of Hamilton and Jefferson, to which political party would you have belonged? Why?

3. It is argued that capital punishment is cruel and, therefore, unconstitutional. Do you agree with this argument? Why?

4. "Juvenile offenders should not be tried in separate courts; they should stand trial in regular courts and have all the protection given to adult defendants." Do you agree or disagree with this statement? Why?

CULTURE STUDIES

1. "The Soviet Union is a prisoner of its geography." Do you agree or disagree with this statement? How does this explain foreign policy?

2. If the Nile River had dried up, how would Egypt's history have been affected?

3. "The Middle East today is the powder keg of World War III." Tell why you agree or disagree with this statement.

4. "The African people are more diverse than the Europeans." Explain this statement. How do you account for the differences in their influence on our thinking today?

5. What do leaders like Mahatma Ghandi, Hitler, and Churchill have in common?

6. How do these three words describe Japan's response to Western influence: *adopt, adapt, adept?*

These types of questions can frame spirited discussions with gifted students in a social studies classroom from the intermediate grades on, given appropriate background reading. The same approach, however, can be used with current events so that discussion is not dependent on prior reading. The emphasis is on the *meaning and process* of history, not the events themselves.

The teaching of interviewing techniques as a research tool in social science can also be stimulating for gifted students. One approach might be to interview mothers and grandmothers about their lives and perceptions they hold about growing up. Sample questions might include:

1. How did your parents discipline you?
2. What were your responsibilities in the household?
3. What expectations did your parents have for you?
4. Would you like to go back to childhood?

Other types of interviews of mothers or family members might center on some of the topics below:

1. Interview grandparents or other family members about a particularly momentous historic time, such as World War II, the Depression, or the Civil Rights Movement. Some of the questions might concern the interviewee's view of the event or time period, how or whether this event affected the interviewer or her family's lives.

2. Some interview topics concerning women in the family might also concentrate more on role differences, perceived or real, such as whether women's roles changed in various generations, or whether being female affected their roles or activities in a particular event.

Another favorite technique in gifted social studies programs is the use of simulations or scenarios that involve students directly in the ethical decision-making process. One example might be:

> You are a school board member faced with allocating limited dollars to a special program. Six programs have been submitted for consideration, each carrying a political liability if you do not select it. What program will you fund and why? (Groups of five students review the set of programs proposed and deliberate.)

Through such a technique, gifted learners are placed in the role of decision makers, given ambiguous data, and forced to make a decision. Such real-life activities help students to understand how decisions are made in the real world and how to grapple with the problems inherent with decision processes.

Using the Concept Model to Organize a Social Studies Curriculum

Shane (1981) worked with scholars throughout the world in the social sciences to determine key ideas for infusion into a social studies curriculum for the year 2000. These ideas include the following:

- Historical understanding of all the world
- Understanding of systems in the world
- Relationship of government and the governed
- Nature of power
- Sense of community
- The "trade-off"
- Economic equity
- An information economy replacing an industrial one
- Cultural pluralism
- Global interdependence

Social studies programs for the gifted might be well served to treat these themes as central to their curriculum planning effort. The following course outline on peace studies (College Board, 1980) exemplifies a way to weave broad conceptual themes into the context of world history.*

A CONCEPTUAL AND CHRONOLOGICAL
SEQUENCING FOR PEACE STUDIES

Unit I (1st week): Introduction to Peace Studies

A. Main Concept: Man reacts to conflict situations by virtue of conditioning and genetics.
B. Topics
   1. Theories of Aggression
   2. How Human Behavior Developed
   3. How We Study Human Behavior

Unit II (2nd & 3rd weeks): Our Ancient Inheritance

A. Main Concept: Men have gone to war for many reasons.
B. Topics
   1. Egypt—Territorial War at the Crossroads
   2. Sparta vs. Greece—Ideological War
   3. Roman Empire—Pax Romanum—Imperian War and Peace—War as it Contributes to Societal Decline
      Also possibly:
      Alexander—War and Cultural Diffusion
   4. Judeo-Christian Concepts of War and Peace

Unit III (4th week): Middle Ages

A. Main Concept: The instinct of flight is cancelled by operant conditions such as loyalty and honor.

---

* From *Beginning an Advanced Placement Course in European History*, Edition C, 1980, College Entrance Examination Board. Reprinted by permission of the College Entrance Examination Board.

B. Topics
   1. Quest for Security—Feudalism
   2. Code of Chivalry
   3. Growth of Towns and Cities (theories of crowding and aggression)

Unit IV (5th week): Renaissance and Reformation

A. Main Concept: Religion has been a force both for war and for peace.
B. Topics
   1. The New Spirit of Man
   2. Diplomacy as Practiced in Italian City States—Machiavelli
   3. Wars of Religion
   4. Wars of Commerce

Unit V (6th week): Age of Revolution

A. Main Concept: Political revolutions have caused some of the bloodiest wars.
B. Topics
   1. Old Regime
   2. French Revolution
   3. Napoleonic Wars
   4. Congress of Vienna–Suppression of Nationalism

Unit VI (7th week): World War I and its Aftermath

A. Main Concept: Modern warfare is hell.
B. Topics
   1. The Industrial Revolution and the Increase in Man's Ability to Destroy
   2. Causes of War
   3. Results
   4. The League and its Failure

This outline presents an elegant way to combine several approaches to organizing a social studies curriculum for the gifted. It presents the chronological approach so favored by many teachers, yet it gives the chronology a topical focus, namely, peace studies. Furthermore, it frames each unit with a key concept or idea that is representative of both the time period and the broad topic. The topic of peace and its antithesis war are viewed across time and culture so that key ideas can be highlighted at the moment of their greatest relevance. It is a perfect blend of content and concept considerations.

Taba and Hills (1965) focused a social studies curriculum around the process skills necessary to form generalizations through providing a unifying theme and selected content. The step-by-step process outline is delineated below:

STEPS IN THE FORMATION OF A GENERALIZATION*

Goal: Understand the generalization:

CIVILIZATIONS CHANGE WHEN THEY MEET A NEW CULTURE

---

* Source: H. Taba and J. L. Hills, *Teacher Handbook for Contra Costa Social Studies, Grades 1–6* (San Francisco State College, 1965), p. 103.

Specific content: study of Bolivia, Argentina, Mexico

Step 1: **Learning Facts About Various Countries**
    Sample Teacher Questions:
        What is the climate like where the Aztecs lived?
        What are major trade items for this country?
    Sample Assignment:
        Make a map and chart showing centers of populations and chief exports and
        buyers, education, major work of the people, etc.

Step 2: **Discrimination of Unique Elements in Various Cultures**
    Sample Teacher Questions:
        What differences do you notice among these different civilizations?
        How do you account for these differences?
    Sample Assignment:
        Write a short story of a Mexican child visiting Argentina. Emphasize all of the
        things he or she might see that would be different from his own experience.
        Try to explain the reasons for the differences.

Step 3: **Drawing Inferences About Differences**
    Sample Teachers Questions:
        Suppose explorers from a different part of the world (i.e., Japan) landed in
        Mexico or Bolivia; how would life be different there today?
    Sample Assignment:
        Find three or four elements in present day culture that can be traced back to
        the original explorers.

Step 4: **Finding Generalizations About Cultures**
    Sample Teacher Questions:
        What common things can you find in all of these cultures?
        (governments, education, trade, etc.)
    Sample Assignment:
        Rewrite the short story of the Mexican child. Concentrate on the experience
        that would be familiar to him or her.

Step 5: **Generalization Application**
    Sample Teacher Questions:
        Can we see how the kind of influence the discoverers had on Bolivia, Argen-
        tina, etc., was reproduced here in our country?
        How does our current government reflect the nature of our colonizers?
        What is likely to happen if we meet a more primitive culture when we land
        on Mars?
        What changes would we expect to see in that culture?

These concepts then are used as a framework for student activities that promote higher level thinking skills via Bloom's taxonomy.

    VanTassel-Baska and Feldhusen (1981) have edited social studies units for the gifted around four main themes: change, signs and symbols, reason, and problem solving. These units were developed to be used in either pull-out programs or self-contained classrooms and have been field-tested in both. The primary unit for signs and symbols includes the following sample instructional objective and set of activities:

Objective: Gifted students will be able to analyze the history of writing and the development of the alphabet as a code.

Activities:

1. Read, research, and report on the invention of the alphabet in the Middle East, Ancient land of Canaan, about 1000 B.C.
2. Study how Greeks adapted this alphabet and changed it to fit their language.
3. Make a scroll demonstrating Greek transformations of letters.
4. Create your own alphabet, and shape its features with your classmates.
5. Compose a twenty-word telegram using your own alphabet.
6. Make a scrapbook using photographs, drawings, cut outs, and so on, illustrating different methods of communication.
7. Choose one letter of the alphabet and research the development and significance of it. Share with classmates in an oral presentation.

Using *Cities of Destiny* by Arnold Toynbee (1967) as a key resource, the "change" concept unit for intermediate grades focuses on the growth pattern of cities as a strategy for understanding the growth of societal institutions and social systems. Following is a content outline from that unit:

WHAT MAKES A GREAT CITY?

Prototype: Rome

 I. Structures
   A. Design
   B. Architecture
 II. Societal Governance
   A. Classes
   B. Form of Government
   C. Influence of the Military
III. Sustenance Issues
   A. Food
   B. Clothes
   C. Work
IV. Science and Inventions
   A. The Balance
   B. Aqueducts
   C. Arches
 V. The Arts
   A. Sculpture
   B. Drama
   C. Music
VI. Beliefs and Values
   A. Pagan→Christian
   B. Epicureanism/Stoicism
VII. Language
   A. The Oral Tradition
   B. The Written Record

Thus students can come to understand the organism of a city and the degree to which great cities become cultural metaphors over time.

Using Specific Topics to Organize a Social Studies Curriculum

Lebeau (1979) and Fearn and Fearn (1983) have developed curricula for use with gifted students that focus on understanding law and its implications for citizenship, character development, and leadership. The course outline for a gifted high-school offering at Chelmsford High School, Chelmsford, Massachusetts, in Comprehensive Law follows:

COURSE OUTLINE

I. History of U.S. Jurisprudence
   A. Study of pre-Biblical and Mosaic Law and their moral and ethical contributions to standards of justice.
   B. Study of Greek and Roman Law and their contributions to a formalized legal code.
   C. Study of British Common Law as the foundation for the U.S. Constitution and civil jurisprudence.

II. The Bill of Rights
   A. The historic reasons for their inclusions in the U.S. Constitution.
   B. The application of Amendments I, IV, V, VI, VIII, XIII, XIV, IX, XIX
   C. An in-depth study of the ramifications of the proposed Amendment

III. Logic and Values
   A. Study and application of logic
      1. Syllogistics
      2. Judgments
      3. Moral Reasoning
      4. Analysis of data
      5. Cumulative arguments

IV. Supreme Court Decisions
   A. The process of judicial review and its application to the Constitution.
   B. The study of major Supreme Court cases, citing basic problem(s) for both defense and prosecution.
   C. The historic milieu in which the Supreme Court accepted the appeals

V. Visits from Professionals in the Field of Law
   A. Attorneys
   B. Social Workers
   C. Paralegals
   D. Police Officers

VI. Independent Study
   A. Research on any court case of interest to students.

B. In-depth investigation on the facts, issues, evidence, and testimony in the chosen case.

C. Support of or opposition to the court's decision.

Gallagher et al. (1982) have developed a unit for gifted students on leadership from a political science perspective. Usable with students from grades 4–8 in a social studies program, the unit focuses on important concepts regarding the nature of leadership.

LEADERSHIP UNIT—CONCEPTS

1. Leadership is the exercise of power to achieve the goals of the leader or the leader and followers.

2. Influence is the use of persuasion to achieve change; power is the use of force to achieve change.

3. There are many different types of leaders who play different roles (traditional, legal, charismatic, active/passive, positive/negative).

4. Different leaders are needed to meet different circumstances (establishing goals, creating structures to reach goals, maintaining or enhancing these structures).

5. There are many ways to become a leader.

ELEMENTARY PROGRAMS IN THE SOCIAL STUDIES

Most elementary programs are apt to serve the gifted in the regular classroom or in a pullout/resource room framework. In the regular classroom, the regular social studies curriculum serves all, but the gifted may be given opportunities individually or in small groups to study selected topics in depth and thereby learn special study, research, or library skills. In a resource room setting, the same opportunities may be provided but with more explicit guidance from the resource teacher. Developing or adapting specialized units of study in the social sciences may represent the most practical approach to curriculum development in these groupings. If grouping practices can be modified, it would be preferable for the gifted to have an instructional grouping in the social studies areas throughout the elementary grades.

The classic curriculum developed for use at the elementary level that provides for gifted learners in all key dimensions is Bruner's (1970) *Man: A Course of Study*. This curriculum has been used very successfully in school district gifted programs from grades 4–8. It offers learners an opportunity to explore the differences in values, beliefs, and attitudes across cultures. Rich in the variety of activities it provides, MACOS also has films that depict the cultural life studied.

SECONDARY PROGRAMS IN THE SOCIAL STUDIES

At the middle-school level, gifted students either get individualized treatment and special project opportunities in the regular classroom comparable to the elementary model, or they are enrolled in a special honors class or seminar for gifted learners. In the latter case, a greater exposure to the content of the disciplines is likely to occur along with a strong emphasis on inquiry activities focused on major themes, issues, and concepts in selected disciplines (e.g., history, psychology, economics). At the high-school level, gifted learners may be enrolled in an honors section or a College Board Advanced Placement class (e.g., American history or European history) in which the major focus is on the discipline and its methodology, with an emphasis on discussion, research, and problem solving. Gifted students may also elect to take social studies courses early and thereby accelerate their program in this area. This approach can provide time to participate in special programs like the Executive Internship Program, headquartered in Springfield, Illinois, which invites able seniors to spend a semester working in state government and participating in a weekly seminar regarding their experiences.

Issues in Implementing Curricula for the Gifted in Social Studies

Developing and implementing a curriculum for the gifted in social studies involves a priori decisions concerning program goals, program models, meeting individual student needs, the role of the disciplines, and the commitment to acceleration and enrichment approaches. But at the stage of implementation, there may be a need to confront other issues as well.

1. Finding a balance between enrichment and acceleration in the social studies seems judicious. Enrichment in the social studies can often come as a result of acceleration through basic social studies courses, which then frees the gifted student for specialized learning activities. Students who complete the U.S. History material in less time can be freed for an indepth study of the historical antecedents of the War in Vietnam. Or students may undertake an extended study of current political organization in African governments and how those structures grew out of the large infusion of financial aid from European countries, Canada, and the United States.

2. Another implementation issue deals with the modification in the instructional processes needed to move toward actualizing the goals stated at the beginning of this chapter as important for social science programs for the gifted. In order to accommodate content, process, product, and concept goals, the teacher must ensure that instructional time is used effectively and that content material is organized well. Otherwise, the differentiation for gifted learners is lost. At the secondary level, to group gifted learners for American history and then do nothing to modify the curriculum and instructional approach is to defeat the purpose of having a special program. Modifying material without also altering instructional technique is also insufficient.

3. Since using the inquiry approach and teaching research skills are viewed as important goals in social science programs for the gifted, the issue of staff development is crucial. Teachers need to be trained to use inquiry techniques and to be monitored on their effective implementation with students in the classroom through videotape and playback techniques or another form of peer evaluation.

Training in the research methodology of the social sciences would also be useful for teachers who will be engaging students in these procedures.

4. At the secondary level, planning cooperative units of study with teachers from other departments is one way to enhance the study of cultures and their underlying systems. Using foreign language teachers, English teachers, and art and music teachers to reflect their perspectives on a given cultural period may contribute greatly to the education gained by gifted learners.

5. Choosing outside speakers effectively is another issue to consider at the implementation stage of social science programs. Too often choices are made based on the general field that an adult in the community happens to be practicing in, rather than selecting speakers who can address the impact of social policy in a particular field of the social sciences. Establishing criteria for speakers who come into gifted programs is important:

   a. Speakers should be knowledgeable on issues or problems that the group is studying.

   b. Speakers should be willing to engage gifted learners in discussion about this topic.

   c. Speakers should be attuned to the conceptual level that gifted learners can function and gear their presentation accordingly.

   d. Speakers should help meet a predetermined learning objective rather than only be used as an additional resource.

   e. Speakers should be willing to follow-up on their topic with materials, a visit to the workplace, a return engagement, or individual consultation with a student.

6. A strong focus on the well-organized essay as a grading standard in social science programs should be considered. Not only does this approach lend itself well to the interdisciplinary nature of the material, but it also prepares gifted learners in expository writing skills that are necessary to articulate concepts at high levels of abstraction.

Conclusion

Gifted students can experience high-level, challenging interactions with the world of ideas and learn the skills of critical, creative, and logical thinking in the social sciences. There is an abundance of material in the social sciences to provide enriching experiences beyond the regular curriculum, but, above all, that curriculum must be fast paced and accelerated to provide appropriately challenging learning experiences for the gifted.

KEY POINTS SUMMARY

- The major goals of a social science curriculum for gifted learners are to (1) develop critical thinking and inquiry, (2) understand world cultures, (3) appreciate the relationships among social science disciplines, (4) know major developments in history, and (5) be skilled in social science research.

- Social science curricula for the gifted can be organized by either content topic, a set of broad concepts, or a key area for study within the structure of the discipline.
- An inquiry approach to instruction is most appropriate for teaching the social science curriculum.
- Many model programs in social science for the gifted stress topics such as global interdependence, futures study, law, and leadership.
- Implementation issues to consider include: maintaining a balance between accelerative and enrichment practices, modifying curriculum and instructional processes rather than just materials, staff development, interdepartment planning at the secondary level, selecting speakers, and using the essay as a principal evaluation tool.

References

The Association of Teachers of Social Studies in the City of New York (1977). *A Handbook for the Teaching of Social Studies.* Boston: Allyn and Bacon.

Adams, J. E. (undated). *Environmental Studies from a Global Perspective.* Muncie, Ind.: Ball State University (Burris-Ball State School Corporation).

Barr, R. D., Barth, J. L., and Shermis, S. S. (1977). *Defining the Social Studies.* Washington, D.C.: National Council for the Social Studies.

Barth, J. L., and Shermis, S. S. (1981). *Teaching Social Studies to the Gifted and Talented.* Indianapolis: Indiana Department of Public Instruction.

Bruner, J. (Ed.) (1970). *Man: A Course of Study.* Washington, D.C.: Curriculum Associates.

California State Department of Education (1977). *Curriculum Guide for Teaching Gifted Children Social Sciences in Grades One Through Three.* Sacramento: California State Department of Education.

California State Department of Education (1977). *Curriculum Guide for Teaching Gifted Children Social Sciences in Grades Four Through Six.* Sacramento: California State Department of Education.

California State Department of Education (1977). *Curriculum Guide for Teaching Gifted Children Social Sciences in Grades Seven Through Nine.* Sacramento: California State Department of Education.

College Entrance Examination Board (1980). *Beginning an Advanced Placement Course in European History,* Edition C. Princeton, N.J.: Educational Testing Service.

Fearn, L., and Fearn, C. (1983). *Citizenship and Character Development.* San Diego, Calif.: San Diego Unified School District.

Flachner, J., and Hirst, B. (1976). *200 Years: A Study of Democracy.* New York: Aston Program.

Gallagher, J., et al. (1982). *Leadership Unit.* New York: Trillium Press.

Keener, C. (undated). *A Curricular Approach for Global Studies.* Muncie, Ind.: Ball State University (Burris-Ball State School Corporation).

LeBeau, M. (1979). *Comprehensive Law*. Chelmsford, Mass.: Chelmsford High School.

Schug, M. C. (1981). "Using the Local Community to Improve Citizenship Education for the Gifted." *Roeper Review*, 4(2), 22–23.

Scriven, M. (1964). "A Model of the Social Sciences." In J. Schwab (Ed.), *Education and the Structure of Knowledge*. Chicago: Rand McNally and Co.

Shane, H. (1981). *A Study of Curriculum Content for the Future*. New York: College Entrance Examination Board.

Shaver, P. (1984). "Social Studies Education for the Gifted." *Roeper Review*, 7(1), 4–7.

Shermis, S. S., and Clinkenbeard, P. R. (1981). "History Texts for the Gifted: A Look at the Past Century." *Roeper Review*, 4(2), 19–21.

Taba, H., and Hills, J. L. (1965). *Teacher Handbook for Contra Costa Social Studies, Grades 1–6*. San Francisco: San Francisco State College.

Toynbee, A. (1967). *Cities of Destiny*. New York: Weathervane Books.

VanTassel-Baska, J., and Feldhusen, J. (1981). *Concept Curriculum for the Gifted*. Matteson, Ill.: Matteson School District #162.

EXAMPLE 7.A Gifted Social Studies Syllabus: Chicago Public Schools Gifted Program, K–12

YOSSEL NAIMAN
COORDINATOR OF CURRICULUM EFFORT

KINDERGARTEN

GEOGRAPHY

Gifted kindergarten geography curriculum encompasses study of the physical world through the examination of maps and globes. It is expected that children in gifted programs exit with the ability to recognize the names and locations of the world's continents, major oceans, major rivers, the States of the Union, the City of Chicago, the poles, the climate zones, the equator, the hemispheres, the major longitudinal and latitudinal lines of demarcation, and the concepts of right, left, horizontal, vertical, above, below, and up and down.

PSYCHOLOGY

It is expected that children in gifted kindergarten programs exit with the ability to differentiate between basic needs and wants of both the individual and family and to identify the various roles and behaviors of family members and their interdependent relationships.

ECONOMICS

Students will exit kindergarten with the ability to understand the concepts of "right of ownership," title, property and the exchange of goods and services; and will be able to identify and classify various occupations as service, manufacturing, and agricultural.

HISTORY

Students will exit kindergarten with a conceptual framework for past, present, and future, the history of their families, and a minimal awareness of current events. They will be able to perceive the relationship between past events, present events, and the implications for future events.

FIRST GRADE

GEOGRAPHY

Gifted children will leave the first grade level able to define, locate, and give examples of the following topographical terms: desert, forest, island, lake, mountain, peninsula, plain, river, valley, and volcano. They will exit first grade with the ability to read map symbols related to elevation, population, transportation, resources, industries, and topographical features. They will be able to apply coordinates to a map of the City of Chicago to locate major points of interest, transportation, roads, recreational sites, governmental stations, and cultural institutions.

PSYCHOLOGY

Gifted students exit first grade with the ability to differentiate between specific primary needs—food, air, clothing, housing, sleep, and protection from harm; and specific secondary needs for acceptance, approval, respect, and love. They will examine, discuss, and compare various behaviors people have developed to fulfill those secondary needs.

ECONOMICS

Gifted students at the first grade level will define and give examples of the following terms: production, distribution, and consumption; producer, distributor, and consumer; goods and services; technology, and commerce; and the divisions of agriculture, manufacturing, transportation.

HISTORY

History will be examined by the students from two perspectives: that of the individual, and that of the communities from which they emanate. Students will examine and discuss community events, past and present. They will write their personal history. They will survey the history of Chicago covering major topics beginning with early settlement, the advent of the city charter, industrialization, waves of immigration, urbanization, and the major personages. They will investigate the cultural contribution of various communities, and will study important people who made major contributions to American Life who came from Chicago.

POLITICAL SCIENCE

The political science aspect of the program will focus on the definitions of terms as follows: city, state, nation. Students will study the structure of each of these governmental entities and how each impacts on groups in the areas of law, services, taxes, and elections. Using Chicago as an example, students will focus on the "mayor-council" type of city government, the ward system, city departments, the political parties and their structure, and leaders who affect public decisions.

SOCIOLOGY

Students will discuss roles within the school, community, and neighborhood. They will learn of the hierarchies of administrations that exist within each of the three, and show the interrelationships that exist. Beginning with the students' immediate classroom, students will expand knowledge of their school, and community organizations such as the student council, the PTA, the Advisory Council, block clubs and other organizations.

ANTHROPOLOGY

Students will locate the points of origin of racial groups on a world map. Using the class's ethnic composition, students will locate the points of origin of each of the ethnic groups represented on a world map. They will classify those groups according to their language families. After defining the term, students will examine the customs, traditions, and the folkways of the groups studied.

SECOND GRADE
GEOGRAPHY

The geography strand will continue with the study of definitions of geographic terms. To further develop their ability to locate specific places on a map or globe, students will use coordinates accurate to the nearest degree. Other map and globe skills will include the memorization of names and locations of the 50 states and selected major cities.

The students will categorize the following modes of transportation according to air, land, sea: airplanes, ships, trucks, trains, pipelines, ferries, barges, buses, automobiles. They will use maps showing major routes within the United States.

PSYCHOLOGY

The students will define the following terms associated with the growth and development of personality; peer group, identity, self-concept, environment, interaction, and leadership. The students will explore the conflicts that affect the development of their identity and self-concept; individual vs. society, individual vs. nature, individual vs. self. The students will recognize the interplay of aggression, ambition, dominance, and reward/punishment.

HISTORY

The students will trace the history of Illinois from early explorers, settlement, Indians, statehood, immigration, Lincoln, Civil War, famous people and growth of Chicago to the present day. Their studies will include identification of Illinois borders, neighboring states, bodies of water, population centers (including the capital), distribution of resources, and recreational areas.

Students will write a family history in narrative form covering two generations. The concepts of ancestry and genealogy will be introduced and defined.

POLITICAL SCIENCE

Students will define and study concepts of law, government, legislative branch, executive branch, judicial branch, rules, written law, and unwritten law. Students will discuss such questions as: Who makes the law? Why do societies have laws? What might happen in a society without laws? Who enforces the law? Who interprets the law? How are laws changed? What can be done about unfair laws? How is Illinois government organized? How is the United States government organized?

THIRD GRADE

GEOGRAPHY

A continuing focus of the geography strand of the social studies program concerns the study of the various regions of the western hemisphere in respect to the distribution of natural resources, the climates, the industrial development, the cultures represented, the governmental structures in place, and the economics of each of those regions. In that study, students will compare and contrast single product and diversified economies. The entities to be studied include: Canada, the United States, Mexico, Central America, the Carribean Region, and various regions of South America.

PSYCHOLOGY

Continuing in the psychology strand, students will discuss values, beliefs, attitudes as they have observed them. Questions will be presented such as: What beliefs do you have that affect your life? What do you value? What attitudes do you have as a result of the beliefs and values you have? Students will list characteristics of leadership and examine specific types of leaders and leadership. Using what they have learned about beliefs, values, attitudes and leadership, the students will develop a basic understanding of group dynamics.

RESEARCH SKILLS

In order to prepare for research assignments, the students will read and analyze statements for examples of bias, assumption and generalization, conclusion and clarity.

FOURTH GRADE

GEOGRAPHY

Geography will include the study of the following regions: Europe, North Africa/Middle East, Sub-Saharan Africa, Asia, Australia/Indonesia. Students will compare and contrast the distribution of natural resources, climates, industries, and economies. Students will examine indepth, cultures, governmental structures and economies of a country representative of each region, distinguishing between diversified and single product-based economies. Students will also review the political and physical geography of the regions.

HISTORY

In a survey of world history of early man to the decline of the Roman Empire, the students will study the following units: (1) Prehistoric man, (2) Early River Valley Civilizations of the Near East and Far East, (3) Later Civilizations of the Near East, (4) Aegean World/Greece, (5) Roman Civilization to Constantine. The students will develop an understanding of the political, social and economic structures and cultural aspects of the respective units.

SOCIOLOGY

Students will define these terms: conflict, conformity, interaction, leadership, perception, prejudice stereotypes, bias, and propaganda. They will explore how conflict, conformity and types of leadership affect group interaction. Questions to be addressed are: What determines who succeeds as a leader? What determines which leaders a group will accept or reject? Does communication help a group achieve its goals? Why do people conform? When can conformity be good? bad? Can conflict be both positive and negative? They will also explore how prejudice, stereotypes, bias and propaganda affect individual and group interaction. Questions such as: What are the techniques of propaganda? Is it natural for people to believe in the superiority of their group? (ethnocentrism, chauvinism, nationalism, patriotism) Is hatred inherited or learned? Can hatred be learned? How does a group get stereotyped? How might a stereotype be changed?

RESEARCH SKILLS

Students will select a topic, use appropriate sources, organize information, and produce a written report for oral presentation.

FIFTH GRADE

HISTORY

In a survey of world history from the decline of the Roman Empire to Revolutionary Period of the 18th Century, the students will study the following units: (1) Christianity and the Fall of Rome, (2) Rise of Germanic Kingdoms/Vikings, (3) Rise and Expansion of Islam, (4) Byzantine Empire/Russians, (5) Age of Feudalism (including Japan and Mayan), (6) Late Middle Ages-Trade, Monarchies and Cities, (7) Renaissance and Growth of Nation States, (8) Reformation, (9) Age of Exploration (including Incas and Aztecs), (10) Rise of Mercantilism/Colonialism, (11) Political Revolutions/English, American and French, (12) Russia and Prussia. The students will develop an understanding of the political, social and economic structures and cultural aspects of the respective units.

PHILOSOPHY

In their introduction to philosophy, the students will explore philosophy and establish it as a discipline which attempts to explain the human condition. The students will define ethics and examine ethical theories and representative theorists. The following theories and theorists should be included: Aristotle, Plato, Hedonism (Epicurus), Stoicism (Epictetus); Relativism (Spinoza); Utilitarianism (Mill), Naturalism (Rousseau); Pragmatism (Dewey); Existentialism (Sartre) and K'Ling Fu-Tiu Confucius. Questions to be studied will include: (1) What is a good life? (2) How should man behave? (3) What is a good society? (4) Which is the higher virtue—truth or justice? (5) Upon what premise do each of the philosophers base their conclusions?

RESEARCH SKILLS

Students will select a topic, use a variety of sources, organize information, and produce a library research project. It is expected that the student will also review political and physical geography as it pertains to the historical topic being considered.

SIXTH GRADE

HISTORY

In a survey of world history from 18th Century Political Revolutions to the present, students will study the following units: (1) Non-political revolutions (Industrial, Scientific and Age of Reason); (2) Napoleonic Era; (3) National Independence Movements—Italy, Germany, South America; (4) Building of Empires; (5) World War I; (6) Russian Revolution; (7) Chinese Revolution; (8) Rise of Fascism; (9) Worldwide Depression; (10) World War II, (11) Cold War; (12) Emerging Nations.

The students will develop an understanding of the political, social and economic and cultural aspects of the period. It is expected that students will also review the physical, political and economic geography as it pertains to the historical topic being considered.

PHILOSOPHY

The philosophy strand continues as the students define "politics" as a discipline. They will study the following theorists: Plato, Aristotle, Confucius, Machiavelli, Hobbes, Spinoza, Locke, Rousseau, Burke, Mill, and Marx. The students will seek the answers to these questions: What is the ultimate justification for any form of government? Who should rule? What should be the limits of governmental power (individual liberty)? For whose benefit? Within this strand the students will select a topic, use a variety of sources expressing opposing viewpoints, organize the information and produce a library research report.

SEVENTH GRADE

ECONOMICS

Students will develop a foundational understanding of capitalism through the study of economic organizations and institutions, factors involved in production and distribution of goods and services and major economists and their theories. The students will identify the structure and interrelationships of the following institutions and organizations: sole proprietorships, partnerships, corporations, unions (trade labor), cooperatives, professional associations, governmental institutions regulatory agencies, financial institutions, monopoly and oligopoly. It is recommended that these theorists be studied: Adam Smith, T. Veblen, J. S. Mill, M. Keynes, T. Malthus, J. B. Clark, J. K. Galbraith and M. Friedman.

ANTHROPOLOGY

The students will compare and contrast various cultures throughout history, specifically:

At least two of the following: Tasaday, Netsilik, Australian Aborigine, Kalahari Bushman, Hebrews and Sioux.

Mayans with one or more: Iroquois, Pueblo, Kwakiutl, and Norman England.

Periclean Athens with 1 or more: Ancient Ghana, Ancient Maili, Ancient Songhai, Kush and Axum.

Minimally 2 of the following: Asoka India, Chou Dynasty, Tokagawa Shogunate, and Arman Egyptian.

Minimally 2 of the following: the Kenyatti Kenyan Revolution, Ghandi's Indian Revolution, the Castro Revolution of Cuba, Juarez's revolution in Mexico.

Postwar Japan with one or more: Mao's China, Modern Brazil and Stalin's Russia.

Renaissance Venice with one or more: Byzantine Empire, the Abbasid Caliphate, the Mongol Empire and Moorish Spain.

The following topics will be covered: social organization, economic organization, political organization, moral and ethical behavior; education, expression of aesthetic needs, communication and leisure time activities.

PHILOSOPHY

The student will define "aesthetics" as a discipline. He will study the following theorists: Plato, Aristotle, George Santayana, Alexander Baumgarten, Thomas Monroe, Benedito Croce, and John Dewey. The students will seek answers to the questions: What is beauty? Where does beauty reside? What is art? What is the purpose of art? What is the value of art?

EIGHTH GRADE

HISTORY

Students will study key conflicts in American history including:

a. States' rights vs. centralized governments.
b. Open vs. closed immigration.
c. Civil rights.
d. Urban vs. rural settlement.
e. Isolationism vs. internationalism.
f. Territorial expansion.
g. Laissez-faire vs. controlled capitalism.
h. Exploitation of natural resources.
i. Passivism vs. militarism.
j. Civil disobedience.

POLITICAL SCIENCE

Students will analyze the federal and state constitutions, comparing and contrasting the structures and functions of the 3 branches of the various levels of government. They will analyze and evaluate the effect of the following on government: media, peer pressure, political parties, public opinion, surveys and voter participation. Students will compare and contrast the structure and function of the following governments: Great Britain, France and the Soviet Union with that of the United States.

PHILOSOPHY

In an introduction to semantics, the students will study logic as a means of argument. The students will analyze propositions for truth, validity, soundness and they will study inductive and deductive reasoning. They will study the medium of language in terms of the relationships between language and thought, speech and language, signs and symbols, and words and things. The students will be introduced to the informal fallacies of ambiguity, presumption, and relevance.

NINTH GRADE

SOCIOLOGY

One semester in the 9th grade will be spent in the discipline of sociology. They will interpret major theorists including: Durkheim, Summer, Ward Reisman, Owen, Marx, Parsons, Boaz, Mead, and the social criticism of Jonathan Swift and Jane Addams. Students will study the methodologies of language factor, participant observation, comparison of institutions, sample survey, contrasting methods and community studies. They will use those methodologies in analyzing the following topics: aging, hunger and population, ethnic minority groups, family and marriage, urban problems, social stratification and mobility.

MACROECONOMICS

The other semester in the 9th grade will be spent in the discipline of macroeconomics. They will interpret major theorists including: Barbara Ward, J. K. Galbraith, P. Samuelson, Robert Browne, J. S. Jevous, and Karl Marx. They will utilize the vocabulary and the concepts presented by the theorist plus factors of measurement in analyzing changing conditions. They will analyze the interdependency of national markets with a global perspective. They will examine within the same framework specific issues, i.e., gold and silver markets, prime interest, lending rates, oil pricing mechanisms, etc. They will examine the economics of capitalist, socialist, communist and third world developing countries, analyzing the influence of politics and political philosophy on the allocation of scarce resources.

TENTH GRADE

THEORY OF KNOWLEDGE

In one semester of the 10th grade, the students will investigate the Theory of Knowledge (Epistemology) branch of philosophy by examining how selected philosophers answered these questions: What are the sources from which man derives knowledge?

What can man know? What is the nature of truth? What are the standards of criteria by which man can reliably judge the truth or falsity of our knowledge? The philosophers to be studied include: Aristotle, Plato, Descartes, Auguste Comte, Bertrand Russell, and J. S. Mill.

LAW

The other semester of the 10th grade will be devoted to the study of law. A study of the history of the Supreme Court will enable students to determine how the Supreme Court operates, how the concept of judicial review was developed, how justices are selected, how the Court has influenced and affected American life, and how decisions are implemented. The students will analyze and interpret selected Supreme Court cases.

ELEVENTH GRADE
MODERN EUROPEAN STUDIES

The 11th year program is Modern European Studies, incorporating history at the college level that will prepare students if they choose to take an advanced placement modern European History examination. The course will focus on the interpretation of historical philosophers such as: Spengler, Toynbee, Hegel, Marx, Croce, Ranke, Gibbons, Durant and de Tocqueville. Students will write interpretive essays, research papers from original documents and will take notes from lectures and printed sources. Students will analyze major historical themes in Modern European History. In addition to the political approach, students will analyze significant work of individuals and then works in science, art, architecture, music and literature. They will examine the impact their contributions have had on the development of modern European History.

TWELFTH GRADE
AMERICAN STUDIES

In the 12th grade, students will study advanced placement American History. In making demands upon the students equivalent to those of a full year introductory college course, the focus will be to weigh the evidence and interpretations presented in historical scholarship and to arrive at conclusions on the basis of informed judgment. Students will be provided with the analytical skills and factual knowledge necessary to deal critically with the themes of American History. This course will prepare students if they choose to take an advanced placement examination. In addition to political themes, students will analyze significant works of individuals in science, art, architecture, music and literature. They will examine these people and the impact of their contributions to the development of American History.

SELECTED RESOURCES

The American People: A History, published by D. C. Heath and Co., 1986 (secondary level)

This text is structured to help students understand more than the skeleton of historical facts. Its unit and chapter organization, study aids, and supplemental materials are designed to lead students through the continuous flow of history—the causes, the effects, the comparisons, the contrasts and the repetitions. The student text organization is clear, and each chapter begins with an opener that provides an overview of the chapter's material as well as a bridge from the material previously studied. The opener also contains a chapter outline and a timeline. Section reviews contain excellent critical thinking questions.

Comprehensive Law Curriculum, published through Chelmsford High School, Chelmsford, MA, Marcia Lebeau, Coordinator, 1979 (secondary level).

This curriculum provides an extensive course syllabus on the teaching of law to gifted secondary students. It stresses the moral and ethical complexities of the legal system and was developed in cooperation with the local bar association.

Curriculum on Aging, published by the San Diego County Board of Education, Office of the Superintendent, San Diego County, California, 1982 (elementary K–6).

The *Curriculum on Aging* is organized around four themes of aging. They are: Process of Aging, Aging in the United States, Image of Aging, and Preparation of Aging. Guided by topical goals, the material is ungraded and interdisciplinary in nature. The program materials are in kit form and are designed so that they can be utilized in a wide variety of school settings.

Man: A Course of Study (MACOS), published by Curriculum Associates, Washington, D.C., 1970 (elementary/middle school level).

This program features a strong emphasis on understanding cultural differences. It provides a series of cultural vignettes through which students come to understand and appreciate multiple value systems. The inquiry process in discussion and other activities is a dominant instructional approach.

Portraits of Our Mothers by Frances Kolb, published by The Network Inc., Andover, MA, 1983 (elementary/middle school level).

This compilation of resources about women, their ideas and their lives, constitutes an excellent supplement to other materials. Ideas for research projects are included.

8 Science Curriculum for the Gifted

Joyce VanTassel-Baska

Between impulse and action, to interpose evidence, reason, and judgment.

—Paul Brandwein

Perhaps no curriculum area better captures the natural curiosity and intellectual spirit of gifted students than does science. It is the basic area of interest for many gifted children from their earliest years on. Blurton (1983) reviewed the literature on the early backgrounds of famous scientists and found the majority of studies showed childhood interest in science by the age of five years. Also present in their histories was an early home laboratory. However, this early interest of the gifted in science is rarely matched with an appropriate curriculum within the school context.

Given the current outcry regarding the lack of good general science education in our schools, it may be difficult to convince educators of the need to focus on a differentiated science program for gifted learners. In some respects, if the general science program were upgraded, it would result in more appropriate curricular intervention for the gifted, especially at the elementary level. The National Science Teachers Association (NSTA) has published a monograph that cites key areas for general science education improvement (Harms and Yager, 1981):

CURRICULUM
- should be problem-centered, flexible, and culturally as well as scientifically valid.
- should include humankind as the central ingredient.
- should be multifaceted with a local and community relevance.
- should use the natural environment, community resources, and current concerns.
- should share a perspective that scientific information can be used in a cultural/social environment.

INSTRUCTION
- should be individualized and personalized.
- should constitute cooperative work on problems and issues.
- should be based on current research in developmental psychology.

A review of these areas reflects the degree to which current science programs are textbook-centered, project a narrow view of scientific investigation, and train students to find one right answer. Clearly, current practices are as damaging to gifted learners as they are to all other learners.

It is important to stress, however, that the broad applications perspective of science taken by NSTA as the road to improvement may have some pitfalls for gifted learners. They need intensive work in science areas; they need many opportunities to master the inquiry process at a rigorous level. Consequently, in their curriculum, a better balance will need to be maintained between real-world applications of science and the pursuit of learning to do science in sufficient depth. Fortunately, there are excellent models available for science programs for gifted learners that provide a basis for understanding science in depth and that allow the learners to experience the real world of science firsthand.

Key Components of Science Programs for the Gifted

There are several key components to an appropriate science program for gifted learners. One of these is a strong emphasis on inquiry-based activities. Sternberg (1982) has outlined this major focus for gifted learners:

> . . . science education can and should be made more realistic, and should include training in problem finding, problem solving, problem reevaluation, and scientific reporting. Not only can such training be made realistic and representative of what scientists do, but it can serve as a motivator to those whose gifts may lie elsewhere. In this way, those who choose a career in science can make their choice on the basis of what doing science is like, rather than on the basis of a fiction that may resemble the style of academic coursework, but not the style of scientific research (p. 4).

An appropriate science curriculum for the gifted should also reflect an emphasis on more independent laboratory work, more extensive reading and emphasis on the skills of using the library, and more true experimental work (Brandwein, 1958).

A second key component to an appropriate science curriculum for the gifted is the mastery of the content of science, preferably in the context of scientific method. Concern for students' understanding the structure of knowledge in science has been cited as an important goal in science programs (Connelly, 1969). In a recent analysis of the effects of curriculum materials, it was found that students generally learned the specific content areas of science (biology, chemistry, etc.) to which they were exposed. However, in the case of the National Science Foundation curriculum materials, which are strongly content-oriented and which include BSCS biology, Chemistry study, IPS Science, and PSSC physics, students improved more in the areas of process skills, analytical skills, and creativity when compared to students using other curricula (Welch, 1984). Other researchers have also stressed the importance of learning science content. Ausubel (1965) advocated the presentation of an organized body of knowledge within science as an end in itself; and Klopfer (1969) argued for a careful curriculum sequence in science. Thus science curriculum that not only has a significant content base but is strong conceptually can enhance the development of skills critical for doing science.

A third key component of effective science programs for the gifted is the opportunity for students to interact with practicing scientists as mentors, teachers, and role models. One of the scientists who has worked with talented students in special programs presented a number of skills that scientists must master (Haugen, 1984):

- Quantitative observation; attention to detail
- Mathematical approaches (computation, statistics, modeling)
- Skills in learning, acquiring information, inquiry organization
- Deductive reasoning; problem solving
- Oral and written communication (reporting methods, results, conclusions, plans, persuasive communication)
- Use of computers to store and analyze data and information
- Electrical and mechanical skills

The mentor's involvement with students increases their understanding of the real world of science in ways not possible through a typical classroom. Furthermore, scientists can work directly with students on developing research proposals and sharing the nature of their own research. Students can then come to value the scientific method as they see it applied in a specialized setting. In this context, students gain appreciation of scientific work and learn to view it realistically.

A fourth key component relates to the capacity of the curriculum to reflect the latest breakthroughs in scientific research as well as the technological progress made in applied areas of science. Whereas this can be seen as important for all students, it is critical for the gifted who need access to new information at earlier ages in order to conduct meaningful research. One of the major recommendations emanating from several recent national reports stressed the need for updating the scientific information shared with students and for infusing the curriculum with new technological advances (National Science Board, 1983). Specifically, science programs for the gifted should present technological issues as a part of each formal topic in the standard curriculum (VanTassel-Baska, Landau, and Olszewski, 1985).

Because there is much agreement that high-level ability should be pointed in socially constructive directions, science programs for the gifted should include components of values education through which the students can learn to examine their own values as well as the values of others. Research tends to suggest that gifted students are often very concerned about the moral and ethical dimensions of questions (Gallagher, 1966). Consideration of the moral, social, and ethical dimensions of scientific topics such as nuclear energy, genetic engineering, euthanasia, and innovative medical procedures seems particularly relevant to be included in an appropriate science curriculum for this population.

Therefore, an effective science program for talented learners incorporates: (1) opportunities for authentic laboratory experimentation and original research work; (2) high-level, content-based curriculum that is conceptually strong and carefully organized over the grade span of K–12; (3) opportunities for interactions with practicing scientists; (4) a curriculum rich in current technological advances, coupled with the human dimensions associated with those advances; and (5) a strong emphasis on inquiry processes.

Welch (1984) has noted the importance of understanding the activities, beliefs, and personal traits of scientists in order to make appropriate inferences about an appropriate science curriculum for the most talented. The activities of scientists are procedures of investigation by which knowledge of natural phenomena is gained. They are tactics and strategies of science—the ways scientists behave in their pursuit of understanding. There are four major physical activities (observation, measurement, experimentation, and communication) and a set of mental activities or processes commonly found in the literature.

In addition, scientists appear to operate in accordance with a set of beliefs about the natural world, their methods of inquiry, and the knowledge these methods produce. For example, they believe that a real world exists that can be understood. They assume events in nature have causes and that nature in not capricious.

Welch also notes that certain personality traits seem to characterize the more successful scientists and may provide us with important guidance on the appropriate way to structure a science program for talented learners. Several of these characteristics have been identified by Brandwein (1955) and Klemm (1977) as curiosity, creativeness, and commitment.

Figure 8.1 reflects the salient features of the domain of science inquiry described by Welch (1984). Hence, one way to organize a science curriculum for the gifted is to use the domain as a conceptual guide to major types of learning experiences to be provided. Activities of a scientist represent major categories of objectives for a student curriculum, whereas the beliefs and personal traits inform the process by which science instruction is carried out with such students and provide a way of assessing teachers who can work effectively with talented students. The degree to which these teachers can model the beliefs and traits of scientists may be a clue as to their capacity to be effective role models for students in the process of scientific inquiry. Effective science programs are those that have curious, creative, and committed teachers. Such programs reward students who exhibit these traits and seek to instill them in students who do not.

Science programs for the gifted should incorporate the following types of goals:

- To provide indepth opportunities to learn special topics in science
- To engage in scientific investigation at an early age
- To master the tools of science by understanding the activities, beliefs, and characteristics of scientists
- To understand the relationship of science to all other areas of the human

FIGURE 8.1 Domain of Science Inquiry

Activities	Beliefs	Personal Traits
	About Nature	
Observation	Intelligible	Curiosity
Measurement	Causal	Creativity
Experimentation	Noncapricious	Commitment
Communication		
Mental processes		
	About Method	
Induction	Objectivity	
Deduction	Skepticism	
Form hypotheses	Replication	
Create theories	Parsimony	
Analysis		
Synthesis	*About Knowledge*	
Extrapolation	Structure	
Evaluation	Explanation	
Estimation	Prediction	
Speculation	Tentative	

Source: Wayne W. Welch, "A Science-Based Approach to Science Learning." In D. Holdzkom and P. Lutz (Eds.), *Research Within Reach: Science Education*. Washington, D.C.: National Science Teachers Association. Reprinted with permission.

enterprise and thus to study moral and ethical implications of scientific advancement

- To foster curiosity about the world of science
- To understand the role of science in society, including careers and other real life applications.

Through the infusion of these goals in a science curriculum for the gifted, students can better approach an understanding of the real world of science rather than a cookbook approach often advanced through many science programs used in schools, particularly at the elementary level.

Elementary Science Programs for the Gifted

Although the overall goals of a special science program for the gifted may not differ based on the age of the science students, the core emphasis may vary. Consequently, the nature of the activities will be different. Elementary science programs for the gifted need to stress the following types of approaches: discovery learning, small group investigatory experiences, opportunities for independent learning, and active experimentation.

EXAMPLES OF SCIENCE ACTIVITIES FOR GIFTED ELEMENTARY STUDENTS

Follis and Krockover (1981) developed key activities in science for use with young gifted children at the primary and intermediate levels. Demonstration lessons on discrepant events was one technique suggested. Since the outcome of a discrepant event is seldom what it would seem to be, demonstrations should challenge able students to consider outcomes other than those that are obvious to them. In the discussion following the demonstration of a discrepant event, students should be allowed to speculate on the possible causes and effects of the phenomenon. Examples of discrepant events are:

1. Can paper stay dry under water? How can we put a piece of wadded paper towel under water without getting it wet? Crumple a piece of paper toweling into the bottom of a clear container. What do you observe? Why does this happen?
2. Why does the balloon cling to the wall? Rub an inflated balloon with wood and touch the balloon to a wall. What happens? Why?
3. When doesn't a paper cup burn? Put water into a paper cup. Place a lighted candle beneath it. What happens? Why?
4. Place a coin under a clear glass tumbler; observe the coin closely as water is poured into the glass. What happens to the coin?

Game activities are appropriate for improving children's observational skills as well as giving them the opportunity to apply techniques for identification and classification of objects (Bennett and Bassett, 1972). For example:

Arrange several objects on a table for children to observe carefully for thirty seconds. Then cover the objects and ask the children to generate a list of the items they observed. This can be combined with attribute listing by asking children to list all the heavy items observed, all the red items, and so on.

Science and mathematics can be combined for activities incorporating set theory and attribute listing. Sorting and classifying objects into set defines the concept of set theory and gives children experience in dealing with the attributes of an object. For example:

Give the students a set of objects to sort into two sets, determined by the criteria the objects suggest (e.g., soft and hard, or heavy and light). When the objects are sorted, another criterion should be established, and the items resorted. When several different criteria have been used to sort and classify the objects, ask the children to list the attributes of each object, based first on the previously established criteria, then expanded to include other observable attributes. This manner of sorting and classifying gives examples to the concept of intersection sets—some objects may fit totally or partially into more than one set.

When students are familiar with attribute listing, the strategy can be reversed. Ask the students to name an object when given its attributes. This can begin with familar objects in the classroom then be expanded as children become adept at the process. This exercise could take the form of a game or activity.

Observational skills are also utilized in noting similarities and differences between like and unlike objects. Students should be encouraged to make comparisons. For example:

How is a goldfish like a snail? How is a dandelion plant like a mushroom? How are these items different from each other? Activities of this nature will draw on the child's observational skills and his or her knowledge of attributes.

The development of communication skills is important to gifted young students in the areas of science and mathematics as well as other areas of the curriculum. Students should be encouraged to measure, collect, and record data; to report observations in words and/or pictures; and to discuss ideas with their teachers and peers. For example:

Students could keep a dated diary of the changes noticed as frog eggs mature to tadpoles, using words and/or pictures to communicate their findings. Students could record the growth of plants by measuring the height of a plant, and tearing off a strip of paper each day to equal the new height of the plant. These strips, pasted on paper, will serve as an introduction to bar graphs, and will open another area of investigation. Students can experiment with prisms, drawing the colors of the spectrum observed when the light from prism falls on to paper of various colors.

Measuring activities give gifted young children concurrent experiences in science and mathematics activities. Metric measurement activities should be utilized to provide young children early experience in using metrics. Children need opportunities to develop skills in estimating and inferring as well as taking part in actual measurement experiments. This also involves students in discussion, record-keeping, measuring and estimating. For example, the Elementary Science Study (ESS) unit "Peas and Particles" offers opportunities for estimation as well as for forming systems of measurement.

Brandwein (1955) cautions that at the elementary level the focus should be on the science environment rather than on selection of students as gifted in science. He states: "In describing children in the primary (grades one through three) and middle years (grades four through six), the term 'science prone' should be used rather than 'gifted in science.'" Students who are gifted in science are identified not mainly by high IQ (whether 130 or higher), but by their remarkable achievement; that is, by deeds, not by promise. In fact, achievement (usually, but not always, coupled with high IQ) presages promise. In the elementary school, the concern, then, is with the curriculum, methods, and materials that sustain and support the interest of aspiring young scientists.

Secondary Science Programs for the Gifted

Over the last fifty years, the United States has taken a livelier interest in science offerings for its most able population than it has in any other curriculum area at the secondary level. The perception of this country's world standing is frequently equated with how well students are provided for in the basic sciences. Thus it is not unusual to find long-standing and intensive science programs for the gifted having been successful over a period of years.

The Bronx High School of Science has a fifty-year tradition in offering excellent science opportunities for highly able students in New York City. While the focus of the school's nomenclature centers on science, it offers an excellent program to gifted students across the curriculum. Thus far the program has produced three Nobel laureates in the sciences and it has a long list of distinguished graduates who have gone on to make outstanding science contributions. The ingredients of success for the school's strong science effort rest on three variables: the quality of the student, the quality of the teaching staff, and the strong course offerings in science. Students at the school take four years of science and are exposed to a heavy emphasis on inquiry training in the scientific method. In essence, they learn how to think about science and how to question. The Bronx offers a full load of Advanced Placement courses in the sciences, including AP Biology, AP Chemistry, and AP Physics. In addition, it provides specialized courses that allow students to pursue their own independent work in science, both during the academic year and in the summer. An innovative curriculum was developed in 1975 to foster creativity in science at the school (Galasso, 1977). It has proven to be especially successful with younger science students who need the motivational focus that the curriculum provides. The features of the school curriculum are carefully structured to provide multiple student outcomes. Listed below is an outline used for developing curriculum at the school:

FEATURES OF A SCIENCE LESSON

1. **Philosophy**
   a. Comparison with other subject areas
   b. Problem solving
2. **Lesson Structure and Lesson Planning**
   a. Motivation—aim sequence
   b. Gathering and/or giving information
   c. Hypothesizing
   d. Testing hypotheses
   e. Summaries
   f. Homework

g. Instructional objectives
h. Reading and writing skills
i. Demonstrations
3. **Other Types of Lessons**
a. Laboratory lesson
b. Reading lesson
c. Review lesson

The sample lesson that follows illustrates the inquiry process approach used in science classes at the school.

Lesson Topic—The control of heart rate

Motivation

1. Ask students "What is an easy way to determine heart rate?"
2. Have students take pulse at rest and after exercise.
3. Graph results and interpret.

Pulse rate (heart beats/min.)

Rest   Exercise
          Time

Aim—How is heart rate maintained within narrow limits?

Instructional Objectives

Students will be able to:

1. Relate pulse to heart rate.
2. Identify the nerves going to the heart.
3. Determine experimental procedure for determining the function of nerve that lead to the heart.
4. Draw conclusions regarding the nerves innervating the heart, based on data provided.
5. Discuss advantage of dual innervation of the heart.

The North Carolina School of Math and Science represents a more recent intensive focus on the sciences for gifted learners. Begun in 1980 at the behest of the governor as a device to upgrade education in the state as well as provide exemplary programming to the most able, the school already has distinguished itself as a landmark institution. The quality of graduates is high, and they have enjoyed successful placement in the prestigious higher education world. Furthermore, the school is proving itself to be a successful economic development tool for the state, luring high-powered scientists to work in the research triangle and creating a whole new generation of students who will wish to remain in the area.

Key features of this school in respect to its science curriculum include:

• Up-to-date scientific equipment available for student use
• Access to practicing scientists in the research triangle area surrounding

the school; internships with selected scientists is an integral part of the program

- Employment of scientists as instructors for special courses in the sciences
- A thematic orientation to much of the school's coursework, blending biology, chemistry, and physics together in one unified course around basic scientific principles, for example.

New efforts based on the North Carolina model have also developed in other parts of the country. The Louisiana School for Math, Science and the Arts is flourishing, and the state of Illinois has opened a similar special school organized on the North Carolina model. Located in proximity to two national laboratories, Argonne and Fermilab, the school developed its curriculum to take advantage of the high technology and the human resources available from these laboratories.

A special curriculum project evolved from a two-year summer program for gifted students in science sponsored by Northwestern University and Argonne National Laboratory. This program had three distinct goals:

- To provide talented students with the opportunity to learn specific topics in a discrete area of science or applied mathematics
- To provide talented students with skills in the scientific method sufficient to develop an individual research proposal in an area of their choice
- To provide talented students the opportunity for interactions with practicing scientists, young mentors, and high-quality teachers in pursuit of science learning

A total of 220 junior high-school students scoring at or above 800 on the combined Scholastic Aptitude Test (SAT-M + V) were served by this three-week experimental science program. Typically, students would engage in lecture, laboratory, problem solving, tutorial, and consultative contact with scientists for five hours a day. Teachers and teaching assistants were involved with the students in large group lectures and demonstrations, small group discussions and problem-solving activities, and individual consultation patterns of instruction. The pupil-teacher ratio was 15:1. High-school level texts and specifically designed materials were used. A specific science topic framed each of the courses for students; ecology, genetics, energy, and computer modeling were content foci for the second year of the program. In the first year, more traditional science content was used. Results from the program indicated the program richness associated with the use of practicing scientists was beneficial to students in giving them a more realistic sense of what science was, yet it also pointed out the difficulty of sustaining the inquiry process independently, as only 30 percent of the students followed up after the program in carrying out their research proposal even though all students in the program developed one (VanTassel-Baska and Kulieke, 1987). Course guides were developed in the areas of genetics, energy, ecology, and computer science, based on the program.

Curriculum Development in Science

Excellent science curriculum materials were produced in the 1960s, including BSCS biology, chemistry study, and PSSC physics at the secondary level, and AAAS science and EES science at the elementary level. Unfortunately, the science curricula, like the mathematics curricula, have slowly been replaced by less and less rigorous and challenging materials. The "new science" materials were regarded as inappropriate for most students; the emphasis on learning by *doing* was time-consuming, the reading was too demanding, and the conceptual orientation of the materials was too difficult. These shortcomings of the 1960s curricula are precisely the characteristics that make them an appropriate foundation for gifted curricula today.

Yet it is important to recognize the fundamental importance of teacher training in the use of these materials in order to render programs effective. Existing materials must also be adapted to reflect the accelerated rate of development of new information in the sciences that has resulted from the enormous technological advances of the intervening decades. Furthermore, the role of techology as a tool for gifted learners must be considered. And, if coupled with a vigorous mathematics program, an appropriate science program can rely more heavily on mathematical methods.

By the time they reach sixth grade, students who have outstanding abilities in science are ready for a program that fosters an indepth understanding of the major science areas while emphasizing that science is a dynamic, creative field (Martin, 1979). Rapid change, advanced technology, and the use of more sophisticated science must be incorporated into the curricula while retaining a strong conceptual focus and an emphasis on problem finding, problem solving, evaluation, and reporting. The overall aim, then, is the development of a curriculum that will facilitate the learning of both the content and methods of the sciences.

VanTassel-Baska, Landau, and Olszewski (1985) present a possible scope and sequence of courses in the physical and life sciences covering grades 6–12 that would be appropriate for academically gifted students (see Figure 8.2). Science courses that are typically available to high-school students (i.e., biology, chemistry, and physics) are included in this curriculum; however, students would begin the formal study of specific science subjects such as biology and physical science at the junior high level, allowing them to take more science courses and to achieve advanced placement credit for more science subjects during high school. This curriculum in its entirety is particularly appropriate for students who wish to enter honors science programs at the university level, for students who wish to pursue further study in an integrated science program at the university level (involving more than one science subject), for students who plan a career that involves major intensive study in several science fields (e.g., bio-physicist), and for students who plan to pursue study in a science field to the doctoral level.

The curriculum would begin in the sixth grade, with a course in the history and philosophy of science, with a particular emphasis on the scientific method and its component skills of critical and deductive thinking. The scientific method as a process would be introduced to students at this level but would be a major recurrent theme throughout the curriculum. Entry into and exit from the

FIGURE 8.2 Science Scope and Sequence, Grades 6–12 Appreciation of Science (The History and Development of Scientific Systems)

	6 Philosophy of Science and Technology: The Scientific Method	7 IPS Physical Science	8 BSCS Biology	9 AP Biology	10 Honors Chemistry	11 Physics (PSSC)	12 Course Options: AP Physics/AP Chemistry/or Geology
History of Science	X						
Cycles of Nature		X	X	X			
Doctrine of Limits	X	X			X	X	
Conservation of Energy-Minimization of Entropy	X	X	X	X			
Growth, Development, and Transformation		X	X				
Interdependence	X		X			X	
Humans as Actors/Reactors in the World	X	X	X	X	X	X	X
Moral and Ethical Dimensions of Science	X			X			X

curriculum would be flexible, depending upon the students' interest and ability level and career or college goals. High-school credit for courses taken at the junior high level would be accomplished via proficiency examinations in each content area by the local schools and/or through the use of College Board achievement tests.

Incorporated into the science curriculum for gifted students is an emphasis on the major ideas or concepts within both the physical and biological sciences as determined by scientists within those fields (Shane, 1981) and include: the cycles of nature, interdependence, growth, development, and transformation; and humans as actors and reactors in the physical world.

An emphasis on these ubiquitous concepts will help to elucidate the structure of the individual science disciplines as well as their interrelatedness. Objectives of the science curriculum would be to give students information about the scientific advances that are at the cutting edge of knowledge in the field, as well as to teach them the methodology of research and scientific inquiry.

Curriculum Development in Technology

Science curriculum for the gifted should include a strong component on technology, its history, and its development as a field. This component could emphasize the linkages among advances in science and technology. That is, since science typically provides the underlying knowledge base for technology, each science content area, physics, biology, and chemistry, would include units focusing on the technological advances that have been possible as a result of specific discoveries within that content area. These units could be developed independently so as to be easily integrated into the study of the content area where appropriate (i.e., when students have sufficient knowledge of the underlying scientific basis to permit a thoughtful and indepth examination of some of the technological results). The impact of technology on furthering scientific discoveries that make a contribution to the knowledge base—or the reciprocity between science and technology (e.g., the telescope causing a revolution in astronomy)—could also be examined. An example would be a unit on the atom bomb (a technological result of the field of chemistry). An understanding of the periodic table and the patterns and regularity within it as a result of the structure of the atom and its properties would be necessary before one could proceed to the topic of nuclear fission and the results of this process on the element of plutonium. This topic could be introduced in the chemistry curriculum at the point where students have the prerequisite knowledge to fully understand its evolution within the content area.

Woven throughout such units would be an emphasis on overarching and recurrent themes and issues that relate to the field of technology as a whole and to specific technologies somewhat more cogently or urgently. These include the power of technology as a force which causes exponential growth; the impact of technology on society—movement from an industrial society to an information society; the results of technology—societal progress versus societal regression; the effects of technological advances on the quality of life; and the strategies that society and individuals can employ (problem solving, problem prediction, decision making) to cope with the rapidity of changes wrought by technological and scientific advances and their potential results. Key areas of societal impact to include in a curriculum might be:

1. Environmental pollution through toxic wastes, acid rain, etc.
2. The beginning and ending of life through in vitro fertilization techniques, life support systems, organ transplants, etc.
3. National defense through nuclear arsenals, STAR wars, etc.
4. Improved medical treatment through laser surgery, cat scans, etc.
5. Improved communication access through computer mail, videotape, etc.
6. Improved transportation networks through structural redesign and computerized systems

Conceptual Approaches to Science Curriculum

There are many fine books on science already available that organize science ideas according to conceptual themes. One such example is Judson's (1980) book called *The Search for Solutions*. This text organizes scientific ideas according to nine key issues and themes.

1. Investigation: The Rage to Know
2. Pattern
3. Change
4. Chance
5. Feedback
6. Modeling
7. Strong predictions
8. Evidence
9. Theory

Using exemplary photographs, paintings, and diagrams to illustrate these key ideas in science as well as featuring interviews with current scientists, Judson creates a "feeling" for science in his readers that deepens their understanding of science as the art of knowing. Filmstrips and teaching guides have also been developed for use with the text.

Another book and PBS television series that also has a strong conceptual organization is *Connections* by James Burke (1978). He has chosen to focus on eight recent inventions that account for phenomenal change in our modern environment and daily lives: the atomic bomb, the telephone, the computer, the production-line system of manufacture, aircraft, plastics, the guided rocket, and television. Burke links each of them, however, to earlier inventions that take the reader back to ancient times. These "chains of discovery" allow students to understand the nature of scientific and technological breakthroughs over time and culture.

A third example of such materials is the fine intellectual masterpiece by Jacob Bronowski, *The Ascent of Man* (1976). His work chronicles the progress of man according to key scientific discoveries, yet the text also bridges these discoveries to issues of social progress. His description of our current conception of science and its relationship to an earlier view of architecture is typical of the interplay of ideas he uses throughout the text:

> The fact of the matter is that our conception of science now, towards the end of the twentieth century, has changed radically. Now we see science as a description and explanation of the underlying structures of nature; and words like *structure, pattern, plan, arrangement, architecture* constantly occur in every description that we try to make. . . . The spiral structure of DNA has become the most vivid image of science in the last years. And that imagery lives in these arches.
>
> What did the people do who made this building and others like it? They took a dead heap of stones, which is not a cathedral, and they turned it into a cathedral by exploiting the natural forces of gravity, the way the stone is laid naturally in its bedding plane, the brilliant invention of the flying buttress and arch and so on. And they created a structure that grew out of the analysis of nature into this superb synthesis. The kind of man who is interested in the architecture of nature today is the kind of man who made this architecture nearly eight hundred years ago. There is one gift above all others that makes man unique among the animals, and it is the gift displayed everywhere here: his immense pleasure in exercising and pushing forward his own skill (pp. 112–113).

The Bronowski work can be used as a teacher reference for organizing an interdisciplinary program in science, or as a direct teaching tool with students from sixth grade on. A PBS film series highlights each section of the book.

The three examples provided here are excellent beginning resources in building a conceptually based science program that could focus on some of the most fascinating scientific ideas of our time.

At a more basic level, the concept of change is explored in a science unit developed for gifted learners at the primary, intermediate, and junior high levels (see Example 8.A at the end of the chapter).

Women in Science and Mathematics

The curriculum implications for encouraging girls to continue studying mathematics and science have emerged as a major issue over the last two decades. Several studies have cited the lower incidence of women in advanced coursework in these areas and fewer women in careers related to science. Whereas studies have cited several possible reasons for this discrepancy that may be found in the social (Eccles, 1984), psychological (Astin, 1969), and biological (Benbow and Stanley, 1980) milieus, it is a difficult discrepancy to ignore when addressing the needs of gifted females. Consequently, it may be important for curriculum planners to be conscious of the need for emphasizing certain issues in the context of a gifted science program for both genders.

Project Link in Minnesota is a prototype of a program for gifted girls in grades 4–6 who are potentially interested in science and math careers. The program seeks to establish career role models for girls from the local community. Adult females come into the classroom to address various career-related issues. Opportunities to visit the professional women at work are also arranged. Such a program emphasizes careers in mathematics and science for girls, and at the same time it provides real-life role models in science and science-related professions.

Helping gifted girls understand the importance of taking four years of high-school math and science is another important thrust of a program. Since only 1 out of every 300 gifted girls ever pursues a doctorate, it is important for them to see the relationship of early educational attainment in the specific areas of math and science as an indication of their later broadening of future educational and career paths. Small group discussions and films like *Count Me In: Educating Women for Math and Science* may be excellent ways to foster these ideas.

Another way to deal with some gifted girls' lack of self-confidence may be to use bibliotherapy techniques that focus on reading biographies of women scientists and/or other works that they may have written. The following is a list of famous women scientists, about whom much has been written.

Elizabeth Blackwell (1821–1910): Physician. First woman in America to become a doctor; established the New York Infirmary for Women and Children; organized Women's Central Relief Association which trained nurses; assisted in developing examinations long before they were compulsory; founded the New England Hospital for Women and Children in 1859.

Rachel Fuller Brown (1898–1980): Organic chemist. Co-developer with Elizabeth Lee Hazen (1885–1975) of Nystatin, the first antifungal antibiotic for use in human disease; received the Squibb Award in Chemotherapy and was the first woman to receive the Chemical Pioneer Award of the American Institute of Chemists.

Mary Bunting (1910–   ): Microbiologist. First woman member on the Atomic Energy Commission; made discoveries on the effects of radiation on bacteria.

Eleanor M. Burbridge (1919–   ): Astronomer. First woman Royal Astronomer at the Royal Greenwich Observatory in England.

Rachel Carson (1907–1964): Biologist. Alerted the country to the dangers of pollution through her book *Silent Spring*.

Gerty Cori (1896–1957): Biochemist. First American woman to receive the Nobel Prize in Medicine/Physiology in 1947; researched carbohydrate metabolism on how the body uses its fuel supply of starches and sugars as related to certain hormone secretions.

Marie Curie (1867–1934): Chemist. First person to receive two Nobel Prizes: Physics in 1903 for the discovery of radium and Chemistry in 1911 for her research into radioactivity.

Lilian Gilbreth (1878–1972): Industrial engineer. Developed time and human motion studies to reduce waste and increase efficiency in the office, factory, hospital, and home settings.

Hetty Goldman (1881–1972): Archeologist. Interpreted the stages of pre-historic life in Greece; first woman professor at the Institute of Advanced Study at Princeton.

Jane Goodall (1934–   ): Animal behaviorist. Conducted detailed studies to show that chimpanzees are intelligent, tool making, social animals.

Dorothy Crowfoot Hodgkin (1910–   ): Crystallographer. Received the Nobel Prize in Chemistry in 1964 for research on the crystal structure of biochemical compounds, particularly penicillin.

Hyatia (c. 370–415): Mathematician. Mathematics and philosophy professor at the University of Alexandria in Egypt; developed the astrolabe and planesphere, instruments used for studying the stars.

Shirley Jackson (1946–   ): Physicist. First and only black woman currently in theoretical physics; participant in the International School of Subnuclear Physics in Italy.

Irene Joliot-Curie (1897–1956): Physicist. Received the Nobel Prize in Chemistry for discovering a technique for making artificial radioactive elements.

Maria C. Mayer (1906–1972): Physicist. Received the Nobel Prize in Physics in 1963 for her work during World War II on isotope separation for the atomic bomb.

Barbara McClintock (1902–   ): Research scientist. Received the Nobel Prize in Medicine/Physiology in 1983 for her research in the cytogentics of maize.

Margaret Mead (1901–1978): Anthropologist. Studied and wrote on the cultures of the South Sea Island, childrearing, and the role of women in society.

Florence Sabin (1871–1953): Physician. Teacher of anatomy and histology at the Johns Hopkins University; discovered the origin of red corpuscles and made contributions to tuberculosis research; received the National Achievement Award in 1932.

Rosalyn Sussman Yalow (1921–   ): Medical physicist. Received the Nobel Prize in Medicine/Physiology in 1977 for the discovery of randioimmunology, a method of measuring minute concentrations of hundreds of substances in body tissues important in determining the differences between diseased and normal tissues.

Other ways of encouraging girls to stay in math and science programs relate to strategies used by teachers in the delivery of the content of such courses. In classroom teaching, try to emphasize the following approaches:

1. Teach problem-solving strategies.
2. Use holistic presentations of a mathematical idea rather than only a step-by-step procedure.
3. Emphasize real-life applications of science and math.

4. Allow enough time for solution finding.

5. Emphasize diverse ways to solve problems.

6. Use math/science-related problems, games, and puzzles as rewards.

Such techniques can lower the math anxiety experienced by many gifted females in advanced math and science courses. The use of special seminars for gifted girls to discuss ideas of math anxiety can also be helpful. Other direct and indirect teaching strategies may also be useful to consider:

DIRECT TEACHING

- Present information about women who have careers in science and technology.
- Help girls to understand the effects of sex-stereotyping and bias in science and career materials on their perceptions and science-related interests.
- Provide information about contributions of women in science.
- Explain the projections for science and engineering careers over the next decade.
- Relate the changing roles of men and women to the career potential for women in science.

INDIRECT TEACHING

- Select materials that avoid sex stereotypes in their illustrations (e.g., pictures in which women are actively engaged in science, outdoors as well as indoors, and in which as many men are looking over women's shoulders and vice versa).
- Invite women scientists into the classroom to talk about relevant topics.
- Encourage girls to develop manipulative hobbies, such as constructing models and radios.

Implementation Issues in Science Programs

The issues associated with implementing a sound curriculum for gifted students in science are fairly straightforward in terms of understanding what the goals of such a curriculum should be, based on the characteristics and needs of able learners as well as the nature of the activities, beliefs, and characteristics of successful scientists. And it is fairly clear that developmental differences can be handled through differentiating activities and topical choices at the elementary level as compared to the secondary level. What remains more difficult to handle from an administrative perspective are the resource needs to carry out such an ambitious program. Perhaps it would be useful to focus on some of these needed resource areas and how they might be handled.

1. *The choice of teacher.* It is vitally important that the teacher of gifted students in science know science. This is as important in the elementary-level program as

it is in a secondary one. The individual should have advanced content knowledge in science but also have the skills to manage a science classroom effectively. Using high-school staff to work in an elementary science program may be one way of getting the level of expertise required. Another way would be to differentiate the teaching staff so that one individual teaches predominantly science. Use of student help from universities as well as scientists in the area also will enhance the learning process for these students.

2. *The scientific environment.* Up-to-date science equipment in a laboratory that is conducive to conducting group and individual experiments is vital to carrying out the nature of the programs suggested in this chapter. And yet there can be exciting science going on for students with a creative teacher who uses the world around us as a scientific laboratory. For young students, in particular, collecting and analyzing the natural world is a wonderful context for scientific inquiry. Thus classrooms need not be equipped with everything to make science viable. However, the need to create a conducive environment for doing science is a vital aspect of implementation.

3. *The emphasis on problem finding and problem solving rather than merely "problem doing."* Although canned experiments are easier to use in a classroom setting, they do little to instill a love of science in the gifted or to further the cause of real scientific inquiry. Engaging students in original research questions is an important aspect of implementing a successful science program for them. Using everyday tools, simple designs, and curiosity about natural phenomena constitute the best resources for students indulging in problem-finding behavior.

4. *Selection of texts that focus on broad conceptual issues rather than isolated topics or skills.* Several texts that are organized by key themes in science have been discussed in this chapter. Even if a core text is necessary, conceptually based materials provide a good supplement to a core text, and can be easily adapted for classroom use, particularly in a discussion format.

5. *Opportunity for individual scientific research work through hosting science fairs and junior science symposia.* Encouragement in scientific investigation can be enhanced by deliberately structuring an event to display and evaluate student work and utilizing scientists from the community as participants and critics. Programs like Science Olympiad or science fairs provide a chance for students to test themselves against other students who have similar interests and abilities as well as tap into the ideas of real practicing scientists.

6. *Connections to the real world of science through mentorships and internships.* Having students assigned to a hospital laboratory or a corporate research lab is one way of their gaining valuable insights into science as a profession. Such placements also enhance understanding scientific inquiry as an internalized process.

Conclusion

Science programs for the gifted need to be available at kindergarten and continue as a strong thread in their education through high school. A much stronger focus on the process of scientific investigation and the moral and ethical dimensions of scientific discoveries need to be infused. Original work in science conducted by the students themselves from an early age should be carefully nurtured so that scientific curiosity is stimulated and not extinguished. It will likely take scientists some time to solve problems like those cited by Judson as the critical eight currently in search of solutions (see Judson, 1980, p. 200):

1. What was the origin of the universe?
2. Needed: a unified theory in physics for four kinds of observable forces—weak, strong, electromagnetic, and gravitational.
3. What was the origin of the solar system?
4. What is the origin of life?
5. Establishing the quantitative bases of natural selection and evolution.
6. What are the controlling processes that cause the fertilized egg to become the organism?
7. What are the mechanisms by which aging and death occur?
8. How does the human nervous system perceive, think, and process information?

Effective science programs for gifted learners, however, can begin to nurture the process.

KEY POINTS SUMMARY

- Science programs for the gifted should emphasize inquiry-based activities in an original research mode, an understanding of scientific method in the context of specialized scientific areas, opportunities for modeling scientific behaviors, and an appreciation of the interplay of science and technology.
- Gifted students should understand and emulate the total domain of science inquiry: the activities, beliefs, and personal traits of scientists.
- Elementary science programs for the gifted should stress exploratory learning in science, both in small groups and independently.
- High-school programs for the gifted should focus on more opportunities for real-world connections to practicing scientists, to the community, and to the ethical and moral considerations underlying scientific discovery.
- Excellent materials for use as curriculum for the gifted already exist in discrete areas of science, particularly as an outgrowth of the National Science Foundation work in the 1960s.
- Interdisciplinary materials can assist in teaching gifted students the serious implications of science study in our world.
- Gifted girls need special encouragement to continue in science programs and to relate to the field as a potential career path.

Selected Resources

Biology: A Molecular Approach. BSCS Blue Version, 5th ed. Lexington, Mass.: D.C. Heath, 1985.

A molecular approach to understanding contemporary bio-related issues, such as DNA engineering, evolution, cellular engineering, environmental science. Encourages understanding of major biological concepts to make biology useful. Major sections: Overview; Life Processes; Genetics; Human Biological Systems; Higher Organization; and Inter-related Systems.

The Philosophy and Method of Science. The Center for Talent Development, Northwestern University.

This curriculum guide considers the basic philosophical position underlying scientific research, the components of the scientific method, and the skills of critical and deductive thinking involved in its application. Emphasis is on the history, process, and application of experimental design illustrated by classic as well as current research problems from the physical and behavioral sciences.

Applications of Technology in Science. The Center for Talent Development, Northwestern University.

Highlighted in this curriculum guide is the role of technology in several areas of science. The curriculum focuses on the contribution of technological advances to the understanding and development of basic scientific concepts and the power of technology as a force (positive and negative) in determining the future of the human condition. Specific topics addressed in the guide include Energy Sources and Uses, Genetics, Ecology, Space Travel, Conservation, and Electronics.

Unified Sciences and Mathematics for Elementary Schools (USMES). Moore Publishing Company, P.O. Box 3036, West Durham Station, Durham, N.C. 27705.

The USMES curriculum is organized into twenty-six problem areas, or units, that have been developed in the classroom by teachers and students in a wide variety of schools. Each unit is a challenge, such as "Promote changes that can make eating in school more enjoyable" or "Make your own weather predictions." Each challenge, stated in a Teacher Resource Book, is general enough to apply to many situations.

Discovery Activities for Elementary Science. Arthur A. Carin and Robert F. Sund. Columbus, Ohio: Charles E. Merrill.

This program provides a diversity of activities involving environmental, physical, and life sciences. The paperback guide clearly informs teachers what background they need before undertaking each discovery lesson.

Concepts in Science, Curie Edition. Paul F. Brandwein, et al. New York: Harcourt Brace Jovanovich, 1980.

The series emphasizes "sciencing" as a method of learning. The breadth and depth of the study of the concepts which increase throughout the program are intensified at each level.

Other Resources

Elementary Science Study. Educational Development Center, 55 Chapel Street, Newton, Massachusetts. McGraw-Hill.

Introductory Physical Science (IPS). Educational Development Center, 55 Chapel Street, Newton, Massachusetts. Prentice-Hall, Inc.

Intermediate Science Curriculum Study (ISCS). 508 South Woodward, Florida State University, Tallahassee, Florida. Silver Burdett.

Science—A Process Approach. Commission on Science Education, American Association for the Advancement of Science, 1515 Massachusetts Avenue, N.W., Washington, D.C. Delta Corporation.

Secondary School Science Project (Time: Space, and Matter). 10 Seminary Place, Rutgers University, New Jersey. Webster Division—McGraw-Hill.

References

Academic Preparation for College. (1982). New York: The College Entrance Examination Board, Educational Equality Project.

Astin, H. (1969). *The Woman Doctorate in America.* New York: Russell Sage.

Ausubel, D. P. (1965). "An Evaluation of the Conceptual Schemes Approach to Science Curriculum Development." *Journal of Research in Science Teaching, 3,* 255–264.

Benbow, C., and Stanley, J. (1980). "Sex Differences in Mathematical Ability: Fact or Artifacts?" *Science, 210,* 1262–1264.

Bennett, L., and Bassett, G. (1972). "Games and Things for Preschool Science." *Science and Children,* 9(1), 25–27.

Blurton, C. (1983). "Science Talent: The Elusive Gift." *School Science and Mathematics,* 83(8), 654–664.

Brandwein, P. F. (1955). *The Gifted Student As Future Scientist.* New York: Harcourt, Brace, and Jovanovich.

Bronowski, J. (1976). *The Ascent of Man.* Boston: Little, Brown.

Burke, J. (1978). *Connections.* Boston: Little, Brown.

A Celebration of Teaching: High Schools in the 1980s (1983). Reston, Va.: The National Association and the Commission on Educational Issues of the National Association of Independent Schools. A Study of High Schools, NASSP.

Connelly, F. M. (1969). "Philosophy of Science and the Science Curriculum." *Journal of Research in Science Teaching, 6,* 108–113.

Eccles, J. (1984). "Sex Differences in Mathematics Participation." In M. Steinkamp and M. Maehr (Eds.), *Women in Science.* Greenwich, Conn.: J. A. I. Press.

Educating Americans for the 21st Century: A Report to the American People and the National Science Board (1983). The National Science Board Commission on PreCollege Education in Mathematics, Science, and Technology. Washington D.C.

Follis, H., and Krockover, G. (1981). "Selecting Activities in Science and Mathematics for Gifted Young Children." *School Science and Mathematics,* 82(1) 57–64.

Galasso, V. (1977). *Model Program for Developing Creativity in Science.* Washington, D.C.: U.S. Office of Education, Office of Gifted and Talented.

Gallagher, J. (1966). *Ethics and Moral Judgment in Children: A Pilot Investigation*. Boston: Unitarian Universalist Association.

Harms, N., and Yager, R. (1981). *What Research Says to the Science Teacher, Volume 3*. NSTA Monograph. Washington, D.C.

Harré, Rom (1981). *Great Scientific Experiments*. New York: Oxford University Press.

Haugen, D. (1984). Presentation to Summer Institute on Curriculum Development for Teachers, Northwestern University.

High School: A Report on American Secondary Education (1983). The Carnegie Foundation for the Advancement of Teaching, supported by the Atlantic Richfield Foundation and the Carnegie Corporation of New York.

Holdzkom, D., and Lutz, P. B. (1984). *Research within Reach: Scienced Education*. Charleston, W.V.: Appalachia Educational Laboratory.

Judson, H. (1979). *The Eighth Day of Creation*. New York: Simon and Schuster.

Judson, H. (1980). *The Search for Solutions*. New York: Holt, Rinehart & Winston.

Klemm, W. R. (Ed.) (1977). *Discovery Processes in Modern Biology*. Huntington, N.Y.: Robert E. Krieger Publishing.

Klopfer, L. E. (1969). "The Teaching of Science and the History of Science." *Journal of Research in Science Teaching*, 6, 87–95.

Lockard, J. D. (Ed.) (1977). *Twenty Years of Science and Mathematics Curriculum Development: The Tenth Report of the International Clearinghouse on Science and Mathematics Curricular Developments*. College Park, Md.: The International Clearinghouse, Science Teaching Center, University of Maryland.

Martin, K. (1979). "Science and the Gifted Adolescent." *Roeper Review*, 2(2), 25–26.

National Science Board Commission (1983). *Educating Americans for the 21st Century*. Washington, D.C.: National Science Foundation.

Rensberger, B. (1986). *How the World Works*. New York: William Morrow & Company.

Shane, H. (1981). *A Study of Curriculum Content for the Future*. New York: College Entrance Examination Board.

Sternberg, R. J. (1982). "Teaching Scientific Thinking to Gifted Children." *Roeper Review*, 4(4), 4–6.

Vandervoort, G. (Ed.) (1986). *Northwestern University and Argonne National Laboratory Curriculum Guides*. Evanston, Ill.: Center for Talent Development, Northwestern University.

VanTassel-Baska, J., and Kulieke, M. (1987). "The Role of Community-Based Scientific Resources in Developing Scientific Talent: A Case Study," *Gifted Child Quarterly*, 31(3).

VanTassel-Baska, J., Landau, M., and Olszewski, P. (1985). "Toward Developing an Appropriate Math/Science Curriculum for Gifted Learners." *Journal for the Education of the Gifted*, 8(4), 257–272.

Welch, W. W. (1966). "The Development of an Instrument for Inventorying Knowledge the Development of Educational Paradigms." *Educational Research*, 12(10), 6–14.

Welch, W. W., Klopfer, L. E., Aikenhead, G. S., and Robinson, J. T. (1981). "The Role of Inquiry in Science Education: Analysis and Recommendations." *Science Education*, 65(1).

Welch, W. (1984). *Proceedings from the National Institute of Education, National Conference on Science.* Washington, D.C.: National Institute on Education.

Welch, W. (1986). *A Science-Based Model for Science Learning.* Unpublished paper presented at Kalamazoo Mathematics and Science Academy Conference, Kalamazoo, Michigan.

EXAMPLE 8.A A Science Unit on Change* ━━━━━━━━━━

DEVELOPED BY DR. GERALD KORCKOVER
PURDUE UNIVERSITY

INTRODUCTION

Everyone makes many observations every day, but only a few people make scientific observations. Scientific observations are made to obtain information. With the information, the scientist attempts to answer questions raised by ideas using special procedures called experiments.

In an experiment, a scientist is interested in changes—before, during, and after the experiment has been conducted. Once it has been established that a change has occurred, the scientist is almost certain to be curious about what is responsible for the change.

This unit explores the differences between physical and chemical changes, the effect of change overtime, and identification of the components of an observed change.

PRIMARY

Motivation: Have students experiment with food coloring to make different colors. What combinations result in certain colors such as orange, purple, etc.?

Objective: Gifted students will be able to observe and distinguish between physical and chemical changes.

Activities:

1. Give students an ice cube and have them weigh and observe it. Record what happens to the ice cube after 1 minute, 5 minutes, 10 minutes, 50 minutes (or every 5 minutes for 50 minutes). What caused the ice cube to change? Collect the water from the melting ice cube and weigh it. Does the mass of the water equal the mass of the ice

---

* *Source:* Adapted from "A Guide for Teaching the Concept of Change in Science," by Gerald H. Krockover, Purdue University, West Lafayette, Indiana 47907. Adapted with permission.

cube? Why or why not? Pour the water into a container and refreeze it. Does the mass of the "new" ice cube equal the mass of the original one? Why or why not? This is an example of a physical change. Design an experiment to illustrate a chemical change. Hint: what if the water evaporated?

2. Take a sheet of paper and cut off a corner. How has the paper changed? Put the paper back to its original shape. What other physical changes can be used to illustrate that it can be returned to the original state? Try crushing a can versus a sheet of paper or aluminum foil. Next try mixing finger paints. Mix yellow and red—what color results? Separate the resulting color back to red and yellow—If this cannot be done, is this an irreversible chemical change?

Objective: Gifted students will be able to identify the physical and chemical changes that occur in one's environment.

Activities:

1. Have students select a deciduous tree to observe over a period of time. Have them prepare observation charts based upon the tree characteristics that they wish to observe. Point out that the observations should be quantified if at all possible. Variables that could be selected include: number of leaves, tree height, number of limbs of a certain size, tree girth, or leaf colors. Identify the changes (physical) that have taken place based upon the variable(s) selected. Prepare a graph of the variable used over time. Locate other physical changes that are related to the changes observed for the tree. What chemical changes can be identified for investigation. Why do leaves fall off some trees and not off others? What makes leaves fall off? Why don't leaves fall off evergreen trees?

2. Discuss what is needed for a plant to grow. Soak lima (either yellow or white) or mung beans overnight (clean first with a bleach solution). Place one dry and one wet seed on a paper towel. Observe the differences with a hand magnifying glass. Plant both seeds in separate cups. Set the cups in the sunlight and water them as required. Observe their growth. Record the growth pictorially or cut strips of paper to record the growth of the plant and glue the strips on construction paper each day. Next select a garden site, prepare it and decide upon the garden seeds to be used. Plant the seeds, care for the garden and observe its growth over time.

Objective: Gifted students will be able to observe and describe the changes that take place in organic material over time.

Activities:

1. Collect a series of photographs of famous movie or television stars over time (watch "Face the Music" to get the idea). Observe the photographs and try to identify the famous person. Why do physical changes take place as one gets "older"? Have children bring in a series of photographs of parents, grandparents, themselves, pets, etc., that show a change over time. What changes are most noticeable? Least noticeable? Next try products and how their advertisements have changed over time. Try Coke, Pepsi, or McDonalds. Have children illustrate how they will look when they are 10, 20, 30, 40, 50, 60, and 70 years old.

Evaluation:

1. Provide students with pictures that illustrate a sequence of events and have the students order the pictures. Try plant growth, seasons, or events.

2. Have the students design two experiments that illustrate change using an apple. One experiment should illustrate a physical change and the other experiment should illustrate a chemical change. Have them graph their results.

3. Provide pictures or samples of unpopped and popped corn, bread and toast, cake and cake cough, burned splint and unburned splint, etc. Have students match changed and unchanged materials and describe the properties changed. Then have the students prepare five of their own examples.

INTERMEDIATE

Motivation: Have students select five objects that they think will change when water is added. Have them test their predictions.

Objective: Gifted students will be able to identify the physical and chemical changes that occur in one's environment; observe and describe the changes that take place in organic material over time; solve genetic problems involving single dominant recessive traits.

Activities:

1. Prepare a fruit fly culture. When it is one week old, have the students observe the larvae. The second week have the students observe the increase in population and the need for food refills. Record changes in the life cycle. Predict how many flies there will be by the fourth week. Make a fruit fly graph over a period of six weeks. Count the fruit flies by laying the glass vial containing the fruit flies on the overhead projector and projecting the image on a sampling grid drawn on the chalkboard. The record will probably show a population increase and decline over the six weeks. Have students identify habitat factors which cause change such as: sunlight, air, water, food, space, pollution, soil, etc. Identify factors which are necessary for the survival of the fruit fly, beans, dogs, people, frogs, etc. Using the fruit fly graph, discuss why the population decreased. Next relate the fruit fly experiment to the problem of endangered species. Discuss: Is man an endangered species? Why or why not?

2. These activities illustrate the fact that only some chemical changes can be reversed. Begin by pouring water into two small containers. Pour enough bromothymol blue into each container to get a strong blue color. Blow through a straw into one of the containers. The observation should be that the color changes to yellow or green. Infer why the color changes. Leave both containers overnight and compare the colors the next day. Both containers will be blue again—an example of a reversible chemical change.

Pour clear soda water into a container. Pour an equal amount of water into another container. Put several drops of bromothymol blue into each container. Note that the soda water turns yellow or green while the plain water turns blue. Find out what soda water contains that causes this chemical change. Is it the same material as that in the first experiment? Prove your answers.

To illustrate irreversible chemical changes weigh a sheet of paper on a gram scale or balance scale. Place the paper in a pie tin. Burn the paper (carefully and use caution) and weigh the remains. Observe the color, odor, texture, thickness, and mass of the product. Where did the lost mass go? Design an experiment to collect this lost mass.

Place an ordinary iron nail and a painted (use waterproof paint) iron nail into a clear container of water. Observe what happens for one week. Find out the chemical reaction that is taking place.

Place a ball of wet steel wool into a test tube. Invert the test tube in a tray of water that is only a few centimeters deep. Observe what happens to the water as the steel wool "rusts" over time. Graph the change in water level over time. Infer that the water has taken the place of something (oxygen in the air) which has combined with the steel wool to form "rust." Test the inference by placing a glowing splint into the test tube (a lack of oxygen will make the splint go out).

3. Test a number of household and school substances (Caution: make sure that they are safe to test) with litmus paper of pH Hydrion paper to determine whether the materials are acidic, basic, or neutral. Students should record the original color of the litmus paper and the materials used. It is a good idea to use only one drop of solution in the center of the litmus paper. Solids must be mixed with neutral (distilled) water. Have the students also try "homemade" indicators such as beet juice, cherry juice, grape juice or red cabbage juice. Add the juice (one teaspoon to a half glass of water) and note the color changes. Test all the foods eaten for a specific meal, Tums, Rolaids, aspirin, vitamins, etc.

Using an eyedropper as a titration, test how many drops of a certain combination are needed to make a solution neutral. Try lemon juice and baking soda; vinegar and soap; vinegar and household ammonia (use caution for the fumes); and orange juice and garden lime.

Evaluation:

1. Collect photographs of people in a variety of environments such as: after earthquakes, in drought areas, crowded cities, etc. Discuss and predict what changes may happen to the future populations and why. Relate these changes to the fruit fly experiment.

2. Obtain brine shrimp eggs and prepare the brine shrimp water by placing tap water in a container and letting it stand for one day. Add about 30 ml of rock salt to 1 litre of water. Put 50 to 100 brine shrimp eggs into a vial of brine. Cap and observe for a few days. After 3 days, count the hatched brine shrimp by using a sampling technique. One sampling technique might be to place a clear plastic container over graph paper. Pour the content of the vial into the plastic container. Count the shrimp in one square of the graph paper and multiply by the number of squares covered. Record the data. Compare the number of hatched shrimp to the number of unhatched shrimp to determine a hatching ratio.

Then predict the change in the brine shrimp population when the environmental conditions are changed (heat in this case). Cut a circle (37 cm in diameter) out of stiff cardboard. Draw concentric circles at regular intervals from the center of the circle. Glue aluminum foil to the bottom side of the circle. Trim the edges. Cut the top off of a small cardboard box. Place a lamp with a 25 watt bulb in the box (observe caution when using this apparatus due to the heat developed). Cover with a coffee can which has had both top and bottom removed and holes punched along the ridges of the top and bottom (see figure).

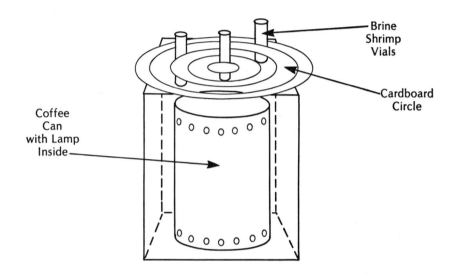

Place the circle on top of the box. Place brine shrimp vials in various concentric circles. Record the number of shrimp hatched every day and from which circle they came. Thermometers can be used to measure the heat output at each location. (Note: keep tops on vials.) State conclusions based upon a graph of the data collected. Investigate the effect of factors other than heat upon brine shrimp such as: detergent, bleach, or ammonia. No brine shrimp? Try fruit flies or mealworms. What do brine shrimp eat? Try one grain of yeast per vial per day.

JUNIOR HIGH

Motivation: Using litmus or pH paper, have the students classify common household items into acids or bases. Students could make predictions first and then record their observed results.

Objective: Gifted students will be able to observe and describe the changes that take place in organic material over time.

Activities:

1. Obtain a variety of seeds such as mung beans, lima beans, green beans, pumpkin, etc. Design an experiment to test the effect of the germination rate of seeds in a water and detergent combination using no phosphate and low phosphate detergents. Remember to use a control for the experiment and to identify the manipulated (independent) and responding (dependent) variables. Discuss the effect of detergents with and without phosphate upon the germination of primary producers in our ecosystem. Should phosphates be banned from all detergents used in the United States? Why or why not? Find

out which states ban phosphates in detergents and which do not. Design a plan to change your state from its present stance.

2. Set up a culture of Daphnia (water fleas). Sample a preselected quantity at specific intervals, for example, one eyedropper full every 24 hours. Count the number of Daphnia to obtain an estimate of the population increase. Graph the results.

Objective: Gifted students will be able to record and organize weather data over a period of months.

Activities:

1. Recognize and organize weather data based upon the following variables: temperature, barometric pressure, precipitation, relative humidity, cloud type, wind speed and directions, and dew point. Prepare a weekly weather observation chart to observe the weather for one month using the above variables. Then design the weather instruments needed to measure the variables stated above. Once data are recorded, students should draw inferences related to the relationship between weather changes and each of the above variables. To illustrate some of the weather observation techniques students should visit the nearest office of the National Weather Service to learn how weather data is received and so that they can learn to read surface weather maps and teletype printouts. Furthermore, students can check their weather data by using a NOAA Weather Radio. A subscription for the monthly weather data for your area from NOAA should also be purchased.

Students should prepare their own weather reports including extended weekend forecasts. All measurements should be made in both the Imperial and metric systems of measurement. If only one measurement system is used, it should be the metric system.

Objective: Gifted students will be able to compare the rate of transfer of heat through different building materials.

Activities:

1. Construct a material tester by using a light bulb in a socket (use caution) set at a fixed distance from a slot into which materials can be placed. Use equal area and thickness squares of different materials such as fiberglass, wood, and ceiling tile. Construct a thermometer holder so that it can be placed against the tile at the same spot for each test. Test the temperature change when the light bulb is turned on for a specific period of time such as one or two minutes. Test the effect of thickness and air space. Test the effect of color by using the same material painted different colors.

Then design experiments to measure sound conductivity through different materials and/or heat conservation in a home.

Objective: Gifted students will be able to identify the components of a characteristic property for a given material.

Activities:

1. Obtain marble chips, iron filings, and lead shot or equivalent substitutes. Prepare a

data table similar to the following one for each of the three materials previously stated:

Marble Chips

Mass, grams   *Volume, millilitres*

Weigh six samples of marble chips and then record the corresponding volume displace-
ment. Use a graduated cylinder and read an initial water volume and then a final water
volume with the marble chips immersed in the water. The difference in water level is
the volume of the marble chips. Repeat this for six samples of iron filings and for six
samples of lead shot.

Graph the resultant data using one pencil color for marble chips, another for lead
shot, and a third color for iron filings. Use the x-axis for volume (ml) and the y-axis for
mass (g). Note that each material data set falls into a certain area of the graph. Calculate
the slope of each line drawn for each of the three materials used

$$\frac{Y\ (g)}{X\ (ml)}$$

Marble Chips	2.9
Iron Filings	6.8
Lead Shot	10.8

The accepted values are given above for comparison. The ratio of mass to volume
that we have used is called the *density* of an object. This experiment illustrates that
density is independent of the amount of material involved. Thus, changing the amount
of material does not change its density. This property of a material is called a characteristic property. Other characteristic properties which could be investigated include:
color, odor, hardness, electric conductivity, and ability to flow. Mass and volume, on
the other hand, are properties of a material which can change from one object to
another.

Is temperature a characteristic property? Why or why not? Try graphing water
temperature (y-axis) to find out. Start with an ice cube and stop when the water is
boiling. Did you find out that temperature is both? The characteristic property part of
temperature is that part between the melting point of a solid and the boiling point of a
liquid called the liquid range.

Evaluation:

1. Design and conduct an experiment to determine whether or not plasticene clay
(non-water soluable) can be used to demonstrate the characteristic property of density.

References

Bainbridge, J. W., et. al. *Weather Study: An Approach to Scientific Inquiry,* Methuen
Educational Limited, 11 New Fetter Lane, London, EC4, England, 1972.

Berger, Gilda and Melvin Berger. *Fitting In: Animals In Their Habitats,* Coward, Mc-
Cann and Geoghegan, 200 Madison Avenue, New York, N.Y., 10016, 1976.

Crocker, Robert K. *Elementary Science Curriculum Study,* Volumes 1 and 2, McGraw-
Hill-Ryerson Limited, Toronto, Canada, 1973.

Crustal Evolution Education Project Modules, Wards Natural Science Establishment, Rochester, N.Y., 1980.

Davis, Hubert, ed. *A January Fog Will Freeze A Hog and Other Weather Folklore,* Crown Publishers, One Park Avenue, New York, N.Y., 10016, 1977.

DeVito, A. and Krockover, Gerald H. *Activities Handbook for Teaching Energy Education,* Goodyear Publishing Company, Santa Monica, CA, 1981.

DeVito, A. and Krockover, Gerald H. *Creative Sciencing: Ideas and Activities for Teachers and Children,* Second Edition, Little Brown and Company, Inc., Boston, 1980.

Elementary Science Study Unit on *Change,* Webster Division, McGraw-Hill Book Company, New York, New York, 1976.

Growth Implications and the Earth's Future, Education Development Center, 55 Chapel Street, Newton, MA, 02160, 1977.

Hounshell, Paul B. and Ira R. Trollinger. *Games for the Science Classroom,* National Science Teachers Association, 1742 Connecticut Avenue, N.W., Washington, D.C., 20009, 1977.

Intermediate Science Curriculum Study, *Investigating Variation Minicourse,* Silver Burdett Company, Morristown, N.J., 1977. (also *Winds and Weather Minicourse,* 1977).

Lawrence Hall of Science, *Outdoor Biology Instructional Strategies,* University of California, Berkeley, CA, 1976.

New UNESCO Source Book for Science Teaching, UNIPUB, Inc., 650 First Avenue, New York, N.Y., 10017, 1973.

Pringle, Lawrence. *Death is Natural,* Four Winds Press, 50 West 44th Street, New York, N.Y., 10036, 1977.

Sagan, Carl. *The Dragons of Eden,* Ballatine Books, New York, N.Y., 1978.

Think About, Agency for Instructional Television, Box A, Bloomington, IN, 47402, 1979. (Sixty—15 minute color programs)

Troyer, Donald L., et al. *Sourcebook for Biological Sciences,* Macmillan, Inc., 866 Third Avenue, New York, N.Y., 10022, 1972.

Utgard, Russell O., et al. *Sourcebook for Earth Sciences and Astronomy,* Macmillan, Inc., 866 Third Avenue, New York, N.Y., 10022, 1972.

Wentworth, Daniel F. et al., *Examining Your Environment Series.* Toronto: Holt, Rinehart and Winston of Canada, Limited, 1976.

Wichers, David and John Tuey. *How to Make Things Grow,* Van Nostrand Reinhold Books, 120 Alexander Street, Princeton, N.J., 08450, 1972.

Wichers, David and John Tuey. *How to Be A Scientist At Home,* Van Nostrand Reinhold Books, 120 Alexander Street, Princeton, N.J., 08450, 1971.

9 Mathematics Curriculum for the Gifted

Grayson H. Wheatley

It is a law of Nature with us that a male child shall have one more side than his father, so that each generation shall rise (as a rule) one step in the scale of development and nobility. Thus the son of a Square is a Pentagon; the son of Pentagon a Hexagon; and so on.

—Edwin Abbot, *Flatland*

Although mathematics is considered by some to be fixed and unchanging, school mathematics is actually quite dynamic and variable. From new math in the sixties, to back to basics in the seventies, to problem solving in the eighties, the mathematics curriculum has undergone major shifts in goals and emphases. The availability of calculators and computers has forced a rethinking of traditional approaches (Wheatley, 1983), and a variety of instructional approaches abound even though the typical classroom adheres to a very staid format (Fey, 1979). As we consider mathematics for the gifted, it is important to recognize the larger mathematics education framework.

Rather than describing a variety of options for gifted mathematics classes, this chapter suggests a particular approach based on recognized assumptions. The focus will be on content rather than instructional methods. With the richness of availability of new ideas in mathematics education, it would be unwise to build a mathematics program for the gifted based on conventional mathematics textbooks that are not appropriate for gifted learners. They are slow paced, rule oriented, and fail to include important topics being recommended by national groups (e.g., the National Sciences Board and the Conference Board of Mathematical Sciences). "Even the best of the existing mathematics texts are very incremental in approach and therefore not appropriate for academically talented youths who prefer and can benefit from a more accelerated, conceptual presentation of course material" (VanTassel-Baska, Landau, and Olszewski, 1985, p. 261). The National Science Board Commission on Precollege Education in Mathematics, Science and Technology (1983) suggested that school mathematics include the following topics: discrete mathematics (combinatorics, graph theory, dis-

The author would like to acknowledge the assistance of Dr. James Hersberger in the final preparation of this chapter.

crete probability, matrices, algorithms, difference equations), statistics, computer programming, philosophical basis of calculus, algorithmic thinking, and student data-gathering and exploration of mathematical ideas to facilitate learning mathematics by discovery. Whereas it is unlikely that the standard school mathematics curriculum will include these topics in the near future, it is crucial that programs for the gifted do so.

Therefore, important components of a mathematics program for the gifted would include:

1. *An articulated K–12 mathematics sequence.* By building a program for all mathematics courses as one package, an effective program can be developed. Too often school systems will develop an elementary and junior high program and use existing high-school courses. The work of each year should be a recognized part of an integrated sequence.

2. *Self-contained classes for the gifted at all grade levels.* Significant and sustained progress requires classes to organize so that the gifted study together. Pull-out programs, while possibly having a short-term positive effect on the learners, are of dubious value over the long term. However, when gifted students are in class with other students of similar ability, a curriculum can be designed that goes well beyond the regular content in both depth and breadth. The syllabus for average learners can be compacted and the topics elaborated, but most importantly, the thinking can be on a higher plane with topics unified and synthesized. No other grouping model offers such potential.

3. *Selected strands of study.* At the elementary school level, substantial units on probability, statistics, estimation, mental arithmetic, spatial visualization, algebra, geometry, and discrete mathematics should comprise the curriculum.

4. *Encouragement of self-generated methods.* It is important that students recognize that they can generate their own ways of doing mathematics—that they do not have to wait to be shown how to perform each succeeding task. Although many educators champion the use of manipulatives in teaching number ideas, there is still strong support for teaching fixed procedures for addition, subtraction, multiplication, and division. In fact, it is virtually universally accepted that elementary school pupils should learn the "efficient" computational methods found in every math textbook. The fact of the matter is that the elementary school mathematics curriculum as exemplified by commercial texts is primarily a matter of learning rules for special situations. But children can construct their own methods for dealing with most situations (Labinowicz, 1985).

Shown is an example of a bright second-grade student who developed an efficient algorithm for adding two-digit numerals. Shawn was presented with the task shown below.

$$37$$
$$\underline{+\ 54}$$

His method was this: take 3 from the 4 to make 40 (37 + 3), 40 and 50 makes 90, the answer is 91. This is a general algorithm that works quite well, but more importantly, Shawn *understood* it because he devised it. On another level, a more significant event occurred. Shawn experienced the satisfaction of creating a method. He found that mathematics is understandable and that the process of constructing meaning is an enjoyable and rewarding activity. Throughout the study of mathematics, gifted students should be encouraged to develop their own procedures rather than always depending on the teacher to show a method to be practiced. In fact, if students develop their own methods, little practice is needed (Maddell, 1985).

5. *Emphasis on problem solving at all grade levels.* Helping the gifted learners focus on the heuristics of problem solving increases their capacity to approach successfully new mathematical tasks and enhances their efficiency in dealing with difficult problems.

6. *Fast-paced courses for the highly gifted.* The top 2–3 percent of learners are not always well served by the program designed for the top 15–25 percent. The very best students can frequently study material at a much faster rate. They can learn the content of two or more years of mathematics in a single year. It will often be necessary for smaller school districts to work together to offer such courses for the few students that may be in this category.

7. *A formal Algebra I course offered no later than the eighth grade.* Such a course should be meaningfully organized, stress the concept of variables, and not emphasize manipulation of symbols at the expense of relationships. The scope of the course should go well beyond the content of a conventional Algebra I course.

8. *Advanced placement calculus.* Because previous courses have been compacted, this course may well be offered in the eleventh grade, providing a year for advanced study at a nearby university or to facilitate early college admission.

Essential Topics

The mathematics curriculum for gifted students should differ from the conventional curriculum in pace, scope, and organization. The pace of learning can be greatly accelerated for more able learners, allowing them to experience the exhilaration of unifying ideas; they can study many more topics in greater depth. These are topics that would be beyond the range of average learners. For example, gifted fifth- and sixth-grade students can profit from a study of probability, intuitive algebra, functions, and limits (Hersberger and Wheatley, 1986).

Every effort should be made to challenge gifted students with advanced material. It would be unwise to program all gifted students into algebra at the seventh or eighth grade; some may be ready for it earlier. The content recommendations below should be adjusted to the appropriate grade level. The following list of essential strands should be a part of a student's mathematical experience before beginning a formal course in algebra. (Actually, a more desirable but difficult plan to implement is an integrated approach in which students study "real" algebra and "real" geometry throughout the elementary grades as the Europeans do.)

1. *Problem solving.* When basic skills in mathematics are identified, strong consideration must be given to problem solving. Computational skill is a means

to an end, where the end is solving problems. Schools have not been teaching problem solving; the word *problems* in texts are there to provide practice on skills. Problem solving is the means by which an individual uses previously acquired knowledge, skills, and understanding to satisfy the demands of an unfamiliar situation (Krulik and Rudnick, 1980). Problem solving is highly motivating for gifted students; they enjoy the challenge and respond well to problem solving once they dispel the belief that mathematics is computation. Students can become aware of the strategies and approaches they use when stuck on a problem. Emphasis on strategies, such as look for a pattern, guess and test, and draw a diagram, has been shown effective in developing problem-solving proficiency with gifted students (Hersberger and Wheatley, 1986; Wheatley and Wheatley, 1982). Throughout the K–12 curriculum, attention should be given to solving novel problems. As much as 20 percent of each year should be devoted to teaching such strategies and to problem solving in general.

2. *Estimation and mental arithmetic.* For many years cries have been heard for more estimation in the mathematics curriculum. Little progress was made because the rounding approach of the standard curriculum does not work well. Recently, Reys and Reys (1983) developed an approach to computational estimation that involves a different method. Strategies such as front-ending, adjusting, and using compatible numbers have proven quite effective in building estimation proficiency. Once computational methods have been introduced, estimation should be an integral part of the year-long study of mathematics.

For example, consider a front end strategy for the problem shown below.

$$
\begin{array}{r}
642 \\
\times\ \ 5 \\
\hline
\end{array}
$$

The strategy consists of two steps: a front-end estimation, followed by an adjustment. So, for the problem shown here, the estimator would say $5 \times 600 = 3000$, 5×42 is at least 200, so 5×642 is about 3200. Front-end strategies exist for all four arithmetic operations, and they work equally well with whole number, fraction, or decimal arithmetic.

Mental arithmetic should also receive major attention (Reys, 1985). Hope, Reys, and Reys (1986) discuss ways of helping students become effective in performing computational tasks mentally. For example, 6×99 can be done mentally by subtracting 6 from 6×100, or $37 + 28$ can be done by thinking 37, 47, 57, 65. It is important that students realize there are alternatives to performing the standard algorithms on their "mental blackboard." Over several years students should develop methods for mentally performing all four operations with whole numbers, decimals and, fractions (see Schoen and Zweng, 1986).

3. *Spatial visualization.* Although not usually treated in conventional texts, spatial visualization is actually a critical mathematical ability. Research studies by Battista, Wheatley, and Talsma (1982), Talsma, (1986), and Turner (1982) document the importance of spatial visualization in mathematics. Of all intellectual factors, spatial visualization is the most highly correlated with mathematics achievement and least addressed in the mathematics curriculum. Gifted learners frequently have great capacity for using imagery and they should have the opportunity to enhance their ability to visualize. Activities such as the construction

of three-dimensional models from nets, tangrams, tessellations, Mira Math, and graphing are effective in learning to think visually. This topic, like estimation, should begin early in the program and continue throughout.

4. *Computer problem solving.* Hersberger and Wheatley (1986) developed a fifth- and sixth-grade curriculum for the gifted that featured computer problem solving as a major component. In this approach, little time is devoted to teaching a programming language such as BASIC, instead, students are presented with a problem to solve after learning only a few programming statements. The problems are ones for which a computer program can be written to determine solutions. Students work in small groups, select their own problems from an available set, and write a computer program to hand in. Through this activity students come to see the power of a computer, and incorporate computer problem-solving strategies in their thinking. The computer is used as a medium to learn mathematics through problem solving, and as a medium to learn more about problem solving itself.

5. *Probability.* Probability provides a way of reasoning that complements the absolutist thinking that dominates school mathematics. It is important that children begin early to build probabilistic models of thought into their reasoning patterns. The applications of probability are many and diverse; for example, chemistry, physics, and economics are conceptualized in terms of probability models. Since gifted students are likely to study in the sciences, an early beginning with this topic will facilitate their progress.

6. *Statistics.* Societal changes over the past ten to twenty years have created the need to process vast amounts of information. The ability to interpret, analyze, and represent information has become a basic skill. Textbook publishers and school systems change slowly, and thus we have educational programs designed for a previous era. A mathematics program for gifted students should allocate significant amounts of time to statistics. This can be accomplished by using supplementary materials such as the Quantitative Literacy program of the American Statistical Association and others described in Shulte and Smart (1981).

7. *Rational numbers.* With the advent of electronic computing devices and the metric system that is based on the decimal system, some educators have advocated less attention to fractions and more on decimals. This naive reaction fails to recognize the major role of rational numbers in the conceptualization of scientific principles and expressing mathematical ideas. In building a K–12 rational number strand, the work at the primary level should be primarily intuitive and conceptual, with much use of physical representations (e.g., The Pattern Factory from Creative Publications). At the intermediate level, equivalences and computations can be introduced, but since rational number computation is quite complex, care must be exercised not to introduce complex computations such as addition of fractions with unlike denominators too soon. Finally, a pre-algebra course can complete the work on use of rational numbers and introduce rational expressions, which will be a major topic in high-school algebra.

8. *Geometry and measurement.* Hoffman (Bloom, 1986) has recommended that geometry for gifted students emphasize transformational and coordianate ap-

proaches with much attention to ruler and straight edge constructions. Traditionally, geometry at this level has been a collection of terms and definitions (e.g., "This is a parallelogram. A parallelogram is . . ."). Geometry is rich in relationships to be explored, and a problem-solving approach is highly effective in this subject with gifted students. In the study of measurement, after students have constructed the meaning of linear, square, and cubic measures, problems can be posed that can prove most interesting. Surface area and volume of prisms, pyramids, and other polyhedra provide a rich setting for establishing relationships and building intuitions. All work with formulas should be approached meaningfully, and rote applications of given formulas should be very limited.

9. *Ratio, proportion and percent.* Proportional thought serves as the basis for much work in the sciences. It is critical that mathematics for the gifted establish a strong background in thinking proportionally. Since this topic requires formal operational thought, in the Piagetian sense, the topic should normally occur in grade five at the earliest, with major work in grades six and seven.

10. *Intuitive algebra.* Algebra textbooks are essentially collections of procedures for manipulating expressions and solving special types of equations. A thoughtful view of the subject reveals that algebra is expressing relationships in symbolic form. With gifted students, it is essential that we get beyond changing the form of an expression [e.g., writing $x^2 - 9$ as $(x - 3)(x + 3)$] and putting the emphasis on using the language of algebra to express relationships (e.g., writing the nth term of the sequence 5, 8, 11, 14 . . .). By focusing on functions and their graphs, students can build spatial intuitions that give meaning to what they do. Mason and Pimm (1985) provide excellent suggestions for an algebra course based on understanding and meaning rather than special methods. Effort should be made to approach each topic as problem solving so that students can construct meaning for themselves.

Exemplary Programs

FAST-PACED COURSES

Highly precocious youth profit greatly by studying material at a faster than normal rate. As has been shown at Johns Hopkins University in the Study of Mathematically Precocious Youth, students with high SAT-M scores can complete two or even three years of high-school mathematics in a four-week summer session. Based on these results, it is not unreasonable to expect similar results in a school setting. For example, gifted thirteen-year-olds can complete Algebra I and Algebra II in the same year. It is important that the most able students have the opportunity to study mathematics at a pace that matches their potential learning rate. Otherwise they unconsciously adjust their learning to accommodate school demands; gifted students respond to high expectations if they are consistent and reasonable. In school programming, several school systems may cooperate to provide fast-paced courses, as has been done in the suburban Chicago area.

An example of radical acceleration that works well is the summer algebra course offered for gifted junior high-school students at Purdue University. In 1985, twenty-four students mastered the equivalent of two years of algebra skills in a two-week period. The instructor was a mathematics educator with a rich background in gifted education. The students attended class five hours a day, with help sessions available in the evenings. The remarkable aspect of this program was the content. Even though most of these students had not previously studied algebra, the textbook was for second-year algebra. Algebra II texts usually devote the first third of the book to a review of Algebra I. This pace is just about right for gifted students. At the end of the course, the students took the ETS Cooperative Algebra I and Algebra II tests and scored quite high on both tests. Based on their performance in the course, the instructor wrote letters to the students' high-school staff, recommending particular courses as next steps for these students. Follow-up studies have shown that the course is highly effective—most students establish credit in algebra and perform well in subsequent courses, usually high-school geometry. Other universities offer similar programs (Simpson, 1983; Stanley, 1980).

THE CUMBERLAND ACCELERATED MATHEMATICS PROJECT

At Cumberland Elementary School in West Lafayette, Indiana, a fifth- and sixth-grade mathematics program for gifted students operates to challenge students without radical acceleration. Students are identified for the program at the end of the fourth grade. The curriculum emphasizes problem solving by using computers and calculators. Skill work is approached using a diagnostic-prescriptive model; students practice only those computational skills that need strengthening. Little or no time is allocated to discussing arithmetic in class. Instead, class time is used for such topics as cooperative small group heuristic problem solving, probability, graphing of functions, limits of sequences, geometry, measurement, and spatial visualization. Much of the problem solving is done with computers. Students working in groups of two or three write computer programs to solve nonroutine mathematics problems. In grade six, as much as one-third of the year is devoted to this activity. Typical of the problems they solve is:

> In 1960, the population of the U.S. was 180,000,000 and the population of Mexico was 85,000,000. The annual growth in population was 1.23% for the U.S. and 2.23% for Mexico. If these growth rates remain constant, in what year will the population of Mexico exceed that of the U.S.?

An evaluation of this program showed that students in the program out-performed a comparable control group on problem solving and math concepts and on computation, even though the time spent on computation was minimal (Hersberger and Wheatley, 1986).

COMPREHENSIVE SCHOOL MATHEMATICS PROGRAM (CSMP)

Several programs have been based on the program developed within CSMP for gifted students. The program, Elements of Mathematics (EM), was designed for the top 5–10 percent of mathematics students, and is intended as the mathematics to be considered in grades 7–12. It is a unified, spiral approach that emphasizes understanding, concept attainment, development of process skills, and problem solving. The program contains numerous opportunities for discovery through teacher-student dialogues and a strong individualized component. Major content areas include probability, statistics, logic, discrete mathematics, geometry, and measurement. The basic skills emphasized in EM are identical with those proposed by the National Council of Supervisors of Mathematics (NCSM).

Of the programs using the EM material, the Mathematics Education for Gifted Secondary School Students (MEGSSS) program is the most established and well known. Begun in 1978, this ongoing effort provides gifted learners with the opportunity to learn a great deal of sophisticated mathematics at an early age, and it provides the student with an opportunity to earn substantial college mathematics credit prior to graduation from high school. A similar program at the State University of New York (SUNY) at Buffalo has been developed, with the major difference being that the students in the SUNY gifted program actually enroll in mathematics course at SUNY Buffalo during the last two years of the program (see Harpel, 1983; Kaufman, Fitzgerald, and Harpel, 1981; Krist, 1985). It should be noted that the EM-based programs deal with quite sophisticated mathematics at the upper levels, and require a teacher clientele with a more substantial working knowledge of college mathematics than most secondary teachers. The programs are designed to prepare students to step directly into advanced training in either mathematics or the sciences.

Issues in Curriculum Implementation

As an individual school system develops an implementation plan for the gifted, many issues will arise. Some of these issues result from local factors. For example, in the Indian River School District in Delaware, an eighth-grade algebra course for more able students was abandoned because proper standards for admission were not established; consequently, students without sufficient ability were admitted. Several years later, the course was reestablished but with well-defined criteria. Previous educational plans will influence decision making and the type of gifted program established. Discussed below are issues that are likely to arise.

1. *Placement of the beginning algebra course.* When should gifted students begin the normal study of algebra? This is an issue that must be considered carefully. Some argue for seventh grade, yet others feel that harm is done by offering an eighth-grade course. A popular approach is to offer algebra in the eighth grade for gifted students, and to schedule younger students into the course if they are unusually precocious. The resolution of this issue will be influenced by the size of the school system and plans for transporting students between buildings.

2. *Computer-assisted instruction.* Computers make individualized instruction possible, which suggests that programming for the gifted can be facilitated by acquiring or writing software that will essentially deliver instruction and solve some of the difficult scheduling problems. Although this option seems attractive and may be better than other feasible plans, the quality of learning in such an

environment may be questioned. Clearly, the computer is a powerful tool and should be a part of mathematics for the gifted, but whether entire courses should be delivered by computer is a question that requires careful attention. (For a full discussion of this question, see Chapter 16 in this book.)

3. *The high-school sequence.* There is no one best set of high-school mathematics courses for the gifted. Many options exist and each course can have many orientations. Determining the course sequence (e.g., Algebra I, Geometry, Algebra II, college algebra and trigonometry, and calculus) does not constitute final planning. How does the Algebra I course for gifted students differ from the regular Algebra I course? Does it go well beyond the regular course? Will the content of the geometry course be transformational geometry? Solid geometry? These are important issues and the answers may not lie in just selecting a textbook. Will analytic geometry be taught as a separate course or integrated with calculus? Will a course in discrete mathematics be offered? Will it be taken before or after calculus? How does computer science fit into the program? Where will problem solving be in the high-school curriculum? For an excellent delineation of these issues, see Hirsch and Zweng (1985).

4. *Instructional materials.* Whereas the standard teaching aid is the textbook, the inherent limitations of books written for the lowest common denominator in meeting the needs of the gifted must be considered. Textbooks, which are designed for national distribution, must be appropriate for all types of classes. Such books, if usable at all, require major adaptation for use with the gifted. In many cases, a school system will need to package a course by using materials from several sources. Excellent materials are available and can be used to build strong programs for the gifted, but this approach requires time and money.

5. *Articulation.* School systems usually have good articulation within a building, but this is not always the case between buildings, especially when the buildings house students at different grade levels. Implementation plans should include attention to the articulation issue. Even though a school district may have a strong gifted education program at the elementary level, if there is not proper follow through at the secondary level the students may not be well served. School systems must make decisions about leadership, coordination, communication, and K–12 curriculum committees.

Materials and Content Examples

Implementation of the program described in this chapter calls for a great deal of material outside the mathematics textbook to be utilized. In particular, the problem-solving material must be taken almost entirely from outside sources. When one chooses problem-solving material, special care must be taken to select material that is easy for the instructor to utilize in an educationally sound manner, and that is sufficiently challenging for the students. The main sources for most of the very good problem-solving material available at this time are Dale Seymour Publications, Addison-Wesley, and Creative Publications. (See the Problem Solving Materials List for some of these materials.)

When developing the material for the portion of the program that precedes algebra, two projects developed for middle-school enrichment are quite helpful.

The Mathematics Resource Project from Creative Publications, and *The Middle Grades Mathematics Project* from Addison-Wesley focus on areas such as probability and statistics, geometry and spatial visualization, numeration, ratio and percent, and other areas of critical importance to successful implementation of this program. These materials can be used to form the core of the enrichment material in several of the necessary content areas.

This chapter concludes with examples of lessons typical of those described, and that are similar to those available in the material suggested throughout the chapter (see Example 9.A). They would be used at various places in the curriculum, depending on the students' backgrounds and expertise.

Conclusion

It is clear that gifted learners are greatly underserved by standard mathematics curricula. Part of the problem is that conventional texts are limited and outdated; however, they would not be appropriate even if they did treat the topics identified in this chapter since they are incremental and based on drill and practice. Yet materials do exist from which a mathematics program for the gifted can be designed. This chapter suggests a mathematics curriculum for gifted students, K–12.

Of the grouping models, self-contained gifted classrooms hold the most promise. Although other models have merit, it is often difficult to build a sustained and articulated curriculum in mathematics without ongoing instructional grouping.

Problem solving should serve as a focus topic and as a mode of instruction; students can learn to reflect on problem-solving processes and also learn new material through problem solving. Although we cannot be sure what specific knowledge will be important in the next century, we can be sure that problem-solving ability will be essential. The other nontraditional topics outlined in the chapter have been recommended by the major national organization in the field and form the core of the curriculum. Computational skill, which occupies so much of instructional time, can be achieved as a secondary objective.

Of equal importance to the content is the learning environment. If gifted students are to become competent, creative, and curious, they must learn in an intellectual environment that encourages them to organize ideas in their own way. Teaching strategies that dispense knowledge and show procedures must not dominate. Gifted students must come to believe that they can construct mathematics for themselves and that this process is exciting and rewarding.

KEY POINTS SUMMARY

- Mathematics curriculum for the gifted can best be delivered in self-contained classes or instructional groups.
- Model programs for the gifted in mathematics usually emphasize only one of the three basic curriculum models; such programs either offer advanced content on a fast-paced basis, are problem-solving oriented, or are conceptually unified.
- The mathematics curriculum should emphasize problem-solving approaches as the dominant mode of instruction.

- Highly gifted students can profit from fast-paced and accelerated mathematic experiences.
- Major strands of a gifted student's mathematical experience prior to algebra should be: (1) problem solving; (2) estimation and mental arithmetic; (3) spatial visualization; (4) computer problems; (5) probability; (6) statistics; (7) rational numbers; (8) geometry and measurement; (9) ratio, proportion, and percent; and (10) intuitive algebra.
- Major issues in developing mathematics curriculum for the gifted include: (1) when to teach beginning algebra; (2) how to use computer-assisted instruction; (3) how to sequence the high-school courses; (4) where to find good instructional material, and (5) how to articulate the various components of the curriculum.

Selected Materials List

Charles, R., and Lester, F. (1985). *Problem-Solving Experiences in Mathematics, Grades 1–8*. Menlo Park, Calif.: Addison-Wesley.

Dolan, D., and Williamson, J. (1983). *Teaching Problem-Solving Strategies*. Palo Alto, Calif.: Addison-Wesley.

Fisher, L. (1982). *Super Problems*. Palo Alto, Calif.: Dale Seymour Publications.

Fisher, L., Kennedy, B., and Megidovich, W. (1980). *Brother Alfred Brousseau Problem-Solving and Mathematicas Competition*. Palo Alto, Calif.: Creative Publications.

Fisher, L., and Medigovich, W. (1981). *Problem of the Week*. Palo Alto, Calif.: Dale Seymour Publications.

Greenes, C., Gregory, J., and Seymour, D. (1977). *Successful Problem Solving Techniques*. Palo Alto, Calif.: Creative Publications.

Greenes, C., Immerzeel, G., et al. (1980). *Techniques of Problem Solving (TOPS)*. Palo Alto, Calif.: Dale Seymour Publications.

Greenes, C., Spungin, R., and Dombrowski, J. (1977). *Problem-mathics*. Palo Alto, Calif.: Creative Publications.

Judd, W. (1977). *Problem Solving Kit for Use with a Calculator*. New York: Science Research Associates.

Krulik, S., and Rudnick, J. (1980). *Problem Solving: A Handbook for Teachers*. Boston: Allyn and Bacon.

Krulik, S., and Rudnick, J. (1984). *Problem Solving: A Sourcebook*. Boston: Allyn and Bacon.

Lenchner, G. (1983). *Creative Problem Solving in School Mathematics*. Boston: Houghton Mifflin.

Meyer, C., and Sallee, T. (1983). *Make It Simpler*. Palo Alto, Calif.: Addison-Wesley.

Nelson, D., and Worth, J. (1983). *How to Choose and Create Good Problems for Primary Children*. Reston, Va.: National Council of Teachers of Mathematics.

Pedersen, J., and Armbruster, F. (1983). *A New Twist*. Palo Alto, Calif.: Addison-Wesley.

Roper, A., and Harvey, L. (1980). *The Pattern Factory*. Palo Alto, Calif.: Creative Publications.

Seymour, D. (1982). *Favorite Problems*. Palo Alto, Calif.: Dale Seymour Publications.

Seymour, D. (1984). *Problem Parade*. Palo Alto, Calif.: Dale Seymour Publications.

Enrichment Projects

Mathematics Resource Project. Hermanson, J., Pieters, R., and Sowder, L. (1978). *Geometry and Visualization; Mathematics in Science and Society; Number Sense and Arithmetic Skills; Ratio, Proportion, and Scaling;* and *Statistics and Information Gathering*. Palo Alto, Calif.: Creative Productions.

Middle Grades Mathematics Project. Fitzgerald, W., Lappan, G., Phillips, E., Shroyer, J. and Winter, M. (1986). *Factors and Multiples; Mouse and Elephant: Measuring Growth; Probability, Similarity, and Equivalent Fractions;* and *Spatial Visualization*. Menlo Park, Calif.: Addison-Wesley.

Additional Materials

The Contest Problem Books I–IV. These offer past American High School Mathematics Examinations from 1950 to 1982. The problems are challenging and help reinforce concepts and offer creativity and efficiency in the solutions. Available from the MAA.

Gardner, M. He has eleven books of reprints of articles from *Scientific American*. The books are fascinating and stimulating. They provide motivation for reading mathematics and offer insight into the history, uses, elegance, and recreations of the field. His latest collection is entitled *Knotted Doughnuts*.

Polya, G. *How to Solve It*. Princeton University Press. The Bible of Problem Solving. He offers a mathematician's viewpoint on the processes and the enjoyment of problem solving. The mathematical content is an integral part of his method as it should be in teaching problem solving.

University of School Mathematics Project (UCSMP). This is an Amoco and Carnegie sponsored project design to write an implementable curriculum for *average* students in line with recent recommendations of educational committees. The secondary component, headed by Zalman Usiskin, is writing materials for grades 7–12. The seventh grade text *Transition Mathematics* is designed for those students at grade level 7.0 regardless of age. This has been tested with gifted sixth graders and works well, although it needs supplementing. For information contact Carol Siegel, 5835 S. Kimbark, Chicago, IL 60637.

Usiskin, Z., and Bell, M. *Applying Arithmetic, A Handbook of Applica-*

tions of Arithmetic. The title explains the subject but not the depth at which these authors analyze and categorize these applications. Supported with a National Science Foundation grant. For more information, contact Zalman Usiskin, 5835 S. Kimbark, Chicago, IL 60637.

References

American Statistical Association (1985). *Quantitative Literacy Project.* Washington, D.C.: American Statistical Association.

Battista, M., Wheatley, G., and Talsma, G. (1982). "The Importance of Spatial Visualization and Congnitive Development for Geometry Learning in Preservice Elementary Teachers." *Journal for Research in Mathematics Education, 13*(5), 332–340.

Bloom, N. (1986). "The Teaching of Geometry." In M. Carss (Ed.), *Proceedings of ICME-V,* Boston: Birkhauser.

Carss, M. (1986). *Proceedings of the Fifth International Congress on Mathematical Education.* Boston: Birkhauser Boston, Inc.

Fey, J. (1979). "Mathematics Teaching Today: Perspectives from Three National Surveys." *Arithemetic Teacher, 28,* 10–14.

Harpel, J. (1983). "Project MEGSSS." *Mathematics Teacher, 76,* 286.

Hersberger, J., and Wheatley, G. (1980). "A Proposed Model for the Mathematics Education of Gifted Elementary School Pupils." *Gifted Child Quarterly, 24,* 32–40.

Hersberger, J., and Wheatley, G. (1986). *An Evaluation of a Fifth-Grade Mathematically Gifted Program.* Unpublished paper, Purdue University.

Hirsch, C., and Zweng, M. (1985). *The Secondary School Mathematics Curriculum.* Yearbook of the National Council of Teachers of Mathematics. Reston, Va.: NCTM.

Hope, J., Reys, B., and Reys, R. (1986). *Mental Computation in Middle Grades.* Palo Alto, Calif.: Dale Seymour Publications.

Kaufman, B., Fitzgerald, J., and Harpel, J. (1981). *Mathematical Education for the Gifted Secondary School Student: MEGSSS in Action.* Saint Louis: Cemrel. (ERIC ED 226 960)

Krist, B. (1985). "The Gifted Math Program at SUNY Buffalo." In C. Hirsch and M. Sweng (Eds.), *The Secondary School Mathematics Curriculum.* Reston, Va.: NCTM.

Krulik, S., and Rudnick, J. (1980). *Problem Solving: A Handbook for Teachers.* Boston: Allyn and Bacon.

Labinowicz, E. (1985). *Learning from Children.* Menlo Park, Calif.: Addison Wesley.

Madell, R. (1985). "Children's Natural Processes." *Arithmetic Teacher, 32*(7), 20–22.

Mason, J. and Pimm, D. (1985). *Routes to Algebra.* Milton Keynes, England: Open University Educational Enterprises.

National Council of Teachers of Mathematics (1980). *An Agenda for Action–*

Recommendations for School Mathematics of the 80s. Reston, Va.: National Council of Teachers of Mathematics.

National Science Board Commission on Precollege Education in Mathematics, Science and Technology (1983). *Educating Americans in the 21st Century: A Report to the American People and the National Science Board.* National Science Board, Washington, D.C.

Reys, B. (1985). "Mental Computation." *Arithmetic Teacher, 32,* 43–46.

Reys, R., and Reys, B. (1983). *Guide to Using Estimation Skills and Strategies* (*GUESS*). Palo Alto, Calif.: Dale Seymour Publications.

Schoen, H., and Zweng, M. (1986). *Estimation and Mental Computation.* Yearbook of the National Council of Teachers of Mathematics. Reston, Va.: NCTM.

Shulte, A., and Smart, J. (1981). *Teaching Probability and Statistics.* Yearbook of the National Council of Teachers of Mathematics. Reston, Va.: National Council of Teachers of Mathematics.

Simpson, N. (1983). *Evaluation of Midwest Talent Search Summer Program. Final Report.* Evanston, Ill.: Northwestern University.

Stanley, J. (1980). "On Educating the Gifted." *Educational Researcher, 9,* 8–12.

Talsma, G. (1986). *Individual Differences in Visual Short-term Recognition Memory, and their Interrelationships with Spatial Ability and Problem Solving.* Unpublished doctoral dissertation, Purdue University.

Turner, K. (1982). *An Investigation of the Role of Spatial Performance, Learning Styles, and Kinetic Imagery in the Learning of Calculus.* Unpublished doctoral dissertation, Purdue University.

VanTassel-Baska, J., Landau, M., and Olszewski, P. (1985). "Toward Developing an Appropriate Math/Science Curriculum for Gifted Learners." *Journal for the Education of the Gifted, 7*(4), 257–272.

Wheatley, G. (1983). "A Mathematics Curriculum for the Gifted and Talented." *Gifted Child Quarterly, 27*(3), 77–80.

Wheatley, G. (1984a). "Instruction for the Gifted." In J. Feldhusen (Ed.), *Toward Excellence in Gifted Education.* Denver: Love Publishing.

Wheatley, G. (1984b). "Problem Solving Makes Math Scores Soar." *Educational Leadership, 41*(4), 52–53.

Wheatley, G., and Wheatley, C. (1982). *Calculator Use and Problem Solving Performance of Sixth Grade Pupils. Final Report.* Washington, D.C.: The National Science Foundation.

EXAMPLE 9.A Sample Objectives and Activities in Mathematics ━━━━━━━━

PROBLEM SOLVING

Goal: Students will develop strategies for solving nonroutine problems.

Activity: Organize the class into groups of three. Give each group one copy of one problem. Sample nonroutine problems are provided below. Provide time for the groups to work. Then have representatives of each group present to the class their solutions and strategies.

Problems:

1. The product of three numbers is 6783 and their sum is 57. What are the three numbers?

2. The surface of Clear Lake is 35 feet above the surface of Blue Lake. Clear Lake is twice as deep as Blue Lake. The bottom of Clear Lake is 12 feet above the bottom of Blue Lake. How deep is Blue Lake?

3. When asked how old she is, a teacher responded with this riddle: "My age is a two digit number. When multiplied by seven the result is a three digit number. When the digit six is written after the three digit number, that number is increased by 1833." How old is the teacher?

4. Two flagpoles are each 100 feet high. A rope 150 feet long is strung between the tops of the flagpoles. At its lowest point, the rope sags to within 25 feet of the ground. How far apart are the flagpoles?

5. In a game of simplified football a touchdown results in 7 points and a field goal results in 3 points. What is the largest game score for a team *not* possible?

6. A printer uses 837 digits to number the pages of a book. How many pages are there in the book?

7. Which sums are most likely to occur in adding two numbers?

   a. The 50 numbers shown below were taken from the last two digits of a listing in a phone book.

   b. Find the sum of each pair of digits.

   c. Arrange the sums so that you can see the number of times each sum occurs.

   d. Are all sums just as likely to occur?

   e. How many ways can a sum of 8 occur?

   f. Form a generalization about the pattern of sums and explain.

   g. Obtain a phone book and pick 100 names in a row.

   h. Copy the last two digits and repeat the experiment.

   i. Did your results agree with the first experiment?

63	36	95	63	85	37
59	21	35	84	79	96
70	58	43	27	36	28
33	72	96	48	22	49
55	37	03	43	35	81
71	67	63	34	84	48
05	68	35	59	49	96
47	42	14	23	91	95
01	39				

NUMERATION

Objective: Write numerals in base five.

Activities:
Given the set of xs shown below, we usually write 12 for the number of objects.

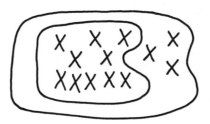

This representation uses a group size of ten. Let us see what happens when we use a different group size. Suppose we use a group size of five. The grouping is shown below.

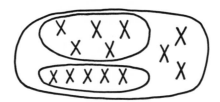

We can write 23 (base five) to show that there are two groups of five and three more.

The system of numbers we usually use is a base ten system. The system used above is a base five system.

We can write 23 (base five) = 12 (base ten).

Write the base five numeral for each set shown on page 268.

Any number can be chosen for the group size. Thus we could write numerals in many different bases. For example, let's choose a group size of three. Write the base three numeral for each of the previous sets.

Choose other base sizes and write the numerals in those bases.

Objective: Write the base five numerals to 444 (five). How can you be sure your work is correct?

Activities:
It is interesting to count in other bases. For example, to count in base five, we only use the symbols 0, 1, 2, 3, 4.

To count in base five we say,

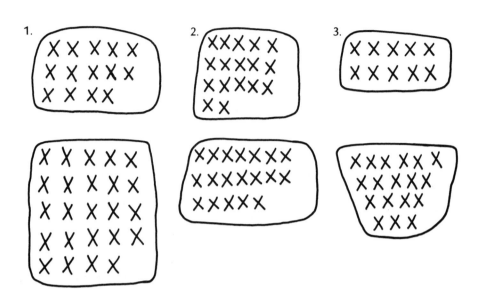

1, 2, 3, 4, 10, 11, 12, 13, 14, 20, 21
Continue counting in base five until you reach 44 (base five).
What comes next?
What is the base ten numeral for 44 (five)?

Objective: Convert from one base to another.

Activities:
To convert from base five to base ten we use the group size.
   Example:
      Write the base ten numeral for 34 (base five).
         34 (base five) = 3 × 5 + 4 = 19 (base ten).
         243 (base five) = 2 × 25 + 4 × 5 + 3 = 73 (base ten).
      Write the base ten numeral for each of the numerals below.
         a. 41 (base 5)   b. 24 (base 5)   c. 110 (base 5)
         d. 100 (base 5)   e. 444 (base 5)   f. 1000 (base 5)
         g. Choose six other base 5 numerals and change them to base ten.

Objective: Perform computations in different bases.

Activities:
Try adding, subtracting, multiplying, and dividing in base 5.
   Sample tasks:

a. 12 (five)	b. 43 (five)	c. 312 (five)	d. 4)132 (five)
+32 (five)	+24 (five)	× 3	___(five)
(five)	(five)	(five)	

How can you be sure your work is correct?

Objective: Write numerals in other bases.

Activities:
Write the base eight numeral for each set shown below.

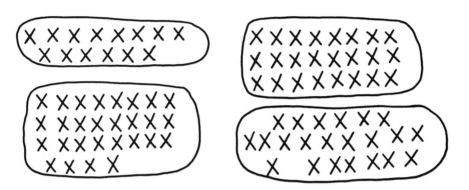

Try counting and adding in base eight.
Can you change numerals form base eight to base five? base ten?
Write the base ten numeral for each:
    a. 17 (eight)   b. 36 (eight)   c. 203 (eight)
Now make up 10 (eight) problems of:
    d. your own and solve them!
    e. 17 (eight)   f. 36 (eight)   g. 111 (eight)
    h. Now make up 10 (eight) problems of your own and solve them!

Objective: Invent a numeration system.

Activities:
Other symbols than 1,2,3 . . . can be used to build a numeration system. Use the symbols A,B,C,D,E to write the first twenty base 5 numerals. If you use A=0, B=1, C=2, D=3, E=4 you should find that 16 (base 10) is DB and that 23 (base 5) is CD.
    Use the symbols, Γ, $\daleth$, L, $\lrcorner$ to write the base four numeral for the first twenty numbers.
    Make up symbols and write the base eight numerals for the first thirty numbers.

Objective: Describe the binary system (base two).

Activities:
Look up the binary system and study it. Learn to count and add in the binary system.

Objective: Write a computer program to convert from one base to another.

Activity:

Do it!

Evaluation:

1. What comes after 24 (five)?
2. 42 (five) = _____ (ten).
3. 102 (five) − 43 (five) = _____ (five)
4. 36 (eight) = _____ (ten)
5. 20 (eight) = _____ (five)

MEASUREMENT

THE WICK EXPERIMENT

Goal: Determine a pattern of change.

Materials: Wick (blotter paper, chromotography paper), container (drinking glass), pencil, watch with second hand.

Procedure:

1. Mark off seven or more dots on the wick at 5 mm intervals with a felt tipped marker (not a pencil or ball point).

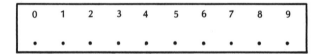

2. Prepare a glass with about two centimeters of water.
3. Suspend the wick from a pencil across the glass so that it just touches the water. DO NOT put the wick in the water until you are ready to begin timing.

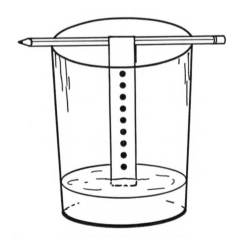

4. Using a table like the one below, record the time in minutes and seconds when the water reaches each dot.

	Watch Reading	Time
0	Ex. 15:00	Ex. 0
1	15:07	7
2	15:37	30
3		
4		
5		
.		
.		
.		

5. Make a graph of the pairs of data as shown below.

Mark number	Time
1	
2	
3	
4	
5	
6	
7	

Your graph should be prepared like the one shown on page 272.

Questions:

1. Does the water rise at a constant rate? Explain.
2. Does the water slow down or speed up as it rises? Explain.
3. Try changing certain parts of the experiment.
   a. Suppose the wick is thinner. Will the curve be the same?
4. Suppose you try a different type of wick. Will the results change?
5. Think of other things to vary.

Comment: You will probably wish to repeat the experiment several times to be sure of your results. Scientists usually do an experiment many times to be sure of their findings.

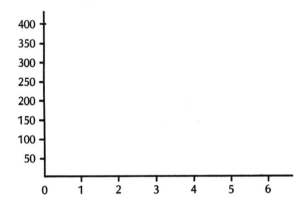

PROBABILITY

Objective: Gifted students will be able to determine the probability that an event will occur.

Activities:

1. Complete the attached sheets.

Objective: Gifted students will be able to describe the meaning of the word "random."

Activities:

1. Look up the word "random" in several reference books. Write a definition of the word.
2. Ask a high school math teacher what "random" means.
3. Check the reference manual for a computer and find out the command to generate a random number from 0 to 1 (for example, 0.4325678). What is the command to generate a random whole number from 1 to 10? Use this command to pick a random number from 1 to 20.
4. What does it mean to draw a ball from a jar at random?
5. In the State Lottery, the winning numbers are drawn at random. What does this mean?

Objective: Gifted students will be able to determine the chance of an event that cannot be predicted.

Activities:

1. What is the probability a thumbtack will land point up? Unlike a coin experiment, it is impossible to predict the chance of this event. However, we can estimate the chance by trying the experiment. Obtain 10 thumbtacks, all

alike. Toss the ten tacks and record the number with point up. Repeat this experiment for a total of 10 tosses. This is like tossing one tack 100 times. Write the fraction of the tosses on which the tack landed point up. This is an estimate of the chance of the tack landing point up. Compare your results with others. How did your answer differ?

2. Carlos wants to get all six baseball cards available. Each pack of gum contains one card. Question: On the average, how many cards must be purchased to get all six different cards?

The answer to this question can be estimated by conducting an experiment. Use a regular six-sided die with sides numbered one through six. (You could also use a computer to pick random numbers from one to six.) Roll the die until you have gotten each side. Make a chart for recording your tries. Repeat this experiment 10 times and then average the results. By using a larger number of tries, you obtain a better estimate of the answer.

A faster way to conduct this experiment is to program a computer to roll the die for you.

3. Problem: Three coins are tossed. What is the chance they will land with exactly 2 heads showing? Try to reason through the answer. Next, perform an experiment to estimate the chance. Prepare a recording sheet with number of tosses down the left and number of heads (0,1,2,3) across the top.

4. Toss three coins 40 times. Record the number of heads on each toss. Based on your findings, what is your estimate of the chance of getting exactly two heads?

Sue Ellen thought about the experiment and said that the chance of getting one head is the same as the chance of getting two heads. Is she correct? Explain.

Pat found a way of computing the chances in the problems above. He made a list of the ways each coin can land. His work is shown below.

Possible outcomes:
H H H
H H T
H T H
T H H
H T T
T H T
T T H
T T T

There are eight possible outcomes. Since there are three outcomes with two heads, the chance of getting exactly two heads is 3/8. Use this information to find the chance of getting three heads. One head. No heads.

5. Repeat this experiment with four coins. Estimate the chance of getting 0 heads, 1 head, 2 heads, 3 heads, and 4 heads. Look for a pattern in your results.

6. Draw a graph of the results in number 3 and 4.

7. Based on your work, predict the chance of 2 heads in the toss of five coins. Estimate the chance of 0 heads, 1 head, 3 heads, 4 heads, and 5 heads.

8. Write a computer program to simulate a probability experiment.

9. To determine whether a game is fair, try selected games. In each case decide whether the game is fair. By a fair game, we mean that each player has an equal chance of winning.

10. Select 10 activities from the book, *What Are My Chances?* (Book A and Book B, by A. Shute and S. Choate, Creative Publications, 1977, Palo Alto, Calif.). Complete the activites.

Evaluation:
Have students generate three probability experiments and present one to the class. Peer critique should follow.

SPATIAL VISUALIZATION

Goal: Students will develop spatial reasoning by determining and comparing constructed geometric shapes.

Activity:
Provide cubes of some sort, Multi-link Blocks work well. Pose the following problem: How many *different* shapes can be made with five cubes? Each cube must share a face with at least one other cube. This is a challenging problem. There is no mathematical formula—the possibilities must be analyzed and a system for determining all shapes constructed. There are 29 different shapes. Have groups compare results as needed. Challenge students to draw the 29 shapes. Ask students to formulate interesting follow up questions.

Examples:

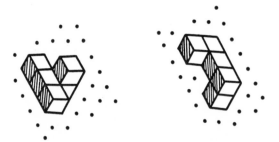

Section Three

Integrating Curriculum from Key Learning Realms _____

10 The Humanities as a Curricular Essential for the Gifted

Joyce VanTassel-Baska

> It is not enough to teach an individual a specialty. Through it he may become a kind of useful machine but not a harmoniously developed personality. It is essential that the student acquire an understanding of and a lively feeling for values. He must acquire a vivid sense of the beautiful and of the morally good. Otherwise he—with his specialized knowledge—more closely resembles a well-trained dog than a harmoniously developed person.
>
> —Albert Einstein

If the proper study of mankind is man, as the poet Alexander Pope has intoned, then perhaps the humanities are the connective tissue that link all of the disciplines needed by gifted learners. A reasonable definition of the humanities for purposes of conceptualizing such a curriculum might be: The humanities are comprised of all formal and informal acts of humankind that have resulted in creative products that deliberately attempt to portray and enhance the human condition in some form. Thus a child's drawing would be an appropriate object for study, whereas a garbage heap would not. The child's drawing represents a deliberate act of expression; the garbage heap is a product created haphazardly and without artistic intent.

Although this definition is rather broad, it has the advantage of allowing educators a wide degree of latitude in structuring humanities programs for the gifted and hopefully allows for a revision of thinking regarding this important area of the curriculum. Too often, the definition of the humanities has been limited to the fine arts. Consequently, the power of the humanities for integrating human experience was viewed merely as a loose amalgam of specific subjects in the curriculum. How can we successfully incorporate a humanities curriculum for the gifted within our current curricular and program structure?

One theoretical reference point for the teaching of the humanities on this grand scale would be the work of Phenix (1964), who categorized all bodies of knowledge into broad realms of meaning that reflect all of the diverse acts of humankind:

Symbolics are concerned with our invention and use of various symbol systems. These would include spoken languages (native, foreign, and computer), mathematics, and nonverbal symbolic forms such as gestures, sign language, etc.

Empirics are knowledge areas in which we are concerned with abstract phenomena and human behaviors and the need to generalize about them. These areas include science, psychology, and the social sciences.

Esthetics focus on our desire to create new forms and perceive objects in particular ways. These areas include music, the visual arts, the movement arts, and literature.

Synoptics allow us to reenact the past and seek ultimate answers related to life's purpose. These areas of study would include history, religion, and philosophy.

Ethics focus on our need to make judgments of good and evil and therefore are concerned with moral knowledge.

Synnoetics are concerned with our relationships to other people and therefore focus on personal and interpersonal knowledge.

Another overarching model to consider for conceptualizing humanities curricula is presented by Brandwein (1971). He probes the meaning of five core concepts as they are perceived and expressed by humankind:

Truth (consistency, relevance, reality)	Individuals search for and express the reality of their experience.
Beauty (significant form, ideal form)	Individuals perceive and express the beauty of experience.
Justice (compassion, mercy)	Individuals seek and express the ideals of justice.
Love (loving-kindness)	Individuals seek and express love.
Faith (ultimate concern, commitment)	Individuals seek and express their faith.

The primary modes of expression used to communicate human experience are described: art, movement and dance, play and drama, music, and language. Individuals then can move through levels of expression within and across modes in search of higher levels of meaning. This model is very useful in integrating separate fine arts areas of the curriculum around key concepts and levels of experience.

Why are the humanities so important for the gifted? There are several reasons that curriculum planners need to consider when organizing curriculum experiences:

1. The humanities, by their very nature, provide a perfect union of cognitive and affective elements, thus providing gifted students with curriculum experiences that directly engage them in equally high-level intellectual and emotional activity.

2. Intellectually gifted children have unusually keen powers to see and understand interrelationships; therefore, the humanities are useful curricular tools, for their whole structure is based on constantly interrelating form and content across knowledge bases.

3. Humanities are an enrichment tool in the highest sense, for they pro-

vide the gifted with an intellectual framework not available in studying only one content area, but rather expose them to many not covered in traditional curricula.

4. The humanities provide a basis for understanding the creative as well as the intellectual process through critically analyzing products, and being actively engaged in the creative process itself.

Goals for humanities-oriented programs for the gifted might be:

- To enhance students' understanding of the power and good in the creative acts of humanity
- To provide opportunities for students to integrate ideas across broad fields of study
- To develop a sensitivity to the process of knowledge production and utilization in the real world
- To appreciate their own and others' capacities for creative production
- To provide a framework for understanding systems of knowledge and their organization

These are K–12 goals that can be addressed through a total framework of study or through carefully weaving this perspective into all curriculum areas. Many secondary schools have not addressed humanities programs in their curriculum. This has been attended by a loss of an integrated vision of learning from our schools. It behooves educators of the gifted to find creative ways to include the humanities element in the curriculum and to see that the total curriculum is suffused with such a perspective.

Although the importance of using the humanities view as a focal point for providing curriculum for the gifted may not be in question, how those humanities experiences for the gifted are organized is an area lacking consensus. There are several ways that school districts and other educators have approached the task:

1. Focus on the past, using chronology, to note the important contributions of men and women across history and fields.
2. Focus on the present and future, using the perspective of contemporary society. Who are we and where are we going (with some homage paid to where we've been)?
3. Focus on universal themes or ideas. Topics like "war" or "love" are popular, yet more intellectually stated topics are also used (e.g., Justice in 19th Century British Society: A Study of Cultural Values).
4. Focus on the common elements across humanities subject areas. For example, the ideas of theme and symbol as they are expressed in literature, art, and music.

In any of these orientations to organizing a humanities curriculum, it is important to note the characteristics of a sound humanities program for gifted learners.

Lindsey (1981) listed six important variables to consider in building such programs.

Value-Focused	The Humanities look at man in the world as his actions reflect his more significant commitments.
Interdisciplinary	The Humanities take their subject matter from all the discrete disciplines—history, literature, the arts, philosophy, theology, etc.—and fuse these into illustrations of Man in the World.
Topical	The subject matter of the Humanities is organized into topical units for study. *The Nature of Honor,* for instance, might address this idea from our time into deep antiquity. David, Peter, Brutus, Don Quixote, Lancelot, Antigone, Nat Turner, all these personages might be used to illustrate the concept.
Student-Centered	In the Humanities, learning outcomes are the result of a rich and meaningful exploration by teacher and student together. Thus everyone continues to grow and develop as a result of the learning.
Intellectual	Study in the Humanities is the manifestation of *intelligence manifest in a healthy on-going curiosity about oneself.* . . . Minds that are intellectually alive continue the quest for knowledge, truth, beauty, wisdom.
Creative	The Humanities allow the gifted to synthesize existing knowledge into novel and improved models for the future.

Can the humanities be taught to gifted students below secondary level? Several theorists have argued that the integration of subject matter disciplines must be preceded by a firm grounding in at least a few of those disciplines. Students developmentally may not be ready to function at such abstract levels at earlier ages (Piaget, 1962). Yet we know that even young gifted children can make extraordinary conceptual connections on their own without a formal learning environment. Clearly, there is much that can be done with a humanities perspective for gifted learners throughout their years in school.

Should the humanities be seen as an area of exploration only for gifted learners during the K–12 years in school? This question is rather complex because it deals with characteristics of a particular type of curriculum and its match to characteristics of a particular type of learner. It would be difficult to consider the teaching of humanities opportunities as they are suggested in this chapter for typical learners at the stages of development advocated. Certainly, the humanities are appropriate for all learners at some stage of development, but it is questionable that all components suggested by Lindsay could be included in a curriculum for all during K–12 schooling. Another consideration here is educational context. Students operating above grade level will very likely profit from humanities approaches at each stage of their schooling. In each school district, however, the percentage of learners that would be included in that criterion would vary considerably. Therefore, it is reasonable to state that students would require a threshold competence in core domains of inquiry before they might profit from the interdisciplinary exploration implied by the humanities. The more intellectually rigorous the curriculum, the less it would be appropriate for any group but the gifted. In the final analysis, how the humanities are defined and approached will best determine which students might profit most from the curriculum. What is clear is that gifted learners can profit immensely from such curriculum approaches. Therefore, why not begin with this population and translate to other levels as it seems appropriate, rather than doing the reverse.

Concept-Based Curriculum: Model C Revisited

The humanities represent the embodiment of Model C curriculum introduced in Chapter 1. They provide the focus on key ideas, issues, and themes that have haunted humans over the centuries and that have expressed themselves in various forms—literature, art, mathematics, and the social sciences. The task of organizing concept curriculum, even once you have made a decision on an ongoing organizational model, is very complex. VanTassel-Baska and Feldhusen (1981) used Adler's *Syntopicon* as a large universe of ideas from which to choose a select few to develop interdisciplinary curriculum at the K–8 levels. The key concepts used were: change, reasoning, and signs and symbols. The matrix in Figure 10.1 shows the way each of these concepts was interpreted in core domains of study.

The next task was to write curriculum guides that flowed from these myriad interpretations of the three concepts. These guides were formalized by grade-level clusters, K–3, 4–6, 7–8, according to each of the concepts. This approach to concept curriculum making provided a broad unifying framework within which objectives and activities were developed for the requisite levels and content fields.

Another approach to concept curriculum was used in the Phoenix Project curriculum in Toledo, Ohio. This program was developed to integrate curriculum experiences for disadvantaged gifted learners at the high-school level, grades 9–10. The techniques employed to achieve this integration were through the organization of the program and cooperative staff planning as well as through writing integrated curriculum. The curriculum used special projects, field trips, and speakers as agents of unification. An example of the project unification approach follows:

PHOENIX CURRICULUM AREAS

Math

Science

Social Studies

English

PLANNED PROJECTS

1. A project that focuses on showing the relationship of equality and inequality in each of the content domains.
2. A paper that describes the use of symbol in all knowledge areas.
3. A seminar that explores issues of space according to the perspective of a mathematician, scientist, social scientist, and writer.

FIGURE 10.1 Matrix of Key Concepts by Subject Area

Key Concept	Language Arts	Social Studies	Mathematics	Science
Change	*Seasonal change as viewed in children's literature *Life cycle issues in literature	*Differences between peoples of the world *Growth of cities as cultural centers *The evolution of major cultures	*Modeling Theory *Techniques for representing changes: graphing	*Differences between physical and chemical changes *The effects of change over time *Methods for describing observed change
Reasoning	*Discrimination of fact from fiction *The relationship of syntax to meaning in literature	*The power of reason: critical thinking *The collapse of reason in advertising and propaganda *Applications of reason in the twenty-first century	*Probability reasoning *Prediction theory	*Reasoning as the scientific art of problem solving *Reasoning as a scientific attitude
Signs and Symbols	*Punctuation *Literary symbols *The conversion of symbol to theme	*Common nonverbal signs and symbols in everyday life *Learning language systems as a code to culture *Symbols within a culture	*Numeration systems as symbols in mathematics *The computer as a tool to manipulate symbols	*Symbols as communication in science *Archaelogy as a study of symbols *Maps as symbols of the real world

*Source: J. VanTassel-Baska and J. Feldhusen, *Concept Curriculum for the Gifted.* Matteson School District, Matteson, Illinois, 1981.

A key integration technique used in Phoenix was team teaching and team planning, carried out on a block-scheduling model. Each of the four Phoenix teachers was assigned four Phoenix periods, back to back, within which the team could make decisions on daily time allotments. Typically each teacher taught for three periods and planned with at least one other team member for the fourth, accommodating a total of sixty students in the process. Consequently, long-term projects could be planned that involved all areas of the curriculum. The project model for unifying ideas and concepts could be implemented in other school contexts as well at both elementary and secondary levels.

Another approach to humanities education for the gifted has been through the incorporation of philosophy as a core element in the curriculum experience. The teaching of philosophy as an integrated learning experience for the gifted was first suggested by Ward (1961), and used as the "cement" to hold together the North Carolina Governors School's course structure, later popularized by Matthew Lipman's fine national program, *Philosophy for Children.* Yet its importance as a fundamental subject in gifted students' curriculum is not assured. If we view the humanities as the seamless web of human experience embodied in works like the *Great Books of the Western World,* then we must recognize the importance of logic as a tool skill to be mastered in understanding and interpreting such experience. Schroeder (1981) has suggested the study of philosophy as a subject for the gifted by fourth grade. He advocates the teaching of a continuum of concepts around the subject area core shown in Figure 10.2.

Gallagher's leadership curriculum, cited earlier in Chapter 7, utilized a unit level approach to working on key concepts. He chose to focus on basic ideas in the definitional structure of the term *leadership;* namely, power and influence as well as exploring the characteristics of leaders, their dependence on circumstance for success, and the multiple paths by which one can become a leader. By limiting both the number and type of concepts to be studied as well as the grade levels at which they might be offered, he has limited the scope of his curriculum effort.

FIGURE 10.2 Philosophy Continuum for the Gifted by Grade Levels*

4th Grade	5th	6th	7th	8th	9–12th	13+
Formal Logic ⟶	Syllogism ⟶		Verbal & Rhetorical Fallacy ⟶	Classics of Philosophy & Persuasian ⟶		Ethics Aesthetics Religion
Philosophy for Children	(Lewis Carroll's silly syllogisms)		(use in politics, advertising, etc.)	(Plato, Descartes, Berkeley, Hume)		
Program	Fallacy (Darryl Huff's *How to Lie with Statistics*)					

* *Source:* Adapted from F. Schroeder, "Trends for the Future in Humanities for the Gifted Student," *Roeper Review* 4(2).

The seminar model represents another approach to the delivery of a humanities curriculum. Typically special seminars for the gifted are held biweekly or even monthly and are scheduled for three- to four-hour sessions. Topics are delineated for the year and may be loosely linked to a single concept or may explore several concepts. Frequently outside speakers are employed to provide indepth commentary on a particular idea or issue. Examples of seminar topics and speakers in the humanities follow:

HUMANITIES TOPIC	SEMINAR LEADER
Urban Architecture	Urban planner
Contemporary Art Forms	Local artist
The Work of Hemingway as an Example of 20th Century Alienation	Writer-in-the-schools
Cultural Archetypes: The People of Chicago	Studs Terkel, Chicago philosopher
Conservation: The Key to Survival in the Future	Futurist
The Search for Meaning: Developing a Philosophy of Life	Humanities professor

Key Questions Regarding the Humanities

Some key questions may be helpful to consider at this point regarding a humanities curriculum:

1. *According to what scope do you want to organize humanities experiences?* The examples cited thus far in this chapter range widely in terms of scope. Figure 10.3 demonstrates this continuum. School districts can start with any of the approaches cited, but need to consider carefully how to broaden the scope of their humanities opportunities to students over an extended period.

2. *How do you want to ensure that a study of the humanities is considered basic for the gifted learner?* One way of ensuring the inclusion of the humanities perspective is to see that any curriculum that is implemented for gifted learners contains a concept strand, an aspect that addresses big ideas, issues, and themes. In the teaching of algebra, for example, ensure that there is some focus on the idea that algebraic notation is one of several symbol systems within mathematics, the idea that mathematics is an invented system, and the idea that mathematics shares many form characteristics with music and art. Also ensure that students learn about the people who do mathematics, the processes they use, the way they think, and what mathematics means to them. By including such information in the curriculum, students are assured of gaining insights into the larger issues in mathematics beyond individual problems assigned from the book.

3. *What are some curriculum examples of integrated work in the humanities?* Using the humanities to structure an integrated curriculum is a very powerful way to address the needs of the gifted. Incorporating history, literature, philoso-

FIGURE 10.3 Humanities Models Based on Scope

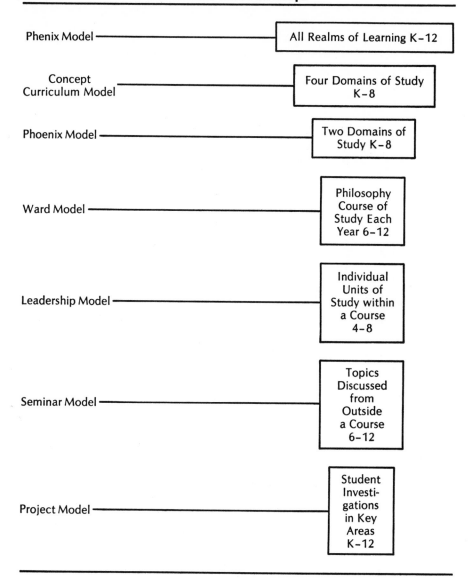

Phenix Model —————————————— | All Realms of Learning K–12 |

Concept Curriculum Model ————— | Four Domains of Study K–8 |

Phoenix Model —————————————— | Two Domains of Study K–8 |

Ward Model —————————————— | Philosophy Course of Study Each Year 6–12 |

Leadership Model ————————————— | Individual Units of Study within a Course 4–8 |

Seminar Model —————————————— | Topics Discussed from Outside a Course 6–12 |

Project Model —————————————— | Student Investigations in Key Areas K–12 |

phy, art, and music into a curricular whole can provide gifted students with an extraordinary grasp of how integrated knowledge really is, and the various forms in which it is effectively utilized. The matrix chart from the Phoenix Program employs a thematic structure superimposed on a chronological time frame in order to generate sample readings, artworks, and musical pieces (see Figure 10.4).

FIGURE 10.4 Phoenix Curriculum in the Humanities

Humanities—Aspects for Integration—Literature

	Communication	Search for Identity and Psychological Security	Power and Authority	Justice	Tolerance	Survival	Change
Man Emerges from Nature Pre-410 A.D.	• Socratic method • Cicero's orations • "Pyramus and Thisbe" myth	• Pericles—"Funeral Oration" • Romulus and Remus myth • Virgil (Aeneid) • Ovid	• Antigone—Sophocles • "Ozymandias"—Shelley	• Oresteian Trilogy • Parable (Matt 18: 23–35) • Myth	• Parable (Luke 10:30–37) • Medea Euripedes	• The Odyssey • Aeneas, Jason, Theseus, Hercules as heroes	• "Genesis" • Plato "Allegory of the Cave" and The Republic
Man Fashions Security with Faith (410–1453)	• Trombador and Trouvere stories, songs, poems	• Everyman (film-record) "Our Lady's Juggler"	• St. Thomas (Proofs of the existence of God) Summa Theological • "Sir Patrick Spens" (anon. form)	• Dante's Inferno—"Third Canto"	• "Prodigal Son" (Luke 15)	• "Lord Randal" (anon. poem)	• "Song of Roland" • Alchemy • Gold Art
Man Rediscovers His Freedom (1453–1650)	• Romeo and Juliet—Shakespeare	• "Letter to Posterity"—Petrarch • Voices	• Machiavelli—excerpts from Voices • Canterbury Tales—Chaucer • Julius Caesar—Shakespeare	• "Mother Goose Rhymes" • Voices	• Luther—Osborne • "Musee des Beaux Arts"—Auden • "No Man Is an Island"—Donne	• "Of Warfare"	• "Shall I Compare Thee to a Summer's Day?"—Shakespeare • "Even Such Is Time"—Raleigh • "To The Virgins"—Herrick

Man Attempts to Order His World (1650–1900)	• "Gulliver's Travels"—Swift • "There is No Frigate Like a Book" and "I Would Like to See It Lap the Lilies"—E. Dickinson	• "Essay on Man" (Epistle II, 1)—Pope • "Songs of Myself"—Whitman	• "Eve of Waterloo"—Byron	• "Rime of the Ancient Mariner"—Coleridge • "Civil Disobedience"—Thoreau	• Declaration of Independence • "The Quaker"—Hawthorne • Letters from the Earth—Twain • "On Tolerance"—Thoreau • Billy Budd—Melville	• Spenser and Darwin—Laws of the Universe • Great Expectations—Dickens • Swiss Family Robinson—film • "The Outcasts of Poker Flats"—Harte	• "Essay on Man" (Epistle I)—Pope • Thoreau and Emerson Poetry • The Time Machine and War of the Worlds—Wells
Man Fragmentizes His World (1900–?)	• The Miracle Worker—Gibson • "Paul's Case"—Cather • "Too Early Spring"—Benet	• A Doll's House—Ibsen • "Invictus"—Henley • "The Road Not Taken"—Frost • A View from the Bridge—Miller • A Raisin in the Sun—Hansberry • The Glass Menagerie—Williams • Catcher in the Rye—Salinger • The Learning Tree—Parks	• 1984—Orwell • "The Catbird Seat"—Thurber • "The Lottery"—Jackson • Lord of the Flies—Golding • Occurrence at Owl Creek—Bierce • A Different Drummer—Kelley	• "Cask of Amontillado"—Poe • "The Coup de Grace"—Bierce • "Richard Cory"—Robinson	• Who's Afraid of Virginia Woolf—Albee • Of Mice and Men—Steinbeck • "The Baby Party"—Fitzgerald • "And the World Will Be Purified"—Pegler • "Go Tell It On the Mountain"—Baldwin	• "Flight" and The Pearl—Steinbeck • "Death in the Woods"—Anderson • "To Build a Fire"—London • Diary of Anne Frank—Frank • Hiroshima—Hersey • The Uprooted—Hamlin	• "The Second Coming"—Yeats • "By the Waters of Babylon"—Benet • Chariots of the Gods—Damiken • 2001 Space Odyssey—Clarke

(Continued)

FIGURE 10.4 (continued)

Humanities—Aspects for Integration—Arts and Music

	Communication	Search for Identity and Psychological Security	Power and Authority	Justice	Tolerance	Survival	Change
Man Emerges from Nature pre–410 A.D.	• Catacomb art • Greek music (Seikilos song)	• Parthenon • Romulus and Remus and Wolf (statue) • Colossus (Rhodes) • Statue of Liberty	• Egyptian sculpture • Pyramids • Athena	• Laocoon (statue)	• Dying Gaul (statue)	• Pont du Gard (Roman bridge) • Appian Way (Roman highway)	• Depiction of human figure: 600 B.C.
Man Fashions Security with Faith (410–1453)	• Gothic sculpture • Illuminated manuscripts	• Medieval Walled City • Ptolemic concept of universe—Basis for Divine Comedy	• Gothic architecture • Charlemagne's throne, church, etc., at Aachen • van Eyck's Adoration of the Lamb	• Gregorian chant (Kyrie Elison)	• Walled City concept	• Mont St. Michel	• Romanesque vs. Gothic styles of architecture
Man Rediscovers His Freedom (1453–1650)	• African drum music • Ghirlandajo—"An Old Man with His Grandson"	• Copernican concept of universe • "Pieta"—Michelangelo	• "Last Supper"—DaVinci	• El Greco—"Laocoon" • Michelangelo—"Last Judgment"	• Bruegel—"Fall of Icarus"	• Michelangelo—"Pieta"	• Development of harmony • Josquin—"Ave Maria" • Transition: God-centered and man-centered art

Man Attempts to Order His World (1650–1900)	• Rembrandt—"Descent from the Cross" • Goya—"Disasters of War" Series	• Picasso—"Tragedy" • Rodin—"The Thinker"	• Bach—"Passacaglia C Minor" • Versailles	• David—"Death of Socrates"	• Bach—"Crucifixion from St. Matthew's Passion" • African sculpture • Japanese woodcuts	• Gericault—"Raft of the Medusa"	• Development of painting (Baroque-Impressionism)
Man Fragmentizes His World (1900–?)	• Abstract painting • Jazz	• Tooker—"Government Bureau," "Subway," "Waiting Room"	• Leadbelly—"John Henry"	• "Sacco and Venzetti" (painting)	• Picasso—"Guernica"	• "Red Staircase" (painting)	• Modern architecture • Duke Ellington's "Kyrie and Credo" (Jazz and Credo) Jazz Suite on Mass Texts

Another example from a high-school seminar for gifted students illustrates the role of the arts in expressing cultural values. In this curriculum, overall goals, objectives, and a course syllabus are articulated from a broad themes perspective (see Figure 10.5).

FIGURE 10.5 Gifted Humanities Seminar

PART I

Long-Term Goals:
1. To understand that the search for knowledge is unending and natural
2. To understand the concepts of art, science, knowledge, beauty, and truth
3. To understand how the individual functions within American culture

PART II

Objectives:
1. The student will be able to compare ideas about the individual's role in society.
2. The student will be able to understand various perspectives about knowledge, art, and science.
3. The student will be able to grow in his or her appreciation of the arts.
4. The student will be able to understand the role of art in a technological world.

PART III

Course Outline:
  I. The Individual: An Examination of Values
    A. The individual and experience
        1. What are values?
        2. What role does experience play in the formation of values?
        3. What causes values to change?
    B. The individual and knowledge
        1. What is the relationship between knowledge and experience?
        2. Is empirical knowledge the best kind of knowledge?
        3. Does knowledge help one attain happiness?
    C. Knowledge and wisdom
        1. Is there a relationship between knowledge and wisdom?
        2. Which is preferable, knowledge or wisdom?
        3. As one grows in knowledge or wisdom, do values change?
 II. The Individual: An Examination of Ideas
    A. Discussions of philosophy
        1. Basic philosophical concepts
            a. What is philosophy?
            b. How can we distinguish between Eastern and Western philosophy?
            c. What are the universal qualities of philosophy?
    B. Discussions of underlying ideas
        1. The nature of science
            a. What is science?
            b. Are there similarities between art and science?
            c. Are there dangers in placing more emphasis on either art or science?
        2. Science and knowledge
            a. What is the relationship between science and knowledge?

FIGURE 10.5 (*continued*)

      b. Is scientific knowledge the same as technology?

      c. Does man control technology or does technology control man?

    3. The nature of art

      a. What is art?

      b. How can we distinguish between good art, bad art, and non-art?

      c. What are some differences between Eastern and Western art?

    4. Art and knowledge

      a. What is the relationship between art and knowledge?

      b. Is man's need to know similar to his need to express?

    5. Quality

      a. What is quality in life? In art?

      b. Does everyone recognize quality?

III. The Individual: The Role of the Individual in Society

  A. The individual as autonomous

    1. Is man basically a social creature?

    2. How important is conformity to most humans?

    3. In what ways are values dictated by society so that pressures are placed on the individual?

    4. What, other than society, may motivate human beings?

  B. The individual as a part of society

    1. Is it natural for an individual to want to contribute to his society?

    2. Is man basically a product of his society?

    3. What must humans do to insure the survival of their society?

    4. What conflicts does the individual face as a member of society?

An eclectic approach to organizing a humanities curriculum for the gifted was taken in the Portland, Oregon, Parkrose School District. Educators decided to treat the humanities as their program core for grades 7–12 and to integrate English, social studies, and career education across the secondary span. Each year of study carried a theme:

Grade 7: The Individual in Society

Grade 8: National Perspectives

Grade 9: Global Perspectives

Grade 10: National Prospectives II

Grade 11: Comparative Governments

Grade 12: Independent Study of Current Issues

Several subthemes or topics were then carefully selected under each year's course of study. A sample concept teaching guide is included here for the ninth-grade theme of Global Perspectives with a subtheme of Power Conflicts.*

---

* Reprinted with permission from Parkrose School District No. 3, *Academic Excellence in the Humanities.* Seattle: The Northwest Clearinghouse for Gifted Education, 1982. Available through the Clearinghouse, 1410 South 200th St., Seattle, Washington, 98198.

THE GLOBAL PERSPECTIVE:
CONCEPT TEACHING GUIDE

I. *Power Conflicts: Talk Softly . . . but Carry a Big Stick*

   A. Theme: Why and how do human power conflicts develop?

   B. Introductory Unit: Students compare and contrast conflicts in their lives, especially *vis á vis* parents, teachers, other adults, peers, and younger children.

   C. Introductory Case Study: *Power Conflict in the Raw: Military Conquest* (at least one is chosen for past and present)

   1. Present: Nazi Invasion of Europe, Korean War, Soviet Invasions of Hungary (1956) and Czechoslovakia (1968), Russo-Japanese War, World War I, etc.

   2. Past: Mongal Invasion, Attila the Hun, Tameriane, Alexander the Great, Napoleanic Wars, etc.

   3. Analysis of past and present military conflicts to show causes, effects, and relationships, to lead the students to form generalizations about the causes and types of power conflicts

   D. Concept Generalizations: Using military conquest as a base, students construct an analytic framework of global power conflicts, which should include the following categories:

   1. Causes (overpopulation, value conflicts, militarism, self-protection, imbalance of power, economics, and others)

   2. Types (military conquest, revolution, civil war, terrorism, genocide, peaceful compromise, passive resistance, submission, and others)

   E. Student Case Studies: Using the concept generalizations discovered in step "D," the students investigate and analyze specific types of power conflicts in their historic settings to discover additional generalizations about the concept in its different manifestations. Following teaching model step #4, these types should be investigated:

   1. Military Conquest (e.g., Nazi, Japanese, European, Barbarians, Islamic, Mongol, Napoleonic, Norman French, Roman, Byzantine, Incan, Mayan, Aztec, Alexandrian, and others)

   2. Revolution (e.g., American, French, Russian, Irish, Hungarian, Greek, South American, Boer, Chinese, and others)

   3. Civil War (American, Russian, Spanish, Chinese, Irish, Indian/Pakistani, and others)

   4. Terrorism—Subversive and despotic (Leftist, Rightist, Irish, Vietnamese, Moslem, Palestinian, Japanese, Nazi, South American, Soviet, African, American Radical, and others)

   5. Genocide (Nazi, Soviet, American, Indian, Chinese, Biblical and others)

   6. Peaceful compromise (Munich, SALT Talks, Cold War, Holy Alliance, Three-Emperors League, Soviet/Finnish)

   7. Passive Resistance (India, Denmark in WWII, American War-Resisters, Quakers, and others)

   8. Submission (Czechoslavakia in 1938, 1948, and 1968; Austrian Anschluss; (Anglo-Saxon submission to Norman French)

   F. Concept Analysis: following the final step of the teaching model, the students will, in writing, analyze, synthesize, and evaluate what they have discovered

> about power conflicts, focusing especially on why there are power conflicts, how they come about, and what might be future developments. In addition, students should attempt answers to the "what if's" of past, present, and future power conflicts.

This approach to planning and implementing humanities curriculum provides guidance to the teacher on how to structure the teaching-learning process for a given unit of study. It also provides an overarching scheme for several years of productive study for the gifted learner.

It is important to note the commonality of each of these treatments of the humanities in school-based programs; they share a common focus on humankind, our issues and concerns, and our creative products. Thus any subject area could be transformed into a humanities approach, for such a focus underlies the framework of all knowledge. By providing students with insights into the person or the culture behind the idea, invention, or the artist's rendering, we have made visible an important perspective in the quest for educational relevance.

Recent general trends in humanities education also provide support for broadening the base of what the humanities might be. Humanities educators have cited the following directions as important:

1. Stress interpretive skills rather than direct recall of names and facts.
2. Make connections among the arts.
3. Place greater emphasis on nonverbal arts: architecture, painting, ceramics, dance, symphonic, operatic, chamber music, etc.
4. Place new emphasis on non-Western arts: Islamic, African, Japanese, Chinese, Indian, Native American, etc.
5. Place new emphasis on emergent and popular arts: film, jazz, folk music, science fiction, mystery.

The Learner in the Context of the Humanities

Just as the curriculum in the humanities is integrative and focused on large ideas and concepts, so too must the perspective of the learner shift from a focus on a right or wrong answer to a position that recognizes the relativistic nature of the world. Not that this shift is unimportant in other areas of study, but in the humanities it is vital to the acquired learning stance that students must make.

Perry (1970) has researched learner positions among college students and has developed an epistemological framework to account for them:

Position #1: *duality* (the student sees everything in black and white terms)

Position #2: *multiplicity* (the student is able to entertain the idea that people could have more than one point of view about the same event)

Position #3: *subordinate relativism* (the student sees that some truths are based on the perspective of the viewer and the circumstances surrounding events)

Position #4:   *relativism* (the student recognizes that all truth is relative to situations and circumstances and the perceptual field of the viewer)

This model represents one paradigm that may be useful in describing the nature and the direction of the change necessary for gifted students to make in their thinking as they are exposed to humanities education over their years of schooling.

The Direct Teaching of Creativity in the Context of Humanities Education

If the study of humankind and our accomplishments is to have real meaning in the lives of students, will they not have to experience the creative impulse for themselves? It seems quite reasonable that the answer to this question is a resounding "yes." One curriculum that addresses creativity in its various components and also uses the context of the humanities for its examples is *Creativity: The Human Resource* developed by Chevron Research Company (1980). A filmstrip and teacher's guide were developed around the following aspects of creative development with corresponding activities. A sample from this curriculum follows:

CREATIVITY COMPONENTS	CORRESPONDING ACTIVITY
Recognizing Patterns	Ask students to bring objects to class that are interesting to them in some way. List properties of selected objects; guess objects correctly from properties.
Making Connections	Listen to two different pieces of symphonic music. Draw the "feeling" of the music on 9 × 12 construction paper. Discuss relational outcomes.
Taking Risks	Have students go on a "smelling" tour of unseen odors. They should write down: how the odor makes them feel, what colors it reminds them of, whether it is pleasant, whether it reminds them of any personal experience in their past.
Challenging Assumptions	Have students plan a school without teachers. Have them write an essay describing a favorite class in such a school.
Taking Advantage of Chance	Have students think up unexpected events that could happen. List the consequences of each, as many as possible. Discuss.
Seeing in New Ways	Have students choose a picture and view it only in 2″ × 2″ frames.

> Choose a frame that is visually
> pleasing, cut it out, mount it, and
> write about it.

The filmstrip that accompanies this curriculum depicts visual images that reflect each of these creativity components. For example, Buckminster Fuller's geodesic dome is used to illustrate risk taking and Duchamp's work is used to illustrate the challenging of assumptions.

Another approach to the exploration of creativity within humanities programs is to have students engage in the "making" of an actual product within each area studied. Thus the following list of creative tasks could be generated for each of the humanities areas named:

Visual Arts———————————→	Create a photographic montage.
Music————————————→	Write and perform a musical composition
Poetry————————————→	Write an original poem about humankind and our environment.
History————————————→	Research and write the history of a small town nearby.
Science————————————→	Create a theory to explain some phenomenon you don't understand; find evidence to support it.
Mathematics———————————→	Create a mathematical model to show how something of interest to you works.
Philosophy———————————→	Develop your own philosophy of life and articulate it on paper.

Such an exercise may give even gifted students no more than the "experience" of creation, but it still is worthwhile in that sense.

More extended manifestations of these ideas can be carried out in long-term individual and group projects within the humanities program. Many gifted students have prepared films, art portfolios, and musical scores; written books; and conducted original research—all within the framework of a humanities program. Thus the teaching of creativity in the manner described here is a reasonable approach in such programs for the gifted.

Issues in Implementing Humanities Programs for the Gifted

As with any aspect of a curriculum for the gifted, there are special issues and concerns that must be considered at the stage of implementation. And in some respects the issues are more problematic in the humanities than they are in the other individual domains of study because of the inherent organizational change that is required to adopt a humanities perpective in schools. The integration of subject matter requires a "breaking down" of the current school operation: scheduling, staffing, and curriculum planning being primary considerations.

1. Selecting the right teachers to work with a humanities curricula is perhaps the most fundamental issue. Qualifications to work with such curriculum include the following: (a) a genuine enthusiam for viewing knowledge in an integrated way, (b) strong training in one area of the humanities, (c) avocational involvements that show interest in other humanities topics or areas of study, (d) flexibility in teaching style, and (e) a strong desire to learn from colleagues also working in this area. It is also useful to consider teachers based on their willingness to engage in team teaching as well as team planning. The complexity of the effort to structure a humanities curriculum requires the combination of conceptual strengths with flexible, open personalities.

2. At the secondary level, scheduling a humanities program is a critical dimension of implementation. Two scheduling models seem particularly facilitative. One is block scheduling that allows periods for humanities work to be scheduled back to back. This model aids students and teachers in terms of coordinating and integrating both the concepts and the logistics of such a program. Another helpful scheduling model is a school within a school that allows identified students and their teachers to be scheduled separately from the total school. This model allows for maximum flexibility in time to be allocated and limits the effects of irregular scheduling on the total system. Scheduling at the elementary level can be accomplished through a self-contained grouping pattern, perhaps across grade levels, that would allow at least two teachers the opportunity to work with the program.

3. Whereas the large issues of planning and implementing a humanities curriculum have been addressed throughout this chapter, it is useful to comment on some common organizational difficulties that tend to emerge:

   a. At the secondary level, the issue of credit to be given for humanities coursework is often a barrier to implementation. It usually is easiest if one, but preferably two, core departments are willing to award credit for the coursework. Typically these are the social studies and English departments. Although fine arts departments are often willing to award credit, the importance of those credits for graduation and college is not seen by gifted students or their parents as highly valuable.

   b. Deciding on the organizational approach to humanities work may be extremely difficult in some school contexts. Strong proponents of theme-oriented curriculum often clash with those who prefer more traditional orientations such as the study of cultures. Since it is important for the institutionalization of the program to build toward consensus, one way to handle differences is by compromise. Since all humanities work involves several levels of study and analysis, it is possible to accommodate global themes and cultural studies that loosely fit them; conversely, it is possible to fit themes within the broad context of cultural study.

   c. Although it is tempting to allow a humanities program to utilize many outside speakers and community resources, it is dangerous to have the overriding impression of the program be one of a potpourri of topics and presentations that do not necessarily fit together except at a very general level. Consequently, guarding against the reliance on multiple instructors, or even total team teaching, may be important to ensure that you are building a rich tapestry of understanding of an idea at several levels and not just superficially exposing students to many different stimuli.

Conclusion

As educators of the gifted, we can point to many noble experiments with these learners that have appeared to succeed. We speak often of their need to understand themselves, other people, and other ways of life. We also anticipate their future "greatness" as creative producers in whatever their chosen fields. And we value their potential contribution to making a better society in which to live. Yet these worthy expectations can only be adequately addressed in a humanities curriculum that deliberately integrates thought and feeling, skill and idea, and subject and object. For it is in this context that the power of the individual can be developed—the character as well as the intellect. American education can ill afford to ignore the importance of such a contribution to human resources.

KEY POINTS SUMMARY

- At the most abstract level of Phenix's "acts of man," the humanities provide an integration of all domains of study.
- Humanities approaches can be incorporated for the gifted at all stages of development.
- Important characteristics of the humanities are that it is value-focused, interdisciplinary, topical, student-centered, intellectual, and creative.
- Humanities curriculum exemplifies the best of model C concept curriculum in its orientation to shared inquiry and epistemological position.
- The program models for integrating humanities curriculum include school-within-a-school programs, seminars, separate courses, philosophy, and individual units of study.
- Humanities teaching and learning is concerned about drawing out the learner to recognize multiple and relative perspectives on issues, themes, and problems.
- The humanities provide an appropriate context in which to teach the heuristics of creativity.

Selected Materials for Use in Humanities Programs for the Gifted

PHILOSOPHY FOR CHILDREN

Philosophy for Children Program. c/o Dr. Matthew Lipman, Montclair State College, Montclair, NJ. *Primary audience:* intermediate middle-school gifted students.

This set of reading materials that focus on students caught in common human dilemmas emphasizes a philosophical orientation to student discussions that promote an examination of values and their role in human decision making. Used as a literary tool, the selections lend themselves well to student understanding of human motivation, conflict, and common literary themes and issues. The program also constitutes a strong critical-thinking vehicle for teaching and learning in that domain.

The Humanities (undated). Louise Dudley and Austin Faricy. New York: McGraw Hill. *Primary audience:* secondary.

This humanities text focuses on literature, the visual arts, and music, and attempts to conceptually present the humanities as the artistic creations by all people at all times, stressing that art lives because it is appreciated and enjoyed at an experiential level. The book is organized around key concepts in the arts: subject, function, medium, organization, style, and judgement. Powerful examples from various art forms are used to illustrate ideas. This is an excellent resource for the teacher in a humanities program.

Civilization. Kenneth Clark. New York: Harper and Row. *Primary audience:* secondary.

This classic book blends the traditional art forms with a strong sense of historical context as a basis for the discussion of what constitutes a civilization. Useful in humanities programs for the gifted, the book also could be used as a social studies text from the perspective of world cultures. It is a compendium of scholarly references and archetypal concepts. A PBS television series captured salient elements of the book and is available on videotape.

Concept Curriculum for the Gifted. Joyce VanTassel-Baska and John Feldhusen. c/o Keystone Consortium, P.O. Box 2377, West Lafayette, IN 47906. *Primary audience:* elementary and junior high.

This set of units is organized around four concepts: change, signs and symbols, reasoning, and problem solving in each of the core subject matter areas, including language arts, social studies, mathematics, and science. Developed for use in pull-out or self-contained programs, the curriculum is organized by primary, intermediate, and junior-high levels.

References

Academic Excellence in the Humanities (1982). Seattle, Wash.: The Northwest Clearinghouse for Gifted Education.

Brandwein, P. (1971). *The Permanent Agenda of Man: The Humanities,* New York: Harcourt, Brace, and Jovanovich.

Creativity: The Human Resource (1980). VanNuys, Calif.: The Chevron Research Company.

Gallagher, J. (1984). *Leadership.* New York: Trillium Press.

Lindsay, B. (1981). "Cornerstones and Keystones: Humanities for the Gifted and Talented." *Roeper Review,* 4(2), 6–9.

Perry, W. G. (1970). *Forms of Intellectual and Ethical Development in the College Years.* New York: Holt, Rinehart, and Winston.

Phenix, P. H. (1964). *Realms of Meaning*. New York: McGraw-Hill.

Piaget, J. (1962). *Plays, Dreams and Imitation in Childhood*. New York: W. W. Norton.

Schroeder, F. (1981). "Trends for the Future in Humanities for the Gifted Student." *Roeper Review*, 4(2), 12–15.

VanTassel-Baska, J., and Feldhusen, J. (1981). *Concept Curriculum for the Gifted*. Matteson, Ill.: Matteson School District.

VanTassel-Baska, J. (1974). *The Phoenix Project Curriculum Guide*. Toledo, Ohio: Toledo Public Schools.

Ward, V. (1961). *An Axiomatic Model for Educating the Gifted*. Columbus, Ohio: Charles Merrill.

11 Arts Curriculum for the Gifted

Ken Seeley

Art is not a means in itself, but a means of addressing humanity.
—Modest Petrovich Mussorgsky

The educational world of most students is comprised of compartmentalized, segmented, and arbitrarily assigned academic domains of study that are taught separately, often in courses by different teachers, from different departments, in different classrooms, at different times of the day. This organization of learning and knowledge may promote efficient schedules for mass education, but it gives little time and attention to aesthetics or the relatedness of knowledge in various disciplines. Given this structure and its inertia, we as educators need to examine alternatives that provide bridges among knowledge, experience, and awareness. It is the arts as well as the humanities that offer such bridges.

The overall goal of teaching the arts to gifted learners is to help these students scrutinize the knowledge, experience, and values they derive from all of their studies and to translate them into unique and satisfying portrayals and explanations of their existence. In order to achieve this broad and complex goal, we must create arts experiences that are:

1. *Interpretive or integrative* of the student's knowledge and experience
2. *Normative* in helping the student move toward an understanding of art forms and the student's own appreciation of these forms
3. *Critical* in strengthening the student's ability to question, confront, deliberate, judge, and create alternative forms

It is also important to adopt a philosophy regarding the arts that will provide the basis for curriculum development activities. Many tomes have been written about the philosophy of art. In his landmark work, *Art as Experience,* originally published in 1934, Dewey provides an excellent philosophical beginning for our treatment of the arts experience. Dewey states,

The real work of art is the building up of an integral experience out of the interaction of organic and environmental conditions and energies . . . . The thing expressed is wrung from the producer by the pressure exercised by objective things upon the natural impulses and tendencies . . . . The act of expression that constitutes a work of art is a construction in time, not an instantaneous emission . . . . It means that the expression of the self in and through a medium, constituting the work of art, is itself a prolonged interaction of something issuing from the self with objective conditions, a process in which both of them acquire a form and order they did not at first possess (pp. 64–65).

The inferences drawn from Dewey's philosophy about "real art" might be summarized as:

- Art requires an integrating and interactive process to produce it.
- Art uses emotion ("natural impulses and tendencies") combined with objective materials and forms.
- Art takes a prolonged period of time to produce.
- Art is an expression of self into a chosen work.
- Art results in both the artist and the medium for the art acquiring characteristics that are new and perhaps unique.

Although some may argue that Dewey's philosophy is too narrow, it can be used as a point of departure for curriculum developers to refine their own philosophy. The resultant philosophy for curriculum development must address a differentiation of "arts for all" versus arts for the gifted. This is not intended to diminish the importance of existing arts curricula for artistically gifted students. Rather, it implies that an arts curriculum for the gifted must extend and enrich what exists because the potential of the gifted student is to become a real artist. Certainly art, theater and music classes, art appreciation, and aesthetics should be integral parts of a good school curriculum. These activities can serve to identify those students with exceptional potential who need their talent developed through specialized experiences.

The Arts for Whom?

Given the reality of limited funding for education, it is important to define early the role of the arts for various types of learners in schools. Early exposure to the arts is important if we are to find talent and develop it. This implies a curriculum philosophy of arts for all students as a means of finding potential talent. In later years of schooling, the instruction needs to become more intense and specialized. Unfortunately, the arts suffer from a value system that sees this area of the curriculum as a frill or fad. As an advocate for the arts, Lorin Hollander, a concert pianist who started as a prodigy with the New York Philharmonic at age twelve, has some important words:

A back to basics mentality in the schools, if it weren't so tragic, would be ludicrous. But that's what they're doing. How dare they? How dare they trust whatever common denominator came up with this theory: that the arts and arts education are expendable to mankind. This is criminal. It is not intelligent. I believe that if arts education is not handled with creativity and care and brilliance in the public schools, then we are asking for severe mental disturbance in our communities. How will people touch, spiritually embrace? We are equipping kids with words and numbers and strong legs and arms, and then they confront each other, spout at each other, have no sense of the humanity in each other, like two points of triangles, with their feelings behind them, never learning how to use them, and these feelings are then turned inward . . . .

If we are to find and develop young artists, we must have active arts programs in schools. This chapter focuses on the arts for talented children, but we must be advocates of a firm general curriculum base in the arts from which to build specialized curriculum. An arts curriculum is essential for the talent development of children with high potential, whether artistically gifted or academically gifted. It heightens sensitivity and creative ability. It provides emotional outlets and a medium for expression that words and numbers cannot. The arts also provide a new means of understanding and explaining complex phenomena of human endeavor and human motivation.

In order to answer the question, "arts for whom?", it is important to wrestle with the value questions of how public education views the arts. If, as Hollander suggests, the arts are seen as expendable, then it may require a course of action that limits arts to the gifted education curriculum, if they are to be included at all. Even within the field of gifted education, the arts are typically given short shrift. It appears at this juncture that in most school settings it will be an uphill battle. However, the struggle must continue if we value the intellectual and emotional well-being of our children. The education of gifted children is a logical vehicle for developing a meaningful arts curriculum in unique ways.

Yet it is necessary to address some of the political realities of public education. It is unlikely that public schools would ever offer sufficient curriculum in all areas of the arts to challenge the most talented students. Indeed, families often need to support the talent development of their children through private study with artists, yet some families may not be able to do so because of economic disadvantage. However, the schools can provide an important set of basic arts exposures from which future opportunities at least have a chance to flower because the talent becomes identified.

Differentiating Curriculum in the Arts

For the purposes of discussion in this chapter, "the arts" refer to the major fine and performing arts, including visual arts, dance, music, theater, and creative writing. Curriculum development that addresses all of these areas is based on the general model presented in Chapter 1 by VanTassel-Baska. The model suggests three areas of curriculum differentiation: modifying the core curriculum, extending the core, and integrating the curriculum areas. There is great variation both within and across public schools on core curriculum in the arts. Within schools the variation is usually by level. Secondary schools typically have more highly developed offerings in the arts than at the elementary level. This variation is particularly problematic for talented young children, but it could be mediated by allowing such children access to secondary classes on a part-time basis. The variation across school districts has to do with the nature and extent of the curriculum offerings in the arts. For instance, some school districts have no special art teachers or music teachers at the elementary level. It is also rare to find specialized drama classes at the elementary or middle-school level. Also, the level of instruction in the arts in public schools is typically too broad-based to challenge the very talented young artist. Therefore the modification of the core curriculum in the arts for the talented student is very situation specific. In some instances there is no curriculum to modify.

The following strategies are suggested for modifying the core curriculum:

1. Allow talented elementary students to attend secondary arts classes.
2. Cluster talented students by using magnet schools and offer advanced instruction such as master classes and individualized approaches.
3. Articulate existing school arts programs for individual talented students who are studying privately.
4. Utilize the artists-in-the-schools program for some specialized offerings for the most talented students.

In order to consider the concept of an extended core curriculum for the arts, it is necessary to do an extensive needs assessment of individual students. Once there is a determination of the talent areas, level of ability, and location of the students, the extended curriculum can be developed. If the strategies suggested for modifying the core are in place, it is much easier to begin the extension process. Programs for gifted young artists need a process/product extension that typically goes beyond what most schools offer. Differentiating curriculum at this stage requires some or all of the following alternatives to be considered:

1. Create master classes in each art area for the most talented students, based on ability and irrespective of age.
2. Utilize community mentors/artists to provide individual talent development on an ongoing basis.
3. Create alternatives within each art area that are not found in the typical core curriculum such as music composition, conducting, theatrical directing and producing, use of nontraditional art media, writing novels or extensive works, or choreography.
4. Generate real audiences and outlets for the students' products or performances such as commercial gallery exhibits, solo or ensemble performances with adult dance, music, or theatrical groups, or submitting creative writing for publication.
5. Develop collaboration efforts in the arts.

CONSIDERING THE VISUAL ARTS

Special attention is given here to the visual arts because they are typically not well addressed in the curriculum for talented youth, nor is there as much private instruction available in this area as in the other arts. Outlets for the performing arts are more common, and creative writing is often well developed in both regular and gifted education. However, the recognition and specific development of young visual artists rarely occurs in school, even though it is important to find these students at an early age.

Gardner (1980) states, "For it is in the activity of the young child, his preconscious sense of form, his willingness to explore and to solve problems that arise, his capacity to take risks, his affective needs, which must be worked out in a symbolic realm—that we find the crucial seeds of the greatest artistic achievement."

Drawing is typically the first artistic activity that children are exposed to. Gifted young visual artists often will skip or accelerate through the normal stages of drawings that are described in most art education texts. However, there has not been a visual arts equivalent of a prodigy who achieved adult eminence as we might find in music, drama, or verbal areas. This phenomenon may relate to the development of fine motor skills and visual-spatial ability required for accomplished visual art. It may also be related to lack of opportunity for intense and sustained instruction in visual art. At present this is merely speculation, but it would certainly make for an important research project to see if accelerating visual art instruction results in precocious ability as in other areas.

Identifying young visual artists for a special program is typically done by three different approaches similar to identifying all gifted children. A product review of the child's art work by artists (typically accompanied by an interview) is a common approach. Another way is to have a special art program open to anyone who wants to come as a means of exposing children to serious peers with opportunities for focused art activities. Finally, there is a self-nomination process after the child has a clear understanding of the program.

Some specialized tests have been developed that may help in the identification. After nine years of research of artistically gifted students, the Wilson Cognitive Instrument was developed, in which a self-evaluation Likert-type scale is used. Wilson (see Hurwitz, 1983) developed another art test—the National Assessment of Art Test for students ages nine to seventeen years, which provides standards for teachers to use in evaluating children's art.

Hurwitz (1983) provides an informative handbook for those who would plan programs for talented students in the visual arts. He gives excellent exemplary program descriptions, such as self-study units for the Gifted in Art from Worcester, Mass. This is an upper-elementary art program that allows the artistically talented students to work in their own regular classrooms on specially designed independent study units. Another example of an elementary-level program is Aesthetic Education for the Intellectually Gifted at William Ward School in New Rochelle, New York. Here, a team of artists (art, dance, drama, and media) worked with intellectually gifted students in a year-long pull-out program. A high-school exemplary program is described at the Milwaukee Art Center (a city museum), which operates a studio course for high-school credit over a semester for a daily two-hour program. Hurwitz also recommends the Advanced Placement Program in art areas.

Magnet High Schools in the Arts

Some large cities offer a specialized high school in the arts. (Certainly this concept has been popularized by the movie and television series *Fame*.) This type of school is a fine resource for meeting the needs of secondary talented students. It has also opened up the world of the arts to less affluent students who could not afford private specialized instruction. One case study is presented here of the New Orleans Center for the Creative Arts (NOCCA) to provide a good example of such a magnet school.

Opened in 1974, NOCCA offers professional arts training in dance, theater, music, writing, and visual arts. It is operated by the New Orleans public schools for 250 students who attend on a half-day basis, spending the other half day in their home schools. The teachers who staff the school are professional performers who work in their arts discipline; they are not typical classroom teachers. Students are selected by audition, interview, and product reviews, with the understanding that they wish to pursue a career in the arts. NOCCA prepares students after three or four years to enter the arts profession for which they were trained. Students also must be academically successful in their home schools to qualify for selection.

Like most arts schools, this magnet school is more rigorous than the normal high school. Balancing the normal academics with the specialized arts classes is extremely demanding. In a way, it helps to screen out the less committed students. The world of fine and performing arts is very competitive, and only those who are absolutely committed to their craft have a chance for success.

A recent study of the students at NOCCA was reported by Kauffman, Tews, and Milam (1986). They summarized their findings as follows:

1. Students appear to enjoy and benefit from the depth, breadth, and qualitative differences in their arts training.

2. Students in disciplines that appear to be less academic (dance and visual art) need to be sensitized to the intellectual and academic aspects of their art.

3. Many students experience isolation or rejection as a result of their artistic endeavors.

4. The development of self-esteem and future goals can be among the most significant outcomes of an arts training program.

Although lacking in number, magnet school programs are valuable models. However, there are many alternatives that smaller communities can develop. A "school within a school" concept that allows flexible scheduling for blocks of time can also provide a valuable arts program. Programs with universities and museums can also be developed to provide the specialized arts training for talented high-school students.

Curriculum Integration in the Arts

The integration of the arts may represent the most appropriate area for gifted education curriculum development, in that most skill development in individual areas is done by specialists or through private study. This section focuses on collaboration in the arts as a means of integration. Other means of integration can be done in more verbal areas such as art history, philosophy of art, aesthetics, and art appreciation.

Collaboration in the arts is often misunderstood as one art form as an adjunct to another. Some examples are the relationship of music as background for dance, or visual art as scenery background for theater. This is not collaboration, however; it is merely a layering of art forms. Collaboration requires an interweaving of the arts to meet the following criteria: (1) each art form must have its own integrity and be able to stand alone, (2) there must be common elements in each art form that relate to the other, and (3) the whole must be greater than the sum of its parts. Collaboration is both a process and a product. As a process, it has artists working together as equals in the development of the ideas and concepts as well as the techniques to implement those ideas. One artist is not more important than the other in the process. The collaborative product must meet the above three criteria and create a unique impact on the audience that would not happen if the individual art pieces were presented by themselves.

Collaboration in the arts is not widely done nor is it easy to do. It requires of artists an openness and vulnerability that may be uncomfortable. The creative writer who writes lyrics with a composer needs to analyze the music critically as it relates to the words, and the musician must do the same with the words as it relates to the music. The teamwork required can be trying and at times a battle of wills between and among artists. It is this human dynamic that makes the collaborative process difficult and has probably limited the number of significant collaborations in the world of art.

Collaboration makes the student think critically about the arts. Criteria are established by which to evaluate a collaboration critically. Three questions are used to analyze each collaborative effort:

1. Does the collaboration find common elements in each discipline? A successful collaboration somehow identifies an idea, a theme, a word, a concept—something about which each discipline has something to say.

2. Can the separate elements from each discipline stand on their own? A successful collaboration is made up of parts from each artistic discipline that have their own integrity and quality.

3. Are the separate elements of each discipline even better for being part of the collaboration as a whole? A successful collaboration is a whole that is greater than the sum of its parts.

Having these defined criteria by which to judge a collaboration, the students develop a critical vocabulary that can also be applied to individual disciplines. Students gain confidence in their own ability to speak critically about the arts, and they learn that criticism is not a personal judgment but rather a constructive tool in the creative process. Criticism is an integral part of any collaboration; it provides the direction and structure for revision and refinement of the work in progress. The students learn to view their work as a work in progress rather than as a final statement that has no room for change or improvement.

Collaboration also contributes greatly to the development of the individual. Interpersonal skills come into play as students learn to interact effectively with a group as the group works toward a common goal. Each student must identify and defend his or her own values and learn how to stand up for those values in the creative process. There is a give and take in the process of collaboration that helps students recognize when to acquiesce and when to stand firm for a given idea or principle. It is through this interaction that a student begins to understand his or her own creative process within the larger context of the group. Students learn how to be supportive as well as critical of one another.

The process of collaboration involves first identifying a common idea or theme that relates in some way to each artistic discipline. Then each discipline is explored to find how it can contribute to the creation of the work, maintaining the integrity of its own expression while going beyond itself to find a unified expression of all of the artistic disciplines involved in the process.

Through the process of collaborating with artists from other disciplines, the student must first define and articulate the concerns and unique qualities of his or her own discipline. Only then is the student able to begin to search for the common ground between artistic disciplines. Indirectly, collaboration embodies the quest for self-expression and the development of the individual that is at the center of the arts.

In order to establish similarities between artistic disciplines, the student must examine the language used in each discipline to try to find a common vocabulary to describe the concerns of each discipline relative to a common goal. Conversely, the student also discovers through this process the differences between disciplines, finding that each discipline has its own unique concerns and language that have no application to other disciplines.

Application of the Collaborative Process

To translate this process into a gifted education program, it is important to discuss the concept at length and build on the student artists' creative powers. Three elements are recommended as an approach to teaching collaboration:

1. Develop a common vocabulary across the arts involved.
2. Teach the basics of artistic criticism as a constructive process that leads to the final element.
3. Employ revision and refinement over time.

At the end of this chapter is a glossary of art terms contributed by Gibson (1986). This glossary is certainly not intended to be a finite listing of terms for integrating the arts. Rather, it is an example for a teacher to use, change, or add to with students as an important exercise to broaden perspectives. If a musician can understand what a visual artist means by *space,* what a creative writer means by *space,* and what a dancer means by space, the common understanding is the basis for good collaboration. More than an exercise in general semantics, the vocabulary-building activity among student artists can help them understand their own art better, as well as other arts.

The second element of criticism is greatly aided by having a common vocabulary and also identifying any vocabulary that is unique to one art form. This understanding facilitates critical analyses of collaborations that may be used as examples, such as professional exhibits and performances in the community. It further facilitates the criticism expressed between student artists about their developing collaborative ideas and products. Formal instruction in criticism would be helpful, particularly in assisting in the development of careful observation and listening skills. This may be introduced as a unit on aesthetics that incorporates the vocabulary-building exercises, all as a prelude to the collaboration effort.

The most difficult of the three elements to communicate to young artists is the final concept of revision. There is a widespread myth that the most creative productions are spontaneous or instantaneous. These creative "Aha's!" are seen as the final product. As Dewey (1934) aptly points out in his philosophy, "A work of art is a construction in time, not an instantaneous emission" (p. 65). Too often the young artists immediately transform their creative ideas into a product and believe they are done. The initial product must be seen as a beginning—not an end. Teachers of the gifted can present many case studies of great artists, writers, dancers, and musicians who take long periods through many iterations and revisions to reach what they felt was close to a final product. Revision must be viewed as a necessary part of the creative process if the product is to have significance and meaning. Revision does not diminish the importance of the initial creative idea. It should be seen as enriching and developing it in a cycle that may generate many products and take many turns over time. This is particularly true for the performing arts, although visual artists may view a completed painting as only one product along the way of the development of their original creative idea. They do not feel "done" even though the canvas or the sculptured piece is on display in a gallery.

When teachers of the gifted attempt this integration of the arts idea by using art teachers or artists from the community, they should not expect an enthusiastic response. Most artists are invested in their own art medium and view integration as one art serving as hand maiden to another. The teacher of the gifted can play the unique role of facilitator and "integrator" among the student artists and adult artists.

Implementation Issues in the Arts

Implementation of arts programs for the gifted present a set of unique issues that require the thoughtful consideration of program and curriculum planners.

1. As in the other content areas, a curriculum in the arts for gifted students should extend from the core curriculum. Implementation becomes problematic when there is not a sufficiently rich core curriculum to use as a beginning point for the arts curriculum development. Such situations require teachers and coordinators to create specialized curriculum unique to the gifted program.

2. Utilization of arts resource people can pose implementation problems, depending on availability, cooperation, and costs. Artists in the community may be available, but schools may not have sufficient funds to bring them into the classes. Other communities may not have artists available in certain disciplines, or arts resource people within the school may not wish to cooperate with the gifted program. Gaining parental support can be helpful in finding resource people and/or sponsoring fund-raising activities for an artist-in-residence program.

3. Developing internal resources to the schools is important if an arts program is to be sustaining and articulated from elementary to secondary levels. Developing and implementing a model curriculum in one area of the arts is helpful in gaining internal support to move to other arts areas. Involving school arts personnel in planning for gifted students is a good way to develop ownership and future cooperation in implementing curriculum.

4. Joining forces with arts organizations in the community for advocacy purposes can assist in gaining broader-based support for arts programs in schools. Such relationships can also lead to mentorships for artistically talented students. The overall advocacy effort should help the general climate for the arts in the community.

Conclusion

Whereas teachers of the gifted are often called upon to be a jack of all trades, they can develop an integrated arts curriculum without being artists. Interdisciplinary approaches are implicit to any quality curriculum for the gifted; the arts are no exception. They provide fertile ground for high-level, challenging learning experiences. The preceding information is built on the curriculum development processes presented in an earlier chapter and provides for the beginning of an integrated arts curriculum for artistically gifted students. These ideas and strategies have been implemented and field tested with elementary and middle-school students in Colorado as part of a state-supported program development effort in gifted education. There is also evidence that these ideas would work with high-school students and could provide an additional dimension to arts magnet schools that have traditionally been single discipline-oriented.

KEY POINTS SUMMARY

- The development of arts curriculum for the gifted should begin with a philosophy of art that is broad so as to demonstrate the value of arts for all gifted students. The philosophy should also be specific enough to guide curriculum for the most talented in the arts disciplines.

- A good basic arts curriculum in the elementary grades is important if we are to find potential art talent, particularly in visual art.

- Curriculum in the arts varies greatly among schools and the most talented students often must rely on private instruction to be sufficiently challenged.

- Schools can offer many alternatives to talented students by allowing access to secondary school instruction for elementary students, and offering advanced placement programs in the arts to secondary students.

- Arts curriculum for gifted students can focus on collaboration and integration with the teacher of the gifted providing facilitation among the artists.

- Collaboration in the arts offers many exciting opportunities for talented students to expand beyond their own discipline into new understandings of art in its broadest sense.

- Criticism and aesthetics are important elements of arts curriculum from which all gifted students can benefit.
- The concept of revision is important to challenge talented students in the arts who have often been praised for a first effort as a final product.

References

Dewey, J. (1934). *Art as Experience*. New York: Capricorn Books.

Eisner, E. W. (1972). *Educating Artistic Vision*. New York: MacMillan.

Gardner, H. (1980). *Artful Scribbles: The Significance of Children's Drawings*. New York: Basic Books.

Gibson, R. (1986). "A Glossary of Arts Terminology." The Clayton Institute for the Arts in the Humanities (occasional paper).

Hollander, L. (1978). Keynote Presentation at the National Forum for the Arts and the Gifted (U.S.O.E., Dept. of H.E.W.), Aspen.

Hurwitz, A. (1983). *The Gifted and Talented in Art*. Worcester, Mass.: Davis Publications.

Kaufmann, F. A., Tews, T. C., and Milam, C. P. (1986). "New Orleans Center for the Creative Arts: Program Description and Student Perceptions." *Gifted Students Institute Quarterly, 11*(3).

Stein, L. (1986). "Artists as Teachers." Clayton Institute for the Arts and Humanities (occasional paper).

Stein, L. (1986). "Collaboration in the Arts." Clayton Institute for the Arts and Humanities (occasional paper).

A Glossary of Integrated Arts Terminology*

ABSTRACT (adj) often contrasted with REPRESENTATIONAL (see), and thus referring to things other than the inhabitants of the everyday (natural or manmade) world; often said about artistic forms or ideas.

ABSURD (adj) (derived from the Latin *ab* "from" and *surdus* "dull-sounding, silent") characteristic of art forms that are reactions against rules and reason; examples: dumb art and theater of the absurd; these represent human existence as ridiculous because it occurs in a universe thought to be meaningless.

AESTHETICS (n) the branch of philosophy that deals with the nature of art and related concepts such as beauty.

BEGINNING-MIDDLE-END (n) Aristotle's (384–322 B.C.) classic ingredients for a well-made presentation, whether written or performed.

---

* *Source:* R. Gibson, "A Glossary of Arts Terminology," The Clayton Institute for the Arts in the Humanities, 1986.

CATHARSIS (n) a traditional objective for classical (Greek and Roman) dramatic tragedy; a purification or "washing out" of the audience's emotions in response to a play; other arts sometimes aim at a similar emotional release, either by the artist during the making of the artwork, or else by the audience in response to it.

CENTER (n) any focus of an artwork in time or in space; (v) to withdraw into oneself in order to gather insight, strength or perspective in preparation for making an artwork.

COMMITMENT (n) a decisive aesthetic choice that involves an artist in some definite course of action.

CRITICISM (n) any thoughtful, reasoned response to an artwork; sometimes divided into "expository" and "evaluative"; sometimes divided into "descriptive," "interpretive," and "evaluative."

DECISION-MAKING (n) an artistic choice based on reasons; such choices are absolutely essential to the artist's work.

DESCRIPTION (n) an account of the details of an artwork as perceived by an observer; in art criticism, the foundation for the INTERPRETATION (see) and EVALUATION (see).

DOMINANCE (n) quantitative measure of an artwork's principal elements; examples of dominant elements may include specific colors (visual art), chords (music), movements (dance), and characters (theater).

EVALUATION (n) a judgment of the worth or quality of an artwork; one of three components (see DESCRIPTION and INTERPRETATION) in a critical review.

EXPOSITION (n) the initial presentation of an artwork's concept, theme or principal idea, typically followed by development and variations.

FORM (n) the structural element, plan or design of an artwork; specifically, the combinations and relations to each other of an artwork's components, such as the lines, colors and volumes of a visual work, or the themes and variations of an aural work.

FUNCTION (n) work done by an artwork's elements, especially in relation to its other elements or to the entire work.

IMAGE (n) an element that appeals to the senses, usually by representation; examples: portraits (painting), busts (sculpture), similes (poetry, plays).

IMPRESSIONISM (n) a movement in several arts and characterized by emphasis on the artist's emotional response to external stimuli.

IMPROVISATION (n) composition of an artwork on the spot, and with varying degrees of planning and organization.

INTENSITY (n) an artwork's power to hold an audience's attention and direct its responses.

INTERPRETATION (n) an explanation of an artwork's meaning; a component in a critical review, along with DESCRIPTION (see) and EVALUATION (see).

METAPHOR (n) an implied comparison between different things; example: Bob Dylan's "evening's empire vanished into sand" (from his song "Mr. Tambourine Man") compares a sunset with an ancient civilization.

MINIMALISM (n) an artistic approach characterized by employing the fewest possible variations of themes or elements.

MODERNISM (n) an artistic approach characterized by breaks in theory or practice with the past; the search for new forms of expression in any of the arts.

NARRATIVE (n) a story line which functions as a principal organizational structure for an artwork; the "backbone" or "spine" of many artworks.

NEGATIVE SPACE (n) the context for an artistic IMAGE (see); example: in a drawing of a tree, the empty areas between leaves and branches.

OBJECTIVE (adj) public and immediate; without interpretation or bias; opposite of SUBJECTIVE (see).

PATTERN (n) any artistic style, SHAPE (see), design, FORM (see) or figure accepted or proposed for imitation.

PERSPECTIVE (n) a way of seeing (either visually, auditorily or intellectually) which permits the observer to organize or understand an object.

PRESENTATIONAL (adj) a type of acting which stresses the actor's understanding, first, himself and only then, the character being played; often contrasted with REPRESENTATIONAL (see) acting.

REALISM (n) an artistic theory and practice involving fidelity to nature or real life and avoiding idealization of artwork's subject or surroundings.

REPETITION (n) an artistic technique in which an element is presented again and again, either for emphasis or else to provide or prepare for variations.

REPRESENTATIONAL (adj) refers to artistic renderings of ordinary, mundane matters of fact; in visual art, the term is contrasted with ABSTRACT (see); in performing art, the term is contrasted with PRESENTATIONAL (see).

REVISION (n) a step in the creative process in which inspiration is organized, given form, and corrected in order to communicate in the best possible way.

RHYTHM (n) the grouping and balancing of strong and weak elements in visual or aural patterns; the regular recurrence of identifying elements.

ROMANTICISM (n) an approach to the arts emphasizing the imaginative and the emotional, the autobiographical and introspective, the primitive and melancholy, and the remote in space and time; often contrasted with classicism's emphasis on the rational and intellectual.

SHAPE (n) the visible or auditory makeup of an object in a more or less permanent form; (v) to alter or manipulate an object's form and thereby bring it into correspondence with a plan or pattern.

SOURCE (n) an artist or artwork that influences a later work or artist; in visual art, often used derogatorily, suggesting that the later work is unoriginal.

SPACE (n) a three-dimensional entity that extends without bounds in all directions; the field of physical objects and events, and for their order and relationships.

SUBJECTIVE (adj) private and indirect; marked by personal feelings or ideas; opposite of OBJECTIVE (see).

TEXTURE (n) the structure of something made of closely interwoven elements; the feel of an object (whether real or imagined) as it appears immediately to the senses.

THEME (n) an idea of considerable importance within an artwork; in music, it is often repeated and leads to VARIATION (see); in other performing arts, the theme is an artwork's general topic or concept.

TRUTH TO MATERIALS (n) an artistic approach which permits qualities of the artist's raw materials to remain in the completed work and even influence its final form or features.

VALUE (n) an object or event important to one or more human beings; in music, the relative duration of a musical tone; in visual art, the relative lightness or darkness of an area; (v) to estimate or assign the worth of an object, an event, or one of its parts.

VARIATION (n) the repetition of an artistic element together with embellishments or modifications.

12 Thinking Skills and Curriculum Development _____

John Feldhusen

Some problems are so difficult they can't be solved in a million years—unless someone thinks about them for five minutes.

—H. L. Mencken

The terms *thinking skills* and *process skills* are bandied about frequently in the field of gifted education. Although there is still very little research to support the teachability of thinking skills, educational practitioners enthusiastically embrace new materials and methods for teaching in this area. We might not be sure about the outcomes or effects of our teaching of thinking skills, but we tend to honor the teacher who does engage children in thinking activities in the classroom.

Much of the impetus for teaching thinking comes from educational programs to teach creative thinking to children in regular classrooms and from more recent emphases on teaching creative thinking in gifted programs. Although the research evidence is questioned, there certainly is some reason to believe that creative thinking can be enhanced (Tannenbaum, 1983; Feldhusen and Clinkenbeard, 1987). Feldhusen and Treffinger (1975) also reported survey research showing that a vast majority of elementary teachers claim to be teaching creative thinking in their classes.

The pioneering work of Guilford (Guilford and Hoepfner, 1971) paved the way for many of our approaches to the assessment of thinking skills and to conceptions of how to teach them. While focusing our attention on divergent thinking or creative thinking skills, Guilford also stressed a number of cognitive skills in the structure of intellect operations (cognition, memory, convergent production, and evaluation) and on reasoning and problem solving. Meeker (1982) continued the work of Guilford and greatly extended it to school applications in both diagnostic testing and curriculum materials to enhance thinking skills. Torrance and Myers (1970) and Williams (1972) carried out extensive curriculum development projects in the area of divergent and creative thinking which led to widespread acceptance of the concept of teaching thinking skills to children in all subjects and from grades K–12.

The impetus to incorporate thinking skills goals in gifted programs also emerges from the widespread availability of instructional materials that purport to teach thinking skills. *Philosophy in the Classroom* (Lipman, Sharp, Oscanyan, 1980) is a massive effort to *teach* the skills of logic and critical thinking to children. The two books on *Critical Thinking* by Harnadek (1980) have been widely adopted in gifted programs in the United States, as have the four books, *Building Thinking Skills* by the Blacks (1984). MACOS (Bruner, 1970) has been revived as inquiry training in many gifted programs. Taba's (1962) inquiry teaching model has enjoyed considerable revival in gifted programs. Sternberg (1985) has shown that certain insight skills can be enhanced with fairly simple game-like teaching materials. The Bloom *Taxonomy* (1956) has also had profound impact as a guide to higher level thinking skills in gifted programs.

All of these thinking skills approaches are buttressed by a revival of interest in tests to measure thinking skills: the *Watson-Glaser Test of Critical Thinking* (1980); the *Ennis-Weir Critical Thinking Essay Test* (1985); the *Developing Cognitive Abilities Test* (1980), which measures skills at the higher levels of the Bloom *Taxonomy;* the *Ross Test of Higher Cognitive Processes* (1976); the *Structure of Intellect Learning Abilities Test* (Meeker, 1985); the *Cornell Critical Thinking Test* (Ennis and Millman, 1985); and the *Torrance Tests of Creative Thinking* (1974). When we have tests to measure thinking skills, we feel more confident that the constructs being measured really exist.

More explicit guidance, linked to sound theory and research, on how to teach thinking skills has come recently in two volumes, *Learning and Thinking Skills* (Chipman, Segal, and Glaser, 1985) reporting the results of a conference held at the University of Pittsburgh Learning Research and Development Center. These volumes are notable for their blend of researchers' and practitioners' (teachers') points of view. In *Thought and Knowledge: An Introduction to Critical Thinking*, Diane Halpern (1984) also provides a comprehensive overview of research and practice in the teaching of thinking skills, even though her title seems to indicate that only critical thinking is covered. Thus, with clear recognition that all this emphasis on thinking skills may lead to neglect of the importance of other learning activities, we nevertheless assert that a goal of all gifted programs should be to develop thinking skills to the highest levels possible. In a comprehensive review, Glaser (1984) presented a strong case, however, for the fundamental role of a knowledge base in teaching thinking skills. Glaser suggests that the proper interaction between youth and knowledge or subject matter is dynamic, interactive inquiry, problem solving, analysis, or synthesis activity. Thus, the process of teaching thinking skills is coterminous with the teaching of concepts and principles, for both must go on simultaneously. There is no teaching of thinking skills in isolation from a knowledge base, nor is a knowledge base developed without a dynamic, thinking type of interaction with the content.

Lipman, Sharp, and Oscanyan (1980) argue for the infusion of thinking skills into the entire school curriculum:

> The integration of thinking skills into every aspect of the curriculum would sharpen children's capacity to make connections and draw distinctions, to define and to classify, to assess factual information objectively and critically, to deal reflectively with the relationship between facts and values, and to differentiate their beliefs and what is true from their understanding of what is logically possible. These specific skills help children listen better, study better, learn better, and express themselves

better. They, therefore, carry over into all academic areas. A thinking skills program must help children think both more logically and more meaningfully (p. 15).

The purpose of this chapter, then, is to review the fundamental rubric for teaching thinking skills as a part of the general process of developing a knowledge base. The knowledge base is conceived of as the ultimate source of creative production when gifted students have achieved the cognitive processing skills of insight as described by Sternberg (1985) in his triarchic theory of intelligence.

The Bloom Taxonomy

The Bloom *Taxonomy* (1956) has been widely adopted as a model for conceptualizing higher level thinking skills for gifted learners. Although originally developed for a quite different purpose (to classify instructional objectives and test items in a hierarchical fashion), it was a natural extension of the *Taxonomy* to its use as a hierarchical model of thinking processes or skills. Indeed, the authors of the *Taxonomy*, the College Board Committee of Examiners, had spelled out quite thoroughly the psychological and cognitive aspects of each level of the *Taxonomy*. Thus, they clearly viewed it as representing a cognitive explanation of learning and/or thinking processes. However, a host of other practitioners began to relate the levels of the *Taxonomy* to the teaching of thinking skills for gifted and talented youth or for children in general. Sanders's (1966) plan for questioning based on the *Taxonomy* is one such early effort.

At this point, a review of the levels of the Bloom *Taxonomy* is appropriate. We begin at level one, which is called the "knowledge" level. This level represents all cognitions that simply represent remembering information or processes. The teaching method may involve lectures, drill and recitation, or having students read. The curriculum goals at this level may be stated as follows:

- Name the major terrestial configurations.
- Detail the phases in the operation of a battery.
- List the characteristics of political essays.
- Show knowledge of the major political issues of the 1940 election.

It is important to recognize that the knowledge level of the *Taxonomy* covers a wide range of types of information to be remembered:

- Specific bits of information
- Terminology
- Facts such as dates, events, places
- Conventions
- Trends and sequences
- Classifications and categories
- Criteria
- Methodology
- Principles
- Generalizations
- Theories

Level two of the *Taxonomy* and all higher levels are referred to as representing intellectual abilities and skills. Level two is called the "comprehension level." Here, higher forms of cognitive activity than memory are expected, such as interpretation, extrapolation, and translation. These might include:

- paraphrasing events
- understanding the concept of peace

Level three is called "application." It refers to those intellectual activities in which students use principles, concepts, theories, generalizations, or other abstractions in solving problems or apply them in new situations. For example, goals might be stated as:

- Able to use principles of economics in solving current financial problems.
- Able to use principles of learning in specifying the best procedures for teaching a new concept.

Level four is called "analysis." This may involve:

- Identifying major elements in a communication
- Analyzing relationships among the ideas in a document
- Recognizing form and pattern in an essay
- Seeing the connections between different aspects of a project
- Breaking a compound down into its constituent elements

Always there is the expectation that the students will be able to dissect, detect elements, or see relationships among the parts.

The next level upward is called "synthesis." It refers to all those intellectual activities in which students combine or integrate ideas, concepts, principles, or information into unified wholes that represent a new pattern or structure. The newness, of course, represents a creative element in the process. Thus, students might do any of the following:

- Write an essay combining elements of the styles of Swift and Lamb.
- Propose a plan for testing a hypothesis.
- Write a scenario depicting life in the year 2000 based on current trends.
- Draw a picture that incorporates the impressionists' views.
- Create a machine based on the principles of weightlessness.

The final level of the *Taxonomy* is called "evaluation." At this level, students are expected to make judgments using standards or criteria. For example:

- What are the flaws in the main character's arguments?
- Compare the artistic qualities of Rembrandt and Titian.
- Judge the scientific arguments for and against evolution.

These levels of the Bloom *Taxonomy* provide a guide for teachers of gifted learners to engage them in intellectual activity appropriate to their levels of ability. The goals of the higher levels call for appropriate instructional activities in which students are actively engaged in practicing high-level cognitive activity. Thus, for the goal "Compare the images used by different writers," an appropriate activity for gifted students might be to have small groups compare the images used by Edgar Allen Poe in "The Raven" and in "The Cask of Amontillado." Similarly, an activity for another gifted class with the goal of synthesizing ideas about propaganda might be to discuss the role of political messages in the election of President Reagan.

Given that teachers seem to spend a lot of class time purveying factual information to students (Goodlad, 1984; Sizer, 1985), the Bloom *Taxonomy* can be a valuable guide to teachers of the gifted in planning discussion questions, in organizing learning tasks for small groups of students, in developing instructional assignments, and in writing curriculum units of instruction. Combined with other approaches or systems for teaching thinking skills, it offers a unique approach to assuring that dynamic, creative interaction occurs between gifted students and course content. The results should be learning with meaning of highly retrievable and transferable concepts, principles, and cognitive strategies.

Critical Thinking

The area of critical thinking was delineated by Ennis (1962) as a special domain of human thinking. He noted that psychologists and educators had addressed creative thinking, concept formation, problem solving, and associative thinking, but had not investigated critical thinking skills. Ennis reviewed the literature on thinking skills, attempted to identify basic dimensions of critical thinking, and proposed the following list of twelve aspects of critical thinking:

1. Grasping the meaning of a statement
2. Judging whether there is ambiguity in a line of reasoning
3. Judging whether certain statements contradict each other
4. Judging whether a conclusion follows necessarily
5. Judging whether a statement is specific enough
6. Judging whether a statement is actually the application of a certain principle
7. Judging whether an observation statement is reliable
8. Judging whether an inductive conclusion is warranted
9. Judging whether the problem has been identified
10. Judging whether something is an assumption
11. Judging whether a definition is adequate
12. Judging whether a statement made by an alleged authority is acceptable

FIGURE 12.1 Ennis's Three Types of Thinking Skills

1. Define and clarify:
   - Identify central issues and problems.
   - Identify conclusions.
   - Identify reasons.
   - Identify appropriate questions to ask, given a situation.
   - Identify assumptions.

2. Judge information:
   - Determine credibility of sources and observations.
   - Determine relevance.
   - Recognize consistency.

3. Infer—solve problems and draw reasonable conclusions:
   - Infer and judge inductive conclusions.
   - Deduce and judge deductive validity.
   - Predict probable consequences.

Source: R. H. Ennis, "A Logical Basis for Measuring Critical Thinking Skills," *Educational Leadership, 43*(2), 1985, p. 42.

Ennis has refined his model or taxonomy of critical thinking skills recently (1985) to include three types of thinking skills and thirteen dispositions of critical thinkers. They are presented in Figures 12.1 and 12.2. (See Sternberg and Baron, 1985, p. 42 for this version of Ennis's theoretical conception as well as Ennis's own presentation of the conception in the 1985 reference above.) Ennis defines critical thinking as follows:

FIGURE 12.2 Ennis's Thirteen Dispositions of Critical Thinkers

The ability to:
1. Be open-minded.
2. Take a position (and change a position) when the evidence and reasons are sufficient to do so.
3. Take into account the total situation.
4. Try to be well informed.
5. Seek as much precision as the subject permits.
6. Deal in an orderly manner with the parts of a complex whole.
7. Look for alternatives.
8. Seek reasons.
9. Seek a clear statement of the issue.
10. Keep in mind the original and/or basic concern.
11. Use credible sources and mention them.
12. Remain relevant to the main point.
13. Be sensitive to the feelings, level of knowledge, and degree of sophistication of others.

Source: R. H. Ennis, "A Logical Basis for Measuring Critical Thinking Skills," *Educational Leadership, 43*(2), 1985, p. 42.

Critical thinking is reflective and reasonable thinking that is focused on deciding what to believe or do. Note that there are creative activities covered by this definition, including formulating hypotheses, questions, alternatives, and plans for experiments (p. 45).

Illustrative Objectives and Activities

Illustrative objectives and activities follow for each of the twelve critical thinking skills in the Ennis hierarchy. Teachers who are developing curriculum for the gifted should note that most of the illustrations are embedded in curriculum content and not presented as abstract experiences. Thinking skills are learned best in the context of subject matter. Such experiences will ensure that the skills will not become task specific but will transfer to a variety of real-life thinking experiences.

An objective and activity for the first aspect or component of critical thinking might be as follows:

Objective: Gifted learners will be able to explicate the meaning of complex excerpts from their reading materials.

Instructional   Reread the following passage which was a part of your assigned
Activity: readings. Then, working in small groups, try to answer the questions which follow.

Grappling with such abstract and complex ideas and trying to derive meaning from them is a first and basic aspect of critical thinking.

The second aspect of critical thinking and all subsequent aspects call for judgment. Whereas judgment is presented as the sixth or highest level of thinking in the Bloom *Taxonomy*, it is likely that all of the thinking skills that involve judging also involve the subordinate cognitive skills of comprehending, analyzing, and synthesizing.

More specifically, the second aspect of critical thinking is judging whether there is ambiguity in a line of reasoning. As an illustration, the following objective and instructional activity are presented:

Objective: Judge whether there is a lack of clarity in a document that discusses a controversial issue.

Instructional   Read the following statements and decide if there is ambiguity
Activity: or a lack of clarity anywhere in the statement. Underline the ambiguous elements, if any, and explain the ambiguity below:

> *We must strive to nurture our environment for future generations. This is the only place that they will have to enjoy. We must respect their right to health and productive lives.*

The third aspect of critical thinking has to do with judging if contradictions exist within a document. The following objective might be written into a curriculum plan:

Objective: Judge whether there are contradictions among or between statements within an essay.

Instructional   Read this statement and decide if there are contradictions
Activity: within it. If there are, be ready to explain them:

> *The United States is committed to the democratic freedoms for all people. The citizens of all nations should have the right to self-determination. The United Nations should have the power to mandate democratic rights for all peoples of the world.*

This activity can be pursued in social studies, literature, composition, or science classes, depending on where the illustrations are found. If the class is composition, there might be a principal emphasis on analyzing the contradictions in writing.

The fourth aspect of critical thinking is judging whether a conclusion necessarily follows. This is essentially a skill in logical thinking. An objective in this area might be stated as follows:

Objective: Judge whether the following conclusions follow logically from the data and results of the experiment.

Instructional   A sword blade is held in a flame. The sword blade curls down-
Activity   ward as though it has melted. The blade is removed from the
in Science: flame and laid on a table with the edge upward whereupon it straightens out quickly. Which conclusions seem warranted and why?

    1. The original bending of the blade was not due to melting.
    2. Gravity caused the blade to bend downward.
    3. The blade was bimetallic, made of metals with different expansion ratios, and thus was bent due to the conflict of the two ratios.
    4. The blade melted.
    5. It straightened out when laid on the table because it was a single metal and it resumed its natural straight shape.

This activity in science is drawn from the inquiry activities developed by Suchman (1965) but adapted for our illustration. It would best be presented to a group of gifted learners first as a demonstration with a bimetallic blade and a flame, followed by an inquiry discussion and a careful review of the possible conclusions to select those that are tenable.

Problems in pure logic may also be used as instruction under this objective. Here are examples adapted from Halpern (1984, p. 58). Judge if the conclusion follows from the premises:

Premise #1:   All boys are athletes.
Premise #2:   All athletes are muscular.

Conclusion: All boys are muscular.
Conclusion: All muscular people are boys.

Premise #1:   Some lawyers are honest.
Premise #2:   Some honest people go to church.

Conclusion: Some lawyers go to church.
Conclusion: Some churchgoers are lawyers.

Premise #1:   Professors are erudite.
Premise #2:   Erudite people are boring.

Conclusion: Professors are boring.
Conclusion: Boring people are professors.

These problems in logic can be taught through discussion, which might begin with Venn diagrams illustrating the inclusiveness of major and minor premises and their relationship to conclusions.

All A are B
All B are C

All A are C
All C are A

All A are B
Some B are C

Some A are C
Some C are A

Lipman's program (Lipman et al., 1980) of *Philosophy for Children* provides some excellent training in the area of logic and critical thinking. The *Mind Benders* published by Midwest Publications (Harnadek, 1978), *Playing with Logic* (Schoenfield and Rosenblatt, 1985), and *Critical Thinking* books (Harnadek, 1980) all offer excellent experiences for children in the areas of logical and critical thinking.

The next aspect of critical thinking is judging whether a statement is specific enough. Here is an objective and an instructional activity:

Objective: Judge whether a statement is specific enough to draw conclusions from it.

Instructional   Read the following statement. Then try to answer the questions
Activity: which follow or indicate that the information is not specific enough to answer the questions.

All of the soldiers were poised at the barricades ready to charge into battle. The captain paced up and down behind them, wringing his hands and sighing audibly.

1. The captain seemed to be agitated or concerned about the battle.
2. The captain was afraid to make the decision to order the troops into battle.

A class discussion could grow out of these questions as to what could be inferred or deduced from the stated condition. Comparable material could be developed in most areas of the curriculum.

The sixth aspect of critical thinking is judging whether a statement is the application of a principle. This calls for students to learn how to assess the relationship between a general rule and a specific application of the rule. (For the remaining aspects we shall not give an illustrative objective and instructional activity, but shall merely give brief illustrations.) For example, it is now a widely held political principle that economic sanctions by one country against another are not effective in changing the political behavior of the target country. Students may be asked to judge whether the economic boycott organized by President Ronald Reagan against Libya in 1986 is truly an application of the principle, and will it be or not be effective? They may also be asked to judge and contrast the value of economic sanctions against South Africa and to try to explain why one might be effective whereas the other is not.

The seventh aspect is to judge whether a statement is reliable. In a discussion of *Hamlet* in an English class, we are asked to judge the reliability of the following assertions:

1. The major issue with which Hamlet is grappling is power and the loss of power to his uncle.
2. Hamlet is a homosexual.
3. Hamlet's mother is an opportunist.

The eighth aspect is judging whether an inductive conclusion is warranted. The following are inductive conclusions:

1. World weather patterns are changing.
2. Nuclear power is too dangerous to be used to generate electricity.
3. Politicians rarely keep their word.
4. Samuel Clemens was really a racist person.

Based on reading of text material and other primary and secondary sources, students can make the judgments as to whether these statements are warranted inductive conclusions.

The ninth aspect is judging whether a problem has been identified. This is a valuable critical thinking skill in all problem-solving activities. Often tense people attempt to solve the wrong problem given the problem situation. For example, cars often have accidents on icy bridges. What is the problem?

1. How to get the bridges sanded early after a storm begins.
2. How to prevent ice from forming on bridges.
3. How to prevent accidents on icy bridges.
4. How to get drivers to exercise more caution.
5. How to get a truck to salt the bridges.

Knowing that the problem is really how to prevent accidents on icy bridges gives the students a broader and hopefully more comprehensive approach to solve this problem.

The next aspect is judging whether something is an assumption. As in several other aspects of critical thinking, Ennis notes that this ability is not unitary but is really a complex of perceptual and cognitive abilities. Ennis gives the following illustration: "When the demand for nucroscopies decreases, the price decreases." What is the assumption regarding this specific situation and the general principle to which it is related?

The next critical thinking skill is judging whether a definition is adequate. Ennis gives rules for definition and various forms of definitions. For example, in definitions that are intended to classify a concept or object, Ennis states the following rules:

1. The defining part should contain (a) a general class, and (b) a feature or features that set this member off from members of the general class.
2. The defining part should be equivalent to the part being defined.
3. The defining part should not use the term to be defined.
4. The defining part should not give more than enough to provide a complete classification.

Science students may now be asked to judge the adequacy of this definition of an isotope:

Any of two or more species of atoms of a chemical element with the same atomic number and position in the periodic table and nearly identical chemical behavior.

The final aspect is judging whether a statement made by an alleged authority is acceptable. As an illustration, an English teacher cites a noted movie critic who asserts that modern interpretations of *Macbeth* are nearly all influenced by Freudian psychology. Is the authority correct? Students in an English class will read several, hopefully representative, interpretations of characters' motives in *Macbeth* and judge whether those interpretations are based on Freudian psychological or philosophical tenets.

These various aspects of critical thinking are now taught explicitly in such published material as Harnadek's two-volume series, *Critical Thinking* (1980), which is intended for average high-school students according to the publisher. We would therefore conclude that gifted junior high-school students could also learn the concepts. It should also be the case that gifted students are given abundant practice to develop these thinking skills in each of the disciplines. This means that math teachers, literature teachers, composition teachers, and science teachers all find ways to structure discussion, small group work, and individual writing assignments in which students get ample opportunity to learn how to use these different aspects of critical and logical thinking in dealing with that area.

Creative Thinking and Creative Problem Solving

The major areas of thinking skills promoted in programs for gifted learners are creative thinking, problem solving, and creative problem solving. The pioneering work of Torrance (1962, 1965), Parnes (1967, 1977), Treffinger (1980), and Feldhusen and associates (1969, 1977) paved the way for a proliferation of instructional materials designed to teach creative thinking and problem solving (Feldhusen and Treffinger, 1985). Most gifted programs, especially at the elementary level, place major emphasis on the teaching of creative thinking and problem solving. The general rationale is that gifted learners have very high potential for creative activity and production in adulthood and that they should begin developing that potential as early as possible. A closely related goal is for gifted learners to become effective as high-level researchers and creators. To develop competence in research, these students need underlying competence in creative thinking and problem solving, a knowledge base in the area or discipline in which they may carry out research, and some specific research competencies or skills.

What are the specific skills of creative thinking and problem solving? Torrance led the way in focusing researchers and developers on the basic divergent thinking abilities of fluency, flexibility, originality, and elaboration. *Fluency* is the ability to think of or to recall many ideas or problems for a given concept or task. For example:

1. What are all the ways we might rewrite this equation and maintain the equality?
2. What are all the possible reasons you can think of for Hamlet's strange behavior toward Ophelia?
3. What are all the ways that might be used to enhance this chemical reaction?
4. Think of all the reasons you can for the anarchist behavior of Sacco and Vanzetti.
5. What are all the types of stitches that would best accommodate the design for this blouse?
6. Name as many alternative hypotheses as you can for the failure of the law of supply and demand to function in relation to food prices during World War II.
7. What were all the problems faced by the Jamestown settlers?
8. Write as many titles as possible for your story.

From these examples it should be clear that creative thinking can be developed or taught in all school subjects. *Fluency* is the skill of being able to recall or think of a number of ideas or problems for a specific stimulus situation. It is one of the essences of insight behavior described by Davidson and Sternberg (1984) called "selective comparison." In selective comparison, one is able to relate new information to information acquired in the past. The process obviously involves fluent recall of information. Pollert, Feldhusen, VanMondfrans, and Treffinger (1969) found that fluency is correlated with memory. Thus, to a great extent fluency is a selective recall process.

During the exercise of fluent thinking, students may also be taught to develop their capacities for flexible and original thinking. Originality implies that selective combination occurs. Davidson and Sternberg describe this as a process of synthesizing or associating hitherto unconnected ideas into a new unique or original whole. Thus, the objectives or directions for some school tasks might read as follows:

1. Think of new and original ways of grafting plants.
2. Develop a whole new set of operational symbols to denote mathematic operations. Try to create signs that look like their function.
3. Combine several forms of essay to create some new genre of essays.
4. What are some new ways to help people better understand the complexities of different cultures?

Flexibility is the capacity to produce new ideas that deviate from normally expected ideas and to be able to produce new ideas that shift categorically during the process of idea production. As with originality, the essential condition for idea production is a fluency-like task demand, and as with originality, the major effort to induce and train the cognition called "flexibility" is through a metacognitive process of becoming aware and striving to use the capacity. The following objectives or tasks are especially designed to evoke flexible thinking:

1. What are all the ways you can devise for weighing very light objects other than a balance or spring scale?
2. Shakespeare's *Macbeth* is a tragedy. What are ways you could change it to become a comedy?
3. Write a short essay that has no active verbs in it.
4. Write alternative forms of a given equation in which there are square root operations on both sides of the equal signs.

All of these illustrations open the door to flexibility or an alternate way of viewing an otherwise familiar concept or process.

Elaboration is a process of filling in details, developing ideas, or bringing an abstract concept to life. Fluent, original, and flexible thinking may yield many ideas. An intermediate process calls for evaluation or judgment concerning the worth of ideas produced. Judgment, of course, always implies criteria. Could this idea be developed and yield some practical payoff? If developed would it alleviate hunger? Would people find it humorous? Once the evaluation or judgment is made and an idea is selected for expansion or development, the elaboration process has begun. Like the fluency function, it involves filling in details, thinking of illustrations, deciding on color, determining quantities, and selecting a mode of communication. Here are some elaboration tasks:

1. Think of many ideas for a story emphasizing characterization. Select the best idea. Develop it as a short story.
2. Think of a number of possible experiments in genetic mutations. Select the most original. Design a complete experiment.
3. Identify major problems facing the homeless in American cities. Select the most serious one. Design a solution to that problem.

Slightly elaborated and usually carried out in groups is the process of *brainstorming* (Osborn, 1963). It combines all of the basic divergent thinking skills described above. Through long experience, a common set of rules for brainstorming has emerged. Feldhusen and Treffinger (1985) propose the following guidelines:

1. Do not criticize or evaluate any ideas produced. Ideas should be free flowing and unhampered at this stage.
2. Crazy or humorous ideas are acceptable. Wild imaginative ideas may become practical when forced into problem situations from a different viewpoint. The emergence of an unusual or bizarre idea may spark yet another idea.
3. Quantity of ideas is important. Quality of ideas is not considered at this point. The more ideas there are, the greater the base for evaluation and selecting viable ideas becomes.
4. Work with others in the combination of ideas. No one person's ideas belong to that person; all ideas at this stage are thrown into the communal pot. Ideas that sprout from other ideas that have been suggested are fair game.

Brainstorming is an excellent method of helping students learn how to think creatively in groups. It can be thought of also as a problem-solving method, but the emphasis is on creating conditions and developing skills for the production of new, unique, or original ideas and solutions.

A more complex form of creative thinking, now widely taught to students in programs for the gifted, is *creative problem solving.* The major model for this skill was developed by Parnes (1967), later popularized by Parnes, Noller, and Biondi (1977), and recently promoted for gifted programs by Treffinger (1980). Six steps or processes characterize the model:

1. Mess-finding
2. Data-finding
3. Problem-finding
4. Idea-finding
5. Solution-finding
6. Acceptance-finding

The main purpose of "Mess-finding" is to sort through a problem situation and find direction toward a broad goal or solution. In "Data-finding," participants sort through all available information about the mess and clarify the steps or direction to a solution. In "Problem-finding," a specific problem statement is formulated. "Idea-finding" is a processing of finding many ideas for solution to *the* problem or parts of the problem. "Solution-finding" is an evaluation or judgmental process of sorting among the ideas produced in the last step and selecting those most likely to produce solutions. Finally, in "Acceptance-finding," a plan is devised for implementing the good solutions. An adaptation of the creative problem-solving model is called "Future Problem Solving." It involves the application of the creative problem-solving model to studies of the future and to problems that are now emerging as major concerns for the future (Whaley, 1981).

A number of other creative thinking techniques have been described by

Feldhusen and Treffinger (1984) in the new edition of their book *Creative Thinking and Problem Solving in Gifted Education.* These include synectics, attribute listing, morphological analysis, and forced relationships. Generally, creative techniques give students opportunities to think and develop thinking skills without the stress or anxiety that is often associated with logic and critical thinking. This is not to say that creative thinking skills are all-purpose alternatives to the rigorous forms of thinking required in logical analysis and critical thinking. Both forms of thinking should be developed in students, and both should be developed in ways that help students learn how to generalize, transfer, and apply them in real problem situations. New skills can profitably be practiced initially in abstracted and artificial forms to help students grasp the cognitive model. They may also profitably learn new models through problem solving or exploratory experiences. Once they understand the nature of the process (e.g., brainstorming), they should then have more and more experience in dealing with real problem situations in which they can apply the model. In school that may mean moving from brainstorming experiences of a contrived nature toward problems and inquiry in the disciplines of mathematics, science, social studies, English, business, agriculture, and home economics. Whereas the initial problem might involve using brainstorming to think of uses of old tin cans, later experiences would include writing as many forms as possible of an equation, identifying a variety of caustic compounds, listing all the major environmental problems facing the United States, or writing alternate titles for a story.

In a concluding statement to his very extensive review of creativity, Tannenbaum (1983) concludes that "[Creativity] consists of a not yet known combination of general and specific abilities and personality traits associated with high potential that can be realized in a stimulating environment with the help of good fortune" (p. 328). Our state of knowledge or understanding of creative thinking, of how to measure it and how to teach it may be no better and no worse than our knowledge of any of the other thinking processes.

Questioning and Inquiry Skills

Questioning skills and inquiry methods have long been a part of the repertoire of thinking skills. In their book *Creative Learning and Teaching,* Torrance and Myers (1970) dealt extensively with the topics of questioning skills of both teachers and students in a series of lengthy chapters. They illustrated all of the techniques, showing how to question for information, how to question for thinking, how to use provocative questions, and how to teach children to become good questioners. They proposed that teachers use the following forms of questions to stimulate students' thinking:

1. *Interpretation.* What does the following statement mean: Conspicuous consumption by Americans living in Africa is a supreme paradox.

2. *Comparison-Analysis.* How are parenting practices and family value systems different now from 100 years ago?

3. *Synthesis questions.* How could you combine elements of the philosophies of the Sierra Club and the Audubon Society to forge a stronger force for environmental protection in the United States?

4. *Evaluation.* Did the United States reveal moral bankruptcy by its failure to intervene when the Pol Pot regime massacred three million Cambodians?

5. *Sensitivity to problems.* What are the major problems of the United Nations Organization?

6. *Clarifying problems.* Why don't teachers enjoy higher professional status?

7. *Provocative questions.* What would be the results if a law was passed banning *all* killings and physical violence on TV?

8. *Hypothetical questions.* If you were principal of the school, how would things change?

9. *Questions to encourage thoughtful reading.* Why was Mozart called the "Boy Wonder"?

10. *Questions to encourage thoughtful listening* (beyond the literal message). Why did it take Morse so long to perfect his telegraph?

11. *Questions to see new relationships.* How is flooding in Pakistan related to the U.S. love of big cars?

Students can be taught to be good questioners and their questioning skills can be developed, but it appears that an appropriate classroom atmosphere is also desirable to foster this development. Some of the major characteristics of such a classroom are the following:

1. The teacher is patient and waits for students to formulate questions.
2. There is no ridiculing of students by teacher or peers for "dumb" questions or ideas.
3. Offbeat and unusual ideas or questions are accepted for discussion.
4. Humor is accepted and encouraged.
5. The classroom is orderly but relaxed.
6. The classroom is a rich, stimulating environment with a lot of material resources.
7. The teacher is "with it" and dynamic.

Good questioning skills can be used in a variety of ways:

1. Analyze and clarify ambiguous situations
2. Secure information
3. Clarify problems
4. Test hypotheses
5. Evaluate possible solutions

Sanders developed an extensive program of questioning skills, as reported in his book, *Classroom Questions, What Kinds?* (1966). The program is based on the Bloom *Taxonomy* (1965) and uses the six levels of the *Taxonomy* as guides to the formulation of questions. It should also be noted that the models for questioning proposed by Torrance and Meyers (1970), as discussed earlier in this chapter, also include several types of questions that are identical to Bloom *Taxonomy* levels.

Two major programs for the development of inquiry skills were developed by Taba (1962) and Suchman (1965). The Taba model is presented very thoroughly in Maker's *Teaching Models in Education of the Gifted* (1982). The major strategies used in the Taba model are (1) concept development, (2) interpretation of data, (3) application of generalization, and (4) resolution of conflicts. Maker notes that the major factors in developing students' inquiry skills are the teacher's questions and the sequencing of learning experiences.

In the first stage, *concept development,* information is listed and tested for relevancy. Then the information is grouped according to common attributes or characteristics. Next it is labeled through abstracting or synthesizing the basic aspects of the information. In the next step, called "subsuming," students search for relationships among the information. Finally in the fifth step, the whole process is recycled to search for new ways of understanding the information.

The second phase of the Taba model is called *interpretation of data.* Students are involved in gathering data and drawing conclusions or inferences from it. Taba stresses that teachers may guide, but students must do their own inquiring.

In the third phase, *generalization,* students use previously learned generalizations and try applying them to new situations. The process may be one of predicting consequences. This would be essentially like some synthesis level activities in the Bloom *Taxonomy.*

Finally there is a phase called *resolution of conflict.* This activity involves students in taking viewpoints, examining alternate positions, analyzing attitudes and values, and making judgments. This phase obviously involves students in activities comparable to level six of the Bloom *Taxonomy* (judgment or evaluation), but it is clear that level four (analysis) is probably also involved.

The Taba model is notable for its comprehensive approach to the involvement of students in a carefully sequenced set of steps through the thinking process. The model is designed to teach a set of inquiry skills that can be used in a wide variety of situations in life.

The Suchman model (1965) might be described as a system to teach students how to become active seekers and questioners in science. A puzzling or ambiguous situation is presented to the students in a film. The most popular illustration depicts a bimetallic strip bending upward at the ends when placed in a flame. Students do not know that it is bimetallic. They can ask questions about the phenomenon, but may receive only yes or no for answers. Suchman proposed that students go through three stages of inquiry in finding the explanation for such a discrepant event. The first he calls *episode analysis;* this is simply clarifying the basic facts of the situation. The second is called *determinance of relevance;* this is a process of figuring out the relevant and necessary aspects or elements of the situation. The third stage is called *induction of relational constructs;* this is the phase of discovery or understanding the relationship.

The author has observed students involved in Suchman's inquiry tasks and has led groups of children who are carrying out the inquiry process. The stages described by Suchman do occur but sometimes out of order. In early stages of training there is little systematic movement through the stages; there is much wild guessing. Later, students begin to cooperate and build upon the discoveries of one another. The excitement grows as they get close to the principle.

These inquiry-discovery oriented thinking programs illustrate well the need for very active roles of students in learning how to think. They also illustrate well the value of small group work in which students interact and stimulate one another. Finally they clearly show the role of the teacher in structuring the experience and guiding students through it.

Conclusion

We have reviewed a variety of approaches to the teaching of thinking skills: the Bloom *Taxonomy*, Ennis's critical thinking skills, creativity and creative problem solving, questioning skills, and inquiry. All of these systems are applicable and useful in all areas of the curriculum. They call for active involvement of students in thinking, analyzing, inquiring, probing, synthesizing, and evaluating, and they demand teachers who are effective in structuring and guiding the experience.

The California State Department of Education has developed and published (1979) an extensive set of curriculum guides covering art, literature, science, music, and social studies across all the grades. These guides incorporate many of the thinking skills and illustrate many of the methods presented in this chapter. (See, for example, the volume on *Literature and Story Writing* for elementary and middle schools, which can be ordered from the California State Department of Education, P.O. Box 271, Sacramento, CA 95802.)

Teaching thinking skills requires not only a well-developed curriculum plan, but also teachers who have learned the prerequisite skills of questioning, leading inquiry, small group work, discussion techniques, and problem solving, which are essential in guiding youth through complex cognitive activity. There are great risks in trying to incorporate thinking skills in the curriculum. It is easier to prepare and teach didactic lessons by lecturing, but the payoffs in learning for gifted students are infinitely superior when the teacher can guide them through the intricate maze of ideas to a clear understanding of concepts and principles and to enhanced skills of thinking.

KEY POINTS SUMMARY

- Thinking skills should be a vital aspect of the goals of programs for gifted and talented youth.

- The Bloom *Taxonomy* is one valuable guide in teaching higher level thinking skills to the gifted.

- There is a set of critical thinking skills that should be mastered by the gifted.

- The teaching of all thinking skills should turn quickly to the application of those skills in knowledge bases, disciplines, or real-world problem contexts.

- Creative thinking and creative problem solving are vital skills that gifted students need as prerequisites to productive thinking.

- Questioning and inquiry skills give gifted students the background they need for analytical activities.

References

Black, H., and Black, S. (1984). *Book 1: Building Thinking Skill.* Pacific Grove, Calif.: Midwest Publications.

Bloom, B. S. (1965). *Taxonomy of Educational Objectives, Handbook I, Cognitive Domain.* New York: Longman.

Bruner, J. (1970). *Man: A Course of Study.* Cambridge, Mass.: Educational Development Center.

California State Department of Education (1979). *Principles, Objectives and Curricula for Programs in the Education of Gifted and Talented Pupils—Kindergarten through Grade Twelve.* Sacramento: California State Department of Education.

Chipman, S. F., Segal, J. W., and Glaser, R. (1985). *Thinking and Learning Skills.* Hillsdale, N.J.: Lawrence Erlbaum.

Davidson, J. E., and Sternberg, R. J. (1984). "The Role of Insight in Intellectual Giftedness." *Gifted Child Quarterly, 28,* 58–64.

Ennis, R. H. (1962). "A Concept of Critical Thinking." *Harvard Educational Review, 32,* 81–111.

Ennis, R. H. (1985). "A Logical Basis for Measuring Critical Thinking Skills." *Educational Leadership, 43*(2), 44–48.

Ennis, R. H., and Millman, J. (1985). *Cornell Critical Thinking Test.* Pacific Palisades, Calif.: Midwest Publications.

Ennis, R. H., and Weir, E. (1980). *Ennis-Weir Critical Thinking Essay Test.* Pacific Palisades, Calif.: Midwest Publications.

Feldhusen, J. F., Bahlke, S. J., and Treffinger, D. J. (1969). "Teaching Creative Thinking." *Elementary School Journal, 70,* 48–53.

Feldhusen, J. F., and Clinkenbeard P. R. (1987). "Creativity Instructional Materials; A Review of Research." *Journal of Creative Behavior.*

Feldhusen, J. F., and Treffinger, D. J. (1975). "Teachers' Attitudes and Practices in Teaching Creativity and Problem Solving to Economically Disadvantaged and Minority Children." *Psychological Reports, 37,* 1161–1162.

Feldhusen, J. F., and Treffinger, D. J. (1975). *Teaching Creative Thinking and Problem Solving.* Dubuque, Iowa: Kendall-Hunt.

Feldhusen J. F., and Treffinger, D. J. (1985). *Creative Thinking and Problem Solving in Gifted Education.* Dubuque, Iowa: Kendall-Hunt.

Glaser, R. (1984). "Education and Thinking: The Role of Knowledge." *American Psychology, 39*(2), 893–904.

Goodlad, J. I. (1984). *A Place Called School.* New York: McGraw-Hill.

Guilford, J. P., and Hoepfner, R. (1971). *The Analysis of Intelligence.* New York: McGraw-Hill.

Halpern, D. F. (1984). *Thought and Knowledge: An Introduction to Critical Thinking.* Hillsdale, N.J.: Lawrence Erlbaum Associates.

Harnadek, A. (1978). *Mind Benders*. Pacific Grove, Calif.: Midwest Publications.

Harnadek, A. (1980). *Critical Thinking, Book 1 and 2*. Pacific Grove, Calif.: Midwest Publications.

Lipman, M., Sharp, A. M., and Oscanyan, F. F. (1980). *Philosophy in the Classroom*. Philadelphia: Temple University Press.

Maker, C. J. (1982). *Teaching Models in Education of the Gifted*. Rockville, Md.: Aspen Publications.

Meeker, M. (1982). *Divergent Production of Semantic Units*. El Segundo, Calif.: SOI Institute.

Meeker, M., Meeker, R., and Roid, G. H. (1985). *Structure of Intellect Learning Abilities Test (SOI-LA)*. Los Angeles: Western Psychological Services.

Osborn, A. (1963). *Applied Imagination*. New York: Scribners.

Parnes, S. J. (1967). *Creative Behavior Guidebook*. New York: Scribners.

Parnes, S. J. (1977). "Guiding Creative Action." *Gifted Child Quarterly, 21*, 460–476.

Parnes, S. J., Noller, R. B., and Biondi, A. M. (1977). *Guide to Creative Action*. New York: Charles Scribner.

Pollert, L. H., Feldhusen, J. F., VanMondfrans, A. P., and Treffinger, D. J. (1969). "Role of Memory in Divergent Thinking." *Psychological Reports, 25*, 151–156.

Ross, J. D., and Ross, C. M. (1976). *Ross Test of Higher Cognitive Processes*. Los Angeles: Western Psychological Services.

Sanders, N. M. (1966). *Classroom Questions, What Kinds*. New York: Harper & Row.

Schoenfield, M., and Rosenblatt, J. (1985). *Playing with Logic*. Belmont, Calif.: David S. Lake Publishers.

Sizer, T. R. (1985). *Horace's Compromise: The Dilemma of the American High School*. Boston: Houghton Mifflin.

Sternberg, R. J. (1985). *Beyond IQ: A Triarchic Theory of Intelligence*. New York: Cambridge University Press.

Sternberg, R. J., and Baron, J. B. (1985). "A Statewide Approach to Measuring Critical Thinking Skills." *Educational Leadership, 43*(2), 40–43.

Suchman, R. (1965). "Inquiry and Education." In J. Gallagher (Ed.), *Teaching Gifted Students: A Book of Readings*. Boston: Allyn and Bacon.

Taba, H. (1962). *Curriculum Development, Theory and Practice*. New York: Harcourt Brace and World.

Tannenbaum, A. J. (1983). *Gifted Children, Psychological and Educational Perspectives*. New York: Macmillan.

Torrance, E. P. (1962). *Guiding Creative Talent*. Englewood Cliffs, N.J.: Prentice-Hall.

Torrance, E. P. (1965). *Rewarding Creative Behavior*. Englewood Cliffs, N.J.: Prentice-Hall.

Torrance, E. P. (1974). *Torrance Tests of Creative Thinking, Norms-Technical Manual*. Lexington, Mass.: Ginn and Company.

Torrance, E. P., and Myers, R. E. (1970). *Creative Learning and Teaching*. New York: Dodd, Mead.

Treffinger, D. J. (1980). *Encouraging Creative Learning for the Gifted and Talented.* Ventura, Calif.: Ventura County Supt. of Schools, LTI Publications.

Watson, G., and Glaser, E. M. (1980). *Watson-Glaser Critical Thinking Appraisal.* New York: Psychological Corporation.

Whaley, C. E. (1984). *Future Studies.* New York: Trillium Press.

Wick, J. W., and Smith, J. K. (1980). *Developing Cognitive Abilities Test.* Glenview, Ill.: Scott, Foresman.

Williams, F. (1972). *A Total Creativity Kit.* Englewood Cliffs, N.J.: Educational Technology Publications.

13 Affective Curriculum for the Gifted

Linda Kreger Silverman

Without self-knowledge in depth we can have dreams, but no art. We can have the neurotic raw materials of literature but not mature literature. We can have no adults, but only aging children who are armed with words and paint and clay and atomic weapons, none of which they understand. And the greater the role in the educational process which is played by unconscious components of symbolic thinking, and wider must be this ancient and dishonorable gap between erudition and wisdom.

—Lawrence Kubie

Since its inception, the main focus of gifted education has been on academic advancement. By comparison, the affective development of the gifted has received much less attention. However, neglect of the emotional lives of children impacts their intellectual lives and achievements. The affective realm is not separate from the cognitive realm; they interact in learning and development (Piaget, 1967). In the last several years, interest in the affective domain has awakened. We are beginning to understand the critical importance of emotions to the learning process, to the full development of the individual, and to the future of society.

Although several writers in gifted education have pleaded for the integration of cognitive and affective curriculum for the gifted, the subject matter of affective education remains unclear. The content of an affective program has been variously depicted as the development of:

- Individualized value systems (Krathwohl, Bloom, and Masia, 1964)
- Attitudes, beliefs, and values (Sellin and Birch, 1980)
- Interests and appreciations (Carin and Sund, 1978)
- Persistence, independence, and self-concept (Franks and Dolan, 1982)
- Feelings, emotions, and awareness of self and others (Treffinger, Borgers, Render, and Hoffman, 1976)
- Interpersonal relations (Treffinger et al., 1976)
- Humanitarianism (Fantini, 1981)
- Curiosity, risk taking, complexity, and imagination (Williams, 1970)

Indeed, the term *affective* appears to encompass everything that cannot be considered purely cognitive or intellectual in nature. In this text, affective development refers to all of the personal, social, and emotional aspects of learning.

Affective development plays a unique role in the curriculum. It is both a part of it and apart from it. It is important to design specific learning activities to promote self-awareness and awareness of others. This would seem to be particularly pertinent to gifted education, since educators and parents alike are more concerned with the social development of gifted children than with their academic advancement. Special programs for the gifted, which often have a flexible curriculum, can provide an excellent context for focusing on affective concerns.

However, affective development is not a discipline, like English or mathematics, so it may seem to some to be out of place in a book of this nature, and out of place in the curriculum. After all, one cannot major in affect. And at the middle- and high-school levels, where education is organized in disciplines, there seems to be no room for emotional development. Yet, the need for emphasis in this area increases in adolescence, when the personal curriculum of the fledgling adult is more salient than the desire for mastery that characterized an earlier developmental period. At these levels, seminars, discussion groups, and preventive counseling groups can supplement traditional subject matter offerings.

Schools have been reluctant to respond to the affective needs of the gifted. Among the reasons for this neglect are:

- The traditional lack of concern in education for the affective domain (Tannenbaum, 1982)
- Attitudes on the part of parents that emotions are to be dealt with in the home rather than in the school (Elgersma, 1981)
- Fear of indoctrination (Bloom, Hastings, and Madaus, 1971)
- Lack of agreement as to the nature of affective education
- The position that if the school meets the child's cognitive needs, affective development will automatically follow (Mehrens and Lehman, 1973)
- Lack of reliable and valid tools for assessing affective development (Franks and Dolan, 1982)
- Lack of clarity as to the optimal level of affective functioning to be attained (Franks and Dolan, 1982)

More clarification is needed of the goals of affective education to dispel parental fears that the school system plans to engage in indoctrination or infringe on the belief systems of the family. Instruments for assessing affective development would certainly be useful, although the dearth of such materials should not be used as an excuse to ignore children's emotional needs. Programs that are only concerned with cognitive development often breed competition rather than cooperation, and do not automatically produce responsive citizens. The main obstacle to the incorporation of an affective strand in the curriculum has been the attitude that the school is not responsible for the child's emotional life. The increasing number of adolescent suicides with which school personnel have had to contend has led to marked changes in this belief.

The emotional lives of the gifted are very intense. Topics discussed on an intellectual level in school can have a profound impact on them. For example, an eight-year-old highly gifted girl cried nightly for weeks about the possibility of nuclear war, asking endless questions of her parents. When education emphasizes only cognition, neglecting emotional experiences, gifted children can become anxious, depressed, alienated, socially inept, or emotionally blocked. Since it is emotion that fuels commitment to ethical principles (Dabrowski and Piechowski, 1977), there are great benefits to be gained for both the child and society by paying closer attention to the affective realm.

A more supportive climate toward affective education and a growing concern for the total adjustment of the gifted child do appear to be slowly emerging in the schools. Newer definitions of giftedness incorporate nonintellective elements, such as task commitment (Renzulli, 1978). The number of materials available for affective development is burgeoning (e.g., Treffinger et al., 1976). Studies of affective characteristics of the gifted are increasing. Group dynamics, values clarification, and affective activities are popular components of gifted programs, even at the secondary level (Betts and Knapp, 1981; Curry, 1981).

Affective Education vs. Counseling

One reason teachers are often hesitant to initiate an affective program is their concern that they have not had enough training in counseling. They fear that they will not be prepared to deal with the issues that might surface when children begin to explore their emotional lives. They don't want to open Pandora's box. Many teachers of the gifted really would like more of an emphasis on counseling in their training programs (Hultgren, 1981), but the lack of such training need not be a deterrent in providing for the affective needs of the students. An affective education program can be conducted effectively by the classroom teacher, with support services of the school counselor or social worker available as needed.

It is important to distinguish between affective education and counseling, so that the classroom teacher does not become overwhelmed by the responsibility of attending to the children's emotional needs. This responsibility extends only so far; when the children's needs extend beyond the teacher's training and competence, then the counselor must take over. Affective education and counseling are both concerned with emotions and personal development; however, they differ in several important ways. Affective activities are less personal than counseling and deal with emotional issues in less depth. Through these activities, students learn more about their own beliefs and philosophies, and develop greater self-awareness and understanding of others.

The underlying philosophy of affective education is respect for the uniqueness of each student's beliefs and experiences. No attempt is made to change anyone's values or attitudes. Sharing is optional, and privacy is respected. Although some people fear that discussion of values invites imposition of the teacher's values on the students, such an imposition would be antithetical to the purpose of affective education. Unlike counseling, which serves to promote positive changes in an individual's ability to cope with life, affective education promotes awareness, not necessarily change. Integration of affective objectives into the curriculum can prevent the need for counseling in some cases by building self-esteem and better interpersonal relations.

The following list summarizes some of the main differences between affective education and counseling.

AFFECTIVE EDUCATION

- Oriented toward groups
- Usually directed by the teacher (no special training required)
- Involves self-awareness and sharing of feelings with others
- Consists of planned exercises and activities
- Unrelated to therapy
- Students helped to clarify their own values or beliefs
- Personalizes the curriculum, making it more relevant to the student

COUNSELING

- Oriented toward individuals
- Directed by an individual trained in counseling
- Involves problem solving, making choices, conflict resolution, and deeper understanding of self
- Consists of relatively unstructured private sessions or group sessions in which content is determined by students
- Closely related to therapy
- Students helped to change their perceptions or methods of coping
- Unrelated to curriculum

It would be ideal if a counselor could be involved in the planning of an affective program, as a consultant to the teacher, and as a resource if referrals appear necessary. At the very least, teachers should receive an inservice on the signs of depression, sexual or physical abuse, and suicidal ideation, and be instructed as to methods of referral. At the junior and senior high-school levels, the school counselor should be more involved in conducting the affective program, and provide special assistance on career counseling.

Affective Education and Curriculum

An affective program is usually conceived as a specified time period devoted to affective concerns. At the primary level, the curriculum often includes units on the development of self-concept. There have been kits, programs, and book series written on social development. Affective curricula now exist for middle-school and junior high-school students. At the junior and senior high-school level, small group discussions on shared concerns provide a type of preventive counseling that can counteract depression and isolation—two major factors in adolescent suicide.

It is also possible to construct a less visible affective program that is simply a part of every subject area. Affective education can be interwoven with the curriculum by constructing activities in such a manner that they enhance learning in the cognitive and affective domains simultaneously. Dealing with real issues (Renzulli, 1977) or children's interests strongly affects motivation. Designing activities so that the progression of difficulty is within the children's grasp—not so easy that they are bored nor so difficult that they are overwhelmed—builds self-confidence. Allowing children to work in pairs, triads, or small groups expands social development and leadership. Raising ethical issues or creating cognitive dissonance supports moral development. Kaplan (1974) recommends that affective objectives be written along with cognitive objectives when designing learning experiences for the gifted.

Gifted children usually have positive self-concepts about their learning abilities, but they frequently lack confidence in their social skills (Ross and Parker, 1980). Social skills, like other skills, are learned through positive experiences. The gifted often need specific guidance in making friends, building the self-esteem of others, and working cooperatively. The development of these skills can be curricular objectives. They can be addressed on a cognitive level through literature, social sciences, and evaluating the global impact of scientific advances. Learning experiences can be designed to increase students' awareness of the emotional needs of others, and provide opportunities for students to develop leadership and work cooperatively toward group goals.

Developing the Self-Concept

Affective development is rooted in an individual's self-concept. Social skills, leadership ability, and moral development are founded upon self-esteem. One's self-esteem can be likened to tea in a teacup—when the teacup is filled beyond capacity, it spills over into the saucer, and when the teacup is half empty, there is no surplus to share with others. In his "self-theory," Carl Rogers (1951) provides a basis for understanding self-concept. Rogers maintains that the self is the central aspect of personality. He describes self-concept as an organized configuration of perceptions of one's characteristics and abilities that develops out of interpersonal relationships. Since it is formed through interactions with the world, it is vulnerable to feedback from others. The self is a dynamic force, shaping the person's perceptions and behavior. Snygg and Combs (1949) assert that the basic drive of the individual is the maintenance and enhancement of the self.

Reviewing the research on the self, Clark (1983) summarizes as follows:

. . . Researchers found that the view of the self determines achievement and enhances or limits the development of a person's potential.

. . . The beliefs we have about ourselves literally determine our actions and our perceptions of the world and other people. We construct our own reality from these beliefs and often operate as if this is the only view possible (Combs and Snygg, 1959; May, 1967; Rogers, 1961) (p. 108).

Some children are buoyant in the face of daily challenges; others seem to view each challenge as an onslaught against their self-esteem. Gifted children are particularly vulnerable because they react in an intensified manner to experience. A mistake may be experienced as humiliation—proof of the child's unworthiness. The unique characteristics of the gifted—supersensitivity, perceptiveness, perfectionism, and self-criticism—furnish ample opportunities for them to feel inadequate, despite the number of successful achievements to their credit (Sisk, 1982). This paradoxical lack of self-esteem in the face of much success has recently been labeled the "imposter phenomenon" (Clance, 1985; Harvey,

1985). Experience shows that most gifted children suffer from this syndrome to some degree. They believe that they are not as smart as others perceive them to be, and they live in continuous dread of being unmasked as frauds.

Reversing a child's negative self-concept is a difficult task, but it can be done. The first step is recognition of the child's feelings of inadequacy. With many children, negative self-attitudes are apparent, but the gifted often mask these feelings. They may act superior when they are actually feeling inferior; they may appear emotionless to cover up heightened sensitivity and vulnerability. Group discussions with other gifted students are invaluable for helping the gifted recognize that they are not alone in these feelings and for teaching them ways of coping with such feelings.

An Affective Curriculum

A comprehensive affective program for the gifted includes opportunities to discuss common concerns with other gifted students. Researchers, teachers, and counselors have observed a rather consistent set of issues that beset the gifted. For example, Strop (1983) found that a group of seventh- and eighth-grade Talent Search students worried most about universal concerns, performance, and getting along with others. When these students were asked to rank order specific issues, the following ten concerns emerged in order of priority:

1. Establishing and maintaining positive relationships with peers
2. Dealing with over-sensitivity to what others say and do
3. Making appropriate career choices
4. Developing the ability to relax and relieve tension
5. Maintaining the motivation and desire to achieve
6. Developing positive leadership skills
7. Getting along with siblings
8. Developing tolerance
9. Dealing with the striving for perfectionism
10. Avoiding prolonged periods of boredom

Affective curricula have been developed for middle-school students (Beville, 1983) that address these concerns. A similar program developed by Delisle (1980) revolves around four specific adjustment problems of the gifted:

Problem #1: Problems associated with realizing the nature and significance of intellectual differences and the accompanying feelings of inferiority and inadequacy

Problem #2: Problems associated with social alienation or discomfort due to dissatisfaction with the frequency and merit of interpersonal relationships

Problem #3: Problems associated with a dull and meager school curriculum that provides little academic sustenance

Problem #4: Problems associated with locating and pursuing occupational and educational choices commensurate with the gifted's interests and abilities (pp. 22–23)

Delisle (1980) presents activities designed to increase awareness of each problem area: discussion questions, books, films, cartoons, brainstorming activities, and quotations. An example of the activities follows:

Communicate a series of goals that you expect to achieve and a series of goals that others expect you to achieve:

—compare these expectations;

—rate the financial, societal, and emotional benefits of each expectation (Delisle, 1980, p. 24).

Delisle's article also includes an instrument for evaluating the success of a preventive counseling program.

In addition to the generic concerns of gifted children, some students deal with specific problems related to their situations or personalities. Among these specific problems are:

- Underachievement
- Depression (often masked as boredom)
- Hiding abilities
- Understanding their introversion
- Uneven development
- Excessive competitiveness
- Hostility of others toward their abilities
- Feeling overly responsible for others
- Being overshadowed in the family by the eldest sibling
- Hidden handicaps
- Lack of true peers

Taking into account the dominant themes expressed by most gifted students and the specific problems encountered by a portion of the population, the following topics are recommended as ingredients in an affective program.

TOPICS FOR AFFECTIVE DEVELOPMENT

Understanding Giftedness	Introversion
Self-Expectations	Peer Pressure
Fear of Failure	Competitiveness
Expectations of Others	Guilt
Feeling Different	Social Skills
Uneven Development	Dealing with Stress

Sensitivity   Developing Study Habits
Tolerance   Developing Leadership Ability
Family Dynamics   Career Exploration
Responsibility for Others

The order of presentation of these topics and the amount of time spent exploring each one would depend on the needs of the group. In the affective domain, it is difficult to predetermine a scope and sequence, but not impossible. A school district dedicated to incorporating affective objectives into the curriculum in a comprehensive manner could take clusters of these topics and determine which ones would be stressed at each grade level. Some might be recycled at each grade level, and dealt with in a different manner. For example, Understanding Giftedness and Feeling Different could be introductory units in the first year of middle school and high school, whereas Self-Expectations and Expectations of Others might be central themes at all grade levels. Some topics, such as Developing Study Skills and Career Exploration, lend themselves more readily to the development of a scope and sequence through the grades than topics such as Sensitivity and Tolerance.

Flexibility is essential in an affective program, so that the curriculum remains responsive to the immediate needs of the group. For example, if a group of students happens to be facing severe peer pressure, or is dealing with stress from some other source, the discussion group needs to be structured in such a way that these issues can be dealt with at the time they occur, rather than waiting until their scheduled time in the curriculum. In other words, a curriculum can be designed with set activities, but it would be more effective if there were also unstructured times when immediate issues could surface and be discussed.

The presence of a trained counselor at the secondary level would enhance the effectiveness of the group process; however, all teachers of the gifted should be trained to lead group discussions and to respond to the emotional needs of the students. The school counselor or social worker can be asked to participate in at least some discussions, and guest speakers can be invited from the community to discuss their career patterns. If certain topics would be more comfortable for girls to discuss in an all-female group, some group sessions should be designed to accommodate this need.

When affective development is incorporated into the curriculum itself instead of isolated as a separate set of experiences, the most comprehensive framework for doing so comes from Taxonomy of Affective Objectives (Krathwohl, Bloom, and Masia, 1964).

The Taxonomy of Affective Objectives

Since concern for the "whole child" has been a philosophical underpinning of elementary education, it would be reasonable to assume that affective education evolved from the elementary level to the higher educational levels. However, one of the major influences in this area originated at the college level as early as 1948. A committee of college examiners that produced Bloom's Taxonomy of Cognitive Objectives also developed the Taxonomy of Affective Objectives (Krathwohl, Bloom, and Masia, 1964). The original plan was to create one complete taxonomy in three major parts: cognitive, affective, and psychomotor domains (Bloom, 1956). The taxonomy of the cognitive domain was completed first, in 1956, and that of the affective domain followed in 1964.

The committee found the creation of an affective taxonomy to be an extremely arduous task. Due to the imprecision with which affective objectives were usually stated, they defied classification. Teachers were unclear as to the learning experiences appropriate to the objectives. Testing procedures were primitive. Whereas the cognitive domain could be assessed through the observation of overt behaviors, the affective domain was less observable.

> It is difficult to describe the behaviors appropriate to these objectives since the internal or covert feelings and emotions are as significant for this domain as are the overt behavioral manifestations (Bloom, 1956, p. 7).

In spite of these difficulties, the task was completed, and resulted in a much needed framework for the development of affective goals. The taxonomy addresses interests, attitudes, values, the development of appreciations, and emotional sets or biases (Krathwohl, Bloom, and Masia, 1964). It is hierarchically ordered from passive to active manifestations. As is true for the cognitive domain, each level incorporates all of the skills involved in the previous levels.

AFFECTIVE DOMAIN

1.0 Receiving
    1.1 Awareness
    1.2 Willingness to receive
    1.3 Controlled or selected attention

2.0 Responding
    2.1 Acquiescence in responding
    2.2 Willingness to respond
    2.3 Satisfaction in response

3.0 Valuing
    3.1 Acceptance of a value
    3.2 Preference for a value
    3.3 Commitment

4.0 Organization
    4.1 Conceptualization of a value
    4.2 Organization of a value system

5.0 Characterization by a Value or Value Complex
    5.1 Generalized set
    5.2 Characterization (Krathwohl, Bloom, and Masia, 1964, p. 95).

The first level of the taxonomy, Receiving, is concerned with gaining the student's attention. Three levels of attention are outlined, progressing from passive reception to active selection of stimuli. At first the learner is only vaguely aware of particular affective elements, and is unable to verbally describe them. At the next stage, the student demonstrates a willingness to receive the affective information, but has not yet formed any judgments about it. At the final stage, the student shows a preference for certain affective experiences even in the presence of competing stimuli.

An example of this progression of attention is in the enjoyment of classical music. If the teacher played baroque music quietly in the background while the children worked, some children would enjoy it, some would dislike it, and some would not notice it. As the children became more familiar with it, those who disliked it might come to tolerate it, and those who had not noticed at all would probably begin to pay attention to it. They might notice when it wasn't playing or when the tempo of the movements changed. As their awareness increased, they might indicate that they work better with music in the background, and when given a choice of different types of music, perhaps they would select classical music.

The next level, Responding, is characterized by active participation of the learner. This is the level at which interests are born. In the three stages, the student moves from compliance to active initiation and eventually to marked enthusiasm. Continuing with the example of classical music, the student might listen initially simply to satisfy the teacher, then start to ask for particular pieces to be played, and then express enjoyment with the music of certain composers.

Another example is the way in which some students respond to biographical studies. When a student is asked to read about the life of an eminent individual, he might do so at first out of obligation. As he begins to identify with the person, he may decide to read more about the woman on his own. If his interest increases, he may attempt to read everything that was ever written about her. Teaching is often concerned with this level of the taxonomy. Teachers expose their classes to a variety of topics in hopes that some of them will become lasting interests for the students.

Valuing, the third level, is at the heart of affective education. In the process of valuing, the student examines his own beliefs and the beliefs of others, ascribes worth to certain of these values, and then commits himself to living in accordance with the ones he has chosen. In the first stage, the belief is embraced, but not necessarily acted upon. In the second stage, the student actively seeks the value and becomes identified with it. In the third stage, the person displays a high degree of certainty about the value and acts to promote it. An example of valuing would be learning about all sides of the nuclear power issue, taking a firm stand, and then writing letters to legislators or attempting in some other way to promote her position.

Work in values clarification appears to be an elaboration of this part of the taxonomy (Carin and Sund, 1978). Raths, Harmin, and Simon (1978) describe three phases of valuing—choosing, prizing, and acting—which approximate the three stages of this level. They further subdivide the valuing process into seven steps:

VALUING*

Acceptance of a value	Choosing	(1) freely
		(2) from alternatives
		(3) after thoughtful consideration of the consequences of each alternative

---

* Adapted from L. E. Raths, M. Harmin, and S. B. Simon, *Values and Teaching: Working with Values in the Classroom*, 2nd ed. (Columbus, Ohio: Merrill, 1978).

Preference for a value	Prizing	(4) cherishing, being happy with the choice
		(5) enough to be willing to affirm the choice to others
Commitment	Acting	(6) or doing something with the choice
		(7) repeatedly, in some pattern of life

In values clarification, the student chooses values freely, not on the basis of peer pressure or pressure from authority figures. Choice presupposes that the individual is aware of alternatives. The authors suggest that brainstorming many possible responses to a situation increases the likelihood that a value will emerge. Informed choice requires that the person understand the various consequences of all potential options. Prizing or cherishing means holding certain values dear. A value is affirmed when an individual lets others know that she holds it—when she wishes to be identified with it. Acting upon a value means that it shows up in some aspects of one's life. It also tends to be persistent—it shows up repeatedly in different situations and at different times (Raths, Harmin, and Simon, 1978).

In developing a set of values, the individual moves from weakly defined, conflicting values derived from external sources to a cohesive set of internally derived convictions (Dabrowski, 1964). Value construction is a lengthy process, requiring maturation, experience, and some degree of crisis. When values are adopted mindlessly in imitation of others, with no inner conflict, they are more susceptible to change.

Marcia's (1966) research on types of identity status reveals the importance of crisis and commitment to the developing personality. Marcia elaborated upon Erikson's work (1959; 1968) on identity development, observing four different ego-identity statuses in college students: identity diffusion, foreclosure, moratorium, and identity achievement. Identity diffusion involves the inability to make commitments; foreclosure involves commitment without crisis; moratorium is the experience of the crisis itself; and identity achievement involves both ideological commitment and occupational choice.

The hallmark of identity diffusion is lack of commitment. Although Erikson (1968) attributed identity diffusion to unsuccessful resolution of the identity crisis, Marcia (1966) found that some identity diffusion subjects have never experienced a major crisis in their beliefs. Those in the foreclosure status have blindly adopted the values of parents or others, and so have commitment but have not experienced crisis. According to Marcia's research, young people who adhere to authoritarian values tend to have low self-esteem and are highly subject to manipulation by others.

The third status, moratorium, is marked with crisis and vague, changing commitments. According to both Marcia (1966) and Erikson (1968), the experience of crisis is crucial to development. Moratorium subjects are involved in an active struggle to make commitments. Out of this turmoil, they fashion their own set of values and are then able to achieve ideological commitment. The fourth state, identity achievement, is the successful resolution of the crisis period. Identity achievement individuals have seriously considered several occupational choices and several ideologies. They have made their decisions on their own terms, having reevaluated past beliefs. It is not possible to attain identity achievement without first experiencing moratorium. Both moratorium and identity achievement individuals are high in self-esteem and independence and low in anxiety as compared with those in the first two statuses.

Marcia's work highlights the importance of individuals questioning the ready-made values in their world and then choosing their own. Self-chosen values, which flow from a full comprehension of available alternatives, are highly resistant to change and more likely to become life-long commitments (Raths, Harmin, and Simon, 1978).

The last two ranks of the taxonomy, organization and characterization, are normally attained only by high-school and college students, and adults. They require considerable depth and maturity, as well as a capacity for sophisticated thought processes. Organization involves analyzing the internal consistency of one's value structure, dealing with conflicting values, and prioritizing values to form a coherent system. The first step in this process is conceptualization, an analysis of each value in relation to others that are currently held and new ones that are emerging. The values to which one was previously committed are now reviewed, questioned, seen in relation to all others, and then expanded into abstract principles. The individual develops personal goals and ideals that serve as the basis for conscious choices.

The second phase, the organization of a value system, is a process of synthesis. The individual brings together a complex set of values, attitudes, and beliefs into a hierarchical system. Ideally, the value system that emerges from this process would be harmonious and internally consistent. However, since we often tend to hold some values that are diametrically opposed to each other, their integration may be less than perfect. Those values that cannot be harmonized may become less polarized or at least may be held in dynamic equilibrium. Potentialities and limitations are accepted realistically. The person begins to build a philosophy of life.

Characterization by a Value or Value Complex is the highest level in the taxonomy. At this level, the individual acts consisently in accordance with internalized principles. There are two stages to this level: generalized set and characterization. Generalized set is a persistent and predictable response pattern at a very high level of integration. The value structure serves as an inner core to guide behavior. Characterization implies a total way of life based on an internal hierarchy of values. The values exemplified are broader and more inclusive than those at earlier stages. Individuals who attain this level are conscious of their responsibility to all of life. Among the few who have achieved this level of humanitarianism are Lincoln, Gandhi, and Einstein (Carin and Sund, 1978).

> Realistically, formal education generally cannot reach this level. . . . The maturity and personal integration required at this level are not attained until at least some years after the individual has completed his formal education. Time and experience must interact with affective and cognitive learnings before the individual can answer the crucial questions, "Who am I?" and "What do I stand for?" (Krathwohl, Bloom, and Masia, 1964, p. 165).

Since the affective domain and the cognitive domain are inextricably connected (Eiss and Harbeck, 1969; Perrone and Pulvino, 1977; Maker, 1982; Piaget, 1967; Williams, 1979), the cognitive and affective taxonomies developed by Bloom, Krathwohl, and their associates can be used in conjunction with each other for curricular planning. Most affective responses are predicated upon knowledge, and all learning requires, at the very least, attention of the learner.

Vare (1979) recommends that the two domains be addressed simultaneously. She asserts that values and attitudes are transmitted not only by the curriculum, but by the educational process itself: "How we learn is what we learn" (p. 488). She gives as examples of the planned integration of cognitive and affective behaviors Suchman's model for inquiry training (1975) and Williams's model for encouraging creativity in the classroom (1979).

Integration of the two sets of objectives is implicit in their construction. The cognitive and affective taxonomies are related in the following manner:

Receiving	Knowledge
Responding	Comprehension
Valuing	Application
Organization	Analysis
	Synthesis
Characterization	Evaluation

(Krathwohl, Bloom, and Masia, 1964, pp. 49–50)

In their book, Eberle and Hall (1979) indicate how the combined affective and cognitive processes can be applied to aesthetic sensitivity, interpersonal relations, moral and ethical development, and self-knowledge. Carin and Sund (1978) give specific examples of teaching activities related to each level and subcategory of the affective taxonomy. Eiss and Harbeck (1969) provide a complete guidebook for the formation of behavioral objectives in the affective domain. L. Anderson (1981) describes how affective characteristics can be assessed in the schools.

The wealth of materials available today on affective education can be used to provide a climate for affective development in the classroom. The following activities are a small sample of the type often found in classes for the gifted. Other sources of material for affective development are suggested at the end of the section on sample activities.

AFFECTIVE ACTIVITIES

The following affective activities can be used with groups of gifted students. The activities can be done orally in dyads, triads, or small groups. They may also be used as written exercises on an individual basis. If they are written, students may choose to share their responses with others, to share them only with the teacher, or to keep them private. The activities are appropriate for use with all children, not only the gifted; however, since gifted children are extremely perceptive, they are likely to take the activities to greater depths than would their peers.

1. Three wishes (Self-Awareness)
   If you had three wishes, what would they be?
2. Ice Breakers (Sharing Feelings with Others; Feeling Different)

    a. What is your favorite TV program? Why?
    b. What is the best movie you ever saw? Why did you like it?
    c. What was the last book that you read? What did you like about it?
    d. What is your favorite sport?
    e. What is the most beautiful thing you have ever seen?
    f. What is the most unjust situation you know of?
    g. What would you like to be doing ten years from now?
    h. If you could meet anyone who ever lived, who would you want to meet?
    i. What do you love the most?
    j. What do you dislike the most?
    k. What do you look for most in a friend?
    l. What do you dream about?
    m. Who has had the most influence on your life?
    n. What are your three best qualities?
    o. If you could change one thing about yourself, what would you change?
    p. What talents do you wish you had?
    q. What is your biggest worry?
    r. What is the silliest thing you ever did?
    s. When do you feel the most lonely?
    t. When do you feel the most secure?
    u. If you could solve one of the world's problems, what problem would you want to solve?

3. Fantasy Friends (Feeling Different)
    a. Did you have an imaginary playmate when you were young?
    b. How old were you when you first created this friend?
    c. Describe as much about your friend (or friends) as you can remember.
    d. How long did you keep your friend?
    e. How old were you when you gave up this friend? Why did you do it?
    f. Do you miss your friend?
    g. What purpose do you think this friend served? (Davis, 1978)

4. Awards (Building Self-Esteem in Others; Social Skills)
    Pick someone's name out of a hat. Observe this person for a week. Write down everything you like about him or her. At the end of the week, create an award for this person and present it along with a speech in which you incorporate your observations. Each week choose a new individual to honor.

5. Collage Boxes (Introversion; Self-Awareness)
    Paste pictures from magazines on the outside of a shoebox. The magazine pictures should represent qualities that you feel others see in you. On the inside of the box paste magazine pictures that represent the "inside you." Portray the qualities you know about yourself and don't show to others. You may keep the inside of the box secret.

6. Mood Journal (Dealing with Stress)
    Keep a journal in which you write how you feel about things. Each

day rate your mood on a scale from 1 to 10, with 10 being the happiest. Do you find that you are happy most of the time, unhappy most of the time, or mixed? Are there any cycles to your moods? Can you predict your next bad mood? Can you guess how long it will take before you feel better again?

7. Compliment Charts (Building Self-Esteem in Others; Social Skills)

    With masking tape, attach large sheets of butcher paper to the backs of everyone in the group. Distribute marking pens to the group. Write something you like about each person on his or her back. Be specific. Exchange pens often so that the writer cannot be identified by the color of the ink. Write in an unusual manner so that your writing cannot be identified.

8. Collections (Understanding Giftedness)

    Bring five favorite possessions to class. Describe what you like about each one. What does the collection say about you?

9. Put-Downs (Social Skills; Tolerance)

    Keep a list of all the put-downs you hear in a given day. On another day, list all of the compliments you hear. Which list is longer? Start a personal campaign to clean up put-down pollution. Make a pact with your friends to pay a penalty for each put-down. Call attention to self put-downs as well as put-downs of others. Raise consciousness within your group and see if the effect spreads to other groups. How do you feel when you receive and give fewer put-downs?

10. "Pillow Talk" (adapted from a Zen parable) (Family Dynamics)

    When you are angry at someone, hold a pillow firmly in your hands and say aloud all of the reasons why you are right and the other person is wrong. Now turn the pillow upside down and say all of the reasons that the other person is right and you are wrong. Turn the pillow on its side and describe all the ways in which you both are right. Flip the pillow on its other side and describe all of the ways in which you both are wrong (Johnson, 1977).

11. Autobiography (Self-Awareness; Career Exploration)

    Write an autobiography of all the significant events in your life. Have those events helped to shape what you plan to do with your life? How?

12. Cocktail Party (Self-Expectations; Expectations of Others)

    What is the most important thing that you would like others to think about you? Think of a statement that conveys this quality. (For example, for the quality "understanding": "Tell me your problems.") Go around the room repeating your statement to everyone in the room while they do the same. Everyone talks and no one listens. When the teacher says "Freeze!" everyone stops and then says an opposite statement (e.g., "Go away; don't bother me!"). How did you feel after this exercise? Which had more power: the first statement or its opposite? Which is the real you? (Johnson, 1977)

13. Saying No (Self-Expectations; Expectations of Others)

    Choose a partner. Ask your partner to do something completely unreasonable. Your partner should continue to refuse as long as you keep asking. After a few minutes, switch roles and have your partner ask you to do something unreasonable while you practice refusing. Then have your partner refuse while you ask something reasonable. After a few minutes, switch roles. How did each of you feel saying no? Was it easier to say no to an unreasonable request than to a reasonable one? (Wolf, 1977)

14. Family Sculpting (Family Dynamics)

Assign one classmate to role play each of your family members. Tell them just a few things about the person they will pretend to be. Arrange the students in a manner that seems representative of your family. Who is closest to whom? Who is farthest away? Have each person tell how it feels to be that family member.

RESOURCES

There are now some excellent books available for gifted students to help them better understand themselves. There are also novels that feature gifted students, and serve as a form of bibliotherapy. Some of these books are featured below:

Giftedness: Living with It and Liking It. (1984). S. M. Perry. Aurora, Colo.: AGATE Program, Aurora Public Schools.

A workbook for elementary students enrolled in gifted programs, this book is best suited for fourth, fifth, and sixth graders. It contains eight units on understanding giftedness and dealing with it effectively. In the field testing, gifted children found the book informative and enjoyable.

On Being Gifted. (1978). American Association for Gifted Children. New York: Walker.

This book is excellent for high-school students, parents, and teachers. A symposium of gifted high-school students describe their sensitivities, aspirations, attitudes toward their parents and teachers, and programs they felt were effective.

Gifted Children Speak Out. (1984). J. Delisle. New York: Walker.

Interviews were conducted with gifted students about their feelings and experiences. This is a moving book for elementary, middle-school, and high-school students—it is also revealing to their parents and teachers.

The Gifted Kids' Survival Guides. (1983). J. Galbraith. Minneapolis: Weatherall. (1984). J. Galbraith. Minneapolis: Free Spirit. (1987). J. Galbraith and J. Delisle. Minneapolis: Free Spirit.

This popular series includes information and activities for elementary-aged gifted students to understand better their abilities and learn how to get along with others.

Very Far Away from Anywhere Else. (1976). V. LeGuin. New York: Bantam.

An excellent novel for junior and senior high-school students to read, as well as gifted adults, this tiny book focuses on two different types of gifted individuals—one who lives for music and another who has diverse interests. One is supported by her family and the other is not understood at all. The novel provides important insights into the inner world of the gifted.

Further resources on affective activities include: *Thinking, Changing, Rearranging* (J. Anderson, 1981); *Your Child's Self-Esteem* (Briggs, 1970); *Human Teaching for Human Learning* (Brown, 1971); *100 Ways to Enhance Self-Concept in the Classroom* (Canfield and Wells, 1976); *Creative Questioning and Sensitive Listening Techniques* (Carin and Sund, 1978); *Affective Directions* (Eberle and Hall, 1979); *The Centering Book* (Hendricks and Wills, 1975); *Liking Myself* (Palmer, 1977); and *Values and Teaching* (Raths, Harmin, and Simon, 1978).

Conclusion

Affective development, the personal and interpersonal aspects of learning, is a vital part of the curriculum that has often been overlooked. It can be dealt with as a separate strand of the curriculum, with its own scope and sequence. The design of such a scope and sequence would be a highly creative task. At the primary level, activities revolving around self-awareness, developing friendships, learning to say no to strangers, and self-protection are gradually becoming a part of the general curriculum. For the gifted, these can be supplemented with developing appreciations, as suggested in the Taxonomy of Affective Objectives (Krathwohl, Bloom and Masia, 1964).

At the intermediate grades, sensitivity to others, leadership skills, and values clarification appear to be pertinent themes. The activity books developed for gifted students are geared to this age group. They focus on understanding giftedness, feeling different, and getting along with others who are not as gifted. Special times can be set aside in a gifted program for students to engage in these activities.

Middle-school, junior and senior high-school concerns revolve around world issues, performance, and establishing positive relationships with peers. Sensitivity and perfectionism are common themes. Youngsters in these age groups need guidance in dealing with stress, both internal and external. Leadership and career exploration, two key affective areas, lend themselves well to a scope and sequence formate, whereas other areas may be more situational and seem to be best dealt with in discussion groups. Specific activities can be designed or the groups can be kept more open-ended to respond to immediate concerns. Some combination of structured and unstructured activities is also effective.

In addition to having a set time and place in the curriculum, affective aims can be met through instructional strategies, grouping of students, and by imbedding these objectives within cognitive objectives. Suggestions for doing so have been included.

The importance of affective development cannot be overstressed. If school is preparation for life, then students must learn skills for coping with stress, understanding themselves, and developing meaningful relationships with others. We can no longer rely on the family to produce these skills, nor can we assume that this is not our responsibility. Gifted students, because of the intensity of their inner-life, need guidance in these areas to an even greater extent than other children if they are to grow into healthy, happy, productive adults.

KEY POINTS SUMMARY

- Affective development encompasses all of the personal, social, and emotional aspects of learning. It is both a part of and apart from curriculum.
- Much of the affective curriculum for the gifted emphasizes the enhancement of self-concept, self-direction, and social relations.
- Affective needs can be met through the curriculum, instructional strategies, or in preventive counseling groups.
- Affective education differs from counseling in that the former consists of a set of planned exercises for increasing self-awareness of groups of students and requires no special training of the group leader, whereas the latter focuses on helping individuals develop new coping strategies and is directed by a trained professional.
- At the elementary level, affective objectives can be interwoven with cognitive objectives, so that both needs are met simultaneously.
- The Taxonomy of Affective Objectives, developed by Krathwohl, Bloom, and Masia (1964) can be used in conjunction with Bloom's *Taxonomy* as a framework for the development of affective curricula through the grades.
- At the middle-school, junior, and senior high-school levels, seminars are recommended to help gifted students deal effectively with specific issues.
- The recommended topics for an affective curriculum include: (1) understanding giftedness, (2) self-expectations, (3) fear of failure, (4) expectations of others, (5) feeling different, (6) uneven development, (7) introversion, (8) peer pressure, (9) competitiveness, (10) guilt, (11) social skills, (12) dealing with stress, (13) sensitivity, (14) tolerance, (15) family dynamics, (16) responsibility for others, (17) developing study habits, (18) developing leadership ability, and (19) career exploration.

References

Anderson, J. (1981). *Thinking, Changing, Rearranging: Improving Self-Esteem in Young People*. Eugene, Ore.: Timberline Press.

Anderson, L. (1981). *Assessing Affective Characteristics in the Schools*. Boston: Allyn and Bacon.

Betts, G. T., and Knapp, J. K. (1981). "Autonomous Learning and the Gifted." In A. Arnold et al. (Eds.), *Secondary Programs for the Gifted/Talented*. Ventura, Calif.: Office at Ventura County Superintendent of Schools.

Beville, K. (1983). "The Affective Development Curriculum." In S. M. Perry (Ed.), *The Aurora Gifted and Talented Handbook for Middle Schools*. Aurora, Colo.: Aurora Public Schools.

Bloom, B. S. (Ed.) (1956). *Taxonomy of Educational Objectives. Handbook I: Cognitive Domain.* New York: David McKay.

Bloom, B. S., Hastings, J. T., and Madaus, G. F. (1971). *Handbook on Formative and Summative Evaluation of Student Learning.* New York: McGraw-Hill.

Briggs, D. C. (1970). *Your Child's Self-Esteem: The Key to His Life.* Garden City, N.Y.: Doubleday.

Brown, G. I. (1971). *Human Teaching for Human Learning: An Introduction to Confluent Education.* New York: The Viking Press.

Canfield, J., and Wells, H. C. (1976). *100 Ways to Enhance Self-Concept in the Classroom: A Handbook for Teachers and Parents.* Englewood Cliffs, N.J.: Prentice-Hall.

Carin, A., and Sund, R. B. (1978). *Creative Questioning and Sensitive Listening Techniques: A Self-Concept Approach* (2nd ed.). Columbus, Ohio: Charles E. Merrill.

Clance, P. R. (1985). *The Imposter Phenomenon: Overcoming the Fear That Haunts Your Success.* Atlanta, Ga.: Peachtree.

Clark, B. (1983). *Growing up Gifted: Developing the Potential of Children at Home and at School* (2nd ed.). Columbus, Ohio: Charles E. Merrill.

Combs, A. W., and Snygg, D. (1959). *Individual Behavior* (2nd ed.). New York: Harper & Row.

Curry, J. (1981). "Description of a Junior High School Program for the Gifted/Talented." In A. Arnold et al. (Eds.), *Secondary Programs for the Gifted/Talented.* Ventura, Calif.: Ventura County Superintendent of Schools Office.

Dabrowski, K. (1964). *Positive Disintegration.* Boston: Little, Brown.

Dabrowski, K., and Piechowski, M. M. (1977). *Theory of Levels of Emotional Development* (2 vols.). Oceanside, N.Y.: Dabor Science.

Davis, C. (December 1978). Fantasy Friends (classroom activity for junior high school students). Casper, Wy.

Delisle, J. (1980). "Preventive Counseling for the Gifted Adolescent: From Words to Action." *Roeper Review,* 3(2), 21–25.

Eberle, B., and Hall, R. (1979). *Affective Directions: Planning and Teaching for Thinking and Feeling.* Buffalo, N.Y.: D.O.K. Publishers.

Eiss, A. F., and Harbeck, M. B. (1969). *Behavioral Objectives in the Affective Domain.* Washington, D.C.: National Science Teachers Association.

Elgersma, R. (1981). "Providing for Affective Growth in Gifted Education." *Roeper Review,* 3(4), 6–7.

Erikson, E. H. (1959). *Identity and the Life Cycle: Selected Papers.* Psychological Issues Monograph Series, No. 1. New York: International University Press.

Erikson, E. H. (1968). *Identity: Youth and Crisis.* New York: W. W. Norton.

Fantini, M. D. (1981). "A Caring Curriculum for Gifted Children." *Roeper Review,* 3(4), 3–4.

Franks, B., and Dolan, L. (1982). "Affective Characteristics of Children: Educational Implications." *Gifted Child Quarterly,* 26, 172–178.

Harvey, J. C., with Katz, C. (1985). *If I'm So Successful, Why Do I Feel Like a Fake: The Imposter Phenomenon.* New York: Random House.

Hendricks, G., and Wills, R. (1975). *The Centering Book: Awareness Activities for Children, Parents, and Teachers*. Englewood Cliffs, N.J.: Prentice-Hall.

Hultgren, H. (1981). *Competencies for Teachers of the Gifted*. Denver: University of Denver, unpublished dissertation.

Johnson, L. (July 1977). Bioenergetics Workshop. First Rocky Mountain Healing Festival.

Kaplan, S. N. (1974). *Providing Programs for the Gifted and Talented: A Handbook*. Ventura, Calif.: Office of the Ventura County Superintendent of Schools, 1974.

Krathwohl, D. R., Bloom, B. S., and Masia, B. B. (1964). *Taxonomy of Educational Objectives. Handbook II: Affective Domain*. New York: David McKay.

Maker, C. J. (1982). *Teaching Models in Education of the Gifted*. Rockville, Md.: Aspen.

Marcia, J. E. (1966). "Development and Validation of Ego-Identity Status." *Journal of Personality and Social Psychology, 3*, 551–558.

May, R. (1967). *Psychology and the Human Dilemma*. Princeton, N.J.: Van Nostrand.

Mehrens, W. A., and Lehman, I. J. (1973). *Measurement and Evaluation in Education and Psychology*. New York: Holt, Rinehart, & Winston.

Palmer, P. (1977). *Liking Myself*. San Luis Obispo, Calif.: Impact.

Perrone, P. A., and Pulvino, C. J. (1977). "New Directions in the Guidance of the Gifted and Talented." *The Gifted Child Quarterly, 21*, 326–335.

Piaget, J. (1967). *Six Psychological Studies*. New York: Random House.

Raths, L. E., Harmin, M., and Simon, S. B. (1978). *Values and Teaching: Working with Values in the Classroom* (2nd ed.). Columbus, Ohio: Charles E. Merrill.

Renzulli, J. S. (1977). *The Enrichment Triad Model: A Guide for Developing Defensible Programs for the Gifted and Talented*. Wethersfield, Conn.: Creative Learning Press.

Renzulli, J. S. (1978). "What Makes Giftedness? Reexamining a Definition." *Phi Delta Kappan, 60*, 180–184, 261.

Rogers, C. R. (1951). *Client-Centered Therapy*. Chicago: Houghton Mifflin.

Rogers, C. R. (1961). *On Becoming a Person*. Boston: Houghton Mifflin.

Ross, A., and Parker, M. (1980). "Academic and Social Self Concepts of the Academically Gifted." *Exceptional Children, 47*, 6–10.

Sellin, D. F., and Birch, J. W. (1980). *Educating Gifted and Talented Learners*. Rockville, Md.: Aspen.

Sisk, D. A. (1982). "Caring and Sharing: Moral Development of Gifted Students." *The Elementary School Journal, 82*, 221–229.

Snygg, D., and Combs, A. W. (1949). *Individual Behavior*. New York: Harper & Row.

Strop, J. (1983). *Counseling Needs of the Gifted*. Unpublished research. University of Denver.

Suchman, J. R. (1975). "A Model for the Analysis of Inquiry." In W. B. Barbe and J. S. Renzulli (Eds.), *Psychology and Education of the Gifted*. New York: Irvington.

Tannenbaum, A. J. (July 1982). Course notes from "The Nature of Intelligence." Denver: University of Denver.

Treffinger, D. J., Borgers, S. B., Render, G. F., and Hoffman, R. M. (1976). "Encouraging Affective Development: A Compendium of Techniques and Resources." *The Gifted Child Quarterly, 20,* 47–65.

Vare, J. V. (1979). "Moral Education for the Gifted: A Confluent Model." *The Gifted Child Quarterly, 23,* 487–499.

Williams, F. E. (1970). *Classroom Ideas for Encouraging Thinking and Feeling.* Buffalo, N.Y.: D.O.K. Publishers.

Williams, F. E. (1979). "Models for Encouraging Creativity in the classroom." In J. C. Gowan, J. Khatena, and E. P. Torrance (Eds.), *Educating the Ablest: A Book of Readings on the Education of Gifted Children* (2nd ed.). Itasca, Ill.: F. E. Peacock.

Wolf, M. H. (March 1977). Workshop on Theater Games. Jefferson County Public Schools.

14 Leadership Curriculum for the Gifted

William H. Foster and Linda Silverman

No scientific principle can tell us how to make the choice, which may sometimes be forced upon us by the insecticide problem, between the shade of the elm tree and the song of the robin.

—Barry Commoner

Public schools contribute to the creation of our nation's citizens. Of course, other social institutions share in the molding of citizenship; families and communities make major contributions. Yet, the school plays a substantial role in advancing this end. Much of what we do in the classroom makes sense only when understood in light of our desire to develop citizens.

For example, we work to help students understand the basics of representative democracy through the didactics of their history and social studies courses and through the provisions of practical opportunities in self-government such as student council positions, extracurricular club offices, and sports team leadership roles. It is not at all unusual to walk into an elementary or high-school hallway and see youngsters who are campaigning for class offices. Winning or losing such elections is not the only point of the experience. We all know that active participation in the complexity of our political and organizational traditions holds both the promise of winning and of losing. The larger educational point is for the students to encounter the democratic process head on, to learn its subtleties first-hand—subtleties of shared decision making, of power and influence, and the like. In this sense we are instructing our students in leadership throughout our curriculum across the grades.

Since the time of ancient Athens, the idea of citizenship has implied both a responsibility for leadership and for followership. The good citizen is both a leader and a follower. At any moment the circumstance may call the follower to a position of leadership. It is in the nature of a democratic society that all members share in the burden of governing.

A reaffirmation of this ancient model of participatory decision making was, in part, what the American Revolution was all about. The mechanics of representative democracy and standards of individual capability and merit replaced Europe's arbitrary, self-serving "divine right of kings" as the manner in which leaders were selected from among the citizenship. The perplexing task of determining which of our citizens are to lead and which are to follow and how the whole process is be regulated remains with us today. Therefore, our schools are charged with the resolution of this ambiguity through the shaping of students into citizens—citizens who can both follow and lead.

The acquisition of our rights to self-determination are of little value without a concomitant acquisition of the resources of social and organizational mechanisms of government and of experienced leadership. As evidenced by the trials and tribulations involved in the decisions made by the Continental Congress, the process of constructing the mechanisms and structure of government is never easy or simple. But the task of developing among our people a pool of experienced, informed leadership potential for our society is even more challenging. As one generation moves on to the next, the necessity of replacing the old with the new is always before us. The mechanisms of our political, social organization live on in governmental bureaucracy and corporate organizations, but the individuals leading us in the use of these social structures do not. They must be replaced over and over again.

Continuing the upswelling of new leadership in a society that has no formal system for passing on the mantle of leadership, other than the processes of election and meritorious appointment, is problematic. The training of individual citizens in skills and knowledge commensurate with this need for a pool of leadership talent is vital to the realization of a society capable of self-government, in both the public and private sectors.

Thus the role of the school in assisting the larger society in the development of attitudes and skills of citizenship in our young people must go beyond educating them toward followership. It must include an active sponsoring of an understanding of leadership in all, and the acquisition of special attitudes and skills for leadership in those individuals who are disposed toward seeking and accepting such a level of social involvement and responsibility. This task is a large and complex undertaking. It is from this perspective that we address the question of leadership curriculum for gifted learners. We do not assume that there is a special "gift" called leadership; rather, we take the position that gifted learners, like all students in a democratic society, need to know the rudiments of leadership. Much of this instruction will be infused through their currriculum experiences in social sciences and the humanities. However, some students may choose to develop their understanding and skills in leadership beyond this introductory level and are best served through a focused curriculum designed as a separate course experience. What follows is a discussion of the conceptual and practical components of such a school-based model for leadership development.

Some Reasons to Design a Separate Leadership Curriculum

James McGregor Burns (1978) has observed:

> The call for leadership is one of the keynotes of our time. Commencement platforms echo with appeals for high-minded public service—to young graduates, most of whom are worried about finding a job.

. . . Two themes often characterize these summonses. One is that we do not really know just what leadership is. "Why are the leaders not leading?" asks a university president and expert on organization.

One reason, I fear, is that many of us don't have the faintest concept of what leadership is all about. Leading does not mean managing. The "nature of leadership in our society is very imperfectly understood," John Gardner observes, "and many of the public statements about it are utter nonsense." The other theme is the need for moral, uplifting, transcending leadership, a leadership of large ideas, broad direction, strong commitment. Leaders must offer moral leadership, Gardner says. "They can express the values that hold the society together. Most important, they can conceive and articulate goals that lift people out of their petty preoccupations, carry them above the conflicts that tear a society apart, and unite them in the pursuit of objectives worthy of their best efforts." Presumably one can lead others downward—down the primrose path or down the road to barbarism. Yet leadership has—quite rightly, in my view—the connotation of leading people upward, to some higher values or purpose or form of self-fulfillment (pp. 451–452).

If we take Burns's comments to heart, our society as a whole, and our schools in particular, have a large task to perform. We must summon able individuals to leadership roles. But we must do more. Educators must aid those students who respond to the summons with knowledge and training for leadership—what it is and how they can do it. Educators must also raise the students' understanding above a simple understanding and utilization of management techniques to a level of practice that allows a leader to inspire followers to lives characterized by high expectations and moral practices.

Students who show strong interest and high ability in leadership deserve special attention, instruction, and experience. The task that has been set out for them by society is at least as difficult and more complex than that set before the gifted athlete. Tremendous amounts of school and community resources are devoted to the nurturing and developing of such sports talent. Certainly, the nurturing and developing of our young leadership talent is of more value to our free society than the training of our young athletes.

Since the early seventies, leadership has been a formal category among those defining giftedness, a category for the identification and training of students showing high ability as social leaders (Foster, 1981). Prior to this, leadership had been an area of interest for many, both inside and outside the field of gifted education.

In fact, leadership represents one of the most studied areas of human behavior and it has a long history as a primary topic for education and training in business, political, and military institutions. Yet, there is a limited awareness of this long tradition of conceptualization of information and training by members of the gifted education movement. Modest attention has been given to an integration of conceptual frameworks, related research findings, and proven training practices in leadership development. In the past, persons involved in the development of leadership programs in gifted education have developed piecemeal plans, sometimes based on conflicting assumptions and outdated research. We need to coordinate better the current ideas about leadership, developed in fields of psychology, sociology, and management, with those in gifted education, to provide a firmer basis for the education and training of school-based programming for young people who demonstrate an interest in and talent for leadership and for leading. This firmer base is now beginning to emerge as members of the gifted education community turn their concentrated attention to this aspect of curriculum development.

Since the publication of the Marland Report (1972), leadership has been distinguished as one of the categories of giftedness sponsored by both federal and state efforts at training and practice. However, it remains the least articulated of the curricular areas for the gifted learner. But certainly leadership itself is not an unknown quantity. It is one of the most studied of social, psychological constructs, having a venerable history of research and scholarly discussion that dates back eighty to one hundred years. Unfortunately, the more it has been studied, the more elusive its practical character has become.

The Precursor to Curriculum—Identification

Historically, the reliable identification of leaders has been a major concern. Rather than waiting for them to emerge gradually as a result of circumstance and individual initiative, modern business, the military, and certain political groups have set out to identify early on individuals who show leadership potential. Assuming that leadership emanates from a particular set of character traits, elaborate personality instruments have been employed to assess individuals for their leadership potential. Some have been designed specifically for this identification task, whereas other more global measures such as the Minnesota Multiphasic Personality Inventory (MMPI) and the California Personality Inventory (CPI) have been used to develop specialized personality profiles of a set of leadership types (Stogdill, 1974). Such assessment has been done primarily with young adults and adult populations because of an assumption that leadership is, to a degree, a developmental phenomenon and that its identifiable qualities are not in evidence until late adolescence or early adulthood. In addition to these developmental assumptions about leadership, it is assumed that only by the early adult years do potential leaders gain access to social opportunities that allow them to demonstrate the levels of personal initiative and decision making so characteristic of leaders.

From this view, a central task for anyone concerned with leadership curriculum becomes the identification of these special people and the development of opportunities that will allow them to express their leadership across a wide variety of situations. Research attempting to isolate these select personality traits that distinguish leaders from nonleaders has not been very successful, forcing the conclusion that leadership is a highly complex social process that may be very sensitive to changes in situations. So some students may be expected to lead in some situations and some in others. Within the field of gifted education, the task of identifying potential leaders is complicated by the fact that for the implementation of a fully articulated curriculum (K–12), selection must proceed at a very early age. How is it that we are to tell the leader from the follower in kindergarten or first grade? The usual answer is to assess students for their "leadership" potential during childhood and early adolescence so they can be given differentiated educational programming commensurate with their presumed special capabilities and needs.

This is a very difficult thing to accomplish. Heavy dependence on trait-based identification scales and checklists such as the Renzulli-Hartman Behavioral Checklist for the Identification of Gifted and Talented Students (1974), specifically the leadership subscale, should be avoided. Far beyond the power of such simple scales, such early, specialized selection requires careful conceptualizing and administration to preserve the equity of access to special opportunity necessary in our democratic society.

The psychometric character of early identification of those with leadership potential is so tenuous that it is suggested that the elementary level (K–5) be open to all interested students, participation being on a volunteer basis. Following in middle or junior high school, access to specialized programming should be selective, based on applications, personal references, and evidence of leadership behavior in in-school and out-of-school settings.

Educators of gifted learners, dealing with the delivery of a special curriculum on leadership, must be cautious as they make their way through the pitfalls surrounding this leadership domain. Developing early, valid procedures for providing appropriate access to the curriculum is one of the most challenging tasks in gifted education.

If the administrative requirements of a particular school district's gifted program require a formal identification process to provide students access to instructional experiences in leadership, then the implementation of a personal trait model of leadership should be used, especially one based on leadership behavior. Several attempts have been made to describe such behaviorally based characteristics of leadership (Karnes, Chauvin, and Trant, 1984; Renzulli, Smith, White, Callahan, and Hartman, 1976; Richardson and Feldhusen, 1984). Accepting the uncertain nature of such an approach to identifying leadership, Wilder (1979) suggests twelve qualities that can be used to identify children with leadership inclinations and abilities in the school setting:

QUALITIES OF STUDENTS WITH LEADERSHIP POTENTIAL

1. Is liked and respected by most of the members of his class.
2. Is able to influence others to work toward desirable goals.
3. Is able to influence others to work toward undesirable goals.
4. Can take charge of the group.
5. Can judge the abilities of other students and find a place for them in the group's activities.
6. Is able to figure out what is wrong with an activity and show others how to do it better.
7. Is often asked for ideas and suggestions.
8. Is looked to by others when something must be decided.
9. Seems to sense what others want, and helps them accomplish it.
10. Is a leader in several kinds of activities.
11. Enters into activities with contagious enthusiasm.
12. Is elected to offices (Wilder, 1979, pp. 1–2).

Surveying this list reminds us of the critical question: Are leaders born or made? As already noted, although most modern theorists would agree, personality traits alone cannot account for leadership effectiveness (Gibb, 1969; McCall and Lombardo, 1978; Foster, 1981).

A Few Basic Assumptions of the Curriculum

Engaging students in educational activities for the purpose of enhancing the possibilities of their attaining positions of social leadership in later life is certainly a worthy goal. To this end we can adopt numerous curricular and instructional practices. Often selected youngsters are exposed to specific educational experiences designed to introduce them to group dynamics skills relevant to managing small groups. A good example of this would be a curricular objective of teaching selected eighth graders about group decision making, specifically decision by consensus. Such an objective could be implemented through an experiential instructional unit based on an activity like the "Winter Survival Exercise" (Johnson and Johnson, 1975) in which students must determine what they will take from a list of things, such as a compass, a ball of steel wool, and so on, in their efforts to survive. All decisions must be made by consensus.

We must understand that if we use such material we are knowingly or unknowingly accepting and passing on a particular set of assumptions about the basic nature of leadership. Such a training model assumes leadership to be a process, focusing our attention on interpersonal skills training and on a small group view of the arena in which leadership is carried out. It is understandable that educators should be attracted to such an education and training approach as it presumes that the leadership potential we have selected for can be actualized through our direct educational intervention. Many instructional packages exist to complement this basic assumption about curriculum in the area of leadership. Most focus on training in group dynamics and small group process. Much of this material already exists in social science curriculum, such as simulation games or values clarification exercises, and in management training materials developed by groups such as the National Training Institute of Bethel, Maine. Perhaps the most extensive and current of these latter materials are sets of training exercises organized and published annually by Pfeiffer (1985) known as *A Handbook of Structured Experiences for Human Relations Training,* and Pfeiffer and Jones (1985), *Annual Handbook for Group Facilitators.* Most group process/leadership and human relations activities that have been developed over the last decade and a half are recorded in these volumes. Such materials, once adapted from their management training contexts in fields like business administration or organizational psychology, are ideal sources for developing integrated curriculum designs and instructional units for classroom use.

Another difficulty confronts the educator of the gifted learner who is interested in developing curriculum for leadership talent. Though there is no lack of educational and training materials devoted to the education of leaders, especially if the management training literature is utilized, there is little evaluation of materials or approaches to training as to what works best. Therefore, to represent leadership behavior as a broad-based, multifaceted event, an effective program of training must allow for its own organized evaluation of the impact on selected students.

Assuming the limited scope of our present training approaches, intelligent decisions about materials and instructional strategies and settings are difficult. What evaluative evidence does exist is indirect, coming from other fields. Argyris (1976) has shown the great difficulty of and limited success of leadership training with adults. When his findings are extended to the training of young leaders through differentiated educational programs for leadership development, the promise of success in such efforts is tempered. However, the effect of well-formulated programing with our young citizens can achieve desirable outcomes. This remains to be shown through organized implementation and careful evaluation of the utility of training of leadership with our most able students.

Some basic points to keep in mind as the design of the leadership curriculum unfolds are:

1. Be careful not to exclude students from leadership curriculum—particularly young students. An "open door" policy regarding program participation is best.
2. Build your classroom curriculum around leadership as a process, using already existing training material culled from educational, corporate, and military sources.
3. Design your own evaluation of the program, especially of the instructional materials themselves.

Another Key Feature of Any Curriculum for Leadership—Definition

You must decide what you mean by leadership prior to the design of the program. This is obvious. But it is imperative with leadership curriculum because of the conceptual ambiguity surrounding this area. If we design a curriculum in mathematics, we are sure to find a planning committee in agreement on what constitutes introductory algebra. There may be some differences as to the best way in which to instruct the material, but the definition of what constitutes the area is certain. As has already been suggested, this is not the case with leadership.

As many as 130 definitions of leadership can be found in the literature. Like the definition of giftedness, the definition of leadership has changed from a simplistic, innate trait approach to a more complex, person/process/situation interaction definition.

This situational perspective suggests that different students lead best in different situations (i.e., one will be a leader on the athletic field whereas another may lead in social situations). Then there is the question "On which area of situational leadership is the curriculum going to focus—leadership in politics, business, or community affairs?"

Understanding that there is no consensus as to a single definition of leadership, the following illustrate some of the common elements, like interpersonal influence and power, found in most definitions:

> Leadership is the process of influencing the activities of an individual or a group in efforts toward goal attainment in a given situation (Hersey and Blanchard, 1977, p. 84).

> Leadership is the exercise of power or influence in social collectivities, such as groups, organizations, communities or nations, to meet the needs of the group (Gallagher et al., 1982, p. 8).

A decade ago, Colorado State Consultant, Gerald Villars (1976), defined leadership as "human relations talent." This categorical definition was described as follows:

> Empathetic; exhibits high degree of sensitivity to the needs of others.
>
> Values open, trusting relationships among peers.
>
> Demonstrates consistently helping, supportive behaviors in group tasks (p. 2).

A human relations definition of leadership, such as Villar's, incorporates emotional and attitudinal components essential to the development of leaders who serve rather than manipulate the individuals they lead. This accommodates the four models of leadership already outlined, and provides a value-based definition to the curriculum area which makes such leadership training oriented to the ideals of our democratic system. Lamb and Busse (1983) suggest that the best leadership demonstrates a combination of a high concern for task coupled with a high concern for people. Here, the leader nurtures the best that each member can contribute to the whole.

There are several general ways to approach a conceptual definition of leadership. The earliest theory of leadership was the "charismatic leader" or "great man" view. Under this rubric, a person is either born to lead or to follow. This trait-based model holds that there are certain personalities or sets of personal characteristics that differentiate leaders from nonleaders and that these innate traits are applicable from one situation to another.

Beyond being simply a set of personal traits, leadership is most often viewed in terms of the process of managing interpersonal and small group interactions. From this point of view, leaders act toward groups to fulfill the attainment of shared goals. Leadership is carried out through attention to the tasks the group is attempting to accomplish and the process by which it is going about the task. Task-oriented leading focuses on getting the task defined, analyzed, delegated, and completed. Process-oriented leading focuses on maintaining smooth group interactions, encouraging participation, and providing praise and evaluation. Although one person may accept both the task and process functions, most groups are seen to distribute the roles between two people.

This is the most useful of the definitions of leadership from the point of view of designing a curriculum for the area. Our leadership training programs are usually designed to help participating students determine their strengths in relation to either the task or process function and in aiding them to develop skills in their underdeveloped area, thereby increasing their general effectiveness across all the aspects of group dynamics.

Most texts on small group dynamics devote major sections to such topics as task/process dynamics (Cartwright and Zander, 1968; Yalom, 1970). Additional topical areas should include such subjects as stages of group development, group cohesion, decision making, goal setting, conflicts of interest, power, and group problem solving.

This approach to leadership places its emphasis on three major points: (1) leading is a group dynamic motivated by social pressures within the small group itself; (2) it is a skill-based process that is teachable; and (3) it is primarily a situational, rather than a personality-based event.

Leadership Skills for a Leadership Curriculum

If leadership is seen as a general goal for the education of the gifted learner as a whole, then leadership skills are best presented in the regular gifted curriculum. However, when leadership education and training is developed as a separate curriculum, Plowman's (1981) list of skills, which was developed to guide the California State Department of Education's leadership training program, serves as a good model:

LEADERSHIP SKILLS

Cognitive
1. Figures out what is wrong; shows others how to solve problems
2. Handles abstract ideas and sees a broad perspective; sees whole while others focus on parts
3. Plans and follows through
4. Projects into future, seeing consequences of decisions

Personal
5. Gauges appropriateness of decisions, directions, or suggestions and timing for them
6. Copes with unpleasantness

Interpersonal
7. Listens to, observes, recognizes the skills and abilities of others
8. Interacts with others easily and has the ability to inspire confidence in others
9. Perceives and articulates unstated feelings and recognizes and states goals, problems, ideas, and interests of group
10. Follows well
11. Supports members of the group, accepts responsibility, and is able to determine appropriate behavior
12. Organizes others, directs activities, delegates reponsibilities, stimulates action, and establishes the mood of the group (Plowman, 1981, p. 15)

These skills may be used as criteria for identifying children with leadership potential if programmatically necessary, or they may be used as program components in an attempt to help all gifted children develop leadership abilities. Given that one of the prevailing views on leadership is that all members of small groups can be trained in leadership skills (Foster, 1981), it would follow that such training would be an appropriate part of gifted programming.

A large-scale effort at the University of Southern Mississippi to promote leadership training and sort through the educational and training materials, the Leadership Skills Training Program, developed by Karnes and Chauvin (1985), and a Leadership Network Newsletter, rich with resources for developing young leaders, was founded in the spring of 1986.

Some materials for developing leadership skills in gifted students include:

Leadership Education: Developing Skills for Youth (Richardson and Feldhusen, 1984)

Leadership Skills Development Program (Karnes and Chauvin, 1985)

A Leadership Unit (Gallagher et al., 1982)

Leadership: A Skills Training Program Ages 8–18 (Roets, 1981)

Leadership Service (House, 1980)

Learning to Think and Choose: Decision-Making Episodes for the Middle Grades (Casteel, 1978)

Decisions and Outcomes (Gelatt, Varnhorst, Carey, and Miller, 1973)

and *Group Processes in the Classroom* (Schmuck and Schmuck, 1979)

Such materials may be used to organize a leadership program into a scope and sequence plan for the overall curriculum. Figure 14.1 represents on approach to this overall curriculum plan.

Similarly, a curriculum for leadership education needs to be organized according to a planned sequence, K–12, as shown in Figure 14.2. With the application of scope and sequence ideas to leadership curriculum, the basic structure of a differentiated educational and training program is in place. But this skeleton of a curriculum is only a beginning of what may be constructed in the name of a full-blown curriculum. The "Concept Approach" curriculum for secondary instruction by Brash and Burger (1986), found at the end of this chapter (Example 14.A), represents the detail needed in a fully developed plan.

But Are Leadership Education and Leadership Training Enough?

Lindsay (1979) warns that leadership training is insufficient to assure conscientious leadership. He differentiates leadership training from leadership education, indicating that training is concerned only with the development of skills according to preestablished goals, whereas education equips the individual to make intelligent, humane decisions that will result in the enhancement of all concerned. Lindsay asserts that we must be as concerned with the "product" of leadership as with the processes and skills involved. Otherwise, we may be

FIGURE 14.1 Sample of a Leadership Curriculum Plan for the School Year

Grade Level	Concepts and Themes	Content and Information	Independent Study
6th–8th	Leadership as an abstract social, organizational, and personal concept	Introduction of the basics of group processes (i.e., task vs. processes) Introduction of Fiedler's (1967) Leadership/Situation Match Model	Interviews with a series of local political or business leaders. Analysis of two or three biographies of leaders in similar areas

Integration of Thinking Skills and Creativity	Affective/Social Learning	Activities and Experiences Outside the Classroom	Final Project
Evaluating a leader's actions in a decision situation Brainstorm alternative actions for the leader situation above	Setting goals for the student's role in adult leadership positions Time management training	Field trip to State Legislative Session Shadowing of a local business leader for a day	Participation in a school-wide election Work as an editor on the school newspaper as a school opinion leader

FIGURE 14.2 Sample of a Sequence for a Leadership Curriculum Plan 4–12 Across One Area of Instruction

	Grades 4–5	Grades 6–8	Grades 9–12
Contents and Information	Presentation of the personal traits of various types of leaders Description of the various leadership roles in the school and local community	Introduction of the basics of group processes (i.e., task vs. process) Introduction of Fiedler's (1967) Leadership/ Situation Match Model	Presentation and analysis of moral dilemmas for various political leaders in history Study of decision-making processes in group leadership situations

training skillful leaders who exercise their abilities in an egocentric fashion rather than for the good of all.

Leadership education must be conjoined with moral education in order to educate future leaders toward moral choices they will eventually face as they address local, state, or national issues. Like Burns (1978), Lindsay (1979) views leading as being related to issues of moral, ethical behavior:

> The relativism of our time is pernicious; it eats away at the very core of our culture, catalyzing all the various moral fibre into a rather gelatinous soup from which everyone is sanctimoniously, smiling, nodding, excusing, apologizing. . . . For years the schools have for myriad reasons, struggled to educate the nation's children in a relatively value-free environment. Now it becomes evident that we must establish moral education at the core of the curriculum, particularly for students gifted in leadership. If we are to regain our national conscience, our sense of propriety, our hunger for excellence in every endeavor, we must begin with the design of a curriculum in moral education that will provide our future leaders with the appropriate models for reestablishing these values at the center for our consciousness. If leadership education (not training) is imperative it must incorporate moral education (not indoctrination) (Lindsay, 1979, p. 5).

Researchers also have observed that the unique ethical sensitivity of the gifted indicates a special potential for high moral development (Drews, 1972; Vare, 1979). However, this potential cannot develop in a vacuum. Tannenbaum (1972) reminds us that, without prior training, the gifted are not any better equipped to grapple with the value dimensions of their studies than they are to solve problems in non-Euclidean geometry. Rarely has the moral, ethical awareness or potential of the gifted been used as a basis for curriculum development in leadership training. But perhaps it should be.

Kohlberg (1972) suggests that levels of ethical judgment can be raised or lowered through environmental influences. He advocates a type of moral education in which students participate in discussions that involve moral choices. These discussions enable students to understand other viewpoints and the bases used by others to determine what is just. Exposure to high levels of moral judgment can provide the cognitive dissonance that motivates the child to strive toward more comprehensive principles of justice. Actual experience involving moral choices can also further develop ethical awareness.

Higher level moral judgment may indeed require more than the intellectual capability to comprehend abstract principles of justice. A factor that has been overlooked until recently is the capacity to care. The importance of compassion, caring, and reponsibility of oneself and others, are illuminated by Gilligan (1982) in a book depicting the developmental pattern of the moral judgments of women. At the highest levels, there is an interplay between justice and mercy, rights and responsibilities, and a recognition of the interconnectedness of all life.

> The moral imperative that emerges repeatedly in interviews with women is an injunction to care, a responsibility to discern and alleviate the 'real and recognizable trouble' of this world. For men, the moral imperative appears rather as an injunction to respect the rights of others and thus to protect from interference the rights to life and self-fulfillment. . . . Development for both sexes would therefore seem to entail an integration of rights and responsibilities through the discovery of the complementary of these disparate views (Gilligan, 1982, p. 100).

The theme of caring is echoed in Fantini's (1981) plea that all learning be subordinated to the main function of preparing students to create "a humane, CARING society" (p. 3). In order for students to internalize caring values, Fantini recommends that they actively participate in community service as part of their education. He suggests that the curriculum be redesigned to include a section on the desirability of caring values and behaviors as they apply to the self, toward others, and toward nature and the environment. Subjects that might be subsumed under such a section include psychology, health, ecology, contemporary social issues, and ethics. Gifted learners could examine social issues from the perspective of humaneness; in addition, they could be asked to devise ways to complement their cognitive learning with practical experience that would allow them to perform caring behaviors.

When values or moral issues are directly addressed in the schools, two major methods are employed: values clarification (Raths, Harmin, and Simon, 1978), and the cognitive-developmental approach (Kohlberg, 1971, 1972, 1975a, 1975b). Kohlberg's cognitive-developmental model is an elaboration of Piaget's (1948) and Dewey's (Dewey and Tufts, 1936) theories of moral development.

Several other approaches to the enhancement of moral development have been outlined in the literature:

- Critically examining the historical development of philosophies and the effects of these values on the development of societies (Ward, 1961)
- Studying the contribution of the inconspicuous and unsung who show admirable qualities and lead worthwhile lives (Christenson, 1976)
- Examining moral issues shown on television, seen in newspapers, or found in the community (Drews, 1972)
- Attempting to solve some of the problems confronting society and sharing these alternatives with civic leaders (Weber, 1981)
- Exploring humanitarian values and the lives of individuals dedicated to services, in the context of social studies and literature courses (Nelson, 1981)
- Simulations, role play, or perspective-taking exercises (Gallagher, 1985)
- Discussing hypothetical moral dilemmas (Maker, 1982)
- Constructing moral dilemmas (Weber, 1981)
- Involvement in community service programs during or after school (Fantini, 1981)
- Values clarification exercises (Raths, Harmin, and Simon, 1978)

A Special Priority: Using Moral Dilemmas to Enhance Leadership Development

Here students are exposed to moral dilemmas in which a central character must decide between alternative possibilities for action. There should be societal support for any of several actions. After the dilemmas are presented, students are asked to state which action they think the character should take and describe reasons for their decision. The teacher facilitates discussion through skillful questioning, without inserting his or her own opinion. No attempt is made to reach group consensus. Examples of these dilemmas can be found in the recommended resources below.

Blatt and Kohlberg (1975) describe a teaching method that appeared to be effective in bringing preconventional thinking up to the conventional level. Blatt developed moral dilemmas and presented them in class discussions to junior and senior high-school students. In the course of the discussions, he first supported the arguments one stage above the lowest stage represented in the class. When these arguments were understood, he challenged that stage, using new dilemmas, by presenting arguments one stage above the previous one. At the end of the semester, almost half of the students had gained a stage in moral reasoning, which was maintained a year later.

Kohlberg (1964) recommends that adults deal with moral issues from a perspective one stage above the one at which the child is currently functioning. Children understand and prefer judgments that are slightly above their level of reasoning (Rest, 1973). If adults present moral concepts two stages or more above the child's own level, the reasoning is too abstract for the child to be able to grasp. Although discussions at the child's own level will be understood, they will not assist development. Kohlberg (1972) warns that if an adult responds to the child below his or her level of moral development, the child will quickly lose respect for the adult. This too frequently happens to gifted children in their school experiences.

Moral reasoning can be enhanced. In her book, *Teaching Models in Education of the Gifted,* Maker (1982) presents guidelines for applying Kohlberg's theory in gifted classrooms. Other excellent resources include:

Moral Reasoning: A Teaching Handbook for Adapting Kohlberg to the Classroom (Galbraith and Jones, 1976)

Promoting Moral Growth: From Piaget to Kohlberg (Hersh, Paolitto, and Reimer, 1979)

How to Assess the Moral Reasoning of Students (Porter and Taylor, 1972)

Values in a Democracy: Making Ethical Decisions (Guidance Associates, 1976)

Hypothetical Dilemmas for Use in Moral Discussions (Blatt, Colby, and Speicher, 1974)

Getting It Together: Dilemmas for the Classroom Based on Kohlberg's Approach (Mattox, 1975)

Conclusion

There is a substantial distance between the desire to help gifted learners to become familiar with leadership processes and skills and the actual emergence of a leader. But the goal is worthy. The students are there. The training models are available. And responsible evaluation is possible. We need to proceed for the good of the students who are motivated and talented in leadership and for the good of our free society which is always in need of emerging leadership. As Burns (1978) has said:

> The function of leadership is to engage followers, not merely to activate them, to commingle needs and aspirations and goals in a common enterprise, and in the process to make better citizens of both leader and followers. . . . Woodrow Wilson called for leaders who, by boldly interpreting the nation's conscience, could lift a people out of their everyday selves (p. 452).

We need to elevate the leadership knowledge and skills of our gifted learners. They must move out from their own everyday worlds toward a view of leading that transcends the management of government and corporate activities. They must envision better social and moral opportunities for all citizens—leaders and followers alike.

KEY POINTS SUMMARY

- Leadership is an acquired competence, not a special ability. Therefore, access to programming at each stage of development should be based on a motivation in the students to participate in the curriculum.
- There are numerous definitions of leadership. The most useful for the purpose of curriculum development is a process definition of leadership that focuses on the dynamics of small group interaction.
- The leadership curriculum plan should be structured around a concept of scope and sequence that allows for substantial modification of curriculum content as students move from elementary to middle-school to high-school curriculum.
- The instructional activities implementing the curriculum objectives should be experiential in character, using various domains of study as the basis for the experiential learning.
- The areas of management training and small group dynamics are replete with excellent materials that can be adapted for use in school-based leadership programs.
- The substantial portion of the content of the leadership curriculum should focus on values clarification and moral development.

References

Argyris, C. (1976). *Increasing Leadership Effectiveness*. New York: Wiley.

Blatt, M., Colby, A., and Speicher, B. (1974). *Hypothetical Dilemmas for Use in Moral Discussions*. Moral Education and Research Foundation.

Blatt, M., and Kohlberg, L. (1975). "The Effects of Classroom Moral Discussion upon Children's Level of Moral Judgment." *Journal of Moral Education, 4,* 129–161.

Brash, P., and Burger, S. (1986). *Leadership Curriculum*. Pulaski, Ind.: Eastern Pulaski School Corporation.

Burns, J. M. (1978). *Leadership*. New York: Harper Colophon Books.

Cartwright, D., and A. Zander. (1968). *Group Dynamics: Research and Theory*. New York: Harper and Row.

Casteel, J. D. (1978). *Learning to Think and Choose: Decision-Making Episodes for the Middle Grades*. Santa Monica, Calif.: Goodyear.

Christenson, R. M. (1976). "McGuffy's Ghost and Moral Education Today." *Phi Delta Kappan, 58,* 737–742.

Dewey, J., and Tufts, J. H. (1936). *Ethics* (rev. ed.). New York: Holt.

Drews, E. M. (1972). *Learning Together*. Englewood Cliffs, N.J.: Prentice-Hall.

Fantini, M. D. (1981). "A Caring Curriculum for Gifted Children." *Roeper Review, 3*(4), 3–4.

Fiedler, F. E. (1967). *A Theory of Leadership Effectiveness*. New York: Mc-Graw-Hill.

Foster, W. (1981). "Leadership: A Conceptual Framework for Recognizing and Educating." *Gifted Child Quarterly, 25,* 17–25.

Gailbaith, R. E., and Jones, T. M. (1976). *Moral Reasoning: A Teaching Handbook for Adapting Kohlberg to the Classroom*. Minneapolis, Minn.: Greenhaven Press.

Gallagher, J. J. (1985). *Teaching the Gifted Child* (3rd ed.). Boston: Allyn and Bacon.

Gallagher, J., et al. (1982). *Leadership Unit: The Use of Teacher-Scholar Teams to Develop Units for the Gifted*. New York: Trillium Press.

Gelatt, H. B., Varnhorst, B., Carey, R., and Miller, G. P. (1973). *Decisions and Outcomes*. New York: College Entrance Examination Board.

Gibb, C. A. (1969). "Leadership." In G. Lindzey and E. Aronson (Eds.), *The Handbook of Social Psychology* (vol. 4; 2nd ed.). Reading, Mass.: Addison-Wesley.

Gilligan, C. (1982). *In a Different Voice: Psychological Theory and Women's Development*. Cambridge, Mass.: Harvard University Press.

Guidance Associates (1976). *Values in a Democracy: Making Ethical Decisions*. Mount Kisco, N.Y.: Author, 1976.

Hersey, P., and Blanchard (1977). *The Management of Organizational Behavior: Utilizing Human Resources*. (3rd ed.). Englewood Cliffs, N.J.: Prentice-Hall.

Hersh, R. H., Paolitto, D. R., and Reimer, J. (1979). *Promoting Moral Growth: From Piaget to Kohlberg*. New York: Longman.

House, C. (1980). *Leadership Series*. Coeur d'Alene, ID: Listos Publications.

Johnson, D., and Johnson, F. (1975). *Joining Together: Group Theory and Group Skills*. Englewood Cliffs, N.J.: Prentice-Hall.

Karnes, F., and Chauvin, J. (1985). *Leadership Skills Development Program*.

Karnes, F. A., Chauvin, J. C., and Trant, T. J. (1984). "Leadership Profiles as Determined by the HSPQ of Students Identified as Intellectually Gifted." *Roeper Review, 7,* 46–48.

Kohlberg, L. (1964). "Development of Moral Character and Moral Ideology." In M. L. Hoffman and L. W. Hoffman (Eds.), *Review of Child Development Research* (Vol. 1). New York: Russell Sage Foundation, pp. 383–431.

Kohlberg, L. (1971). "Stages of Moral Development as the Basis for Moral Education." In C. M. Beck, B. S. Crittenden, and E. V. Sullivan (Eds.), *Moral Education: Interdisciplinary Approaches*. New York: Newman Press.

Kohlberg, L. (1972). "Moral Education in the Schools: A Developmental View." In J. P. DeCecco (Ed.), *The Regeneration of the School*. New York: Holt, Rinehart and Winston.

Kohlberg, L. (1975a). "The Cognitive-Developmental Approach to Moral Education." *Phi Delta Kappan, 56*, 671.

Kohlberg, L. (1975b). "Moral Education for a Society in Moral Transition." *Educational Leadership, 33*(1), 46–54.

Lamb, R. A., and Busse, C. A. (1983). "Leadership Beyond Lip Service." *Roeper Review, 5*(3), 21–23.

Lindsay, B. (1979). "A Lamp for Diogenes: Leadership Giftedness and Moral Education." *Roeper Review, 1*(4), 4–7.

Maker, C. J. (1982). *Teaching Models in Education of the Gifted*. Rockville, Md.: Aspen.

Marland, S. (1972). *Education of the Gifted and Talented*. Report to the Congress of the United States by the U.S. Commissioner of Education, Washington, D.C.: U.S. Government Printing Office.

Mattox, B. A. (1975). *Getting It Together: Dilemmas for the Classroom Based on Kohlberg's Approach*. San Diego: Pennant Press.

McCall, M. W., Jr., and Lombardo, M. M. (Eds.) (1978). *Leadership: Where Else Can We Go?* Durham, N.C.: Duke University Press.

Nelson, R. G. (1981). "Values Education for Gifted Adolescents." *Roeper Review, 3*(4), 10–11.

Pfeiffer, J. (1985). *A Handbook of Structured Experiences for Human Relations Training, VXI*. San Diego: University Associates.

Pfeiffer, J., and Jones, J. (1981). *Annual Handbook for Group Facilitators*. San Diego: University Associates.

Piaget, J. (1948). *The Moral Judgment of the Child*. Glencoe, Ill.: The Free Press (originally published, 1932).

Plowman, P. D. (1981). "Training Extraordinary Leaders." *Roeper Review, 3*(3), 13–16.

Porter, N., and Taylor, N. (1972). *How to Assess the Moral Reasoning of Students*. Toronto: The Ontario Institute for Studies in Education.

Raths, L. E., Harmin, M., and Simon, S. B. (1978). *Values and Teaching: Working with Values in the Classroom* (2nd ed.). Columbus, Ohio: Charles E. Merrill.

Renzulli, J. S., Smith, F. H., White, A. J., Callahan, C. M., and Hartman, R. K. (1976). *Scales for Rating the Behavioral Characteristics of Superior Students (SRBCSS)*. Wethersfield, Conn.: Creative Learning Press.

Rest, J. (1973). "Patterns of Preference and Comprehensive of Moral Judgment." *Journal of Personality, 41*, 86–109.

Richardson, W. B., and Feldhusen, J. F. (1984). *Leadership Education: Developing Skills for Youth*. West Lafayette, Ind.: William Richardson Enterprises.

Richert, E. S., with Alvino, J. J., and McDonnel, R. C. (1982). *National Report on*

Identification: Comprehensive Identification of Gifted and Talented Youth. Sewell, N.J.: Educational Improvement Center-South.

Roets, L. S. (1981). *Leadership: A Skills Training Program, Ages 8–18.* New Sharon, Iowa: Leadership Publishers.

Schmuck, R. A., and Schmuck, P. A. (1979). *Group Processes in the Classroom* (3rd ed.). Dubuque, Iowa: William C. Brown.

Stogdill, R. (1974). *Handbook of Leadership: A Survey of Theory and Research.* New York: Free Press.

Tannenbaum, A. J. (1972). "A Backward and Forward Glance at the Gifted." *National Elementary Principal, 51*(5), 14–23.

Vare, J. V. (1979). "Moral Education for the Gifted: A Confluent Model." *The Gifted Child Quarterly, 23,* 487–499.

Villars, G. (1976). *Multiple Talent Development.* Unpublished paper. Colorado Department of Education, Denver.

Ward, V. S. (1961). *Educating the Gifted: An Axiomatic Approach.* Columbus, Ohio: Charles E. Merrill.

Weber, J. (1981). "Moral Dilemmas in the Classroom." *Roeper Review, 3*(4), 11–13.

Wilder, L. L. (1979). *The Development of Basic Leadership Skills for the Elementary Level.* Unpublished paper presented for independent study, University of Denver.

Yalom, I. (1970). *The Theory and Practice of Group Psychotherapy.* New York: Basic Books.

EXAMPLE 14.A Sample Leadership Curriculum* ————————

BY PAM BURGER AND SUSAN BRASH

Theme 1: Interaction of Student Leadership with the School Environment.

GOAL 1: STUDENTS WILL BECOME MORE EFFECTIVE COMMUNICATORS IN THE SCHOOLS.

Objective: Students will be able to state the basic fundamentals of public speaking.

---

* *Source:* Susan K. Brash, Director of Gifted Education, and Pamela D. Burger, Home Economics Instructor, Eastern Pulaski Community School Corporation, Winamac, Indiana. Reprinted with permission.

ACTIVITIES:

1. Discuss methods for effective communication in the following areas: giving directions, listening, interpreting nonverbal cues, understanding people, making conversation and introductions, writing letters, and giving speeches.
2. Using a mirror, practice nonverbal communication. Select several attitudes or emotions and try to portray them nonverbally. Present 1 or 2 to the class to see how well your classmates can interpret them.
3. Begin a conversation with someone that you do not know, write a business letter, and make an introduction.

STUDENT ASSESSMENT:

1. Teacher observation of student contribution.

2. Peer interpretation.

3. Be prepared to evaluate each situation and discuss in class.

Objective: Students will incorporate the necessary fundamentals and make a school presentation.

ACTIVITIES:

1. Prepare a short demonstration for the class, explaining how to do something. Try to have enough materials available for everyone in the class to participate in the activity.
2. Review the steps involved in preparing a speech or report. Prepare a 5–7 minute informative speech for the class.

STUDENT ASSESSMENT:

1. Evaluate how well the class follows directions that were given by the leader. (checklist)

2. Peers complete checklist on the speaker.

Objective: Students will listen to an oral presentation and critique it.

ACTIVITIES:

1. Tape record your next group meeting. Play back the tape and write a one-page description of the effectiveness of the communication that occurred. Answer the attached list of questions.

STUDENT ASSESSMENT:

1. Turn in answers to provided questions on the Group Meeting Evaluation Form.

GOAL 2: STUDENTS WILL BECOME MORE EFFECTIVE LEADERS IN THEIR CO-CURRICULAR AND EXTRA-CURRICULAR ACTIVITIES.

Objective: Students will become aware of various leadership styles.

ACTIVITIES:

1. Students will identify who the leaders

STUDENT ASSESSMENT:

1. Are the leaders in the classroom those

are in the classroom and in the extra-curricular activities.

2. *Leaders One and All*   Students create a fictitious, but realistic leader, who will embody the combination of types selected.

who are getting good grades or are they getting in trouble?
Are the leaders in the extracurricular activities the officers and committee chairpersons?

2. Evaluate *Leaders One and All* based on how closely the character reflected the traits of the type of leader chosen.

Objective: Students will compare and contrast leaders in co-curricular activities to leaders in extracurricular.

ACTIVITIES:
1. Analyze the characteristics of the students in each list and chart which students are in one or both.

STUDENT ASSESSMENT:
1. Chart of Analysis:
   Is there a pattern?
   Are there certain leadership characteristics consistently evident in a classroom leader as compared or opposed to an extracurricular activity leader?

Objective: Students will be able to judge various leadership styles.

ACTIVITIES:
1. Students will evaluate the various leadership styles of school leaders they want to emulate.

STUDENT ASSESSMENT:
1. Which type of leader are you?
   Which type of leader would you choose?

GOAL 3: STUDENTS WILL UNDERSTAND THE ROLE OF LEADERSHIP IN SCHOOL GOVERNMENT.

Objective: Students will demonstrate specific principles of parliamentary procedure in conducting a meeting.

ACTIVITIES:
1. Students will be given a list of general guidelines for conducting a meeting and an information sheet on parliamentary motions.

2. Small groups of 8–12 students will plan a meeting in which all motions and parliamentary procedure will be staged.

STUDENT ASSESSMENT:
1. Outside judges, proficient in parliamentary procedure will observe each group and complete a checklist using the guidelines and information that was provided to the students.

Objective: Students will learn the basics of group interaction and use this information to form committees.

ACTIVITIES:
1. Choose a committee and assume that you are the chairperson. Prepare an

STUDENT ASSESSMENT:
1. Evaluation of committee effectiveness after a prescribed time. (checklist)

agenda for your first committee meeting and list your ideas for possible projects. Also describe how you would accomplish the project you propose.
2. You are the president of a new club at your high school. The club has been organized for students who are interested in computers. What standing committees should be established this year? What type of person would you look for to serve as the chairperson of each committee?

2. A paper that outlines the plan with rationale.

Objective: Students will use leadership skills to produce a project for the school.

ACTIVITIES:
1. Students will plan and implement the 8th grade orientation.
2. Students will implement homecoming activities.
3. Students will choose a project to organize and implement an activity within the club to which they belong.

STUDENT ASSESSMENT:
1. Short survey to 8th graders.

2. Survey to principal, coaches, and student council members.
3. Survey to club members.

Objective: Students will appraise their own performances and evaluate the other members in the group or on the committee.

ACTIVITIES:
1. Students will develop a checklist to evaluate members of a group or committee.
2. Students will interview participants.
3. Students will complete a self appraisal.

STUDENT ASSESSMENT:
1. Checklist (self and peer).

2. Log of responses from interviews.
3. Self-appraisal.

Theme 2: Interaction of Students' Leadership Within the Community.

GOAL 1: STUDENTS WILL BECOME MORE EFFECTIVE COMMUNICATORS IN THE COMMUNITY.
Objective: Students will be able to identify various types of communication evident in the community.

ACTIVITIES:
1. List as many potential guest speakers

STUDENT ASSESSMENT:
1. Written lists.

from your community or county as you can think of.

2. Brainstorm a list of resources and forms of communication, other than people, that are available to your group.

2. Written lists.

Objective: Students will be able to differentiate between clear and unclear written and oral forms of communication in the community.

ACTIVITIES:

1. Tape record a radio or news broadcast. Compare and contrast two or more of these in a written paper.

2. Prepare a notebook of written communication and compare and constrast their effectiveness.

STUDENT ASSESSMENT:

1. Written paper.

2. Notebook of the analysis.

Objective: Students will be able to effectively communicate with the community.

ACTIVITIES:

1. Students will give a speech or write a letter to a civic or church organization.

STUDENT ASSESSMENT:

1. School personnel attending the function will be interviewed by the sponsor and their comments on the speech will be evaluated.

Objective: Students will judge the effectiveness in community persons oral and/or written communication.

ACTIVITIES:

1. Students will visit a civic organization in the community and critique its speaker.

STUDENT ASSESSMENT:

1. Written critique.

GOAL 2: STUDENTS WILL UNDERSTAND THE EFFECT LEADERSHIP TRAINING HAS ON COMMUNITY LEADERS.

Objective: Students will learn organization and planning skills.

ACTIVITIES:

1. In a group, brainstorm possible questions to be included on a leadership survey. Evaluate which questions will be used and compile the survey. Present the survey to a selected community leader.

STUDENT ASSESSMENT:

1. Evaluate the results of the survey.

Objective: Students will learn how to develop personal and group goals.

ACTIVITIES:
1. Divide into small groups and list goals of leadership for the group. Categorize the list as personal career and citizenship.
2. Students will respond to items on a checklist which best describes how they would most like to act if they were the leader of a group. (Richardson and Feldhusen, 1984, pp. 28–29).

STUDENT ASSESSMENT:
1. Chart goals by categories.

2. Students role play characteristics of a good leader in front of their peers.

Objective: Students will be able to evaluate their own citizen responsibilities and privileges at various levels.

ACTIVITIES:
1. Develop a philosophy of citizenship and the responsibilities to our country, state and community, family, friend and school. Prepare posters to display in the community showing how the students view citizenship.

STUDENT ASSESSMENT:
1. Evaluate posters.

GOAL 3: STUDENTS WILL UNDERSTAND THE ROLE OF LEADERSHIP IN CITY GOVERNMENT.

Objective: Students will be able to state characteristics of effective city government.

ACTIVITIES:
1. Students will brainstorm and list characteristics of effective city government.
2. Students will learn about the specific functions of community leaders.

STUDENT ASSESSMENT:
1. Objective quiz.

2. Objective quiz.

Objective: Students will be able to emulate characteristics of effective town leaders.

ACTIVITIES:
1. Students will replace different town leaders and conduct business as usual.

STUDENT ASSESSMENT:
1. The leaders who are being replaced will complete a short evaluation of their substitute.

Objective: Students will compare and contrast characteristics of various community governments.

ACTIVITIES:
1. Students will chart the characteristics of three government bodies in the community and list their similarities and differences.

STUDENT ASSESSMENT:
1. Chart.

Theme 3: Interaction of Student Leadership in the World.

GOAL 1: STUDENTS WILL BECOME MORE EFFECTIVE COMMUNICATORS IN THE WORLD.

Objective: Students will evaluate good world communicators.

ACTIVITIES:

1. Students will choose three nationally known news reporters and critique their broadcasts.

STUDENT ASSESSMENT:

1. Written critique.

GOAL 2: STUDENTS WILL LEARN HOW TO BECOME EFFECTIVE LEADERS IN THEIR FUTURE CAREERS.

Objective: Students will analyze their own special talents and abilities.

ACTIVITIES:

1. Students will complete a personality assessment and list their special talents and abilities, noting those that indicate leadership potential.

STUDENT ASSESSMENT:

1. Students will turn in their completed survey and list.

Objective: Students will outline steps for obtaining their leadership goals in life.

ACTIVITIES:

1. Student will be taught a goal planning model (Richardson and Feldhusen, 1984, pp. 66–70).
2. Students will work in small groups to develop values, goals, and objectives for specific assignments.
3. Students will clarify their leadership goals by completing LEAD: A program for Planning Ahead (Richardson and Feldhusen, 1984, p. 72).

STUDENT ASSESSMENT:

1. Peer evaluation of LEAD.

2. Peer evaluation of LEAD.

3. Peer evaluation of LEAD.

GOAL 3: STUDENTS WILL UNDERSTAND THE ROLE OF LEADERSHIP IN THE GOVERNMENTS OF THE WORLD.

Objective: The student will construct examples of influence and power.

ACTIVITIES:

1. Write the definitions for power and influence on the board and give examples of each.

STUDENT ASSESSMENT:

1. Make a poster of pictures of world leaders and categorize them as powerful or influential.

DEFINITION: POWER is the ability to control.

Example: A powerful person may be one who can lift great weights or one who can lead people and make them obey.

DEFINITION: INFLUENCE is the ability to affect what others do or think.

Example: An influential senator can help get a law passed by persuading other senators to vote for it. A newspaper may be influential enough to defeat or elect a candidate.

2. Next give each student two index cards. Direct the students to write on one card an example of a person exerting power over another person or group of people. On the other card have students write an example of person influencing another person or group of people. Collect the cards and read them aloud to the class. Have students indicate if the situation is an example of power or influence.

3. (Optional) Categorize pictures of leaders collected earlier into powerful and influential leaders.

Objective: Students will evaluate leadership qualities in world leaders.

ACTIVITIES:

1. Students will read 3–5 biographies of recognized world leaders. They will choose two and analyze which leadership qualities made them great.

STUDENT ASSESSMENT:

1. Analysis paper.

Section Four

The Process of Curriculum Doing

15 Matching Instructional Strategies to Gifted Learners

Grayson H. Wheatley

Learning without thought is labor lost;
thought without learning is perilous.

—Confucius

Although a variety of instructional strategies can be used with the gifted, some are more appropriate than others. This chapter will examine teaching methods and consider their appropriateness for gifted students. Among the issues to be considered are the effects of instructional strategies on achievement, motivation, and life-long learning.

Choice of an instructional method implies certain assumptions about the learning process. A heavy emphasis on lecturing suggests a belief that the teacher organizes and presents knowledge and the learner "receives" it. In contrast, constructivists such as von Glasersfeld and Cobb (1983) and Wittrock (1977) argue that knowledge is not "out there" to be absorbed but must be constructed by the learner. Ausubel (1978) described learning as a process of presentation by the teacher and reception by the student, whereas Bruner (1960) alerted us to the vital student roles of search and discovery in the learning process.

Building on concepts developed by Gallagher (1985) and Renzulli (1977), Maker (1982a) describes four ways in which curriculum and instruction can be modified to provide a qualitatively different program for gifted students. We can modify what is taught (content), the cognitive processes, the learning environment, and the products expected. Listed below are ways in which these modifications can be made.

1. Learning environment modifications

   a. Student-centered vs. teacher-centered

   b. Independence

   c. Open vs. closed

   d. Accepting

   e. High mobility encouraged

2. Content modifications

   a. Abstractness

   b. Complexity

   c. Variety

   d. Organization

3. Process modifications

   a. Higher levels of thought

   b. Open-endedness

   c. Discovery

   d. Emphasis on reasoning

   e. Freedom to choose solution method

   f. Student-generated methods encouraged

4. Product modifications

   a. Real problems

   b. Read audiences

   c. Transformation rather than summaries

   d. Evaluation by appropriate audiences (Maker, 1982a, pp. 8–17).

These categories can be quite useful in designing instruction for the gifted. They form a framework that reflects the complexity of the task; it is not sufficient to simply modify the content, although that is a critical aspect. Attention must be given to all four of the categories outlined above. In addition to designing content that is more abstract, complex, varies, and organized to reflect the underlying structure, we must also consider the nature of the thought processes that we want students to learn and the environment for learning.

Williams (1972) lists eighteen strategies that can be adapted for use in developing curriculum for the gifted:

Intuitive expression	Tolerance for ambiguity
Paradoxes	Examples of habit
Attributes	Adjustment to development
Analogies	Study creative people and process
Discrepancies	Evaluate situations
Provocative questions	Creative reading skill
Examples of change	Creative listening skill
Organized random search	Creative writing skill
Skills of search	Visualization skill

Williams shows that each of the modes can be united with any of the six curriculum areas (art, music, science, social studies, mathematics, and language arts) in designing curricular experiences for the gifted.

Despite the recommendations by Williams and Maker, didactic methods predominate in programs for the gifted. It is useful in understanding the effectiveness of these methods to consider the perceived student goals for each. First, consider the two contrasting methods—didactic and problem-centered instruction, or, using Bishop's (1985) terms, imposition and negotiation.

Most teachers use some form of didactics as their primary if not exclusive teaching method (Goodlad, 1984). In most cases the choice of an instructional strategy is not consciously made; teachers tend to teach the way they were taught. Teachers of the gifted frequently say, "I would like to use discovery methods but I have so much material to cover." They believe that didactic methods are more efficient and effective. For didactic strategies, the student often sees his or her role as listening, remembering, practicing, and demonstrating proficiences on tests. Pedagogical approaches of the didactic type have the teacher in control of both knowledge (what should be learned) and the learning environment (how it should be learned). That is, teachers using an imposition strategy determine what is to be studied and impose the method by which the tasks are to be completed. For them there is a body of knowledge to be learned and students are expected to acquire that knowledge. The source of authority is with the teacher; authority for correct answers and correct methods as well as classroom behavior lies with the teacher. A teacher who demonstrates a method for dividing 1/3 by 2/5 and then has students practice the method is using an imposition strategy.

On the other hand, problem-centered learning places the student at the center of the decision-making process. Bishop uses the term *negotiation* in contrast to *imposition*. Bishop (1985) defines negotiation as ". . . a goal-directed interaction (teacher and students), in which the participants seek to attain their respective goals" (p. 27). In this definition it is recognized that the goals of the teacher may initially be quite different from the pupil goals, but that through negotiation, mutually respected goals are established and attained. This perspective acknowledges that students can formulate their own goals and that self-formulated goals can be much more effective in motivating students than teacher-imposed goals. Students always have goals and desires, but their goals may be quite different from the teacher's goals. If a teacher ignores the existence of student goals and simply imposes his or her goals on the students, learning will not be optimized. Gifted students are particularly capable of formulating their own goals in a learning situation, and their motivation to learn will be much stronger when they can pursue their own goals.

When negotiation is used in the classroom, the nature of authority is shifted. Correctness of answers is not determined by the teacher but by the content itself; does the answer make sense? Gifted students can decide whether a result has validity. The motivational differences between imposition and negotiation are substantial. Rather than seeing learning as getting answers to please the teacher (or avoid penalties), under negotiation, learning can be viewed as a process of creating meaning for one's self.

This approach may take many forms; for example, whole class discussion, small group work, or individual projects. Williams (1972) suggests that instruction that uses paradoxes, discrepancies, and ambiguity (problem solving) are particularly effective with gifted students. Central to each of these instructional variants is the existence of a problem to be solved or a perplexing situation to be understood. Whether it be in literature ("What are the implied author values in Isak Dinesen's short story, *The Many with the Carnation?*"), in science ("What mechanism could explain a tomato plant's bending toward light?"), or in mathematics ("What is the nth term of the sequence 6, 12, 24, 48, . . . ?"), problem-centered learning can establish a reason for learning. But the problem cannot be an effective stimulant if it is only the teacher's problem. It must become the student's problem or puzzlement. Considerable sensitivity is necessary to assist students in identifying problems. It is essential that students have the experience of sensing, identifying, and clarifying problems before they attempt to solve them. An atmosphere must be established in which students realize that it is acceptable for them to find problems rather than looking to the teacher for the next task to be assigned.

Problem-Solving Strategies

Problem solving is a process of resolving discrepancies. "A discrepancy can be thought of as an inconsistency, a gap, or an exception which is upset" (Copple, Sigel, and Saunders, 1984, p. 18). Sigel (1984) describes intellectual development as a process of recognizing and resolving discrepancies. Although we can create situations in the classroom that might increase the probability that a student will see a discrepancy, we must realize that a problem is personal. Costa (1984) gives an example of a physics student performing a refraction experiment and noting discrepancies: "He (the student) noticed some dark bands in one region of the spectrum. The bands appeared only on the left side and covered a very limited region of the spectrum" (p. 114). This observation led to the problem, "Why were the dark bands in the spectrum and why did they appear only on the left side?" Planned experiments were then conducted, involving the formation and testing of hypotheses and, finally, the resolution of the problem. This student was curious and felt compelled to find an explanation for the phenomena he had sensed. The problem was finally resolved by building an elaborated schema of the light refraction process.

Problem-centered learning is particularly appropriate for gifted students. They have a much greater capacity to sense problems, note discrepancies, and detect ambiguity. Since the gifted are generally more curious and have the ability to follow through, the classroom should be a place where they are free to pursue the questions they raise. Otherwise, potential learning will turn to disillusionment and frustration.

Adam, a first grader, showed a major discrepancy in his performance in different contexts. He did not know his addition facts. He responded to "3 + 1 =" by counting from one, a very primitive response. If we make judgments about Adam based on his response to symbolic forms, we would rate him quite low on number development. However, in another context, a different picture emerged. When shown a set of eight dots arranged in two rows of three and a row of two, he again determined the number of the set to be eight. Adam had developed powerful ways of operating in a visual context but not in a symbolic setting. He could mentally transform the dots to make familiar patterns and thus determine the number. He had not yet developed effective ways of reasoning with numerals. Adam's performance was exceptional with the dots but quite poor with symbols; he could not yet function well with abstract forms such as 4 + 4.

Adam performed quite poorly on typical school mathematics tasks, yet he clearly was a powerful thinker.

In planning for gifted students, we must be open to alternative ways of thinking. By recognizing that students may develop their own ways of thinking about ideas, we can help each student fulfill his or her potential.

Gifted students need many opportunities to encounter such situations as Adam encountered and to exercise their own intellectual capacity to understand such relationships. Through such experiences with discrepancies and problems, they can develop their own intellectual strategies for dealing with new problem situations.

Motivation

Motivation is a critically important variable in the learning equation. Whereas it is clear that gifted students differ greatly in their ability, knowledge base, reflectiveness, and style of learning, it is simply beyond the resources of a teacher to assess every student's understanding, to explain everything they must do to learn, to direct them to the most appropriate materials, to check that they spend the expected time and effort on the task, and to decide what learning mode and style best suits each child. Perhaps it is not even desirable for a teacher to try to deal with all these tasks. However, Nicholls (1983) argues that if the right motivation is established, students will select tasks of suitable difficulty level and work on them in a productive manner. That is, if attention is directed to motivation, many other apparent learning problems will be resolved. Peak motivation is achieved when the learner selects tasks judged to present just the right degree of difficulty (Csikszentmihalyi, 1979; Malone, 1981). Whether it is a reader choosing a book to read, a mountain climber selecting a cliff to scale, or a child playing a video game, motivation is enhanced when the learner makes the choice. Thus, in the classroom for gifted students, learning is facilitated by allowing students to choose, within limits, tasks to attempt and the degree of difficulty. As de Charms's (1984) research shows, there is a need for the learner to be the origin of learning tasks and yet to operate within a structure.

Nicholls (1983) posits three forms of motivation: task involvement, ego involvement, and extrinsic involvement. When a learner is task-involved, he or she is focusing on the task rather than self (not "What will they think of what I am doing?"); learning (understanding) is an end in itself rather than trying to look smart or not to look stupid. Ego involvement is characterized by concern for self rather than with learning, understanding, or finding out. In this condition, one learns only to avoid looking stupid. An extrinsically involved person learns to achieve some reward or to avoid a penalty or to please the teacher. For this individual, learning is a means to an end rather than an end in itself.

Within a class of gifted students, not every student feels confident of his or her ability. Bright girls, for example, tend to have low estimates of their ability to tackle new concepts in mathematics (Dweck, 1986). Because competition to enter the class may be keen and ability has been brought to the forefront by the creation of such a class, some students will feel insecure. If a highly competitive and rigid environment exists within the class, students will not become task-involved. By reducing competition and stimulating student interest in the tasks to be learned, tensions can be reduced and students can be freed from anxieties that block learning.

Problem-Centered Learning and Motivation

Problem-centered learning is facilitated by cooperative learning. In cooperative learning, students work together in small groups, usually to solve a problem. Cooperative learning has many benefits. Noddings (1985) lists the following effects of small group problem solving:

1. Students are stimulated by the thoughts of others.
2. Students assist each other in problem interpretation.
3. Students clarify their thoughts by explaining to others.
4. Students learn useful procedures from others.
5. Students experience increased motivation by cooperative efforts.
6. Students grow from challenges to their stated positions.
7. Students show intellectual growth from peer interaction.

Schools in general, and gifted classes in particular, tend to be competitive. Competitive situations promote ego involvement and an extrinsic orientation to learning. They make it difficult for students to value learning for its own sake. On the other hand, cooperative learning environments foster understanding as a goal; learning becomes an end in itself rather than a means to some other end. Teachers should strive to reduce competition and ego involvement among gifted students and to help students experience the satisfaction of solving problems and making ideas their own.

Realistic Inquiry Experiences

In summary of all that has been said so far, it seems that the ideal learning experiences for gifted learners involve the following conditions:

1. A sense of internal control or self-selection on the part of students
2. Intrinsic interest in the tasks to be learned
3. A sense that the learning tasks relate to the real world, and are not simply "school" activities
4. A real search for meanings, solutions, or understanding
5. A discovery of the plan or system when skilled behavior is the goal

Some of the major forms of realistic inquiry experiences in school include the following:

- Discussion (Good and Brophy, 1984)
- Role playing (Gallagher, 1975)
- Discovery and guided discovery (Anthony, 1973; Bruner, 1960)
- Inquiry (Taba, 1962; Suchman, 1961)
- Small groups (Good and Brophy, 1984; Feldhusen, 1986)
- Seminars (Kolloff and Feldhusen, 1986)
- Games and simulations (Greenblat, 1982; Maker, 1982b)
- Induction and deductive logic (Halpern, 1984; Nickerson, Perkins, and Smith, 1985)
- Critical thinking (Ennis, 1962; Harnadek, 1976, 1980)
- Mentors (Haeger and Feldhusen, 1987; Edlind and Haensly, 1985)
- Field trips (Feldhusen, 1986)
- Experimental research (Dallas Independent School District, 1977)
- Library research (Polette, 1982)
- Tutoring experiences (Ellson, 1976)
- Problem solving (Glaser, 1984; Tuma and Reif, 1984)
- Future studies (Flack and Feldhusen, 1983; Whaley, 1983)

All of these teaching methods can involve gifted and talented students in generative learning (Wittrock, 1977); that is, a process in which students themselves are actively involved in higher level cognitive activities through which they can create their own understanding of concepts and principles and their own cognitive guides for skilled behavior. Wittrock points out that generative learning experiences make it possible for students to relate current learnings to prior experiences and perceptions stored in memory. Generative learning contrasts with reception learning (Ausubel, 1978), an approach to instruction in which the emphasis is on transmission of well-organized information to the student. In the latter approach, the student acts more as a passive receiver of knowledge and less as an active pursuer of understanding.

The sixteen strategies proposed here can all be used by teachers to achieve the following goals for gifted students:

1. Teaching of broad concepts and principles in the discipline
2. Developing a broad range of process or thinking skills
3. Helping gifted students' become self-directed learners
4. Stimulating intrinsic interest in the content

Teachers who are concerned about the teaching of basic skills will see that the relatively automatic behavior that must become a part of every student's repertoire (Samels and Eisenberg, 1981) can best be developed through initial learning experiences in which gifted students develop a cognitive schemata or plan for the skill through their own self-directed exploration or investigation. Automatization of a skill evolves best through repeated experience in using the skill in real contexts or new and more complex learning situations.

General Guidelines for Developing
Strategies to Teach Gifted Learners

The various methods and strategies discussed in this chapter are based on a conception of learning that sees the gifted student as an active, generative, problem-solving learner, creating his or her own understanding and conceptual framework within the disciplines.

We now examine a set of very general guidelines that teachers of the gifted can use in a wide variety of teaching situations. These are general strategies for implementing curriculum plans. Curriculum specifies goals and objectives, subject matter content, concepts and principles, thinking skills or processes, basic skills, attitudes, and values to be learned by gifted students. In this chapter we have focused on instructional strategies that seek to motivate and involve the student in an active, self-directing role in the learning process. The following general guidelines embody the general approaches for such learning for gifted students:

1. Make extensive use of generative instructional strategies such as discovery, discussion, small group problem solving, and other nondidactic methods.

2. Use instructional strategies appropriate to the content. Obviously certain subjects and topics are best taught by one instructional strategy, whereas other topics are best taught with other strategies. While small group problem solving might work well in science, practice might work better in foreign language. Good teachers constantly make their strategy choice based on judgments about the content.

3. Encourage students to develop their own methods of reasoning including self-generated algorithms; encourage alternate ways of thinking and performing tasks.

4. Allow students the freedom to organize their thinking.

5. Provide a learning environment with a variety of options that enable students with different learning styles to choose activities and materials that fit their own learning styles.

6. Deemphasize competition and encourage cooperative learning.

7. Establish a learning environment conducive to task involvement. Nicholls and Burton (1982, p. 376) suggest that "The teacher's task is to create and sustain task involvement and to prevent children's preoccupation with task-extrinsic incentives or with how their ability compares with that of others." This is no easy task, but striving toward it will produce a richer intellectual climate for gifted students. Grading policies and evaluation methods should be examined to consider the effect they have on motivation.

8. Use little or no drill and practice. Since gifted children are often advanced in skills, it is necessary to first assess what the students know, then teach the skills needed. Practice is useless unless the skill is newly acquired, and gifted children need far less practice to acquire skills than average students.

9. Make differentiated assignments to meet the needs of students of different levels of giftedness.

10. Encourage students to set their own goals and to make decisions about what to study. Provide mechanisms such as planning forms and lists of options to enable students to develop their own learning plans (Feldhusen, 1986).

Conclusion

In this chapter, the distinction between two instructional strategies were discussed—one which puts the teacher at the center and another puts the student at the center. It was argued that imposition strategies alone, such as lecture and other modes of "showing students how," have an adverse effect on learning for the gifted. On the other hand, it is argued that negotiation strategies are powerful in establishing a learning environment that allows gifted students to create, integrate, and synthesize ideas. By learning in an environment that encourages cooperation and free exchange of ideas, gifted students become capable of setting goals and achieving them with guidance, not imposition, by the teacher.

Although gifted students vary greatly in their orientation to learning, it is, in a practical sense, impossible for the teacher to design a separate learning experience for each child. Attempting to do this risks having the teacher as the puppeteer and putting the learner in a puppet role. An alternative strategy is to challenge gifted students to set goals and make decisions about how to attack a problem. In this way, learning becomes an adventure in which the students are anxious to participate. The basic thesis of this chapter is that in matching instructional strategies to gifted learners, the matching is best done by the student.

Motivation plays a key role in the learning process. By attending to the motivational effects of classroom moves, it is possible to enhance learning a great deal. It has been said that we learn what we want to learn. Whether gifted students want to learn topic X depends on their beliefs about the learning process and how they feel about their role in the activity. Task involvement is a desirable goal. By deemphasizing extrinsic rewards and competition, we can stimulate students to be interested in the subject for its own sake and enjoy the love of learning.

KEY POINTS SUMMARY

- Instructional experiences for the gifted should involve active cognitive exchange with subject matter.
- Instruction for the gifted should be problem-centered.
- Students should be proactive in setting their own learning goals.
- Problem solving for the gifted should be guided by appropriate learning strategies.
- Motivation is a critical variable to consider in teaching the gifted.
- Inquiry experiences for the gifted should be in realistic contexts.
- Gifted students should be task-involved or intrinsically motivated in learning situations.

• Unnecessary drill and practice should be avoided in delivering instruction to the gifted.

References

Anthony, W. S. (1973). "Learning to Discover Rules by Discovery." *Journal of Education Psychology, 64,* 325–328.

Ausubel, D. P. (1978). "In Defense of Advance Organizers: A Reply to the Critics." *Review of Educational Research, 48,* 251–257.

Bishop, A. (1985). "The Social Construction of Meaning—A Significant Development for Mathematics Education." *For the Learning of Mathematics, 51,* 24–28.

Bruner, J. S. (1960). *The Process of Education.* Cambridge, Mass.: Harvard University Press.

Cobb, P. (1986). Contexts, Goals, Beliefs, and Learning Mathematics. *For the Learning of Mathematics.* Montreal, Canada: FLM Publishing Associates.

Copple, C., Sigel, I., and Saunders, R. (1984). *Educating the Young Thinker.* Hillsdale, N.J.: Lawrence Erlbaum Associates.

Costa, A. (1984). *Developing Minds: A Resource Book for Teaching Thinking.* Alexandria, Va.: Association for Supervision and Curriculum Development.

Csikszentmihalyi, M. (1979). "Intrinsic Rewards and Emergent Motivation." In M. R. Lepper and D. Greene (Eds.), *The Hidden Cost of Reward.* Morristown, N.J.: Lawrence Erlbaum Associates.

Dallas Independent School District (1977). *Up Periscope: Research Activities for Academically Talented Students, Grades 4–8.* Dallas: Dallas Independent School District.

de Charms, R. (1984). "Motivation Enhancement in Educational Settings." In R. E. Ames and C. Ames (Eds.), *Research on Motivation in Education, Volume 1, Student Motivation.* New York: Academic Press.

Dweck, C. (1986). "Motivational Processes Affecting Learning." *American Psychologist, 41*(10), 1040–1048.

Edlind, E. P. and Haensly, P. A. (1985). "Gifts of Mentorship." *Gifted Child Quarterly, 29*(2), 55–60.

Ellson, D. G. (1976). "Tutoring." In N. L. Gage (Ed.), *The Psychology of Teaching Methods.* The Seventy-Fifth Yearbook of the National Society for the Study of Education. Part I. Chicago: The University of Chicago Press, 130–165.

Ennis, R. H. (1962). "A Critical Concept of Critical Thinking." *Harvard Review, 31,* 81–111.

Feldhusen, J., and Kolloff, P. (1978). "A Three-Stage Model for Gifted Education." *Gifted/Creative/Talented, 1,* 3–5 and 53–58.

Feldhusen, H. J. (1986). *Individualized Teaching of Gifted Children in Regular Classrooms.* East Aurora, N.Y.: DOK Publishers.

Flack, J. D. and Feldhusen, J. F. (1983). "Future Studies in the Curriculum Framework of the Purdue Three-Stage Model." *Gifted Children Today, 27,* 1–9.

Gallagher, J. S. (1975). *Teaching the Gifted Child.* Boston: Allyn and Bacon.

Gallagher, J. (1985). *Teaching the Gifted* (2nd ed.). Boston: Allyn and Bacon.

Glaser, R. (1984). "Education and Thinking: The Role of Knowledge." *American Psychologist, 39,* 93–104.

Good, T. L. and Brophy, J. E. (1984). *Looking in Classrooms.* New York: Harper & Row.

Goodlad, J. (1984). *A Place Called School.* New York: McGraw-Hill.

Greenblat, C. S. (1982). "Games and Simulations." In H. E. Mitzel (Ed.), *Encyclopedia of Educational Research.* New York: The Free Press, pp. 713–716.

Haeger, W. W., and Feldhusen, J. F. (1987). *Developing a Mentor Program.* East Aurora, N.Y.: DOK Publishers.

Halpern, D. F. (1984). *Thought and Knowledge: An Introduction to Critical Thinking.* Hillsdale, N.J.: Lawrence Erlbaum Associates.

Harnadek, A. (1976). *Critical Thinking, Book One.* Pacific Grove, Calif.: Midwest Publications.

Harnadek, A. (1980). *Critical Thinking, Book Two.* Pacific Grove, Calif.: Midwest Publications.

Kolloff, P., and Feldhusen, J. (1986). "Seminar: An Instructional Approach for Gifted Students." *Gifted Child Today,* 9(5), 2–7.

Maker, C. J. (1982a). *Curriculum Development for the Gifted.* Rockville, Md.: Aspen.

Maker, J. (1982b). *Teaching Models in Education of the Gifted.* Rockville, Md.: Aspen.

Malone, T. (1981). "Toward a Theory of Intrinsically Motivating Instruction." *Cognitive Science, 4,* 333–369.

Nicholls, J. (1983). "Conceptions of Ability and Achievement Motivation: A Theory and Its Implications for Education." In S. G. Paris, G. M. Olson, and H. W. Stevenson (Eds.), *Learning and Motivation in the Classroom.* Hillsdale, N.J.: Erlbaum.

Nicholls, J., and Burton, J. (1982). "Motivation and Equality." *The Elementary School Journal,* 82(4), 367–377.

Nicholls, J. G. (1983). "Conceptions of Ability and Achievement Motivation." In S. G. Paris, G. M. Olson, and H. W. Stevenson (Eds.), *Learning and Motivation in the Classroom.* Hillsdale, N.J.: Lawrence Erlbaum, pp. 211–237.

Nickerson, R. S., Perkins, D. N., and Smith, E. E. (1985). *The Teaching of Thinking.* Hillsdale, N.J.: Lawrence Erlbaum.

Noddings, N. (1985). "Small Groups and a Setting for Research on Mathematical Problem Solving." In E. Silver (Ed.), *Teaching and Learning Mathematical Problem Solving: Multiple Research Perspectives.* Hillsdale, N.J.: Lawrence Erlbaum.

Polette, N. (1982). *3 R's for the Gifted: Reading, Writing and Research.* Littleton, Colo.: Libraries Unlimited.

Renzulli, J. (1977). *The Enrichment Triad Model: A Guide for Developing Defensible Programs for the Gifted and Talented.* Wethersfield, Conn.: Creative Learning Press.

Samuels, S. J., and Eisenberg, D. (1981). "A Framework for Understanding the

Reading Process." In F. J. Perozzolo and M. C. Wittrock (Eds.), *Neuropsychological and Cognitive Processes in Reading.* New York: Academic Press.

Sigel, B. (1984). "A Constructionist Perspective for Teaching Thinking." *Educational Leadership, 42*(3), 18–21.

Skemp, R. (1979). *Intelligence, Learning, and Action.* New York: John Wiley and Sons.

Suchman, J. R. (1961). "Inquiry Training: Building Skills for Autonomous Discovery." *Merrill-Palmer Quarterly of Behavior and Development, 7,* 147–169.

Taba, H. (1962). *Curriculum Development: Theory and Practice.* New York: Harcourt, Brace and World.

Tannenbaum, A. (1983). *Gifted Children: Psychological and Educational Perspectives.* New York: Macmillan.

Tuma, D. T., and Reif, F. (1984). *Problem Solving and Education: Issues in Teaching and Research.* Hillsdale, N.J.: Lawrence Erlbaum.

von Glasersfeld, E., and Cobb, P. (1983). "Knowledge as Environmental Fit." *Man-Environment Systems, 13*(5), 216–224.

Whaley, C. E. (1983). *Future Studies: Personal and Global Possibilities.* New York: Trillium Press.

Williams, F. (1972). *A Total Creativity Program Kit.* Englewood Cliffs, N.J.: Educational Technology Publications.

Wittrock, M. C. (1977). "Learning as a Generative Process." In M. C. Wittrock (Ed.), *Learning and Instruction.* Berkeley, Calif.: McCutchan Publishing, pp. 621–631.

16 The Role of Computers in Curriculum for the Gifted _____

Grayson H. Wheatley

The computer is the Proteus of machines.
Its essence is its universality, its power to simulate.
—Seymour Papert, *Mindstorms*

The rapidly changing field of technology is opening up rich possibilities for gifted and talented students to gain valuable learning experiences, and is providing a medium for creative expression. In this chapter, the role of technology in programs for gifted students will be explored. Although not exhaustive in its review of possibilities and current practices, uses of computers and related systems will be considered. Guidelines for use of technology will be provided and concerns about computers for the gifted will be expressed.

The Ubiquitous Computer

Of the many markers in the advance of civilization, computers stand out as a significant milestone. Few events in history have had the profound societal impact of computers. Not since the development of language and the printed word have the lives of people been so transformed. Today, computers pervade every aspect of life. Clearly, the potential for computers in programs for the gifted must be thoughtfully considered.

Because gifted students have a propensity for creative expression, the computer becomes a powerful tool for thought. It can perform the tedious detail of a task, freeing the user to form relationships and synthesize complex ideas. For example, by tapping into a data base, students can access more information efficiently. The entire contents of a set of encyclopedias can now reside on a single compact disc. With the compact disc linked to a computer, all entries pertaining to a topic can be immediately obtained. As libraries and specialized data bases store more and more information electronically, research can be conducted in a fraction of the time with much richer sources.

Computers can be used in the classroom in many different ways. Among these many ways, two categories of use will be helpful: delivering instruction and facilitating learning. There are substantial differences in these uses. Thousands of software programs have been created for teaching children specific skills and concepts. Another educational use of computers in schools is to teach children to operate a computer. These computer literacy courses teach students about the computer. Finally, the computer can be used as a tool—to facilitate learning or doing work. In the following sections each of these uses will be discussed.

COMPUTER-ASSISTED INSTRUCTION

Perhaps one of the most pervasive uses of computers in education is to deliver instruction—to teach. Computer-assisted instruction (CAI) has been a focus of educators since their inception. Entire courses are now available on diskettes and many teachers have written short units. In situations where there are too few students for an advanced class, a course on computers could be advantageous. For example, a set of science lessons have been developed at the Educational Technology Center at the University of California, Irvine, which are available through IBM. One of these units, called Batteries and Bulbs, simulates a laboratory experiment on electricity. Students gather empirical data, develop and test hypotheses, and discover a scientific principle. Given a bulb, a battery, and wire, the student is asked to design a circuit to light the bulb. Other units in this series are of a similar nature and are among the best of the CAI materials available.

However, most CAI programs are of poor quality and thus not well-suited for gifted students. A popular type of CAI is drill and practice. If one believes that children learn best by practicing fixed procedures, then CAI is an efficient instructional mode. If, on the other hand, one believes that students construct knowledge in their own idiosyncratic way, then CAI is not as appealing. Certainly gifted students should have the opportunity for creative expression and attention to the major themes of the disciplines. A heavy diet of CAI would be stiffling for gifted and talented students. Even if sophisticated CAI programs were available (intelligent CAI), a gifted child's mind is far too complex to be "read" by a computer.

Furthermore, CAI, with its inherent emphasis on reinforcement and mastery, assumes that mastery is motivating to students. But as von Glasersfeld (1981) argues, understanding is of greater concern to children than mastery. It is a myth perpetrated by the behaviorists that extrinsic rewards such as grades are inherently motivating. Excessive use of CAI seems inappropriate for gifted students. However, it must be recognized that this position reflects a particular philosophic stance. As Walker (1985) writes,

> Much of the present debate about how to use computers for education follow well-worn ideological lines. On the right, representing traditional ideas, are such uses as: drill and practice on basic skills, tutorials on fundamental concepts, and simulations of basic processes in the natural sciences. On the left, representing progressive educational ideals, are such uses as: exploring a microworld, learning to solve problems using software tools, and carrying out personal or group projects on the computer (p. 11).

COMPUTER LITERACY

Computer literacy courses have limited value for gifted students. Too often, schools have viewed the computer as another topic in the curriculum—students must learn *about* computers. Thus we have seen a rash of computer literacy courses in schools. But is this the way computers should be used in programs for the gifted? I think not. First, we must recognize that computer software is transforming the computer into an easily used tool. Many application programs are self-instructional and can be learned, especially by capable students. We do not need to know how a car works to use it for transportation. Similarly, one does not need to know about bits and bytes or be able to name the components of a circuit board to use a computer. Gifted students assimilate the details of keyboards and screens rapidly. Therefore, it is unnecessary to offer a unit of study on how computers work—just have the gifted use computers in applications.

PROBLEM SOLVING

If students construct knowledge for themselves, as Skemp (1979), von Glasersfeld (1981) and Wittrock (1974) argue, using computers in problem solving is an important application of technology in education. By organizing new ideas around a problem, students can build personal schemas that will be available for a broad range of other uses.

Compared to many classroom uses of computers, computer problem solving puts the learner in control as the decision maker and organizer. This learning environment is in sharp contrast to other modes where the user responds to directions and questions and is "programmed" through a set of tasks. Also, in this mode, a programming language can be learned effectively without direct study.

Computer problem solving has been used extensively in the Cumberland Project (Hersberger, 1983) and Super Saturday classes at Purdue University. In the Cumberland Project, gifted fifth- and sixth-grade pupils work in small groups to write programs to solve challenging mathematics problems. This activity is a major component of their mathematics courses during these two years. A careful evaluation of the effectiveness of this pedagogical use of computers has been conducted by Hersberger (1983). The mathematics achievement of students in this program was superior to that of comparable students studying mathematics in a conventional manner.

Computer problem solving can take many forms, from programming in BASIC as described above, using a program such as SemCalc (Sunburst Communications), or using a special purpose program such as Hammurabi. In each case, higher level thought (in the Bloom sense) is required. SemCalc is a problem-solving program that places emphasis on units rather than computations. The user defines the relationships of variables and the units of each, and the program performs the computations. Hammurabi is an economics simulation. The user acts as the ruler of an ancient kingdom and must make decisions on planting and selling grain and allocating resources.

Although computer-assisted instruction has merit in certain situations, care must be exercised in selecting software and designing software uses with gifted students. CAI may provide access to ideas that are unavailable elsewhere, and should be considered under such conditions.

Computers in the Content Disciplines

ENGLISH COMPOSITION

Text processing can greatly extend creative expression and the preparation of reports. Whereas text processing has become routine in many offices and homes in America, few schools have gifted programs that provide computers for writing. Creative persons in all fields are now using computers to increase their productivity and to aid in the expression of new ideas. Text processors are rapidly becoming more powerful. For example, the Apple Macintosh allows the user to easily create diagrams, drawings, and graphs which can be integrated with text. On many computers, the word processor provides choices of fonts and character size which can be intermixed in the text. Built-in dictionaries and automatic spelling checkers increase the quality of student products as well as expand their vistas to new possibilities. Obviously, the power of computers will continue to increase making possible even more varied and creative expression.

It is clear that computers can greatly enhance the learning environment of gifted and talented students. As a high school designs a gifted program, provisions should be made for technology to be integrated into the program. Text processing capability adds an important dimension to composition of ideas and prepares students for the next wave of technological invention. In fact, some gifted students are likely to contribute substantially to this field.

FOREIGN LANGUAGES

Recent advances in speech synthesis and the ability of a computer to provide practice makes computer-aided learning particularly effective in learning a foreign language. A gifted student at any age who becomes interested in learning another language can do so with available computer programs, even though no formal class is available. Thus the computer becomes a mechanism for meeting the needs of students when there are insufficient numbers of students to make scheduling of a class economically feasible. But even in a regularly scheduled class, the computer has proven to be a valuable aid in learning other languages. Many of the objections to CAI that apply to conceptual and relational subjects such as science and creative writing do not apply to foreign language.

SCIENCE

Computers can be used to simulate complex processes in the classroom, to aid in the collection and analysis of data from experiments, and in diverse other ways. Computers have the potential of revolutionizing laboratory and classroom activities. Powerful simulation programs allow students in a chemistry laboratory to explore potentially dangerous or inaccessible processes. Simulations can also provide experiences with ideas that would otherwise require prohibitively expensive equipment. Experiments that would take weeks or even years can be simulated with computers in one class period, thus providing rich experiences in a safe and economical environment.

As an example of gifted students using computers in a nontraditional way, consider the following case. Through a gift from industry in Ft. Wayne, Indiana, a robot manufactured by Zenith/Heath was made available to gifted students in several high schools. The robot, named Hero, was delivered in kit form. The first task was assembly. Because of the complexity of the project, several months were required to complete and debug the assembly. Once Hero was operative, the students were challenged to write programs to control the robot. Students from the participating schools entered their robots in competition for the best performing robot. This year-long activity provided a motivating challenge to students that went far beyond didactic classroom instruction. With the progress of technology, such projects will become less expensive and even more challenging. Students interested in engineering, electronics, and computers can gain rich experiences by assembling and programming robots. A field trip to a nearby university or industry that designs or uses robots would be an excellent activity.

MATHEMATICS

Fey and Heid (1984) used computer support to teach a concepts-first calculus course. Computer software was available for any complex computation, allowing attention to be focused on concepts and relationships rather than computational techniques. At the *end* of the course, the necessary computational procedures were taught. Students studying this program did as well as those in a standard calculus course on a common examination and they also showed a superior grasp of the calculus concepts. Use of technology in this manner seems particularly appropriate for gifted students.

One of the software packages available in the Fey and Heid study was MuMath. MuMath is a symbolic calculator that operates in integer rather than decimal arithmetic. Using MuMath, it is possible to add fractions, factor a polynomial, solve equations, and even differentiate functions. Use of such software in mathematics can allow gifted students to focus on relationships rather than skills.

Both computers and calculators can be important tools for exploration. For example, using computer software that will allow the graphing of any equation allows students to view functions and relations in broad, conceptual ways rather than only experiencing such ideas from a computational perspective. This computer application essentially removes the veil of computation so that the mathematical relationships can be seen and grasped. Wheatley and Wheatley (1982) found that sixth-grade pupils made many more exploratory moves in problem solving when calculators were available, and their mathematics achievement was greatly enhanced.

MUSIC AND ART

With the advent of synthesizers, music takes on a new dimension. The opportunities for composing original pieces and exploring musical forms has been greatly increased. At the North Texas State University, extensive work is done in both theory and skill courses with computers. Musical compositions are composed and performed on computers. Tones and rythmns are studied in the laboratory at other times. Current developments in hardware make this work feasible for high-school students. Programs now exist (Musicworks) that display staff and clef, allow modifications, play the music, and in general allow nearly any manipulation desired.

In the field of art graphics, programs such as MacPaint and MacDraw for the Macintosh computer allow the expression of shape and form on a computer screen, which can then be manipulated, modified, and then printed. Although this procedure is by no means a substitute for actual performing, students who are talented in music or art will find the computer a rich environment for generating and expressing ideas.

CAUTIONS

Bork (1985) states "Over the next 25 years the computer will become the dominant delivery system in education. In most subject areas, more people of all ages will learn more things from computers than from lectures, textbooks, or other modes" (p. 4). But for each topic in the curriculum we must always ask, "Is the computer the best educational media for learning this topic?" The answer may not always be yes. At times it is quite important for events to be experienced as they occur in the world—the world of objects, feelings, purposes, and others. An uncritical rush to teach everything via electronic technology would seem ill-advised.

We must also be cautious about prescribing computer education for young learners. Precocious youngsters take to computers instantly. They find them powerful tools and fascinating toys. With appropriate software, such as Logo Writer, young children can stretch their minds and accomplish amazing things at an early age. However, care must be taken to insure that young children gain varied and rich experiences in interacting with others. Although the computer is a powerful tool for young minds, it would be unfortunate if computer games substitute for more comprehensive life experiences. In school, great care should be exercised in using computers in the primary grades; a strong rationale should be required rather than simply arguing that children need to begin to use computers early. With the many popular drill and practice programs on the market, care must be exercised in selecting appropriate software at this level.

Guidelines

The following guidelines provide a sound basis for the utilization of computers with gifted learners.

1. *Use the computer as an intellectual tool.* As indicated earlier, the computer can be a powerful educational tool. The various uses listed show how the computer can enhance learning in many disciplines. As better software becomes available, the power of this electronic tool will increase. Computers and video systems will become increasingly easy to use, just as the automobile has become easier to use.

2. *Use computer-assisted instruction judiciously.* Although certain software packages can enhance the learning environment for gifted students, great care must be exercised in selecting software. Since gifted students learn at rapid rates, any program that takes the student through a linear step-by-step topic may be limiting. On the other hand, CAI may be very effective for learning vocabulary in a foreign language.

3. *Avoid computer literacy courses.* Although it is important for the leaders of tomorrow to be knowledgeable about technology, this does not translate into courses about computers. Gifted students can acquire such knowledge more efficiently and more effectively by using computers as intellectual tools rather than taking a course in them.

4. *Prevent technology from dominating instructional programs for the gifted.* It is quite easy to become influenced by those who believe computers are ushering in a new era in education. Claims are being made about greatly enhanced learning, and surely that is possible. But just as all important learning cannot be accomplished with textbooks, computers should not be the only medium for learning. Most importantly, students must interact with other people. Gifted students must set goals and make decisions in light of their purposes. The computer will not always be their choice, and we must respect that. Furthermore, when pedagogical analyses are honestly made, the computer will not always figure in the subsequent instructional plan—another setting may be more appropriate. Teacher-led classroom discussion, small group problem solving, visiting a museum, conducting a field trip, attending a musical performance, and reading a classic will continue to be significant educational experiences. The difficult question should be asked: Will the computer make this lesson a better learning experience?

5. *Develop an implementation plan for computer utilization.* It is unlikely that any well-thought-out plan can be implemented in its entirety. By formulating phases for implementation, greater progress can be made. It is important to avoid potential disappointments and disillusionments, which are likely to accompany a crash program. Furthermore, refinements can be made by phasing in a carefully designed program.

6. *Recognize that educational systems change slowly.* Although technology will continue to pervade education, it will not happen rapidly. Teachers do not easily alter their modus operandi—our habits are strong factors in the way we teach. Teachers may believe that cooperative learning is beneficial, understand the rationale, have the materials, know how to use the method, and know they should use small groups in their class, and still stand at the chalkboard and explain the material. In retrospect they may then say, "I should have used small groups," and yet they will repeat the scenario described above. Computers may sit in the back of the classroom unused because the teacher has not incorporated their use into their instructional practices.

Many other obstacles to computer utilization exist. Computers must be purchased, software must be selected, facilities must be prepared, and then a curriculum has to be written for inclusion of computers. Once these steps have been taken, staff development must proceed and, finally, teachers must change the way they teach. We must not expect effective use of computers to be developed in a year or even two. But with careful long-range planning, a computer-enhanced learning environment can be established.

Conclusion

Gifted education can be greatly enhanced by utilizing the new instructional tools of the information society. It is crucial that curriculum developers plan for computers in programs for gifted students. Examples of pedagogical applications have been provided in this chapter, along with guidelines for implementation. The power of computers for greater learning is well-established, but we must be careful in planning their use. Although it is easy to identify potential uses of computers in education, there are many issues to be resolved before computers take their place in the classroom alongside the textbook as a major instructional device. Among the questions being asked about computers in the classroom are: (1) Should schools invest the capital necessary to make computers available to all students? (2) How can teachers be prepared to utilize the new technologies? (3) Is it appropriate for young children to be in front of a CRT for extended periods of time? (4) How does the curriculum become restructured to integrate computers into the curriculum? By asking these questions, a school system can avoid many of pitfalls associated with use of technology with the gifted.

KEY POINTS SUMMARY

- Technology in education of the gifted is dominated by the computer.
- Computers are often used as didactic media of instruction.
- Instructional programs on computers can be inquiry-oriented.
- Gifted students should develop basic computer literacy through experience with computers.
- Computers can be very effective in teaching the skills of problem solving.
- Computers are widely used in teaching the disciplines.

References

Bork, A. (1985). *Personal Computers in Education*. New York: Harper and Row.

Broughton, J. (1984). "The Surrender of Control: Computer Literacy as Political Socialization of the Child." In D. Sloan (Ed.), *The Computer in Education: A Critical Perspective*. New York: Teachers College Press.

Hersberger, J. (1983). *The Effects of a Problem Solving Oriented Mathematics Program on Gifted Fifth Grade Students*. Unpublished doctoral dissertation, Purdue University, West Lafayette, IN.

Fey, J. and Heid, J. (1984). "Imperatives and Possibilities for New Curricula in Secondary School Mathematics." In V. Hansen and M. Zweng (Eds.), *Com-*

puters in Mathematics Education. 1984 Yearbook. Reston, Va.: National Council of Teachers of Mathematics.

Papert, S. (1980). *Mindstorms: Children, Computers, and Powerful Ideas.* New York: Basic Books.

Piaget, J. (1985). "Piaget's Theory." In P. Mussen (Ed.), *Handbook of Child Psychology* (4th ed. Vol I). New York: John Wiley and Sons.

Skemp, R. (1979). *Intelligence, Learning and Action.* New York: John Wiley and Sons.

Sloan, D. (1984). *The Computer in Education: A Critical Perspective.* New York: Teachers College Press.

von Glasersfeld, E. (1981). "The Concepts of Adaption and Viability in a Radical Constructivist Theory of Knowledge." In I. Sigel, D. Brodzinsky, and R. Golinkoff (Eds.), *New Directions in Piagetian Theory of Knowledge.* Hillsdale, N.J.: Lawrence Erlbaum.

Walker, D. (1985). *Computers and the Curriculum.* Unpublished manuscript, Stanford University.

Wheatley, G., and Wheatley, C. (1982). *Calculator Use and Problem Solving Strategies of Sixth Grade Pupils.* Final report, National Science Foundation.

Wiggington, E. (1985). *Sometimes a Shining Moment: The Foxfire Experience.* Garden City, N.Y.: Anchor Press/Doubleday.

Wittrock, M. (1974). "Learning as a Generative Process." *Educational Psychologist, 11,* 87–95.

17 Instructional Leadership ————————

Ken Seeley

There is nothing more difficult to take in hand, more perilous to conduct, or more uncertain in its success than to take the lead in introducing a new order of things.

—Niccolo Machiavelli

For the purposes of this discussion, it is important to differentiate instructional leadership from curriculum leadership. Curriculum leadership implies that there are educators who assume the major responsibility for planning and developing the curriculum. This is an on-going process, as indicated in Chapter 2. Instructional leadership is different in that it involves the implementation of the curriculum, which involves staff development, curriculum field testing, evaluation, and curriculum modification. In many cases curriculum leadership and instructional leadership are performed by some of the same persons or teams of professionals. Building principals often have input into curriculum development, but they rarely enjoy the unilateral influence they exercise as instructional leaders. In its simplest form, curriculum leadership creates what would be taught in schools, and instructional leadership implements and monitors the curriculum. Curriculum leaders confer with the instructional leaders over time to decide what changes are needed in the curriculum.

Instructional leadership has become the central focus of the school principalship in recent years. The literature in school administration, as well as programs designed to train principals, reflect this emphasis. In examining the past twenty years in school administration, one can see the evolution of emphasis from humanistic leadership to management systems leadership and now, again, to the roots of the principalship: instructional leadership. The term *principal* was originally *principal teacher*. The dropping of *teacher* is historically significant as an evolution of social and professional status, but even more significant, it signaled a greater distance of the principal from the instructional process. Although the occasion to act as instructional leader was always inherent in the principalship, few principals cared to act on the opportunity. "The principals were slow individually and as a group to take advantage of the opportunities for professional leadership which were granted them" (Pierce, 1935). In 1968, the National Educational Association conducted a large study on the elementary principalship to ascertain, among other things, how much leadership principals

404

assumed. Principals reported that they had little influence over decisions and they attributed their lack of leadership to strongly centralized school systems (NEA, 1968). A ten-year follow-up study was done in 1978 by the NEA, again to look for differences in the role of principals. Again, the principals reported that they were not in instructional leadership roles, with very little difference from the 1968 study (NEA, 1978).

In this evolution, from "principal teacher" to the present role of the principal, new educational positions emerged, creating a whole middle management that had not previously existed. As a result, instructional leadership became a complex network of professional positions with multiple responsibilities. It is perhaps the formation of this middle management centralized network that led the principals to their responses on the 1968 and 1978 NEA surveys.

In order to view instructional leadership through the lens of educating gifted children, it is necessary to examine the complex set of relationships that typically constitute instructional leadership in most contemporary school districts. Figure 17.1 presents a three-dimensional model of instructional leader-

FIGURE 17.1 A Model for Instructional Leadership

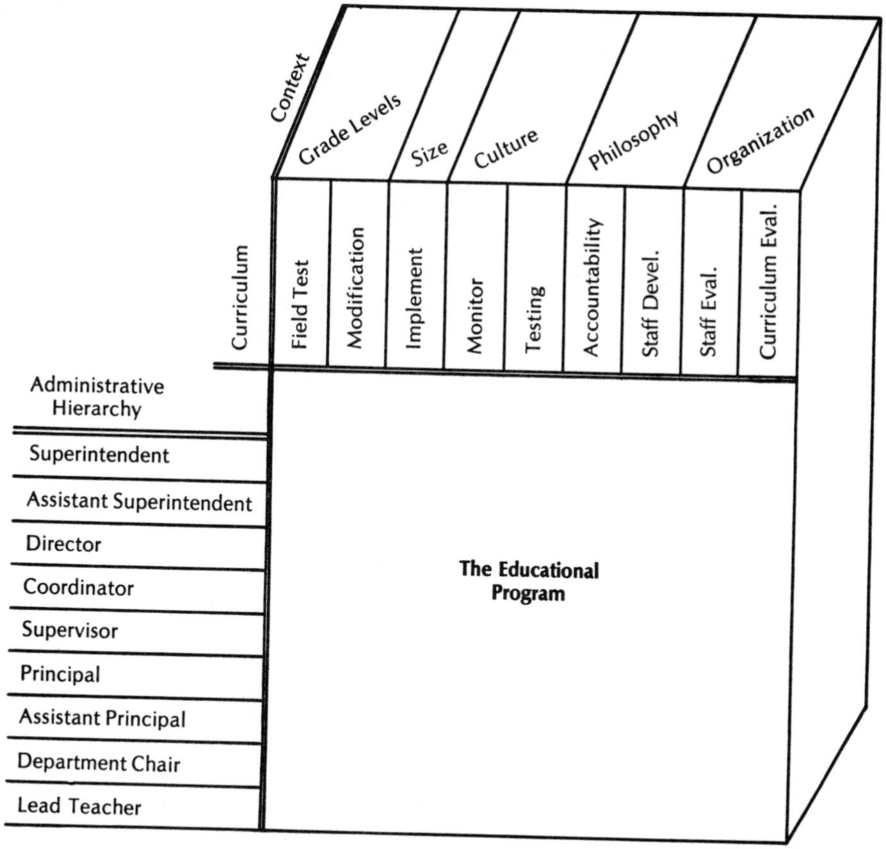

ship. The three dimensions are: administrative hierarchy, context, and curriculum. The administrative hierarchy represents the personnel roles in leadership that vary from central administration to building-level administration. The context dimension deals with variables at the school building-level that affect leadership, such as grade levels, size of school, and culture of the school. The final dimension is the curriculum that constitutes the content of the instruction.

Administrative Hierarchy

Implicit in the administrative hierarchy are various leadership roles that are typically found in schools. Sergiovanni (1984) describes the leadership in school organizations as "a balance between delegation (differentiation) and coordination (integration)" (p. 95). To be effective, leadership personnel along the administrative hierarchy need to be constantly aware of differentiating roles by delegating tasks, and also to fulfill the coordination function in order to integrate the leadership of the organization. This balancing act interacts constantly with the other two dimensions of the model when we consider instructional leadership.

There is an old expression among school administrators that says, "Don't keep a dog and bark yourself." The joke speaks to the importance of delegating leadership responsibility, but it overlooks the coordination function of knowing what, how, and when the dog is barking. Merely delegating responsibility through different roles in the hierarchy does not qualify as effective leadership, unless the roles are also integrated in an interactive leadership model working toward the goals of the organization.

There are good delegators and good coordinators in schools, but it is the combination of these skills that is our best quality indicator. Those in the administrative hierarchy need to understand the differentiation of leadership roles and the coordination of those roles for the entire hierarchy, not just those above them or below them in the hierarchy.

No discussion of school administrative hierarchy would be complete without some attention to the military model upon which many schools operate that hierarchy. This notion is that the hierarchy is a series of ranks, moving from greater to lesser power that proceeds in lockstep fashion with communication only taking place between immediate superior and subordinate. Administrators are often chastised by superiors for "jumping the chain of command" because they shared ideas or information with someone in the hierarchy not immediately above or below them. Whereas the military organizational format maintains an orderliness to communication and decision-making, it is not very successful in coordination and integration. Furthermore, it does not work well in nurturing effective instructional leadership in schools.

The military model falls apart in the middle management of public education. One could clearly state that the assistant superintendent for secondary education was the superior to the high-school principal in the military model. However, is the secondary coordinator of mathematics superior to the high-school principal? Is the director of elementary education superior to the elementary principals if those principals report directly to the superintendent in the organizational plan?

The Middle Management

It is the middle management of public education that is charged with both instructional leadership and curriculum leadership. The greatest ambiguity of the line and staff relationships exists at this level. The application of the military chain of command fails in middle management, and the greatest loss is effective leadership in curriculum and instruction.

With the recent move to assign greater leadership of instruction to principals, there is question concerning whether the authority has gone with the responsibility. Many middle managers believe that the power for instructional leadership is elsewhere in the organization. Principals may feel that they are the pawns of the central office. Central office administrators believe that the principals must provide the leadership because they are closet to the instructional process, but these same administrators keep budgetary control, curriculum control, and control over staff development. In the worse case scenario, this leads to a cycle of helplessness where no one feels he or she can exert leadership.

Clearly there is not one answer for all school organizations as to the most effective administrative hierarchy that will facilitate instructional leadership. As the model indicates, instructional leadership is a function of the interaction of the hierarchy with the curriculum and the context. To address the issue of leadership merely by delegating along the hierarchy overlooks the coordination with other key elements of the organization. Unfortunately, administrators make pronouncements like, "The principal is responsible for instructional leadership." It is an attempt to differentiate a role by delegating responsibility. However, it seems doomed to fail if the other side of the balancing act is not considered—coordination with others in the organization. This area of coordination will be discussed after we examine the other two aspects of the model.

Implications for Gifted Education

Traditionally, the building principal has enjoyed a large measure of autonomy in administering activities within her or his building. A coordinator of gifted education has not established much tradition as a public school administrator. For most school districts, the coordinator is a "new breed of cat" without an academic home in some content area of curriculum like other coordinators. The role and function of a reading coordinator, for example, is usually understood by most educators even though there is an overlap with the principal's role. The coordinator of gifted education enjoys no such general understanding, relates to all areas of curriculum, and is often viewed with suspicion by all in the administrative hierarchy. This lack of clarity in role often leads to conflict between the coordinator of gifted and the building principal in the following areas:

1. Planning and implementing district-wide programs for gifted students at the building level

2. Identification and placement of selected students for special programs
3. Selection and assignment of special personnel to work with gifted students
4. Developing and maintaining parent education programs for parents of gifted students
5. Allocation of categorical funds for personnel and materials for programs for gifted students
6. Basic attitudinal differences about who should be educated and in what manner in the public schools
7. Decision making among all middle managers in the hierarchy in curriculum modification at the building level
8. Implementation of effective data management systems for accountability requirements on gifted students and attendant personnel

Although principals have building-level autonomy, they are expected to carry out the district program. This program usually comes in the form of board policies, administrative procedures, and established curriculum. The coordinator of gifted education is often perceived as somewhat apart from the district program. This is a direct reflection of the whole issue of how gifted education relates to "regular education" as a temporary add-on to the regular education programs, so the coordinator of gifted education may be viewed as a temporary interloper impinging on the regular program.

It is therefore incumbent upon coordinators of gifted education to continually "sell" themselves as legitimate members of the middle management team with a unique but complimentary role to offer their colleagues. As tradition accumulates to the role, so with the level of credibility within the hierarchy. However, the most expedient way to build credibility is to demonstrate continually one's relatedness to the general education enterprise. As a trusted and valuable member of the administrative team, the coordinator of gifted programs can offer much to enhance curriculum and instruction in a school district.

The Context for Instructional Leadership

The context for leadership is certainly as important a dynamic as either of the other two dimensions in that it imposes variability that is situationally based. Sensitivity to context necessitates that there is not *one* approach to instructional leadership that can work in all situations. Some contexts require dictatorial leadership, whereas others might need very subtle nuances to be effective in impacting instruction.

Instruction takes place in a school building that has certain physical features that affect learning and teaching. The variable of school size, usually interpreted as pupil population, also includes the physical size and features of the building in relation to the people in it. Typically, the number of pupils dictates the number of staff for a building, and therefore the number of administrators is determined. Many schools have one principal as the only administrator, which allows for leadership to emerge from the teacher ranks in the form of team leaders or lead teachers. In larger schools, assistant principals can be assigned that instructional leadership or management role so that the principal can provide that kind of leadership.

Grade level is a major variable in determining the nature and extent of instructional leadership. Schools where individual teachers teach all or many different subject areas (elementary or middle schools) dictate a very different context for leadership than departmentalized approaches where teachers teach one subject area only. This subject-oriented approach of most secondary schools, coupled with larger pupil populations, often result in intricate building-level hierarchies with department chairs, curriculum committees, assistant principals, and various other professionals who might be called supervisors or coordinators. Secondary schools exemplify the extreme of middle management. The instructional leadership and curriculum leadership in secondary schools is the middle management of middle management. It is mind boggling to envision the complexity of attempting to implement any reform in curriculum or instruction at the secondary level. That probably explains why secondary schools have been the slowest and most resistant to change. It is an organizational nightmare.

Let us take an example of interest to educators of gifted students. Assume that a person in the administrative hierarchy wants to implement a small instructional change in the high school, such as allowing freshmen access to all Advanced Placement classes offered if they can document readiness either through previous courses or test performance. Such a plan would require review and approval by the following individuals: the principal, the assistant principal for instruction, the head of counseling services, the chairpersons of departments offering the Advanced Placement classes, the subject area curriculum coordinators from the central office, the Advanced Placement teachers, the high-school curriculum committee, and perhaps even the assistant superintendent for secondary education. It is clearly middle management gone wild. With all the best intentions and commitment to participatory decision making, we have created a monster that almost defies effective instructional leadership at the secondary level.

All is not entirely bleak in secondary schools, however. New instructional leadership roles are emerging at the departmental levels from department chairpersons, supported by the principal and assistant principal. These departmental leaders are being encouraged to improve instruction and to experiment with new ideas. This is a small beginning toward improving instructional leadership by empowering those closest to the instructional process to assume responsibility that heretofore was the principal's duty, who was just too busy to do it well.

The context of grade level at the elementary school influences instructional leadership through a central building principal and how he or she delegates and coordinates the leadership functions. Too often there is a disproportionate amount of energy spent on curriculum leadership and too little attention paid to the instructional process. There is much to do about progress on curriculum objectives, and what reading series to purchase, rather than how well the teachers are teaching, how students might be grouped differently, and staff development needs. Most elementary schools offer a more manageable context for effective instructional leadership to occur. The size of the school and the staff usually permits easier delegation and coordination.

The culture of a school constitutes the complex network of relationships and values of all the people who enter therein. A classic quotation by Waller (1932) best describes the culture of a school:

> There are, in the school, complex rituals of personal relationships, a set of folkways, mores, and irrational sanctions, a moral code based upon them. There are games which are sublimated wars, teams, and an elaborate set of ceremonies concerning them. There are traditions and traditionalists waging their world old battle against innovators. There are laws, and there is the problem of enforcing them. . . . There are specialized societies with a rigid structure and a limited membership (p. 103).

What the culture of a particular school might be results from the interaction of all those variables that Waller so well identifies. Anyone who wishes to exercise effective leadership needs to have a level of human sensitivity that can perceive the culture, develop a level of trust or respect from those in the culture, and build on the strengths of the culture.

Out of culture grows philosophy. The culture of the school building or of the school district largely determines what philosophy of education will prevail in the context for leadership. The values and traditions of the community and the educators who serve that community interact to produce a philosophical tone for education. It is rarely articulated, and yet those in the system feel its presence. It may be characterized as progressive or conservative, centralized or decentralized, and ultimately broken into subsets of characterizations by building. There is often wide variation among buildings as to the philosophy that is usually set by the administrative hierarchy in the building. The influence of a centralized philosophy in the school district on the building philosophy varies widely. Its greatest impact seems to be on the organizational patterns that a central administration imposes on the school building (e.g., personnel assignments, grade-level organization, curriculum accountability). Figure 17.2 illustrates the interaction of the variables that form the organization that creates the context for instructional leadership.

The Curriculum

In its simplest form, curriculum is what is taught to students. This chapter attempts to separate curriculum from instruction as a means of differentiating leadership roles and responsibilities along school district hierarchies and context. In reality, curriculum is very complex and is inextricably tied to instruction. It is the successful collaboration of curriculum and instruction that promotes learning.

All curriculum is subject to adjustments of instruction which vary as to depth, breadth, and pace. Any instructor must decide these issues in order to teach any curriculum. These three dimensions of instruction are largely influenced by the nature and extent of curriculum material (usually texts), supervisory expectancies, and the instructor's experience. A wise curriculum professor once said, "The curriculum starts when the door closes." Schools spend enormous amounts of time and money producing curriculum guides in an often futile effort to create uniformity among grade levels and subject matter.

Curriculum for gifted learners implies modification of certain curriculum

FIGURE 17.2 The Context for Instructional Leadership

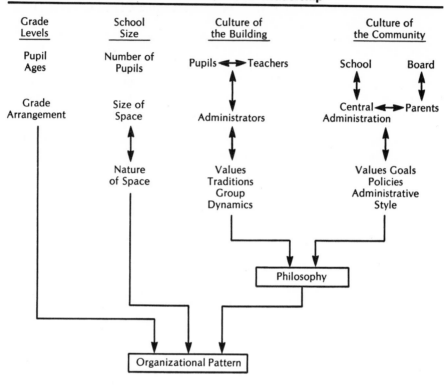

areas and instructional strategies (e.g., assessment of student's level of knowledge). Section Two of this book presented the idea that the content areas provide the base for appropriate curriculum for gifted learners. That curriculum base needs to be modified, extended, and integrated. This is done through instructional intervention requiring careful leadership.

The relationship between curriculum and instruction produces a three-part paradigm to which both curriculum leaders and instructional leaders must be sensitive. There is the curriculum that is published, the curriculum that is taught, and the curriculum that is learned. We know a good deal about the published curriculum. Months and years are spent on writing the published curriculum for each content area by grade level. One can refer to these curriculum guides to see what is to be taught and when. Some teachers try to stay within the published curriculum actually taught and the prescribed texts, but even here we find great differences among classrooms at the same grade level. Instructional leaders attempt to monitor the curriculum that is taught by observing the instruction and reviewing teachers' plans. However, there is limited time devoted to these activities. The curriculum about which we know least is the curriculum that is learned. Testing programs provide some indication about students' abilities to recall factual information. We also know something about reading, writing, and language skills of the students. However, rarely is this information used to adjust the curriculum for the student. Rather, it is a culminating accountability exercise.

Figure 17.3 presents the curriculum-instruction steps with associated leadership tasks. In order to provide instructional leadership to curriculum for gifted learners, it is important to reconfigure the three-curriculum paradigm, as shown in the lower portion of Figure 17.3. We must start with the learned curriculum and compare it to the published curriculum. Sufficient individual assessment information is needed to identify what the student knows and how he or she learns best. Instructional leaders must also ensure that there is sufficient mastery of basic skills and information required by the published curriculum. With these two curricula as a starting point, the taught curriculum for the gifted then requires modification, extension, and integration of the basic content areas. The leadership tasks here necessitate the support of teachers with staff development

FIGURE 17.3 Leadership Tasks for Curriculum Development

Traditional Curriculum Process

STEPS:	The Published Curriculum $\longrightarrow$	The Taught Curriculum $\longrightarrow$	The Learned Curriculum
LEADERSHIP TASKS:	Develop and Prescribe the Curriculum	Monitor and Evaluate the Teachers	Test, Evaluate, Report Quantitative Performance of Learners (Group Only)

Curriculum Process for Gifted Learners

STEPS:	The Learned Curriculum $\longrightarrow$ (Compared to the Published Curriculum)	The Taught Curriculum $\longrightarrow$	Learner Outcomes (Individual and Group)
LEADERSHIP TASKS:	Assure Individual Assessment	Support Teachers with Staff Div.	Evaluate and Report both Quantitative and Qualitative Outcomes
	Assure Mastery of Basic Skills	Support Curriculum Changes	
	Report Differences Between Learned and Published Curriculum	Conduct Formative Evaluation	

to perform the curriculum changes needed, and to provide formative evaluation data to adjust the curriculum to individual differences. The learner outcomes of the taught curriculum are different from the traditional learner curriculum in that they are quantitative and qualitative and must be reported by an individual learner as well as aggregated for the group of gifted learners. These outcome data cycle back to become the learned curriculum in another iteration of the steps, and are compared to the published curriculum to assure accountability requirements and mastery of basic skills.

Summary: Leadership Tasks to Job Description

By examining the leadership tasks at the bottom of Figure 17.3, and the Model for Instructional Leadership (Figure 17.1), we have the basis for a job description for a curriculum/instruction leader in gifted education. The three dimensions from the Instructional Leadership Model form the basis for the job description, and the leadership tasks from the Curriculum Process for Gifted Learners provide more specific duties.

To summarize this chapter, the models and ideas are synthesized into the job description for the curriculum and instruction leader for gifted education. These are the key elements that can guide the selection of leadership personnel:

GENERAL QUALIFICATIONS

1. Demonstrate an understanding of gifted and talented learners and their needs in the classroom context.

2. Be able to communicate effectively to an administrative hierarchy, from lead teachers to the superintendent, in articulating the program for gifted learners as an integral part of the educational program.

3. Be sensitive to the variations of educational settings in different school buildings and among different personnel where philosophy, values, size, level, organizational, and cultural conditions may affect the gifted program in different ways.

4. Demonstrate strong skills in curriculum development and implementation with special attention to modification and evaluation of curriculum for gifted learners.

SPECIFIC DUTIES

1. Design and implement an identification program that assures the individual assessment of potentially gifted students' knowledge and abilities.

2. Implement an appropriate curriculum for gifted learners that assures mastery of basic skill requirements of the general curriculum and allows for modification, extension, and integration of this general curriculum into any specialized curriculum for the gifted.

3. Articulate to the administrative hierarchy the curriculum for the gifted program within the context of the general curriculum and what differences for a specialized curriculum are required.

4. Develop and implement a comprehensive staff development program for teachers of the gifted, as well as regular classroom teachers, that supports and improves the curriculum and instruction for gifted learners.

5. Design and conduct formative and summative evaluation of the gifted program that focuses on both quantitative and qualitative outcomes and leads to necessary revision of the curriculum and instructional approaches used in implementing that curriculum for gifted learners.

Instructional leadership for gifted education programs evolves from good leadership. It is not unique unto itself, but rather borrows from the best of systems intervention theory and learner-based program development. This chapter has presented a generic three-dimensional model for instructional leadership and discussed its application to middle management in education in general, and gifted education specifically. The concept of context for the leadership was presented with general guidelines that any instructional leader might find useful in approaching an individual school building. Finally, the chapter presented curriculum and its close ties to instruction. A model of traditional curriculum and instruction was contrasted with a model for gifted learners to demonstrate some fundamental differences in approach with attendant leadership tasks.

The perceived quality of gifted education is largely determined by the quality of its leaders. That leadership must develop as a logical extension of the broader instructional endeavor of general education. There can be no room for "empire builders" or "saviors" who repudiate and denigrate the mainstream curriculum and instruction. Such leadership results in esoteric programs that are viewed as irrelevant and ultimately cast out as expensive frills. Effective instructional leadership that builds and extends the general education enterprise for gifted learners will result in enduring programs.

KEY POINTS SUMMARY

- Instructional leadership involves implementing curriculum in different contexts and within an administrative hierarchy.

- Instructional leadership is different from curriculum leadership in that it implies the implementation, monitoring, staff development, and evaluation of curriculum. Curriculum leadership is the planning and development of the content to be taught.

- Within the context of gifted education, instructional leadership is a middle management function that requires coordinators of gifted programs to offer skills that are both unique and complementary to the general education enterprise.

- The context for instructional leadership involves the influence of grade level, school size, culture of the school building, and culture of the community on the school philosophy and organizational pattern that evolves.

- The curriculum process for gifted learners requires a comparison between the published or prescribed school district curriculum and the curriculum that the student has already learned.

- The curriculum that is taught to gifted learners evolves from the comparison of prescribed and learned curriculum and it is modified, extended, and integrated based on the learners' needs.
- Formative and summative evaluation of gifted programs must focus on both qualitative and quantitative outcomes of student learning.
- The ideal role of the coordinator of gifted programs involves both instructional leadership and curriculum leadership.

References

"Information—A Key Ingredient to Successful Leadership." (1986). Unauthored article in *NASSP Bulletin,* April, pp. 41–51.

Pharis, W. L., and Zachariya, S. B. (1979). *The Elementary Principal in 1978: A Research Study.* National Association of Elementary School Principals.

Pierce, R. (1983). In D. C. Baltzell and R. A. Dentler (Eds.), *Selecting American School Principals: A Source Book for Educators.* National Institute for Education.

Sergiovanni, T. (1984). *Handbook for Effective Department Leadership: Concepts and Practices in Today's Secondary Schools,* 2nd ed. Boston: Allyn and Bacon.

18 Toward Synthesis: A Vision of Curriculum Processes That Build Comprehensive Articulated Experiences for Gifted Learners

Joyce VanTassel-Baska

Alice: *"Would you please tell me which way I ought to go from here?"*
Cheshire Cat: *"That depends on where you want to get to."*
—Lewis Carroll

Toward Synthesis

While each of the chapters has addressed various aspects of curriculum for the gifted, no one piece has attempted to integrate all of the various components that constitute an appropriate curriculum experience for gifted learners as they move through the continuum of K–12 schooling. That task lies ahead in the content of this final chapter. For it is ultimately in the understanding of important changes and adaptations of that *total* curriculum that the gifted are best served.

In the first section of this book, we dealt with issues related to the curriculum development process itself. First providing a philosophical framework for thinking about curriculum, we then presented the process of development that school districts need to consider in making progress on curriculum issues. Also integral to this section was a discussion of central design elements that ought to be present in any written curriculum. These fundamental chapters are further supported by a close look at unit development and scope and sequence work.

What is central to our thinking about the processes involved in curriculum making for the gifted is the interrelationship of them, one to the other. Too frequently educators become entranced with one model or design as if it constituted the universe of consideration regarding a topic. What we have presented has relevance only to the extent that it is viewed comprehensively. To proceed into curriculum without a philosophy about curriculum, a way of "seeing" it, is as foolish as creating a design with no way to feed it into a relevant system of people who can critique, alter, and hopefully use it.

We were also sensitive to issues of level in this section. For many practitioners, particularly teachers, the level of their work with curriculum will be limited to the development of units. Thus this process is highlighted as one of the most important arenas for curriculum development. Since units come the closest to our ideas about the "delivered" curriculum, it is very important that those curriculum pieces are thoughtful and well-designed. For other practitioners, like gifted program coordinators or curriculum directors, the focus on scope and sequence is crucial to their understanding of how to map out the larger picture of curriculum. Scope and sequence work provides the framework for curriculum articulation throughout the grades in key areas of learning and it is necessary for planning the continuity of experiences for gifted learners. Obviously, at some point in the curriculum development process, these two strands of work must merge in a meaningful way so that the unit efforts are integrated appropriately into the total process.

In the second section of the book, we focused heavily on traditional content areas and ways to modify and adapt them to the needs of gifted learners. Since the verbal arts, mathematics, science, and the social sciences constitute the fundamental domains of study in schools, it seems reasonable to focus on making them more appropriate for the gifted learner rather than trying to work around them in some way. Thus these chapters provided direction and focus for the adaptation of these subjects through differential goal setting, an exploration of the application of our fundamental curriculum models in Chapter 1, examples of successful curriculum that has been adapted, and strategies and resources to consider in undertaking the task.

Our chapter on the humanities provided a detailed look at interdisciplinary approaches to curriculum making for the gifted and wove together the core domains of study in schools with other areas of value to the gifted students. In that sense, the humanities chapter is the keystone for this section of the book in that it reflects a more abstract level of conceptualizing curriculum in which all of the domains of study have a place. We illustrated in that chapter the complexities of structuring a humanities curriculum, but we also stressed its ultimate value to the gifted learner. As with the content chapters that precede it, the humanities chapter provides rich examples of curriculum that has been organized for such programs. Whereas all of the core domains of study relate to more than one learning realm, it is only in the humanities that students come to apply cognitive, affective, social, aesthetic, and psychomotoric capacities in an integrated way. We have tried to demonstrate that, at the highest level, the humanities constitute just such an insightful self-portrait.

The third section of the book explored important areas of a curriculum for gifted learners not generally considered by schools. Yet for gifted students, work in the areas of thinking skills, affective curriculum, leadership, and the arts all constitute important components of their total curriculum experience. Because we believe these areas to be so important in a curriculum for the gifted, we structured the chapters to demonstrate two fundamental approaches to including them. One approach taken is to view these areas as separate domains of study in and of themselves. Our chapters thus provided examples of curriculum that constitute this view. By the same token, a second approach treats these areas as part of all the core domains of study cited earlier. Thus critical thinking, for example, could be a separate course of study for the gifted at fifth-grade level, but it could also be integral to the teaching of reading at that same level. This dual perspective on these vital areas of curriculum represents an important way of ensuring their inclusion in a program for the gifted as both content and process.

These chapters also provided another important service in this book. They distilled the essence of powerful learning realms and provided us with the keys to unlock them. Thus they allow us to access directly a side of learning not frequently utilized through the route of traditional subject matter teaching and learning. We believe that these areas need to be systematically tapped in programs for the gifted. It is important that students have insight into how they think and learn in the cognitive realm—insight into feelings of self-worth and identity in the affective realm, insight into understanding human relationships and the concepts underlying them in the social realm, and insight into various forms of human artistic expression in the aesthetic realm.

In the final section of the book, we addressed important issues of support for implementing the curriculum. At the classroom level, we stressed the importance of the interaction between teacher and learner, and we suggested facilitative modes for enhancing that relationship. We also cited the role of technology in facilitating instruction at the classroom level. Special attention was given to the use of the computer because of its emerging influence in recent years as an instructional tool. At the school and district level, we illustrated the key role that effective instructional leadership plays in facilitating the implementation of curriculum. Ideas were shared about how gifted program coordinators, in particular, might assume this role and move the curriculum development process along. We presented a model in this chapter that illustrated the interlocking aspects of our ideas about curriculum and instruction for the gifted student with the structure and organization of schools. Thus in this final support structure we reconcile the total curriculum effort, which has been expanded on throughout the book, with the real world of schools. It is in this reconciliation, moreover, that the relationship of the institutional framework of schools and the processes of curriculum and instruction becomes fully integrated.

Finally, then, we have evolved to a different level in our view of curriculum for the gifted. Instead of seeing the curriculum effort as separate pieces or models to be merely added together, curriculum work for the gifted can be envisioned as a negotiated set of interlocking systems, each contributing in significant ways to the realization of appropriate, comprehensive, and articulated opportunities for gifted learners. Figure 18.1 illustrates this systems perspective.

To provide final insights for practitioners regarding these systems, we conclude our book with a set of practical recommendations and guidelines to consider, not as a step-by-step process, but as an integral set of knowledge and skills

FIGURE 18.1 The Chain of Curriculum Systems

necessary for teachers and administrators to create and implement a viable curriculum for the gifted learner.

RECOMMENDATIONS AND GUIDELINES FOR PRACTITIONERS IN CURRICULUM DEVELOPMENT

1. *Practitioners in gifted programs need to understand the basic strands of thought in general curriculum and how they are translated into appropriate curriculum models for the gifted.* As we have noted in our opening chapter, these models are derived from the characteristics of gifted learners, research, and informed practice. Thus they provide a common core of understanding about fundamental curriculum and instructional dimensions in gifted programs.

2. *Practitioners need to recognize the importance of the curriculum development process as an on-going cycle and the school district leadership tasks needed to energize it.* We have outlined the stages of curriculum development and provided practical guidelines for proceeding through each stage of the process. It is important that practitioners view this process as a blueprint for action over a three- to five-year period.

3. *Practitioners need to understand the curriculum design process and its fundamental importance in curriculum planning.* Important aspects of differentiation are encompassed at this crucial design level. Questions like "Where is our curriculum going?" "How do we get there?" and "How will we know when we have arrived?" are answered by using a formalized design process. We have provided a translation of the design elements to salient issues in structuring curriculum for the gifted.

4. *Practitioners should be able to develop a scope and sequence in curriculum areas that provides a broad framework for curriculum work from kindergarten through grade twelve.* Organization of such scope and sequence work should occur at several levels, based on the focus of the curriculum. Thus, content, process, product, and concept issues need to be considered. We have provided guidelines to consider in developing scope and sequence and also gave examples of several such efforts.

5. *Practitioners should be able to develop instructional units for use in gifted programs.* Manipulation of all the curriculum models at this level is important: content-based curriculum, process-oriented curriculum, and concept curriculum. We have described the process by which such units can be developed and we provided illustrative examples of completed units.

6. *Practitioners should be able to facilitate the development of curriculum for the gifted in the core content areas that schools currently address.* Since the study in these areas of verbal arts, mathematics, science, and the social sciences comprise the majority of instructional time gifted students are in school, it is crucial that modifications in these areas be made at all stages of development. We have suggested several ways to modify these core areas for the gifted through both acceleration and enrichment strategies.

7. *Practitioners should be able to incorporate the humanities as an integrating force into curriculum for the gifted.* A broad-based humanities program can underscore and enhance concept learning within subject matter disciplines as

well as provide a strong interdisciplinary focus. Using a creative process-product paradigm for teaching the humanities can also foster student growth in understanding "how man creates."

8. *Practitioners should be able to implement strategies for the inclusion and infusion of particular learning realms within a curriculum for the gifted.* These areas include thinking skills in the cognitive realm, affective curriculum in the affective realm, leadership in the social realm, and the arts in the aesthetic realm. Treatment of these areas might be considered as a separate part of the curriculum experience as well as embedded in the core subject matter areas. We have noted key models for use under both sets of conditions in Chapter 12. We have demonstrated that affective curriculum experiences can be treated as content in and of itself in addition to being an integral part of the teaching-learning process. We have cited leadership programs that are intact yet note leadership experiences that can occur in any classroom context. We have treated the arts as interrelated domains of study for the artistically gifted and as strands of experience for the intellectually gifted.

9. *Practitioners should carefully consider both the dynamic interaction of curriculum with instruction and the effects of instructional pattern on the gifted learner.* We have explored the realm of instructional practice in Chapter 15 to introduce those approaches that are most facilitative for gifted students' learning.

10. *Practitioners should be able to select appropriate new technology to enhance the instructional process.* As we have cautioned that it is important to recognize the power of technological tools in the instructional process but to find equally powerful ways to harness them to the complex task of learning. Ideas for using computers effectively with gifted students were presented in Chapter 16.

11. *Practitioners should recognize the importance of instructional leadership in the context of gifted program administration.* In Chapter 17, we have provided a realistic view of how schools function and the problems that coordinators of gifted programs face in that context. Yet central to the issue of curriculum development is the need for a system that supports the effort.

12. *Practitioners need to build comprehensive articulated curricular experiences for the gifted over the span of years they engage in the schooling process.* Gifted education is not a frill; it is not an extra in the school budgeting process. It is an essential and complete set of experiences for a targeted group of learners in our schools. Understanding and meeting the needs of the gifted means addressing all of those needs that can reasonably be undertaken in a school context and doing so over time.

Conclusion

Given the shifting perspectives through which one might view the total curriculum picture for the gifted, it may be useful to conclude on a singular note. It is through the fine-grained lens of experience that ultimate curriculum decisions will be made for gifted students. All of the chapter "frames" of this book should be filtered through the successful experiences of educators who, in the end, best know their own students and their unique needs. These pages have provided several views of the comprehensive house of curriculum for the gifted and marked the direction toward a higher synthesis in understanding it.

Appendix A ▬▬▬▬▬

Useful Paradigms in Conceptualizing Curriculum for the Gifted

PHENIX'S REALMS OF MEANING

- symbolics
- empirics
- esthetics
- synoptic
- ethics
- synnoetics

Phenix, P. H. (1986). *Realms of Meaning*. Ventura, Calif: Ventura County Superintendent of Schools.

GARDNER'S FRAMES OF MIND

- linguistic
- musical
- logical-mathematical
- spatial
- bodily-Kinesthetic
- personal (interpersonal and intrapersonal)

Gardner, H. (1983). *Frames of Mind*. New York: Basic Books.

EISNER'S WAYS OF KNOWING

- aesthetic
- formal
- epistemological

Eisner, E. W. (1982). "Aesthetic Education." In H. E. Mitzel (Ed.), *Encyclopedia of Education* (Volume I). New York: The Free Press, pp. 87–94.

PERRY'S EPISTEMOLOGICAL POSITIONS IN LEARNING

- basic dualism
- multiplicity
- relativism subordinate
- relativism

Perry, W. G. (1970). *Forms of Intellectual and Ethical Development in the College Years.* New York: Holt, Rinehart & Winston.

CHILD DEVELOPMENT

- cognitive development
- psychosocial development
- moral development
- environmental influences
- creativity

Horowitz, F. D., and O'Brien, M. (1985). *The Gifted and Talented. Developmental Perspectives.* Washington, D.C.: American Psychological Association.

Useful Models for Teaching Thinking Skills

ENNIS'S MODEL FOR CRITICAL THINKING

TWELVE ASPECTS OF CRITICAL THINKING

1. Grasp the meaning of a statement.
2. Judge whether ambiguity exists.
3. Judge if contradictions exist.
4. Judge if a conclusion necessarily follows.
5. Judge the specificity of a statement.
6. Judge if a statement relates to a certain principle.
7. Judge the reliability of an observation.
8. Judge if an inductive conclusion is warranted.
9. Judge if a problem has been identified.
10. Judge if a definition is adequate.
11. Judge if a statement is credible.
12. Judge if something is an assumption.

Ennis, R. H. (1962). "A Concept of Critical Thinking." *Harvard Educational Review, 32,* 81–111.

PARNES CREATIVE PROBLEM-SOLVING MODEL

CREATIVE PROBLEM-SOLVING STEPS

Fact-finding (brainstorming)
Problem-finding and defining
Idea-generation and Alternative Solution-finding
Evaluating among solutions
Developing a plan of action (acceptance-finding)

Parnes, S. J. (1967). *Creative Behavior Guide Book.* New York: Scribners.

STERNBERG'S METACOMPONENTS (EXECUTIVE PROCESSES)

1. Recognizing a problem
2. Defining the problem
3. Steps for solving the problem
4. Ordering
5. Deciding on a form for information
6. Allocating resources
7. Monitoring
8. Using feedback

Sternberg, R. J. (1985). *Beyond IQ.* New York: Cambridge University Press.

Useful Paradigms for Implementing Curriculum

WILLIAMS'S MODEL FOR IMPLEMENTING COGNITIVE-AFFECTIVE BEHAVIORS IN THE CLASSROOM FOR THE GIFTED

DESIRED STUDENT BEHAVIORS	TEACHER BEHAVIORS
Fluent Thinking	Parodoxes
Flexible Thinking	Attributes
Original Thinking	Analogies
Elaborative Thinking	Discrepancies
Curiosity (willingness)	Provocative Questions
Risk Taking (courage)	Examples of Change

Complexity (challenge)
Imagination (intuition)

Examples of Habit
Organized Random Search
Skills of Search
Tolerance for Ambiguity
Intuitive Expression
Adjustment to Development
Study Creative People and Process
Evaluative Situations
Creative Reading Skill
Creative Listening Skill
Creative Writing Skill
Visualization Skill

Williams, F. E. (1977). *Classroom Ideas for Encouraging Thinking and Feeling.* Buffalo, N.Y.: DOK Publishers.

Useful Paradigms for Organizing Curriculum and Instruction for the Gifted

BLOOM'S TAXONOMY
- knowledge
- comprehension
- application
- analysis
- synthesis
- evaluation

Bloom, B. S. (1956). *Taxonomy of Educational Objectives, Handbook I: Cognitive Domain.* New York: David McKay.

KRATHWOHL'S TAXONOMY
- recurring
- responding
- valuing
- organization
- characterization by a value or value concept

Krathwohl, D. R., Bloom, B. S., and Masia, B. B. (1964). *Taxonomy of Educational Objectives, Handbook II, Affective Domain.* New York: David McKay.

Appendix B ─────────

Publishers of Curriculum Materials for Gifted/Talented Students

Creative Publications
P.O. Box 10328
Palo Alto, CA 94303

Curriculum Associates
1211 Connecticut Ave., NW,
  Suite 414
Washington, D.C. 20036

Dale Seymour Publications
P.O. Box 10888
Palo Alto, CA 94303

D.O.K. Publishers
P.O. Box 357
East Aurora, NY 14052

Educational Impressions
Resource Materials for the G/T
249 Goffle Road
Hawthorne, NJ 07507

Engine-uity, Ltd.
Box 9610
Phoenix, AZ 85068

G/C/T Publishing Co., Inc.
350 Weinacker Avenue
P.O. Box 6448
Mobile, AL 36601-0448

Good Apple
Box 299
Carthage, IL 62321-0299

The Great Books Foundation
40 East Huron St.
Chicago, IL 60611

The Keystone Consortium
P.O. Box 2367
West Lafayette, IN 47906

Midwest Publications
P.O. Box 448
Pacific Grove, CA 93950

National Association for Gifted Children
Materials Catalog
5100 N. Edgewood Drive
St. Paul, MN 55112

National/State Leadership Training
Institute on the Gifted and the Talented
316 West Second Street, Suit PHC
Los Angeles, CA 90012

A. W. Peller and Associates, Inc.
Bright Ideas for the Gifted and
    Talented (K–12)
Educational Materials
294 Goffle Road
Hawthorne, NJ 07507

SOI Institute
343 Richmond St.
El Segundo, CA 90245

Sunburst Communications
Room WV4
39 Washington Avenue
Pleasantville, NY 10570

Synergetics
P.O. Box 84
East Windsor Hill, CT 06028

Trillium Press
Box 921
New York, NY 10159

Zephyr Press
430 South Esset Lane
Tucson, AZ 85711

Index ━━━━━━━━━━━━━━━